Prefaces

TO PEACE

Prefaces
TO PEACE

A Symposium consisting of the following:

One World *by Wendell L. Willkie*
(COMPLETE)

The Problems of Lasting Peace
by Herbert Hoover and Hugh Gibson
(COMPLETE)

The Price of Free World Victory *by Henry A. Wallace*
(FROM THE NEW BOOK
"THE CENTURY OF THE COMMON MAN")

Blue-print for Peace *by Sumner Welles*
(FROM THE NEW BOOK
"THE WORLD OF THE FOUR FREEDOMS")

———

Cooperatively published by
SIMON AND SCHUSTER • DOUBLEDAY, DORAN & COMPANY, INC.
REYNAL & HITCHCOCK, INC. • COLUMBIA UNIVERSITY PRESS

ABOUT THE APPEARANCE OF BOOKS IN WARTIME

A recent ruling by the War Production Board has curtailed the use of paper by book publishers in 1943.

In line with this ruling and in order to conserve materials and manpower, we are co-operating by:

1. Using lighter-weight paper which reduces the bulk of our books substantially.
2. Printing books with smaller margins and with more words to each page. Result: fewer pages per book.

Slimmer and smaller books will save paper and plate metal and labor. We are sure that readers will understand the publishers' desire to co-operate as fully as possible with the objectives of the War Production Board and our government.

Contents

THE ATLANTIC CHARTER

3

ONE WORLD

By Wendell L. Willkie

v

THE PROBLEMS OF LASTING PEACE
By Herbert Hoover and Hugh Gibson

THE PRICE OF FREE WORLD VICTORY
By Henry A. Wallace

BLUE-PRINT FOR PEACE
By Sumner Welles

Introduction

IN 1917, the American people were unprepared for war. In 1918, the American people were unprepared for peace.

They did understand that, if there were to be a good and lasting peace, they would have to carry on with their associate nations until some kind of international co-operation was put on a permanent basis. In 1918, they favored the League of Nations and their representatives were active in planning it. They did not understand that, if the peace were to be kept, they would have to step out of isolationism in peace as well as in war, and take some real responsibility for a world order. So, when the inevitable jealousies, fears, and greeds of a peace settlement began to show their ugly heads, they refused to join the League they had helped to make. It was a weak League to begin with, and, when the most powerful nation in the world turned its back and went home, it became too weak an agent to guarantee a durable peace, although it was successful, more successful than is generally recognized, in healing the wounds of war and promoting social, economic, and intellectual co-operation among the nations. But, politically, it became a weak congress, run by pressure groups representing the great European powers, unable to agree upon any action which could stop the slide of Europe toward another war.

If the Americans had joined the League, it might, or might not, have grown into success. Nevertheless, if we had gone in, the money and lives which we probably would have spent over twenty years in the attempt to begin a better world order, would not have been as much as we are going to lose in any week of this present war, into which we were as inevitably drawn as if we had assumed some responsible share in making or preventing it. And, in any case, if we had taken real responsibility for keeping the peace we would have been armed and ready for the new world war when it came, instead of being caught in an undignified position as regards our pants.

The American people were unprepared for war in 1939, and still unprepared for war in 1941.

The American people must not be unprepared for peace when it comes. Otherwise, we may share another futile victory like the last one, passing on to the next generation the certainty of another and perhaps finally destructive war. And if we come to the end of war with no policy of our own, and no national unity as to whether we shall take responsibility in peace as we have in war, we shall present an unhappy picture of a great nation able to make war, but unwilling or unable to throw its weight into the vital problems of peace. Defeatism among the democracies made this war inevitable. The question is whether Americans will return to defeatism, when they have helped to win a victory.

There have been sinister forces at work for the last twenty years, and before they can be checked, the Axis and Japan, which have become their armored divisions, must be unconditionally defeated. Why not then in this year of 1943 forget about peace and concentrate on winning the war! The answer has already been given. If no unity in peace aims is reached, we may begin to lose the war on the day we win it. That happened before. It must not happen again. Yet in spite of doubts and fearful difficulties in the road, which no intelligent man will minimize, the prospects for a better peace than last time are in no sense hopeless. They are even hopeful—provided we prepare (and in this country particularly) for peace while we are at war, as we should have prepared for this war (or prepared to prevent it) while we were at peace. And of this fact, not only the leaders of the United Nations, but the outstanding leaders in the political life of the United States, are already aware. No final plan has, or can be, presented yet. No entire agreement is to be expected with so much still uncertain in the course of the war. Nevertheless, there is already a surprising agreement upon some things which must be done if this war is not to lead quickly to another one. Both agreements as to principles, and the disagreements as to how to make them work, are of the greatest interest and importance.

The American public, in general, is not aware of how far their lead-

ers have already looked into the future. The public has only recently
begun to think about war, and they have done very little thinking yet
about the peace after the war. Therefore, we American citizens are
in danger of approaching the actual peace-making, when it comes, as
ignorant and as easily led by the nose, as we were in 1918. This book,
which is really an assemblage of books and important speeches, by men
who have been, or are, or are likely to be in positions of great responsibility in the conduct of American foreign affairs, is an attempt to
bring together what might be called blueprints for peace. With President Roosevelt's addresses, such as his speech on the Four Freedoms,
and the Atlantic Charter, which are too familiar to need reprinting here,
these documents fairly represent what our outstanding leaders are proposing, where they agree, where they disagree.

Wendell Willkie reports on a world transformed by rapid communication and economic interdependence, as he sees it after his now
famous global trip. Sumner Welles, in a survey made from the heart
of his important addresses, sets down simply and clearly the minimum
essentials for a better world-order and a safer and more prosperous
America after the war. Vice-President Wallace, following a somewhat different line, does the same in a series of statements which represent the essence of his ideas on what can be made to happen after
the war. Ex-President Hoover, working with one of the ablest and most
far-sighted of our diplomats, Ex-Ambassador Hugh Gibson, makes a
more detailed and elaborate study of principles, ways, and means,
arranged like a text book for easy and satisfactory study.

Even those readers of this *Prefaces to Peace* who have been following
the controversies in the magazines and the newspapers over what shall
be done after the war, will find many surprises in the book. The proposals for organizing a constructive instead of a destructive world contain many pills which will be hard to swallow for men and women who
still think that it is going to be possible to come back to the *status quo
ante*. Of course, these blueprints are only a *preface* to peace, and upon
such vital questions as to just *how, when, where* the United States is
to take its stand, the authors do not usually commit themselves. It is
too early for that. But it is not too early for the American citizen, whose
own safety and prosperity and the future of his children, are deeply
and irretrievably involved in the post-war settlement—indeed, it is

growing late for him to find out what is being thought and planned by his leaders, and what they already know is indisputable and what they hope.

And let the readers of this *Prefaces to Peace* note that there is already an agreement upon at least a minimum of actions which have to be taken, and let him remember that it is upon a minimum of agreement that all great statesmanship has been based in free countries.

These proposals should be discussed until they sink home. If there is indifference or ignorance in the thoughts of the general public, this is the time to turn on the searchlight. If there is criticism, now is the time for it. America must get its mind on some program for peace. There must be national unity as to principles, and national intelligence at work when it comes to the inevitably controversial ways and means. This book is a first step in education for the hoped for peace.

HENRY SEIDEL CANBY

THE ATLANTIC CHARTER

THE President of the United States of America and the Prime Minister, Mr. Churchill, representing His Majesty's Government in the United Kingdom, being met together, deem it right to make known certain common principles in the national policies of their respective countries on which they base their hopes for a better future for the world.

1 Their countries seek no aggrandizement, territorial or other.

2 They desire to see no territorial changes that do not accord with the freely expressed wishes of the peoples concerned.

3 They respect the right of all peoples to choose the form of government under which they will live; and they wish to see sovereign rights and self-government restored to those who have been forcibly deprived of them.

4 They will endeavor, with due respect for their existing obligations, to further the enjoyment by all States, great or small, victor or vanquished, of access, on equal terms, to the trade and to the raw materials of the world which are needed for their economic prosperity.

5 They desire to bring about the fullest collaboration between all nations in the economic field with the object of securing, for all, improved labor standards, economic advancement and social security.

6 After the final destruction of the Nazi tyranny, they hope to see established a peace which will afford to all nations the means of dwelling in safety within their own boundaries, and which will afford assurance that all the men in all the lands may live out their lives in freedom from fear and want.

7 Such a peace should enable all men to traverse the high seas and oceans without hindrance.

8 They believe that all of the nations of the world, for realistic as well as spiritual reasons, must come to the abandonment of the use of force. Since no future peace can be maintained if land, sea or air armaments continue to be employed by nations which threaten, or may threaten, aggression outside of their frontiers, they believe, pending the establishment of a wider and permanent system of general security, that the disarmament of such nations is essential. They will likewise aid and encourage all other practicable measures which will lighten for peace-loving peoples the crushing burden of armaments.

FRANKLIN D. ROOSEVELT
WINSTON S. CHURCHILL

August 14, 1941

One World

BY WENDELL L. WILLKIE

TO

MAJOR RICHARD T. KIGHT, D.F.C.,
who piloted The Gulliver, the plane in which we flew
around the world, and to whom on November 24, 1942,
the War Department awarded the Oak Leaf Cluster for
extraordinary achievement in completing that "difficult
and hazardous mission in excellent time and without
mishap, despite extreme weather conditions and the
presence of enemy aircraft over
part of the route,"

AND TO

the members of the tireless and skillful crew of
The Gulliver,
CAPTAIN ALEXIS KLOTZ, CO-PILOT
CAPTAIN JOHN C. WAGNER
MASTER SERGEANT JAMES M. COOPER
TECHNICAL SERGEANT RICHARD J. BARRETT
SERGEANT VICTOR P. MINKOFF
CORPORAL CHARLES H. REYNOLDS

INTRODUCTION

Today, because of military and other censorships, America is like a beleaguered city that lives within high walls through which there passes only an occasional courier to tell us what is happening outside. I have been outside those walls. And I have found that nothing outside is exactly what it seems to those within.

I had an opportunity to fly around the world in the middle of this war, to see and talk to hundreds of people in more than a dozen nations, and to talk intimately with many of the world's leaders. It was an experience which none of those leaders and few private citizens have had. It gave me some new and urgent convictions and strengthened some of my old ones. These convictions are not mere humanitarian hopes; they are not just idealistic and vague. They are based on things I saw and learned at first hand and upon the views of men and women, important and anonymous, whose heroism and sacrifices give meaning and life to their beliefs.

In this book I have tried to set down as dispassionately as possible some of my observations and—perhaps not quite so dispassionately—the conclusions I have drawn from them.

I was accompanied on my trip by Gardner (Mike) Cowles, Jr., a noted publisher, and by Joseph Barnes, an experienced foreign correspondent and editor—both perfect traveling companions, both my friends. They have been most generous and helpful in the preparation of material for this book. And though I am sure they would agree with many of my conclusions, they bear no responsibility for this expression of them.

Captain Paul Pihl, U. S. Navy, and Major Grant Mason, U. S. Army, went with me as representatives of those services and gave me valuable advice on the trip from their special knowledge. Everyone in the party and crew alike was helpful and companionable. But I know I am gratifying the wish of all when I pay special tribute to Major Richard (Dick) Kight, our equitable, engaging pilot, for his amazing skill in the operation of the bomber in which we flew.

W. L. W.

New York
March 2, 1943

I EL ALAMEIN

IN a four-engined Consolidated bomber, converted for transport
service and operated by United States Army officers, I left Mitchel
Field, New York, on August 26, to see what I could of the world and
the war, its battle fronts, its leaders, and its people. Exactly forty-nine
days later, on October 14, I landed in Minneapolis, Minnesota. I had
encircled the world, not in the northern latitudes where the circum-
ference is small, but on a route which crossed the equator twice.

I had traveled a total of 31,000 miles, which—looked at as a figure—
still impresses and almost bewilders me. For the net impression of my
trip was not one of distance from other peoples, but of closeness to
them. If I had ever had any doubts that the world has become small
and completely interdependent, this trip would have dispelled them
altogether.

The extraordinary fact is that to cover this enormous distance we
were in the air a total of only 160 hours. We usually flew from eight
to ten hours a day when we were on the move, which means that out of
the forty-nine days given to the trip, I had about thirty days on the
ground for the accomplishment of the purposes in hand. The physical
business of moving from one country to another, or from one continent
to another, was no more arduous than the trips an American businessman may make any day of his life to carry on his business. In fact,
moving about the world came to seem so easy that I promised the president of a great central Siberian republic to fly back some week end in
1945 for a day's hunting. And I expect to keep the engagement.

There are no distant points in the world any longer. I learned by this
trip that the myriad millions of human beings of the Far East are as
close to us as Los Angeles is to New York by the fastest trains. I cannot
escape the conviction that in the future what concerns them must con-

cern us, almost as much as the problems of the people of California concern the people of New York.

Our thinking in the future must be world-wide.

On the way to Cairo, at the end of August, bad news came to meet us. At Kano, Nigeria, there was open speculation as to how many days it might take General Rommel to cover the few miles which lay between his advance scouts and Alexandria. By the time we reached Khartoum, this speculation had become hard reports of what is known in Egypt as a "flap"—a mild form of panic. In Cairo, some Europeans were packing cars for flight southward or eastward. I recalled the President's warning to me just before I left Washington that before I reached Cairo it might well be in German hands. We heard tales of Nazi parachutists dropped in the Nile Valley to disorganize its last defenses. The British Eighth Army was widely believed to be preparing to evacuate Egypt altogether, retiring to Palestine and southward into the Sudan and Kenya.

Naturally, I wanted to check these reports. And Cairo itself was the world's worst place to check anything. There were good men there. Alexander Kirk, United States Minister to Egypt, was not hopeful about the future, but I learned from my long talks with him that he used his corrosive, cynical pessimism as a mask to cover what was really extensive knowledge of what was going on and great skill in trying to hold a fragile situation together. There were other well-informed men in Cairo, not least among them the round, laughing Prime Minister, Nahas Pasha, who has so much gusto and good humor that I told him if he would come to the United States and run for office, he would undoubtedly make a formidable candidate.

But the city was full of rumors and alarms. The streets were filled with officers and soldiers coming and going. A very tight censorship made the American reporters in Cairo doubt and feel skeptical of all British reports from the front. In a half-hour at Shepheard's Hotel, you could pick up a dozen different versions of what was taking place in the desert not much more than a hundred miles away.

So I accepted eagerly an invitation from General Sir Bernard L. Montgomery to see the front for myself, at El Alamein. With Mike Cowles and Major General Russell L. Maxwell, then commander of

United States forces in Egypt, we drove out of Cairo on the desert road to the front. I had bought, at a French department store in Cairo, a khaki shirt and trousers, both several sizes too small for me, but the best they had, and we borrowed the simple bedding which every man carries with him in desert fighting.

General Montgomery met me at his headquarters, hidden among sand dunes on the Mediterranean. In fact, it was so near the beach that he and General Alexander and I took our next morning's bath in those marvelous blue-green waters. Headquarters consisted of four American automobile trailers spaced a few dozen yards apart against the dunes for concealment purposes. In one of these, the general had his maps and battle plans. He gave me one for sleeping quarters. In another his aide put up and in the fourth the general himself lived, when he was not at the front.

This was not often. The wiry, scholarly, intense, almost fanatical personality of General Montgomery made a deep impression on me, but no part of his character was more remarkable than his passionate addiction to work. He was almost never in Cairo. He was usually at the front itself, with his men. I was surprised to find that he did not even know General Maxwell, who had been in complete charge of American forces in the Middle East for several weeks. When we drove up to his headquarters he took me aside and asked, "Who is that officer with you?" I replied, "General Maxwell." And he went on, "Who's General Maxwell?" I had just finished explaining when General Maxwell himself approached and I introduced the two.

Almost before we were out of our cars, General Montgomery launched into a detailed description of a battle which was in its last phases and which for the first time in months had stopped Rommel dead. No real news of this battle had reached Cairo or had been given to the press. The general repeated the details for us step by step, telling us exactly what had happened and why he felt it was a major victory even though his forces had not advanced any great distance. It had been a testing of strength on a heavy scale. Had the British lost, Rommel would have been in Cairo in a few days.

It was my first lesson in the strategy and tactics of desert warfare, in which distance means nothing and mobility and fire power are everything. At first it was hard for me to understand why the general kept repeating, in a quiet way, "Egypt has been saved." The enemy was deep in Egypt and had not retreated. I remembered the skepticism I had found in Cairo, born of earlier British claims. But before I left the trailer in which General Montgomery had rigged up his map room, I had learned more about desert warfare, and he had convinced me that something more than the ubiquitous self-confidence of the British officer and gentleman lay behind his assurance that the threat to Egypt had been liquidated.

General Montgomery spoke with great enthusiasm of the American-manufactured General Sherman tanks, which were just then beginning to arrive in important numbers on the docks at Alexandria and Port Said. He also spoke very highly of the 105-millimeter self-propelled antitank cannon of American make, which was just then beginning to prove that a tank *can* be stopped.

Almost his central thesis was his belief that earlier British reverses on the desert front had resulted from inadequate co-ordination of tank forces, artillery forces, and air power. General Montgomery told me he had his air officer living with him at his headquarters, and that complete co-ordination of planes, tanks, and artillery had been chiefly responsible for the decisive check to Rommel of the last few days. He estimated that the Germans had lost some 140 tanks, about half of them high-quality tanks, in the battle just about concluded, against a British loss of only 37 tanks; and he predicted that he would achieve the same supremacy on the ground that he already had in the air.

That evening, we had dinner in General Montgomery's tent with his superior officer, General Sir Harold R. L. G. Alexander, commander of all British forces in the Middle East, General Maxwell, Major General Lewis H. Brereton, then commanding American air forces in the Middle East, and his British counterpart, Air Marshal Sir Arthur Tedder. Air Marshal Tedder, whom I had also seen and talked with in Cairo, is a curiously charming and impressive soldier, with soft, quiet face and voice, who carries water colors with him on every assignment into the desert. He is a flying hero, and a thoughtful man.

Brereton and Tedder talked that night about the future of the campaign, and nothing that has happened since has made their talk seem bold or boasting. They were both convinced of the possibility of reopening the Mediterranean to United Nations shipping. They agreed that this could happen only after Rommel had been driven back west of the Bengasi bulge. Then, they said, we could again provision and garrison our forces in Egypt and farther east along shipping lanes which would hug the African coast under successive umbrellas of fighting aircraft based on Gibraltar, on Malta, on Bengasi, and on the huge United States air bases in Palestine. They also talked of large-scale bombing of Italy as a real possibility if they held the Bengasi region.

The conversation ranged over many subjects, one of the officers even explaining to me that in the British Army a latrine was irreverently called "The House of Lords." But General Montgomery did not want to talk much about anything except the front. He would listen politely to other talk and within a minute or two swing the conversation back to desert fighting. However, later, he and I walked from his mess tent over to my sleeping quarters. He made sure that my bunk was in order and then we sat on the steps of the trailer, from which we could see whitecaps breaking on the sea under the moon and hear at our backs in the distance the pounding of his artillery against Rommel's withdrawing forces. He was in a reminiscent and reflective mood and talked of his boyhood days in County Donegal, of his long years in the British Army, with service in many parts of the world, of his continuous struggle since the war began to infuse both public officials and Army officers with the necessity for an affirmative instead of a defensive attitude.

"I tell you, Willkie, it's the only way we will defeat the Boches"— he always spoke of the Germans as "the Boches." "Give them no rest, give them no rest. These Boches are good soldiers. They are professionals."

When I asked him about Rommel, he said, "He's a trained, skilled general. But he has one weakness. He repeats his tactics. And that's the way I'm going to get him."

He got up to go, wishing me a good rest, and saying, "I always read a bit before I turn in." And then a little sadly he told me that he had a few books with him. In fact, that everything he had in the world was with him. A short while before he left England he had stored his furnishings and his books, the collection of a lifetime, in a warehouse at Dover. "The Boches in a raid destroyed the warehouse," he added.

The next day we toured the front and I saw with my own eyes the clusters of tank and artillery troops, the occasional fighter-plane bases, and the formidable supply units which constitute a front in the fluid, checkerboard type of warfare that goes on in the desert. Again I was enormously impressed by the depth and thoroughness of General Montgomery's knowledge of his business. Whether it was corps or division, brigade, regiment, or battalion headquarters, he knew more in detail of the deployment of the troops and location of the tanks than did the officer in charge. This may sound extravagant but it was literally true. The man's passion for detail is amazing.

We inspected dozens of German tanks scattered over the desert. They had been captured by the British and blown up at Montgomery's orders. As we would climb up on these wrecked tanks, he would open the food boxes and hand to me the charred remnants of British provisions and supplies which the Germans had taken when they captured Tobruk. "You see, Willkie, the devils have been living on us. But they are not going to do it again. At least they are never going to use these tanks against us again."

All the while we were going over the front, the British artillery was thundering steadily and British and American aircraft were harassing Rommel's retreating troops. The Germans, in retaliation, were sending squadrons of Stuttgart planes in quick, sharp strafing raids against British artillery positions. Here and there above us, we would see in the bright sky a plane that had been hit spinning to the earth in a spiral of fire and smoke and occasionally we'd see the floating parachutes of the pilots who had been lucky enough to get out in time— all of them floating, it seemed to me, out over the Mediterranean, under the propulsion of a gentle breeze from the south.

Among the soldiers we saw at the front were Englishmen, Australians, New Zealanders, Canadians, South Africans, and a company of about thirty Americans. The last were a small tank corps which had been sent by air from the United States for training in actual battle conditions. I talked with each of the Americans and found that they represented eighteen different states. They seemed well and were frank about their desire to get back to the United States and they plied me with eager questions about the Dodgers and the Cardinals, who were then in the final race for the pennant. These men had just come out of the fighting and expected to go back in an hour. But there were no heroics, no big talk. They were just a group of physically hard, alert American boys who were wondering when they'd next see Texas, Broadway, and the Iowa farm.

At noon we stopped for lunch at the headquarters of a divisional commander, another group of automobile trailers. The lunch was sandwiches—and flies. At the front, the flies annoyed the soldiers almost as much as the Germans did. They get into your mouth and ears and nose. They are an irritation peculiar to desert warfare but as real, I should judge, as the mud of the trenches in France. Many of the officers also complained of the fine sand blowing constantly into their eyes and skin. It causes tremendous wear on all mechanical equipment, too. One flier told me that the usual types of airplane engine last only twenty-five per cent of normal expectancy in desert conditions, and everywhere I went in Egypt I found top-notch British and American air engineers talking about the intricacies of filters.

On the way back to General Montgomery's headquarters, he summed up what I had seen and heard. He minced no words at all in describing his situation as excellent, and the battle just concluded as a victory of decisive significance.

"With the superiority in tanks and planes that I have established as a result of this battle and with Rommel's inability to get reinforcements of matériel across the eastern Mediterranean—for our air forces are destroying four out of every five of his matériel transports—it is now mathematically certain that I will eventually destroy Rommel. This battle was the critical test."

I had seen his operating figures on his own and the enemy's tank losses and tank reserves. Many of the enemy's losses I had also seen with my own eyes. He affirmed the information I had been given earlier about the supplies that were even then being unloaded from American ships east of Alexandria.

And he asked a favor of me. He said that a spirit of defeatism permeated Egypt, North Africa, and the Middle East; that successive British failures had led many to believe that the Germans were going to capture Egypt. That because of this, Great Britain had lost prestige. And this loss interfered with his secret service and helped the enemy's. He had stopped Rommel but he was anxious for him not to begin to retreat into the desert before some three hundred American General

Sherman tanks that had just landed at Port Said could get into action. He estimated this would take about three weeks. He figured that if he made a formal public announcement of the result of the battle, Rommel's withdrawal might be hastened. But he thought that an unofficial statement made by me would not be regarded by Rommel as a sign of aggressive action on his part, while at the same time it would have an even greater effect than a formal British communiqué in stiffening the morale of Egypt and Africa and the Middle East.

I was convinced from all I had seen and heard that he was not over-estimating the importance of what he had accomplished and I was glad to do as he wished.

He accordingly called the representatives of the press to his head-quarters, and I told them the results of the battle in the language which he and I had agreed upon in advance: "Egypt is saved. Rommel is stopped and a beginning has been made on the task of throwing the Nazis out of Africa."

It was the first good news from the British side that these newspaper-men had had in a long time. They had been fooled many times and were wary. The battle line, to their eyes, had hardly sagged, Rommel was still only a few miles from the Nile, while the road to Tripoli, from where we were, seemed long and a little fanciful and the road to Cairo painfully short.

I saw in the faces of many of the reporters that afternoon a polite sort of skepticism. They had grown accustomed to generals who predict. They had had no experience with generals who perform.

From Montgomery's headquarters I flew in a little German scout plane, its cabin constructed almost entirely of glass so that one could see in all directions, low over the battlefield to the American and British air base. Air Marshal Tedder piloted the plane.

We saw, at the base, hundreds of American and British aviators, some just returned from fighting, some just taking off. Others sat about exchanging experiences, discussing the wind and the weather, all quite nonchalant. I inquired with some concern about the probable fate of the boys I had seen that morning floating with their parachutes toward the Mediterranean. They could not be identified, but the officer in charge said: "It's surprising how many of them drift back. Some fall behind enemy lines, some into the sea, and some far into the desert. But their ingenuity and self-reliance bring an amazing number of them back to headquarters."

After talking with a number of the American fliers, whom I found in much the same mood as the American soldiers I had seen on the desert, the Air Marshal and I flew on to Alexandria. This was an interlude which served to remind me that all this war is not so direct, so hard, and so essentially simple as the sand or the tanks or the long, clean gun barrels I had been looking at.

Two memories stand out in my mind today of Alexandria. The first was a long discussion with Rear Admiral René Godfroy, in command of the forlorn units of the French fleet in the harbor. His ships were visible from all over town. Their breechblocks were on the shore, their hulls were covered with barnacles, they had oil for only a short run. But still they represented an important potential striking power. And their presence there, great machines of death into which French peasants had poured their savings and French engineers and sailors their skill, useless, crippled, and without honor while France was still enslaved by the Nazis, was a tragic reminder that this war was still a confused and dirty business in which too many men and groups have not yet chosen sides.

Admiral Godfroy spoke good English. He impressed me as a high-grade, competent French officer, and the British officers who had introduced me to him confirmed my impression. He was sorely troubled by the turn of events in France, and almost uneducated in any meaning of the war outside his simple officer's discipline. He had obviously been deeply embittered by the naval actions of the British against French ships after June, 1940. But he expressed great friendship for the United States and a desire for our victory. Although, he said, he took his orders only from Marshal Pétain so long as the Marshal was alive, it was obvious from what he said to me about his own feelings, as well as the feelings of his sailors, that he hoped that American forces would come, and he gave me every indication that if they did the resistance of his fleet would be only a token one.

Since my talk with him and with other French officers, sailors, and soldiers in North Africa, I have never accepted without discount stories of the probable losses we would have sustained at the hands of the French if we had gone in directly as Americans without dealing with

Darlan. I have always suspected tales that can be neither proved nor disproved and which too aptly support a political policy.

My second memory of Alexandria is of a dinner that night at the home of Admiral Harwood, hero of the epic fight of the *Exeter* against the *Graf Spee* in South American waters, and now commander of the British Navy in the eastern Mediterranean. He invited to dine with us ten of his compatriots in the naval, diplomatic, or consular service in Alexandria. We discussed the war in the detached, almost impersonal way in which the war is discussed all over the world by officers engaged in fighting it, and then the conversation turned to politics. I tried to draw out these men, all of them experienced and able administrators of the British Empire, on what they saw in the future, and especially in the future of the colonial system and of our joint relations with the many peoples of the East.

What I got was Rudyard Kipling, untainted even with the liberalism of Cecil Rhodes. I knew that informed Englishmen in London and all over the British Commonwealth were working hard on these problems, that many of them, for example, were trying to find a formula which will go farther toward self-government than the older concept of "trusteeship." But these men, executing the policies made in London, had no idea that the world was changing. The British colonial system was not perfect in their eyes; it seemed to me simply that no one of them had ever thought of it as anything that might possibly be changed or modified in any way. The Atlantic Charter most of them had read about. That it might affect their careers or their thinking had never occurred to any of them. That evening started in my mind a conviction which was to grow strong in the days that followed it in the Middle East: that brilliant victories in the field will not win for us this war now going on in the far reaches of the world, that only new men and new ideas in the machinery of our relations with the peoples of the East can win the victory without which any peace will be only another armistice.

Next day we drove back to Cairo for long conferences with King Farouk, the Prime Minister, and later with Sir Miles Lampson, the British Ambassador to Egypt, and, for all practical purposes, its actual ruler. All along the way we passed through a strange medley of the ancient and the modern. Long camel trains with their native riders streamed by loaded with products of the Nile Valley, and rows of modern trucks hauled back to Cairo high-powered modern fighting planes to be repaired in modern machine shops—and always in the distance we could see those reminders of ancient Egyptian glory, the Sphinx and the pyramids.

II THE MIDDLE EAST

FROM Cairo to Teheran, we flew above trade routes and over cities which are as old as anything in our civilization and which have kept the variety and the contrasts of thousands of years of history. The blindfolded water buffaloes walking in endless circles around irrigation pumps in the valley of the Nile seemed at the time to have little to do with the great American repair depots I saw in Egypt. Underfed and scrawny children playing in the dirty streets of the old city at Jerusalem, young French cadets on the airfield at Beirut, Arab boys and girls of ten working in a blanket factory in Bagdad, Polish refugees camped in great barracks outside Teheran—the first picture I had of this region we call the Middle East was one of contrasts, sharp colors, and confusion.

In the air, between stops, an airplane gives a modern traveler a chance to map in his mind the land he is flying over. From Beirut to Lydda, to Bagdad, to Teheran, we had fairly long flights on which to compare notes and to sort out impressions. Before we left Iran for the Soviet Union, I had made up my own mind about the answers to some of the most immediate and pressing questions I had asked myself about the Middle East.

In the first place, I was convinced that all these peoples were more on our side than against us. Partly, this was simply because America was far away and not exercising any control over them. These are important reasons, by the way, for such popularity as the Germans still enjoy—in Iran, for example. In addition, America's entry into the war had convinced large numbers that whatever might be the temporary setbacks, the United Nations would eventually win. In other words, these peoples of the Middle East who have been overrun by successive conquerors since before the days of Alexander the Great have a large element of the purely practical in their thinking and an instinct for survival that leads them to pick the winning side before the conclusion becomes obvious.

In the second place, I was convinced that some sort of yeast was at work in nearly all the places I visited. Even the strictest kind of neutrality cannot keep the war from working its profound and violent changes on all the peoples who live in this region. Their lives will change more in the next ten years than they have in the last ten centuries.

In the third place, I found no automatic guarantee that these changes will be in our favor. The magic of our Western political ideas has been sharply challenged in the minds of many Moslems, many Arabs, many Jews, many Iranians. They have watched us now at close range, for almost a generation, while we have been fighting each other and ourselves and questioning the central structure of our own beliefs. Everywhere I found polite but skeptical people, who met my questions about their problems and difficulties with polite but ironic questions about our own. The maladjustments of races in America came up frequently, and I believe every government official I talked to wondered about our relations to Vichy. Arab and Jew were curious to know if our expressions of freedom meant only new and enlarged mandated areas which in the Lebanon and Syria and Palestine, rightly or wrongly, had come to mean to them a form of foreign tyranny.

Finally, everywhere I went in the Middle East I found a kind of technological backwardness along with poverty and squalor. Any American who makes this comment lays himself open, I realize, to the charge of being overconscious of bathtubs. But I understood in Jerusalem for the first time how so many other Americans have gone there with a real feeling of returning to Biblical times. The reason was that they were in truth returning to Biblical times, where little has changed in two thousand years. Modern airlines, oil pipe lines, macadam streets, or even plumbing constitute a thin veneer on the surface of a life which in essence is as simple and as hard as it was before there was any West. The only major exceptions to this one finds in the developments, industrial, agricultural, and cultural, which have been made under the supervision of the world Zionist movement or where the Arabs have, as in Bagdad, achieved a measure of self-government.

Four things, it seemed to me, these peoples need, in varying degree and in different ways. They need more education. They need more public-health work. They need more modern industry. And they need more of the social dignity and self-confidence which come from freedom and self-rule.

No one can travel down the Nile, I believe, even when it is the backdrop to a war, without realizing what education could do to help restore to the Egyptian people the national virility that history itself claims for them. The country has started schools; Americans and English have helped; I met Egyptians, from King Farouk and the Prime Minister, Nahas Pasha, to engineers and doctors, who would be recognized as educated men anywhere. Yet nowhere in Egypt—or in the whole Middle East, for that matter, except in Turkey—did anyone suggest showing me a native school as a matter of national pride. The only school that anyone urged me to see was a girls' school operated by an American woman who, under great discouragement, had been attempting to teach Egyptian orphans for thirty years.

I met pashas at every reception I went to. Many of them are married to foreign wives; they are socially attractive, genial men. Public squares are filled with statues of them. "Pasha" is a title which has survived in Egypt from Ottoman times. It was formerly a rank conferred on military leaders or provincial governors who served the empire well. Now it has become a courtesy title, bestowed by the king. Egyptian people figuratively and literally roll out the red carpet for a pasha whenever he appears, for he has the money with which to hire such services.

But when I asked one of my hosts, a young Egyptian newspaperman, "Does a man become a pasha by writing a great book?" he answered, "I suppose he could, except that almost no one in Egypt writes books."

"Do you get to be a pasha by painting pictures?" I asked.

"There is no reason why you couldn't, except that no one here paints pictures."

"Does a great inventor ever get to be a pasha?" And I was told once more, "We've had no great inventors that I know of since the time of the Pharaohs."

I was not in Egypt long enough to learn all the reasons for this cultural sterility. The fact that culture and education in Egypt's great cosmopolitan city of Cairo are dominated by non-Egyptians has something to do with it; as does the predominant ownership of Egypt's fertile

land by a small group of pashas who, for the most part, have attained
their titles not even by political activities but through the use of their
wealth.

But the major reason seemed to be the complete absence of a middle
class. Throughout the Middle East there is a small percentage of
wealthy landowners whose property is largely hereditary. I met a number of them and found them largely disinterested in any political movement, except as it affected the perpetuation of their own status. The
great mass of the people, outside of the roaming tribes, are impoverished, own no property, are hideously ruled by the practices of ancient
priestcraft, and are living in conditions of squalor. The urge and the
strength to create do not come, as a rule, from those who have too much
or from those who have nothing. In the Middle East there is little in
between.

Yet, strange as it may seem, one senses a ferment in these lands, a
groping of the long-inert masses, a growing disregard of restrictive
religious rites and practices. In every city I found a group—usually a
small group—of restless, energetic, intellectual young people who knew
the techniques of the mass movement that had brought about the revolution in Russia and talked about them. They knew also the history of
our own democratic development. In their talk with me they seemed to
be weighing in their minds the course through which their own intense,
almost fanatical, aspirations should be achieved. Likewise I found in
this part of the world, as I found in Russia, in China, everywhere, a
growing spirit of fervid nationalism, a disturbing thing to one who
believes that the only hope of the world lies in the opposite trend.

I found much the same discontent, hunger, and impatience in Iraq,
in the Lebanon, in Iran, and much the same time lag in official recognition of the problem, though the Prime and Foreign Ministers of those
countries are knowing and able men.

In Beirut, in Teheran, and in Cairo, Americans have begun to help
by founding and maintaining schools open to everyone. In Beirut, I
drank tea with Bayard Dodge, president of the American University of
Beirut, in his garden. That same day, I had met General Charles de
Gaulle, leader of the Fighting French, General Georges Catroux, their
Delegate General, and Major General Edward Louis Spears, the British
Minister, and had talked with each of them about the future of Syria

and the Lebanon. But it is no exaggeration to say that Dr. Dodge gave me more hope and confidence for the future of those regions than all the others combined.

I shall, however, never forget my visit with General de Gaulle. I was met at the airport at Beirut, received by an elaborately uniformed color guard and band, and whisked several miles to the house where the general was living—a great white structure, surrounded by elaborate and formal gardens, where guards saluted at every turn. We talked for hours in the general's private room, where every corner, every wall, held busts, statues, and pictures of Napoleon. The conversation continued through an elaborate dinner and went on late into the night, as we sat out on a beautiful starlit lawn.

Frequently the general, in describing his struggle of the moment with the British as to whether he or they should dominate Syria and the Lebanon, would declare dramatically, "I cannot sacrifice or compromise my principles." "Like Joan of Arc," his aide added. "When I referred to my great interest in the Fighting French movement, he corrected me sharply. "The Fighting French are not a movement. The Fighting French are France itself. We are the residuary legatees of all of France and its possessions." When I reminded him that Syria was but a mandated area under the League of Nations, he said, "Yes, I know. But I hold it in trust. I cannot close out that mandate or let anyone else do so. That can be done only when there is a government again in France. In no place in this world can I yield a single French right, though I am perfectly willing to sit with Winston Churchill and Franklin Roosevelt and consider ways and means by which French rights and French territories can be momentarily and temporarily used in order to help drive the Germans and the collaborators from the control of France.

"Mr. Willkie," he continued, "some people forget that I and my associates represent France. They apparently do not have in mind France's glorious history. They are thinking in terms of its momentary eclipse."

Later I was talking with one of the high officials of the Lebanon about the struggle that was then going on between the French and the British for the control of Syria and the Middle East. I asked him where his sympathies lay, and he replied, "A plague on both their houses."

The intellectual leaven in the Middle East has little faith in a system of mandates and colonies, whatever power controls.

From Beirut I went on to Jerusalem. Never was the contrast between old and new more dramatic. For from the windows of our modern, smoothly, swiftly flying plane we could look down through the clear air upon the hills where once stood the cedars of Lebanon, upon the Dead Sea, the Sea of Galilee, the river Jordan, the Mount of Olives, and the Garden of Gethsemane.

In Jerusalem I was the guest of Sir Harold MacMichael, the athletic, pipe-smoking, very able and very British Resident High Commissioner for Palestine and Trans-Jordan. He showed me the old city and explained with infinite patience and good humor the distinctions an American finds it hard to see between a colony and a mandated area.

But it was Lowell C. Pinkerton, American Consul General at Jerusalem, who arranged for me to see at first hand the real intricacies of the problems of Palestine. Through his hospitable house, he ushered in order representatives of all the conflicting factions of Jews and Arabs, and for one crowded day Joe Barnes and Mike Cowles and I interviewed them. Major General D. F. McConnel, commander of British forces in the area, came in, and Robert Scott, acting chief secretary of Sir Harold's administration; able and understanding Moshe Shertok, head of the political department of the Jewish Agency, and Ruhi Bey Abdul Hadi, Arab member of Sir Harold's secretariat; Dr. Arieh Altman, head of the Revisionist faction of Zionism which claims the entire country for the Jews; and Awni Bey Abdul Hadi, Arab lawyer and nationalist leader who claims the whole country for the Arabs. All told us their stories.

By the end of the day, I felt a great temptation to conclude that the only solution of this tangled problem must be as drastic as Solomon's. But then I went to call on Miss Henrietta Szold, founder of Hadassah, in her small, simply furnished apartment. I told her of my day of interviewing and of my talk with Sir Harold MacMichael, of my confusion and of my anxiety to find the answer. I asked her if she thought it true that certain foreign powers were deliberately stirring up trouble between the Jew and the Arab to help sustain their own control.

She said: "With a sad heart I must tell you it is true." Then she said to me, "Mr. Willkie, this problem has been with me for many years. I cannot live comfortably in America while it is unsolved. There is no other appropriate place in the world where the persecuted Jews of Europe can come. And no matter how much we may wish it, that persecution will not end in your lifetime or in mine. The Jews must have a national homeland. I am an ardent Zionist, but I do not believe that there is a necessary antagonism between the hopes of the Jews and the rights of the Arabs. I am urging my fellow Jews here in Jerusalem to do those simple things that break down the prejudices, the differences between people. I urge each of them to make friends with a few Arabs to demonstrate by their way of life that we are not coming as conquerors or destroyers, but as a part of the traditional life of the country, for us a sentimental and religious homeland."

She told me of her belief in the possibilities of education, and though she is an old lady, nearing eighty, her stories of what had already been done on many of the Jewish farm colonies and in Jewish industry under Zionist direction were full of youth and vitality.

It is probably unrealistic to believe that such a complex question as the Arab-Jewish one, founded in ancient history and religion, and involved as it is with high international policy and politics, can be solved by good will and simple honesty. But as I sat there that late afternoon with the sun shining through the windows, lighting up that intelligent, sensitive face, I, at least for the moment, wondered if she in her mature, selfless wisdom might not know more than all the ambitious politicians.

Coupled everywhere with the problem of education in the Middle East was that of medicine and public health. It is hard to travel anywhere in those lands without being uncomfortably conscious all the time of disease and pestilence, and it is hard to see a future for these peoples without a determined drive to improve their health and vitality.

As with education, a few natives and a few foreigners, especially Americans, have already shown what can be done. The malaria record of the United States Army detachments I saw in Egypt, Palestine, or Iran will be one of the exciting disclosures to be made after the war. Screened windows, double doors, careful inspection of servants, drainage of standing water, mosquito boots and mosquito netting have left a mark, I believe, on the imaginations of the peoples of the Middle East. After all, nobody likes malaria.

As public health is improved in these countries, it will have interesting consequences not to be found in any medical book. For health measures must be universal to be effective; disease is no respecter of persons. And as the ordinary man or woman shares in the advantages of a lower mortality rate and a more vigorous life, he is likely, unless I miss my guess, to grow fond of sharing.

Sleeping arrangements for visiting foreigners like our party were certainly not typical. In Jerusalem, as a guest of Sir Harold Mac-Michael, I found no mosquito bar on the bed but a long coiled snake of green punk on a table. I left mine strictly alone, but one of my companions lit his. He reported that it smoldered gently and agreeably through the night and gave him at least a sense of great security. In Bagdad great fans set in the ceiling whirled all night in the Bilat, the special guest palace where we were lodged. It had been constructed to house Prince Bertil of Sweden a few years ago. In Beirut, Syrian boys with fly swatters stalked carefully through the rooms of General Catroux's *Résidence des Pins* before we went to bed. You begin to understand the problem, though, not in watching these time-honored precautions for the privileged, but in examining a mosquito that seems as big as a dragonfly that has escaped all the traps set for him and is about to settle on your arm in the morning, while you uneasily remember the lectures and the warnings that have met you at every stop from New York to Bagdad.

The real public-health problem, of course, is poverty. Bilharziasis takes a frightening toll of lives in Egypt. It is a disease carried by snails which inhabit the Nile. Egyptians drink and bathe in the Nile and its tributary canals and suffer terribly from the devitalizing effects of the disease they catch from the water. The problem, however, is not only to eliminate the snails from the river but also to give the Egyptians a filtered water supply. And this costs money.

Trachoma blinds the eyes of little children in all hot countries, and we saw it on the streets of Cairo, of Jerusalem, of Bagdad. Even with medical care and prevention, however, we shall not eliminate it until people come to want a way of living that will makes flies undesirable. That means adequate housing and refrigeration and screening.

Perhaps the most startling example we saw of bad health on a large scale was in Teheran, capital of Iran. The city's water supply runs

through open gutters along the sides of the streets. People wash themselves and their clothes in it, pump it upstairs to their apartments, drink
it, cook in it. The old proverb that water cleans itself after it turns over
seven times may keep them quiescent, but it does not keep them from
dysentery, cholera, malaria, and a dozen other water-carried diseases.
Only one out of every five children born in Teheran lives to the age of
six.

It is all very well to say, as some people did say to me in Cairo
and Jerusalem, that "the natives don't want anything better than what
they have." That is the argument that has been used everywhere for
centuries against the advancement of the underprivileged, by those
whose condition makes them satisfied with the *status quo*. Yet the history of civilization shows that the creation of economic conditions under
which those who have little or nothing can improve their lot is not a
dividing process but a multiplying one, by which the well-being of all
society is advanced. Both education and public health in the Middle
East, it seemed to me, depend on the achievement of a higher standard
of living, and this in turn requires the introduction of modern technical
and industrial methods of producing goods and services.

Undoubtedly such improvement in living standards will add to the
markets of the world. For the Middle East is a vast, dry sponge, ready
to soak up an infinite quantity and variety of goods and services. There
is potential practical advantage, then, in encouraging better living
standards among these peoples. But there is an even stronger and more
urgent reason for facing this problem. For the present lack of equilibrium between these peoples and their world is a potential source of
conflict, the possible origin of another war.

The facts are simple enough. If we had left the olive groves and
the cotton fields and the oil wells of this region alone, we might not
have had to worry about this equilibrium—at least not yet. But we
have not left them alone. We have sent our ideas and our ideals, and
our motion pictures and our radio programs, our engineers and our
businessmen, and our pilots and our soldiers into the Middle East; and
we cannot now escape the result.

In effect, this result has been to render obsolete and ineffective the
old ways of life. A few miles from Cairo, I saw Egyptian boys not ten
years old pumping water into irrigation ditches with pumps as primi-

tive as the first wheel. Those little boys seemed docile enough, but they won't be for long. All of Egypt, in its curious position of "non-belligerent alliance" with Great Britain, has shown as clearly as a nation can its fundamental indifference as to which side wins. This is not wholly Britain's fault, but it seems to me intimately linked with the way both the British and we ourselves have disregarded our obligations.

This problem, as it seems to me, of bringing the peoples of the Middle East into the twentieth century in technical and industrial terms is, in turn, intimately linked with the question of political self-government. Many Westerners whom I met and talked with in these countries told me the several reasons, valid in their minds, for the extremely primitive backwardness in which most Arabs live. These reasons ranged from the charge that Arabs actually prefer to die young to the statement that their religion prevents them from accumulating the capital with which to make the improvements they need in their way of life. To my mind, these reasons were mostly nonsense. Give any Arabs I saw a chance to feel that they were running their own show, and they would change the world they live in.

Freedom or self-government, talked about in the context of the Middle East, is too absolute a concept to be useful to an American. On the one hand, people who are against it point to the chaos and confusion which would result if all these peoples were suddenly left free to rule themselves. On the other hand, people who are for it paint too black a picture of Western influence in the Middle East, describing it as sheer imperialist exploitation and forgetting the very real gains which have come with French and British and American commercial expansion there.

The pragmatic, realistic truth lies in the middle. I found only very few Arabs or Jews or Egyptians or Iranians who wanted the West to get out lock, stock, and barrel, and at once. For the most part, they wanted an orderly, scheduled plan under which Britain and France would transfer to them a steadily increasing share of responsibility for their own government.

This seems to me a reasonable enough desire. In a country like Iraq, I saw that it can be satisfied. Iraq is one of the very few countries in the world which has passed through colonial status to that of mandated area and then become, technically, a free and sovereign state. I had some chance to see that its sovereignty was still circumscribed by British needs, but at least these were military needs, connected with the winning of the war.

I liked the men I met in Iraq. Prince Abdul Ilah, the Regent, gave me a state dinner under the stars in Bagdad that I shall remember all my life. He stood on a handsome carpet on a vast lawn to greet his guests. On other carpets near his stood the chiefs of his government. Some of them were in robes and turbans, including the Minister of Economics, curiously enough, and the President of the Senate, who is known locally to irreverent foreigners as "God," because of his handsome desert costume, and his long beard. Others were in Western dress. Nearly every minister, I learned, had at some time held nearly every portfolio in the government.

"With a small deck of cards," an Iraqi friend told me, "you must shuffle them often."

A couple of nights later, another dinner was given, this time by Nuri as-Said Pasha, the Premier of Irak. He is a small man, with a keen, inquisitive look on his face and one of the shrewdest minds I have ever met. He had been returned to power only in 1941 after the British had had to use troops to throw out Rashid Ali al Gailani, his predecessor, who had been bought by the Germans. Nuri was running Iraq as a nonbelligerent ally of Great Britain, with a keen desire to get into the fight, which he has since done. Sir Kinahan Cornwallis, British Minister at Bagdad and another of the tall, pipe-smoking, able, quiet, and very British Colonial Office empire-builders whom I met all through the Middle East, was undoubtedly a man to whom Nuri listened with, to put it mildly, respectful attention. But I suspected that Nuri was a realist, that he was not likely to bog down in any dispute over theoretically complete freedom from British control, and that he knew time was playing on his side in his struggle to build the first really modern and independent Arab state.

Nuri's dinner was an Arabian Nights picture of the Middle East. We had spent the day seeing Bagdad, its fantastic Shi'ah mosque sprouting gold minarets into the sky, its dusty adobe walls and houses, a bazaar where copper and silver craftsmen were making bowls and pitchers but the stores sold only machine-made trinkets from New York or Liverpool, one of the finest museums in the world filled with the Ur-Chaldee finds which date from the very beginning of our history, a café where we drank Arab coffee with crowds of people talking, reading papers, or playing backgammon around us. Even against this background, the dinner was fabulous.

After a few formal speeches, the dinner became a concert, and the concert became an exhibition of Arab dancing girls, and this in turn became a Western ball with English nurses and American soldiers up from Basra on the Persian Gulf and Iraqi officers dancing under an Arabian sky. No man could have sat through that evening and preserved any notion that the East and the West will never meet, or that Allah is determined to keep the Arabs a desert folk, ruled by foreigners from across the seas.

The next day, flying from Bagdad to Teheran, I was thinking over the events of the night before. And I became aware of certain sober undercurrents that had been beneath the gaiety, the same undercurrents I had noticed before in talking with students, newspapermen, and soldiers throughout the Middle East. It all added up to the conviction that these newly awakened people will be followers of some extremist leader in this generation if their new hunger for education and opportunity for a release from old restrictive religious and governmental practice is not met by their own rulers and their foreign overlords. The veil, the fez, the sickness, the filth, the lack of education and modern industrial development, the arbitrariness of government, all commingled in their minds to represent a past imposed upon them by a combination of forces within their own society and the self-interest of foreign domination. Again and again I was asked: does America intend to support a system by which our politics are controlled by foreigners, however politely, our lives dominated by foreigners, however indirectly, because we happen to be strategic points on the military roads and trade routes of the world? Or, they would say, to put it your way: because we are strategic points which must be held to prevent Axis or some other non-democratic domination of the key military roads and trade routes of the world? Because our canals, our seas, and our countries are necessary to the control of the eastern Mediterranean and constitute the road to Asia?

I know this problem can be oversimplified in its statement and is not susceptible of easy answers. I know that the retention of points such as Suez, the eastern Mediterranean, and the roads through Asia Minor to the East obviously, if our Western democracy is not to be threatened by hostile forces, must be kept in both friendly and stabilized hands. Likewise, I know there is much historical and even present-day justification for the current "protective" colonial system. Pragmatically, however, in view of the ferment which is going on, it is a question whether that system can be maintained. Idealistically, we must face the fact that the system is completely antipathetic to all the principles for which we claim we fight. Furthermore, the more we preach those principles, the more we stimulate the ferment that endangers the system.

I know all this. But I am here reporting what is in the minds of Prime Ministers, Foreign Ministers, awakened intellectual groups to be found in every city of the Middle East, and even vaguely in the minds of uneducated masses. Somehow, with a new approach and a patient wisdom, the question must be answered or a new leader will arise with a fierce fanaticism who will coalesce these discontents. And the result will be of necessity either the complete withdrawal of outside powers with a complete loss of democratic influence or complete military occupation and control of the countries by those outside powers.

If we believe in the ends we proclaim and if we want the stirring new forces within the Middle East to work with us toward those ends, we must cease trying to perpetuate control by manipulation of native forces, by playing off one against the other for our own ends.

III TURKEY, A NEW NATION

THAT vast and ancient portion of the globe which stretches from
North Africa around the eastern end of the world's oldest sea and
up to Bagdad on the road to China may well be the area in which our
war will be won or lost. It is still a potential battleground; American
tanks and planes are there with those of the British and the Fighting
French and other United Nations. But it is more than a battleground;
it is also a great social laboratory where ideas and loyalties are being
tested by millions of people in the slow but inexorable process by which
the war is also being fought, and won or lost, in the minds of men.

One's feeling that the Middle East is stirring and changing finds conviction in Turkey. For the Republic of Turkey has in one generation
offered a possible prototype for what is happening to all the vast area
that used to be the Ottoman Empire. And, in one form or another, the
ideas which Turkey plants in the mind of an American today are reinforced by everything he sees all the way to the borders of Russia, China,
and India.

Turkey is a new republic; it celebrated its nineteenth birthday last fall.
It is weaker than some of its European neighbors; when I was there
every Turk I spoke to was acutely conscious that his country might be
attacked any day. Finally, it is far smaller than it once was—a sprawling
empire become a neat, cohesive nation.

In spite of being young, and comparatively weak, and small, Turkey
looked good to me. It looked good because it was quite clearly determined
to defend its neutrality with every resource at its command. It looked
good because it had set its face toward the modern world and was building, hard and fast. It looked good because I saw a great many tough and
honest faces, some in uniform and some not, on people who quite obviously had a future to fight for. Finally, it looked good to me because I

thought I saw, in Turkey, a nation which had found itself—a sign that the ideas of increasing health, education, freedom, and democracy are as valid in the oldest portions of the world as they are in the newest.

Ankara is not one of the world's large capitals. It is modern, with part of an ancient village left on a hill as if to remind the Turks how far they have already gone. From another hill, on which Ataturk, the father of the new republic, built his own home, you can walk down tree-shaded streets, with broad pavements, to the center of the city. The streets are full of cars; the people are well dressed and busy; the buildings are new and good-looking.

One day I drove out of Ankara, some forty miles into the country to the east. Outside the city's limits, you find yourself in ancient Anatolia. There are a hardness and strength about this countryside which help you understand why Ataturk so resolutely turned his back on Constantinople, the traditional Ottoman capital, now called Istanbul, and put his capital city here in the middle of the Anatolian plain.

For one thing, it is tough country to attack. A small army, well trained and well equipped, could hold this kind of countryside for a long time against invading, mechanized armies.

Shepherds graze their flocks in the hills. But even in the country, there was evidence of the reconstruction which Turkey has pushed so hard in the nineteen years since it became a republic. Men were building a new highway to the east; we drove by steam rollers and stone crushers at work on this road. There is a good deal of modern irrigation—the kind of irrigation which might someday transform large parts of Anatolia into prosperous farming country. The Turks are proud of their progress in public education, irrigation, and industrial developments and were anxious for us to see what they were doing.

In a village we visited, primarily to see a teachers' training school, they had built a house around the village spring. The house was of concrete and glass; it stood in the exact center of the village. On one side was water for drinking; on another there was provision for washing clothes; the children of the village had a stream to play in. As I stood and looked at this pleasant development, I saw veiled women sitting motionless on the roof of a house in their traditional fashion. But I also saw boys and girls who were looking at the clean spring as I was—at something new and good and exciting.

I saw as much of Turkish industry as I could in a short stay. It is not impressive in size compared to the industries of the German nation which may attack it. But it is impressive in its quality and in the promise it holds for the future. I saw airfields and mechanized army equipment, and railroads, and the most advanced type of building construction. I saw all of these and more, and I convinced myself again that the industrial revolution is not the monopoly of any one nation or of any one race. The combustion engine has awakened millions of people in the Middle East—awakened and disturbed them. To these Turks, it has already brought new skills and new hungers. Now that they want the modern world, and have begun to learn how to handle its tools, it is going to be very hard to stop them.

Even more impressive than the industrial and economic reconstruction of Turkey, going on in the middle of the war, is the social and educational revolution which has taken place. To the visitor's eye in any country clothes furnish a surface indication of the attitude toward change. In Bagdad I had seen government officials, some wearing Western garb, others wearing the traditional robes of the Moslem. In China the President is reverenced for his compliance with the customs and the dress of old China, while Mme Chiang dresses in the Chinese manner but manages to give the effect of at least a glance at *Vogue*. In Turkey every official proudly and exclusively wears Western dress. The fez has been legally abolished as one of the symbols of the change. The few veiled women one encounters already seem an anachronism. Under the leadership of Ataturk and the determined, capable men who succeeded him, the Turks have literally and figuratively abolished the veils of the ancient East. They have stripped them from the faces of their people and the light that has replaced them is there, one feels, to stay.

And this revolution in age-old custom was brought about without badges or uniforms or mass hysteria. It was achieved without attacking any other country.

America has some reason for special pride in this. Robert College, outside Istanbul, which I unfortunately could not visit, remains today what it has been for years—an unselfish experiment in the internationalism of education. Its graduates are now sitting behind some of the most important desks in Turkey. They are turning to good use the knowledge and ideas given them by American teachers who had no other purpose than to make the whole world richer by fighting against superstition and ignorance in one part of it.

But even Americans may have difficulty in understanding how deep this question of education cuts all over Asia. We take our schools and our books for granted. Our children are students without our wondering why or how.

In the Turkish countryside you see education for what it is to people who do not take it for granted. I stood in a plain little school, built by the children and their teachers, and listened to young Turkish boys sing their national anthem. I watched them learn their own national folk dances, embodying the gestures of the ancient crafts which once flourished in Anatolia. But they were being taught according to modern educational methods and they were studying scientific agriculture. It is my deep conviction that opening the books to people in this way is one of the decisive events of history. It is a turning in the road, and one from which there is no turning back.

Modern Turkey is a country which, in spite of its youth and the relative inexperience of its people with freedom and self-government, very definitely has something to fight for. You see this in the faces of people you talk with; you hear it in their speech. It is written large in their new cities, like Ankara, and in their old villages, like those I saw in the Turkish countryside.

But, very naturally, the Turks do not want to fight, knowing how terribly destructive to all their new accomplishment would be an invasion of the German legions. Turkey is a small country. Its sixteen million people have no ambitions outside their own frontiers, and they have no illusions about what they can do to swing the balance in this global war. So they have decided on a policy of armed neutrality. Last fall, they had more than a million of their men in the Turkish Army. They have developed a military machine which makes up in resoluteness and in training much of what it lacks in some branches of modern military equipment. I talked to the assistant chief of staff of the Turkish Army, and I saw his soldiers everywhere I went in the country, standing sentry duty, on maneuvers, in military schools. They impressed me as a very respectable problem for any aggressor nation that might want to use Turkey as a highway to conquest of the East.

Besides seeing Turkey's soldiers, I talked at very considerable length to the leaders of the country's government, the men who were watching Europe with the fearful anxiety of men who did not know when, or even if, they were going to be plunged into a war to save their country.

That is a terrible anxiety to live under. But not a single man in Turkey gave me the slightest hint that there would be anything other than bitter, determined, savage resistance to any threat which jeopardized their peace and safety.

I think this was more than a tale men might fix up to impress a visiting foreigner. I talked with Mr. Saracoglu, the talented and attractive man who is now Turkey's Prime Minister. I talked with Noumen Bey, the wise and distinguished diplomat who succeeded Mr. Saracoglu as Foreign Minister. I talked to many other members of the government, and to Turkish newspapermen, and to soldiers and to peasants and to workingmen. And the story each of these men told me was the same: "We don't want a war or any part of it. But the first soldier who crosses our frontier will be shot, and before we have stopped shooting in our hills and along our roads and in our forests, there will be a lot of dead foreigners."

They always spoke of "foreigners," and they always insisted that their determination to fight was directed against any country which might attack them, from any direction. But it was clear without their saying it that their immediate fears were riveted in one direction. Today they do not fear us, or our English allies who are also Turkey's allies, or the hard-pressed Russians, although they are troubled about Russia's ultimate designs. Their immediate anxiety lies in the West, in the top-heavy power which has been built up in Europe in the last few years and which threatens to spill over into Asia, across their territory. They look with anxiety and with fear, because they do not want to fight, but not with panic and not with any notion of appeasement. Germany has twice attempted a major "peace offensive" in their capital. And it has twice failed.

They would like to deal with us. They are prepared to trade goods. They produce, in Turkey, nearly one-quarter of the world's supply of chrome. Their tobacco and their cotton are badly needed by other countries. With these assets, the Turks can buttress their neutrality, for a time, at any rate. They need foodstuffs—wheat especially—and they need manufactures and machinery, as I was at pains to discover. And I have been greatly pleased that since my return we have been sending them increasingly large quantities of foodstuffs and other materials. For we are today the only country which can adequately supply them. I deeply believe that it is to our interest to do so, as far as we are able, to prevent Turkish resources from going to our enemies, and to preserve the neutrality of a country which wants to be our friend.

And of that there can be no doubt. Nearly a decade of the heavy pounding of Dr. Goebbels and his Nazi propaganda machine has not changed the slower but deeper trend of the awakening people of Turkey toward closer relations with the world's great democracies. The Turks are our friends. They both like and admire us. They do not fear us, nor do they envy us.

Their neutrality, however, is honestly administered. They refused, for example, to allow me to come to their country in the United States Army plane which took me around the world, and I had to change at Cairo into a Pan-American Airways plane to fly up the eastern coast of the Mediterranean and over the bleak and bumpy Taurus Mountains to Ankara. At the airfield where we landed we saw the three carefully guarded Liberator bombers which the Turks had interned after American fliers had been forced down on their return from raids on the oil fields at Ploesti, in Rumania.

But underneath this neutral correctness, there was a cordiality no one could mistake. When the Axis radio during my visit complained of my presence in Turkey, I told the newspapermen that the answer was simple: "Invite Hitler to send to Turkey, as a representative of Germany, his opposition candidate." The remark, I found afterward, caused much quiet amusement among Turkish government officials.

Interestingly enough, although nationalism in Turkey has been the slogan under which so much has been accomplished, Turkey and its officials have more receptiveness to the necessity of international co-operation beyond and outside its own immediate needs than any other country I visited. This was emphasized to me in all the long and frank talks I had with the Prime Minister, the Foreign Minister, and the leading publishers.

Of course, as in all capitals, one sees amusing manifestations of an international society. One night, Noumen Bey, the Foreign Minister, gave a dinner outside of Ankara. It was at the country house of Ataturk, a model farm and dairy which he started outside the city limits. At least, they told me it was a model farm; all I saw was a handsome modern palace on a hill with terraced flower gardens stepping down toward the lights of Ankara in the distance.

In one room of this house, used now by the Foreign Minister for official entertainments, there was a telephone that had been used by Ataturk, made of solid gold. In another room was an old-fashioned Turkish machine for making "shish-kebab"; a chef turned slowly an enormous cylinder of mutton over an open charcoal fire slicing its cooked surface into bowls of rice.

In the main ballroom stood Noumen Bey, our host. He is one of the most accomplished foreign diplomats of this generation, on his record, and he looks the part. His health is not good, but his pallor and a general frailty only emphasize the courtly skill with which he seems to be watching Europe and the world. I found his mind, like his appearance, a little sad, a little cynical, very strong, and very subtle.

Around him danced or drank or talked the diplomats of all the countries on our side. Axis-inspired newspapermen had come to the press conference I held in Ankara, but the Axis diplomats in Turkey do not mix at parties with those of the United Nations. There was still variety enough. The Soviet Ambassador was in Moscow on a trip, but his chargé d'affaires was at the party, very correct in evening clothes—I had none —but with a grim, unlaughing manner. A tall English lady in marabou feathers seemed in striking contrast. Later I learned her husband had fought in Crete. The representatives of Greece and Yugoslavia came up to me with their arms around each other's shoulders to tell me their plans for the confederation of Europe. Another diplomat, whose name I never learned, told me with excitement but with bewildering inaccuracy that he had heard that an American boxer named Conn had just knocked out Joe Louis. The magnificent-looking Ambassador of Afghanistan complained to me that he had taken his post at Ankara chiefly for the hunting and now found that Turkey's preparedness measures barred him from his favorite sport.

In all this confusion, which mirrored well enough the world we live in, the figure of my host, Noumen Bey, grew in stature. Like his predecessor in the Foreign Ministry and present chief, Saracoglu, he drew his strength from no aristocracy of birth or of doctrine. He had fought hard through a long life, first by the side of Ataturk and the Turkish people, and now with the Turkish people alone. I watched him that night at his own party, at which we drank English whisky and ate Russian caviar and danced to American music in the curious internationalism of the diplomatic world, and I was more than ever convinced that the Turkish people have put their bets on a different world emerging from this war.

Like the redheaded, blue-eyed children who surprised me every time I saw them in Turkey, or the hard, iron-faced soldiers on the streets, or the schoolteachers who had learned their soft, pleasant English at Robert College, Noumen Bey seemed to me to personify a vast leaven which is now working deep in the lives of something more than half the human race. He was the product of an ancient people, and a proud tradition, but he was living through, in his own generation, one of the most profound changes ever experienced by any people.

In the last war, Turkey was on the German side. The Ottoman Empire, out of the ruins of which this new republic grew, was popular nowhere in the world. Even the word "Turk" was an evil word.

The change has been so quick that many of us have missed it. For something less than two decades, the phenomenal struggle of Ataturk and his friends, like Noumen Bey and Saracoglu, has channeled the energies and ambitions of their people into new ways of living.

Like the Arabs of the Middle East, like the peoples who live around the borders of China or on the islands of the southwest Pacific, like the Indians, they had no experience with self-government until a generation ago. They had almost no education, wretched standards of public health and sanitation, and a long history of exploitation and poverty and misery. In a few brief years they have completely transformed their habits of life, their ancient customs, and their ways of thinking.

A woman I came to know in Turkey brought these changes home to me in a peculiarly real fashion. She was pure Turk, an attractive, middle-aged woman who spoke English well and whose conversation was that of any intelligent woman today. She was a resident of Istanbul but was in Ankara arguing a series of cases before the Turkish Supreme Court. For she is a lawyer, one of Turkey's most distinguished lawyers, with a large practice. The fact that she was a woman and a lawyer excited no particular comment that I could see. In fact, I met several other young women who were studying law, including daughters of government officials.

And this was in Turkey. I could not help thinking of my boyhood days when, only forty years ago, my mother's active practice of the law and interest in public affairs were considered unusual—almost peculiar—in central Indiana.

IV OUR ALLY, RUSSIA

On Thursday, September 18, I flew into the Soviet Union over the Caspian Sea, across the salt, red mud flats at the delta of the Ural River, and up to the Volga River at Kuibishev. I left Russia ten days later, flying down the Ili River along the old silk route to China from Tashkent in central Asia. Later, on the way home from China, our plane again made three landings in Russia, in Siberia.

I was in Russia a total of only two weeks. I had never been there before. I do not speak a word of Russian, but I had Americans with me to act as interpreters. I had read a great deal about the Soviet Union, but nothing I had read had ever given me a very clear picture of what was going on in that vast country. Finally, I suspected before I went to Russia, and became more and more certain as I stayed there, that the country is so vast and the change it has gone through so complicated that only a lifetime of study and a shelfful of books could begin to tell the whole truth about the Soviet Union.

It is true, and worth reporting, that the Soviet government gave me every chance to find out what I wanted to learn. It permitted me to examine in my own way its industrial and war plants, its collective farms, its schools, its libraries, its hospitals, its war front. I came and went as freely as though I had been making a similar trip through the United States, and I asked questions—unexpected questions of unexpected people—without limit or interference, and always in the presence of an American who understood and spoke Russian.

A visitor for the first time to Russia inevitably reflects now and then upon the past. One late afternoon in Kuibishev I found myself thinking of pre-revolutionary times. I walked alone to the edge of the steep bank on the western side of the Volga and sat on a park bench looking down

44

at the river. The government had given us a Red Army rest home right at the river's edge. There was a biting cold already in the air, but the leaves were still on the trees. Along the bank stretched small, unpainted *dachas*—the country bungalows of which Russians are so fond—and pine trees, and there was an air of deep quiet and strength, like the great river below. Beyond the pine trees was wheat land rolling down the river to Stalingrad, where Russian soldiers were holding a mass of rubble against Nazi tanks and planes.

At the river's edge, below me, a boat had finished unloading its cargo of birch logs. The logs were stacked in a pile that must have covered several acres. With the Don Basin lost, with war industries getting every lump of coal available, this was the only fuel Russian cities would have to burn in the cold winter to come. A shepherd led a flock of sheep along the shore. In the middle of the river a tanker, loaded full, was moving slowly upstream. A young Russian soldier walked along the path behind the sheep, kicking pebbles into the river with his foot. When he took off his hat, the wind ruffled his hair to make him look even younger, and it was only then that I noticed his hat had the insignia of the NKVD, or secret police.

I thought of the pre-1917 shipbuilder who had built the resthouse behind me as a summer home. I had been told that he had been a power in the land, a tight-fisted shipowner and grain merchant who had prospered in the commerce of the Volga when the town had been called Samara and been liquidated when it was called Kuibishev, for the Samaran revolutionist who devised the first Five-Year Plan. The house had stayed, a little less shabby than its neighbors, because the Red Army had found it useful.

I could see, it seemed to me, the entire generation of men and women who had been destroyed, the families that had been scattered, the loyalties that had been broken, the thousands who had died from war and assassination and starvation, in the name of the revolution.

The true story of that period will probably never be told in detail. For except for those who escaped to other lands, and they were relatively few, practically the whole upper and middle classes of Russia have been completely exterminated. And Russians today find the story a heroic achievement.

I had not realized before coming to Russia to what extent that is true.

For I had not sufficiently taken into account, in appraising modern Russia, that it is ruled by and composed almost entirely of people whose parents had no property, no education, and only a folk heritage. That there is hardly a resident of Russia today whose lot is not as good as or better than his parents' lot was prior to the revolution. The Russian individual, like all individuals, naturally finds some good in a system that has improved his own lot, and has a tendency to forget the ruthless means by which it has been brought about. This may be difficult for an American to believe or like. But it was plainly the explanation among all sorts of people, everywhere, and it was clearly expressed during a stimulating evening I spent in Moscow when I was trying to put a group of intelligent modern Russians on the spot to defend their system.

But I had not gone to Russia to remember the past. Besides my concrete assignments for the President, I had gone determined to find an answer for myself to the actual problems posed for our generation of Americans by the simple fact that the Soviet Union, whether we like it or not, exists.

Some of these answers I believe I found, at least to my own satisfaction. I can sum up the three most important in a few sentences.

First, Russia is an effective society. It works. It has survival value. The record of Soviet resistance to Hitler has been proof enough of this to most of us, but I must admit in all frankness that I was not prepared to believe before I went to Russia what I now know about its strength as a going organization of men and women.

Second, Russia is our ally in this war. The Russians, more sorely tested by Hitler's might even than the British, have met the test magnificently. Their hatred of Fascism and the Nazi system is real and deep and bitter. And this hatred makes them determined to eliminate Hitler and exterminate the Nazi blight from Europe and the world.

Third, we must work with Russia after the war. At least it seems to me that there can be no continued peace unless we learn to do so.

Those conclusions were reinforced by what I saw and heard in various parts of the Soviet Union. I saw one portion of the Russian front, close enough to know something at first hand of what the Red Army has done. I saw a good many of the factories behind the front, where the Soviet workers have fooled too many of our experts by keeping up a steady flow of supplies to the fighting men. And I saw collective farms. Behind the factories and the farms, I saw and talked with the Soviet newspapermen and writers who have given all Russians the strangely exalted feeling of being in a crusade. Behind the journalists, I saw the Kremlin, having talked twice at great length with Mr. Stalin, and observed something of how power is really exercised under the dictatorship of the proletariat. Finally, behind all these, I saw the Russian people from one end of Russia to the other, and if my sampling of the 200,000,000 was absurdly small, it had the advantage of being chosen entirely by chance.

One of the most enlightening experiences I had was a trip to the fighting front at Rzhev. To get to Rzhev from Moscow, you must drive up the Leningrad highway running to Kalinin, which used to be called Tver, then westward to Klin and on a little farther to a small country town called Staritsa. We had started out in comfortable cars, riding all night. At dawn, at Staritsa, we changed to American-made jeeps. With me were General Philip Faymonville, Major General Follet Bradley, Colonel Joseph A. Michela, the American Military Attaché in Russia, as well as four members of my party and our Russian guides.

The jeep is a great invention, and as an American I am proud of it. After fourteen hours in one, however, I had acquired an intimacy with its structure, its angles and corners, and its bucking gait that dulled some of my feeling of pride in its American origin. For endless hours, over what seemed endless miles, we bumped and bounced on roads so rough and muddy and rutted and corduroyed that for the first time I really understood the stories my father used to tell me of conditions in pioneer Indiana.

At last we came to the headquarters, north of Rzhev, of Lieutenant General Dmitri D. Lelyushenko, a man so colorful and engaging that among all the personalities I have met he stands out vividly. He was only thirty-eight years old, but a lieutenant general in charge of sixteen divisions of fighting men at one of the most important fighting fronts in the world.

He is a man of medium height, powerfully built, a born horseman with bowed legs betraying his Cossack origin, ruddy, vital, alert, full of animal spirits. He took us to his underground headquarters. He explained his battle maps, the placement of his troops, his plan of attack, the momentary changes in the battle then raging ahead of and around us.

He was then beginning the move to bypass Rzhev and cut the railroad to Vyazma which was accomplished some weeks after we had returned to the United States, preliminary to the dramatic lifting of the siege of Leningrad. From his headquarters in a grove of fir trees on a hill, we could see and hear the artillery beyond the town about eight miles from us.

I was struck by the eagerness of his staff. The general had only to begin a sentence and two or three adjutants were standing at attention, waiting for his order. I was also struck by the number of girls and women in uniform. Besides communications, sanitary and transport work, they stood guard at the observation posts we saw in trees around the general's headquarters and at the underground dugouts where the officers did their work.

From headquarters we drove on, nearer to the battle, and inspected a German strong point which had recently been captured by the Russians. What had once been a small village, on the brow of a little hill, was a mass of wreckage, mud, hamlets, and corpses which had not yet been buried. In the bottom of a trench, I saw a can, unopened but half buried in the mud, marked LUNCHEON HAM in English, and I wondered on which other front in this global war the Germans had picked it up.

The general told me his troops had just taken some German prisoners and asked me if I would like to see them. I said I would and that I would like to talk to them too. The general replied, "I have been instructed to let you do whatever you wish."

I took one look at his freshly captured prisoners, fourteen of them standing forlornly in a line. I looked again, more closely. Then I said to myself: Are these thinly dressed, emaciated, consumptive-looking men the same terrifying Huns, the unbeatable soldiers about whom I have read so many tales?

Through interpreters I began to talk to them. I asked them where they lived in Germany, their ages, whether they got letters from home, how their families were getting along without them, and a multitude of other simple, kindly questions. With the answers, the last vestige of a German military front disappeared. These soldiers became miserable, homesick boys and men. Some were almost forty and some were only seventeen.

I turned to the general and told him what I was thinking.

"That's right, Mr. Willkie," he answered, "but don't be misled. The

German equipment is still superb, and the German officers are proficient and professional. German army organization is unmatched. Even with such men as you see here, the German Army is still the greatest fighting military organization in the world. But if your nation will send us the equipment we need, the Red Army will outfight them on every front from the Caucasus to the North Pole. For our men are better, and they are fighting for their homeland."

I think his men were better, and it was clear all through that day and the day following that they were fighting for their homeland. A few miles behind the front, we saw Russian peasants with their belongings piled high on farm wagons, a cow hitched behind each wagon, plodding slowly along the roads. The striking thing was that they were moving not away from the front, but toward it, surging back with a kind of elemental strength to the land which the Red Army had won back from the enemy. The villages they found were nothing but gaunt chimneys against the sky, but it was time for fall plowing, so back they went.

A drizzling, cold rain—foretaste of what the Germans were to face a month or two later—delayed our departure, and the general invited us to supper with him. About forty of us, Soviet officers and soldiers and their visitors, managed to squeeze into one tent. We ate cold boiled bacon and rye bread, tomatoes and cucumbers and pickles, and toasted each other in vodka.

Unthinkingly, during supper, I asked the interpreter to ask the general just how large a section of Russia's two-thousand-mile front he was defending. The general looked at me as if offended, and the interpreter repeated after him, slowly, "Sir, I am not defending. I am attacking."

After my visit to the Rzhev front, I realized more clearly than ever before that in Russia the phrase "This is a people's war" has real meaning. It is the Russian people in the fullest sense who are resolved to destroy Hitlerism. What they have been through and what they face in the months ahead cannot fail to stir any American. Stalin had given me certain facts about Russia's great sacrifices and desperate needs before I went to the front and I had seen ample evidence of both with my own eyes.

Already five million Russians had been killed, wounded, or were missing. The great fertile farm lands of southwestern Russia were largely in Nazi hands. Their products were feeding the enemy and their men and women were forced to be his slaves. Thousands of Russia's villages had been destroyed and their people were homeless. Her transportation system was overloaded; her factories, producing to the very limit, required the full output of her remaining oil fields and coal mines.

Food in Russia was scarce—perhaps worse than scarce. There would be little fuel in Russian homes in the approaching winter. Even when I was in Moscow women and children were gathering wood from fifty miles around to make a little warmth against the coming cold. Clothing, except for the army and essential war workers, was nearly gone. Many vital medical supplies just did not exist.

This was the picture I got of wartime Russia. Yet no Russian talked of quitting. They all knew what had happened in the Nazi-occupied countries. The Russian people—not just their leaders—the Russian people, I was convinced, had chosen victory or death. They talked only of victory.

I spent one entire day looking at a Soviet aviation plant. I saw other factories in Russia, candy factories, munition factories, foundries, canneries, and power plants. But this aviation plant, now located outside of Moscow, remains most vivid in my memory.

It was a big place. My guess would be that some 30,000 workers were running three shifts and that they were making a very presentable number of airplanes every day. The plane produced was the now-famous Stormovik, a single-engined, heavily armored fighting model which has been developed by the Russians as one of the really novel weapons of the war. It has a low ceiling, and climbs slowly, so that it actually needs a fighter escort. But used as an anti-tank weapon, traveling low and at high speed and carrying heavy fire power, it has been one of the Red Army's most powerful weapons.

American aviation experts were with me on this inspection, and they confirmed my impression that the planes we saw wheeled from the end of the assembly line and tested on an airfield next to the factory were good planes. And, peculiarly enough, they pronounced the armored protection for the pilots the best of any they knew on any plane anywhere in the world. I am no aviation expert, but I have inspected a good many factories in my life. I kept my eyes open, and I think my report is fair.

Parts of the manufacturing process were crudely organized. The wings of the Stormovik are made of plywood, compressed under steam pressure, and then covered with canvas. The woodworking shops seemed to me to rely too much on hand labor, and their product showed it. Also, some of the electrical and plating shops were on the primitive side.

With these exceptions, the plant would compare favorably in output and efficiency with any I have ever seen. I walked through shop after shop of lathes and punching presses. I saw machine tools assembled from all over the world, their trade-names showing they came from Chemnitz, from Skoda, from Sheffield, from Cincinnati, from Sverdlovsk, from Antwerp. They were being efficiently used.

More than thirty-five per cent of the labor in the plant was done by women. Among the workers we saw boys not more than ten years old, all dressed in blue blouses and looking like apprentice students, even though the officials of the factory pulled no punches in admitting that the children work, in many of the shops, the full sixty-six-hour week worked by the adults. Many of the boys were doing skilled jobs on lathes, and seemed to be doing them extremely well.

On the whole, the plant seemed to us Americans to be overstaffed. There were more workers than would be found in a comparable American factory. But hanging over every third or fourth machine was a special sign, indicating that its worker was a "Stakhanovite," pledged to overfulfill his or her norm of production. The Stakhanovites, strange as it may seem to us, are actually pieceworkers, paid at a progressively increasing rate on a speed-up system which is like an accelerated Bedeaux system. The Russian industrial system is a strange paradox to an American. The method of employing and paying labor would satisfy our most unsocial industrialist. And the way capital is treated would, I believe, completely satisfy a Norman Thomas. The walls of the factory carried fresh and obviously honored lists of those workers and those shops which were leading in what was apparently a ceaseless competition for more and better output. A fair conclusion would be that this extra incentive, which was apparent in the conversation of any worker we stopped to talk to at random, made up for a large part, but not all, of the handicap of relative lack of skill.

The productivity of each individual worker was lower than in the United States. Russian officials admitted this to me freely. Until they can change this by education and training, they explained, they must offset it by putting great emphasis on patriotic drives for output and by recruiting all the labor power, even that of children and old women, that they can find. Meanwhile, and there was nothing done with mirrors here, we could see the planes leaving the cavernous doors of the final assembly unit, testing their machine guns and cannon on a target range, and then taking to the air over our heads.

The director of the plant, a grave-faced man in his late thirties, named Tretyakov, took us to lunch in his office. We walked through long corridors, lit only by dim blue electric lights, to a simple room, entirely blacked out, where he worked. On a conference table were sandwiches, hot tea, cakes, the usual caviar, and the ubiquitous bottles of vodka. In a corner stood two flags, both awarded to the plant by the Kremlin for its successful fulfillment of its plan.

Tretyakov offered to answer my questions. He sat at the head of the table. A small, thin silver star was the only insignia on his dark business suit. I later learned that he was one of only seven Soviet civilians who have been given this star, emblem of the title of "Hero of the Soviet Union."

After an hour of detailed cross-examination, it was clear to me that he would have been an outstanding leader in any society I have ever known. He spoke quietly, gravely, with a full sense of the national and international urgency of his work, with an obviously detailed knowledge of what went on in every corner of his enormous plant. A few questions I put to him, such as the number of planes produced daily, the exact number of workers, the exact top speed of the Stormovik, he turned aside politely but firmly. When I tried to get the same information by more subtle approaches, his eyes twinkled, but he was not fooled into betraying any military secrets, any more than a responsible factory manager in England or America would be.

This plant, he told us, had been picked up bodily from its foundations in Moscow in October, 1941, when the sound of Nazi cannonading could be heard in the Soviet capital. It had been moved more than a thousand miles over a transport system already loaded down with the requirements of a nation in arms. It had been set up again, many of its original workers tending their own machines throughout the transfer, and by December, two months later, it was producing planes at its new location.

During that first winter of 1941-42, he told me, there was no heating in the plant. Workers built bonfires in the shops to keep their machines from freezing. There was no housing ready for the workers, and many of them slept next to their tools. By the fall of 1942, things were better organized. Factory restaurants, for example, which I had seen, apparently served simple but adequate and nourishing food to the workers. But I knew that in the same town the only food that could be bought in the markets was black bread and potatoes, and at exorbitant prices.

As the luncheon broke up, I began to question a short, wiry young fellow whom the director had introduced to me as the superintendent of production, his bright young man. He was dressed in worker's clothes, with the mechanic's cap which is almost the badge of an industrial worker in Russia. He was a trained engineer, with an alert, almost jaunty manner, energetic, intelligent, and with a thorough knowledge of his job; the kind of young man that in American industrial life would make rapid advancement, acquire a competence, and become a leader among his fellows. In fact, he reminded me so much of the promising American industrial type that I decided to try to find out from him what were the urges and the lures under the Communist system that caused him to educate himself beyond his fellows, to work the extra hours necessary to become superintendent over 30,000 men, and to acquire the knowledge that was clearly leading him toward the top.

He said he'd be glad to answer my questions. He told me that he was thirty-two years old, married, and the father of two children. He lived in a comfortable house much better than the average, and in peacetime had an automobile.

"How does your pay as superintendent of this factory compare with the pay of the average skilled worker in the plant?" I asked him.

He thought for a moment: "It's about ten times as much."

That would be on the same ratio twenty-five or thirty thousand dollars a year in America, and actually was about what a man of similar responsibility in America would receive. So I said to him, "I thought Communism meant equality of reward."

Equality, he told me, was not part of the present Soviet conception of socialism. "From each according to his capacities, to each according to his *work*," was the slogan of Stalinist socialism, he explained, and only when they had achieved the Communist phase of their development would the slogan be changed to "From each according to his capacities, to each according to his *needs*." Even then, he added, complete equality would not be necessary or desirable.

"With such an income normally you are able to save, to put aside something, aren't you?" I went on.

He laughed and said, "Yes, if my wife doesn't spend too much."

"What do you do with your savings? How do you invest them?"

"With my first savings, we bought ourselves a nice house," he told me.

"And then?"

"Then we bought a place in the country, where the family could go for vacation and I could go for a rest, or to fish and hunt when I could get away from the factory."

"And now that you have these things all paid for, what do you do with your extra money?"

"Oh, I keep it in cash, or put it in government bonds."

Soviet government bonds are non-interest-bearing, and remembering the first money I accumulated and the thought I gave to getting as much income from it as possible, I asked him, just to see what his answer would be, "Why don't you invest it in something that will give you a good return?"

He looked at me in surprise and, I thought, even with a slight air of superiority. "You mean, Mr. Willkie, to get return on capital? That isn't possible in Russia, and anyhow I don't believe in it."

I tried to get him to tell me why, and for ten minutes I found myself listening to Marxist and Leninist theories which I finally interrupted with the question:

"Well, what does cause you to work so hard?"

He answered, sweeping his arm about him as he spoke, "I run this factory. Someday I'll be the director. Do you see these badges?" pointing to a string of decorations pinned on his blouse. "Those were given to me by the party and the government because I was good." He spoke with frank cockiness. "Someday, if I'm good enough, the party will give me something to do with running the government."

"But who will take care of you when you are an old man?"

"I'll have some cash put aside, and if I don't have enough, the government will provide for me."

"Don't you ever have a desire to own a plant of your own?" I asked.

To which he replied with another deluge of Marxian economic and social philosophy with which he was as familiar as with the working of his plant.

"Well, how about your family?" I persisted. "Don't you want your children to have a better start than you had? Don't you want to protect your wife in case you go before she does?"

He said impatiently, "That's mere capitalistic talk, Mr. Willkie. I started as a worker. My children will have as good a start as I had. My wife works now, and as long as she's well she'll continue to work. When she's unable to do so, the state will take care of her."

"Well," I said, "what happens to you if you don't make good in this job?"

And he said with a grim smile, "I'll be liquidated." I knew that might mean anything from demotion to death itself. But he obviously thought that there was little danger that *he* would not make good.

I then tried to tackle him from another angle.

"Suppose—in ordinary times, not wartime—suppose you don't like your director here. Can you leave and get a job in some other factory?"

"Most workers could, but as a party member, I must stay where the party thinks I can do the most good."

"But suppose you should prefer to work at a different kind of job. Can you change your job?"

"That's for those in authority to say."

"I understand that you are in complete accord with the economic and political theories of the state. But if you happened to hold different ideas, could you express them and fight for them?"

It took me ten minutes of hot colloquy to get him even to consider such a supposition, and then his answer was only a shrug of the shoulders. It was my turn to be impatient and I said, somewhat sharply, "Then actually you've got no freedom."

He drew himself up almost belligerently and said, "Mr. Willkie, you don't understand. I've had more freedom than my father and grandfather ever had. They were peasants. They were never allowed to learn to read or write. They were slaves to the soil. When they sickened, there were no doctors or hospitals for them. I am the first man in the long chain of my ancestors who has had the opportunity to educate himself, to advance himself—to amount to anything. And that for me is freedom. It may not seem freedom to you, but, remember, we are in the developing stage of our system. Someday we'll have political freedom, too."

I pressed him: "How can you ever have political freedom and economic freedom where the state owns everything?"

He poured out his theories in a seemingly endless rush. But he had no answers beyond the Marxian ones in which he was so well grounded, and to that basic question, Marxism gives no answer.

As I turned to go, I overheard Major Kight, our amazingly skillful and intelligent pilot, say to Joe Barnes, "Listen, don't let's get away before you explain to that fellow that Mr. Willkie was just trying to get him to talk. Sure, we in America like what money will buy and want to get ahead a bit, but it's not only money that makes us work. This insignia on my shoulder brought me a big raise in pay when I got it. But at the same time I got this piece of ribbon here," pointing to the ribbon of the Distinguished Flying Cross, "and that didn't bring me a cent. You tell him that I'd give the rank and the pay raise back for nothing, but I wouldn't give away the ribbon for a million dollars."

Russia's farms, just as much as its factories, have been mobilized for total war, and their capacity to support a fighting nation has been one of Hitler's most profound miscalculations and one of the world's surprises.

Day after day we flew over these farms, all the way from the front itself, at Rzhev, to the farthest limits of cultivation in Central Asia and Siberia. For Russia's farming lands stretch nearly six thousand miles behind the front. Only from the air, I suspect, can one get any sense of the immensity of this farming land, or of its infinite variety. Parts of it, with grain crops running to the horizon, made our pilot, Major Kight, homesick for his native state of Texas. Other parts, like the irrigated valley near Tashkent, look like southern California.

On the Volga near Kuibishev, I had a chance to see some of these farms at closer range. We went up the river in a neat, modern river boat. Through the trees along the banks could be seen the rooftops of stately homes, once the country estates of the wealthy from as far away as Moscow and St. Petersburg, now rest homes and sanitariums for workers. They reminded me of the great houses one sees from a Hudson River boat. But the Volga is more tricky than the Hudson—as I found for myself when our pilot once let me try his wheel. Suddenly we were among cross currents that rapidly sent us shoreward, much to the delight of the laughing Volga boatmen. Down the river floated great rafts of logs bound for lumber mills, with little huts built on them and cattle and chickens for the families who float slowly on these rafts all summer from the forests of north Russia to the cities of the south.

I had been told in Kuibishev of plans to dam a great bend in the Volga River for the production of electric power; and on this trip we went over the part of the Volga concerned in the proposed development. I am not one to be easily surprised by vast governmental power developments, but when it became clear that this one development, if completed, would produce twice as much power as all the TVA, the Grand Coulee, and the Bonneville developments combined, I began to realize that the Russians dream and plan on a scale to fit their vast forests and plains.

We left the Volga bend to drive inland to a collective farm which had formerly been a hunting estate of a member of the lesser nobility. It had some 8000 acres, with fifty-five families living on it, a ratio of about 140 acres per family, which is about the size of the average farm in Rush County, Indiana.

The soil was good—a dark, rich loam—but the rainfall was slight, only some thirteen inches per year. In Indiana we have about forty. Crops were cultivated without benefit of fertilizer, and cultivation was almost exclusively mechanical. Largely wheat and rye and other small grains were grown. The season's average yield per acre of wheat was fifteen and one-half bushels; of rye a little less, which I thought pretty good under the circumstances. To get this acreage yield, incidentally, required some concentrated figuring on the part of Mike Cowles and myself, involving the transposition of hectares to acres, and poods to bushels. We gave up trying to arrive at a comparable price per bushel in American money. For all quotations were given us in rubles, and we found that the value of the ruble is subject to rapid fluctuation and varies in different markets. We could, however, judge the quality of the grain, and it seemed to us good.

Each of the fifty-five families on the farm was allowed to own one cow; the scraggly herd, consisting of every known mixture as to breed, grazed together on a common near a cluster of small houses in which the families lived. But the collectivist farm itself owned 800 head of cattle, 250 of them cows, of excellent stock and all well cared for. The cattle barns were of brick and large; the floors were concrete and the stanchions modern. The calves were almost tenderly watched over, in clean neat stalls, and women who were in charge of the barns explained to me their methods of improving the stock by care and breeding. The methods were scientific and modern.

I saw only one able-bodied man on the farm; he was the manager. Most of the workers were women or children, with a few old men. For the farms of Russia have been the enormous reservoir from which the Red Army has been recruited, and the wives and children of the Red Army soldiers are today feeding the country.

The manager was the czar of the farm. He was a man of scientific agricultural training, alert and assured. He planned the crops and directed the work. Every man, woman, and child on the place was under his authority.

He, in turn, was responsible for the success of the project and for the production of the farm's quota in the war economy. He would rise in power and in status if he succeeded; his punishment would be severe if he failed.

I was curious about the economy of one of these farms and asked many questions. A careful record of how much each member works is kept, I was told, in the farm office. The unit is a "workday," but special skills are recognized, so that a tractor-driver, for example, who plows a certain number of acres in a day is credited with two "workdays." The binding of a certain number of sheaves, or the tending of a certain number of cows, similarly constitutes an extra "workday."

This farm, like most of the collective farms of Russia, rented its tractors and mechanical equipment from government-owned machine stations, and payment was made from the farm's harvest, not in rubles but in kind. Then the farm had to pay taxes, which constitute almost a rental payment to the government, also in kind. The balance of each harvest was distributed to the members of the farm on the basis of how many "workdays" each had accumulated on the records.

What each member received in this final distribution of the harvest could be traded for manufactured goods at a small store on the farm property, or it could be sold. The government, however, has put steadily increasing pressure on the collective farmers to sell their crops directly to the government, though in theory they remain free to sell anywhere they wish after they have paid in kind for the machines they have used and their taxes. It seemed to me that most of the farmers I talked to had plenty of cash, with no way to spend it. For goods in the stores were scarce and steadily decreasing as a result of the almost complete absorption of all factories by the war and the needs of the Red Army.

We went to the home of the farm manager for lunch. He was a man of thirty-seven, married, with two children. He lived in a small stone house, simple, and in atmosphere not very different from a prosperous farmhouse in the United States. It was a hearty hospitality, with much laughing good humor. The food was abundant, simple but good, and the wife of the manager, who had cooked the meal, urged me to eat as I have been urged many times in Indiana farmhouses: "Mr. Willkie, do have some more. You've hardly eaten a thing." And then, of course, there was the ever-present vodka. Water was nowhere in sight.

I pressed the manager and his wife, and talked with some of the workers on the farm, trying to find out how it was that they were free of the consuming urge of every farmer I ever knew to own his own bit of land. To some of them it even seemed strange that I inquired. But the manager explained that he and the rest were less than a hundred years from serfdom; neither they nor their ancestors had ever owned the land they worked on; and they found the present system good.

I learned later that this farm was somewhat above the average in physical equipment. But it was run much like 250,000 other collective farms in the Soviet Union. And I began to realize how the collective farms constituted the very backbone of Russia's tough resistance.

Behind the front in Russia stand the factories and the farms, in a form of total mobilization unknown perhaps anywhere else in the world except in Germany. Behind the factories and the farms stands the machine which keeps this mobilization total.

One of the most interesting and important parts of this machine seemed to me to be the newspapers, like every other part, under government control.

In Moscow, for the first time in my life or in that of Gardner Cowles, Jr., American newspaper publisher, who was with me, we saw men and women standing in queues a block long to buy newspapers. The daily press is published in circulations which run into seven figures but still cannot meet the demand.

In smaller towns throughout Russia, I saw small crowds of people gathered around glass cases set up in the streets. Inside the cases were pinned copies of *Pravda* or *Izvestia*, the country's two leading papers. People wanted to read them enough to stand in the cold and read over other people's shoulders.

When we flew to Tashkent, our airplane made the flight faster than any regular commercial service of the Soviets. As the first Americans who had been seen in that Central Asian city in many years, we were naturally enough objects of considerable curiosity. We were, that is, until it was learned that we had brought more recent copies of the Moscow papers than any Tashkent had seen. At this point, even our official hosts deserted us to read the news.

I was curious about this, and everywhere I went I asked questions about it. The press in Russia, I came to believe, is the strongest single agency in the hands of the government for short-term purposes, just as I believe the schools are their strongest agency over the long pull. The present government of Russia has had both the schools and the press in its control now for twenty-five years, and foreigners who still belittle the strength of this government, in cold, matter-of-fact terms of the support and sacrifices it can demand from the Russian people, are talking through their hats.

One night, in Moscow, I had a chance to check the kind of thinking and emotion that goes into the Soviet press. The American newspapermen in Moscow are as able a group of reporters as I have ever known. Walter Kerr of the *New York Herald Tribune,* Leland Stowe of *The Chicago Daily News,* Maurice Hindus of the *New York Herald Tribune,* Ralph Parker of *The New York Times,* Henry Shapiro of the United Press, Eddie Gilmore and Henry Cassidy of the Associated Press, Robert Magidoff of the National Broadcasting Company, and Larry Lesueur of the Columbia Broadcasting System, Wally Graebner of *Time* and *Life*—I know no other city in the world, except possibly London, where there is such a company of lively, honest, and hard-working foreign correspondents and newspapermen. Some of them assembled one night a group of Soviet newspapermen, turned us loose in a big room with food and drink and interpreters but no officials, and let me ask the questions I wanted, with no holds barred.

They were an interesting group. There was Ilya Ehrenbourg, Soviet reporter and novelist who has lived most of his life in France and knows western Europe as well, I imagine, as any foreign newspaperman. There was Boris Voitekhov, a young reporter and playwright, who had written the story of the defense of Sevastopol up to the last moment before its fall, when he escaped in a submarine. There was Valentina Genne, a young Soviet newspaperwoman. Simonov was there, a dour-faced young man in Russian *rubashka* and leather boots. He had come to Moscow that day from Stalingrad. He is the author of the play *Russian People*, and perhaps the most popular newspaperman in Russia today. There was General Alexei Ignatiev, a fine figure of a man in his sixties, who served as military attaché abroad before the 1917 Revolution and is now one of the leading commentators of *Red Star*, the daily newspaper of the Red Army.

We ate smoked sturgeon and drank hot tea and talked most of the night. There was two-way traffic in the conversation. They pounded me on the second front in Europe, on what had happened to Rudolph Hess, on the Russian need for more American supplies and equipment. They were well informed, eager, curious, critical but not antagonistic. I was told later that this had been probably the first frank and off-the-record conversation between Soviet newspapermen and a visiting foreigner for a decade.

None of the professional writers present that evening have violated the confidence in which we exchanged opinions. And I shall certainly not do so. But they will not misunderstand, I am certain, if I report for once in my life on some of the things newspapermen told me.

Two things deserve to be reported. The first was what I can only call a quality of intransigence. Those fellows were uncompromising. Train a man from boyhood in a system of absolutism, and he will think in blacks and whites.

For example, I asked Simonov, just returned from Stalingrad, whether or not the German prisoners taken on that front made the same poor and shabby impression I had got from Germans I had interviewed a few days before on the Rzhev front. My question was translated into Russian. But there was no answer. Someone else picked up the ball and carried it.

After living for a few weeks with interpreters, you learn to be surprised at nothing. So I repeated the question. Again, there was no answer. This time I waited until the conversation had come full cycle on itself and reached a pause. I asked the question a third time. General Ignatiev, a courtly and cosmopolitan gentleman and the only Russian present, by the way, who spoke a little English, finally answered me:

"Mr. Willkie, it is only natural that you should not understand. When this war began, we all sought out German prisoners. We cross-examined them. We wanted to find out why they had come to invade our land. We found out many interesting things about the Germans, and about what the Nazis have done to them.

"But now it is different. Since the offensive last winter, when we pushed the Germans back and recaptured many towns and villages they had taken, we feel differently. We have seen with our own eyes what the Germans did to our people and our homes. Today, no decent Soviet newspaperman would talk to a German, even in a prison camp."

Or take another example. I had been suggesting for a few days, as adroitly as I could, that it would be a good move for the Soviets to send Dmitri Shostakovich, their great composer, to the United States on a visit. The night before, I had sat in the packed Tchaikovsky Hall, Moscow's great concert building, and listened to his Seventh Symphony. It is tough music, and much of it is hard for me to like, but its opening movement is one of the most impressive things I have ever heard.

"We have got to understand each other," I said. "We have got to learn to know each other. We are allies in this war, and the American people will not let you down until Hitler has been defeated. But I would like to see us work together in the peace as well as after it. This will require great patience and great tolerance and great understanding on both sides. Why can't Shostakovich be sent to the United States, where he already has a host of admirers and where he could help immeasurably in this job of understanding that we both face?"

It was Simonov who answered me this time.

"Mr. Willkie, understanding works both ways. We have always tried to learn about America. We have borrowed a lot from you, and sent our best men to study in America. We know something about your country, not as much as we would like to but enough to understand why you extend this invitation to Shostakovich.

"You should send some of your good men to study us. Then you would understand why, perhaps, we do not respond warmly to the invitation. You see, we are engaged in a life-and-death struggle. Not only our own lives, but the idea which has shaped our lives for a generation hangs in the balance at Stalingrad tonight. To suggest to us that we should send a musician to the United States, which is also involved in this war and where human lives also hang in the balance, to persuade you with music of something that is as plain as the nose on your face, is in a funny way insulting to us. Please don't misunderstand me."

I don't think I misunderstood him.

The second quality of the evening which deserves reporting was one of calm, quiet, confident pride and patriotism. It is hard for us Americans, who have read more horror stories about Russia than anything else for many years, to realize that a generation is running the Soviet Union today which knows its own strength. I was to be immensely impressed with this later, in central Asia and in Siberia. It is a quality which I have often known in America, especially in the West.

In Moscow I had two long talks with Joseph Stalin. Much of what was said I am not at liberty to report. But about the man himself there is no reason to be cautious. He is one of the significant men of this generation.

At his invitation I called on him one evening at 7:30. He apparently has most of his conferences at night. His office was a fair-sized room about eighteen by thirty-five feet. On its walls hung pictures of Marx and Engels and Lenin, and profiles of Lenin and Stalin together, the same pictures that you see in practically every schoolhouse, public building, factory, hotel, hospital, and home in Russia. Often you find in addition the picture of Molotov. In an anteroom visible from the office was a huge globe some ten feet in diameter.

Stalin and Molotov were standing to welcome me at the far end of a long oak conference table. They greeted me simply and we talked for some three hours—about the war, about what would come after, about

Stalingrad and the front, about America's position, the relationship of Great Britain, the United States, and Russia, and about many other important and unimportant subjects.

A few days later I spent some five hours sitting next to Stalin, through the numerous courses of a state dinner which he gave for me; later while we all drank coffee at little tables in another room, and finally through a private showing of a motion picture of the siege and defense of Moscow.

It was at this dinner, incidentally, that we toasted the interpreters. We had toasted our respective countries and leaders; we had toasted the Russian people and the American people and our hopes for future collaboration; we had toasted each other. Finally it occurred to me that the only people really working at that dinner were the interpreters who were kept bobbing up and down to translate. So I proposed a toast to them. Later, I said to Mr. Stalin, "I hope I didn't step out of line in suggesting that we toast the interpreters." And he replied, "Not at all, Mr. Willkie, we are a democratic country."

Stalin, I should judge, is about five feet four or five, and gives the appearance of slight stockiness. I was surprised to find how short he is; but his head, his mustache, and his eyes are big. His face, in repose, is a hard face, and he looked tired in September—not sick, as is so often reported, but desperately tired. He had a right to be. He talks quietly, readily, and at times with a simple, moving eloquence. When he described to me Russia's desperate situation as to fuel, transportation, military equipment, and man power, he was genuinely dramatic.

He has, I would say, a hard, tenacious, driving mind. He asked searching questions, each of them loaded like a revolver, each of them designed to cut through to what he believed to be the heart of the matter that interested him. He pushes aside pleasantries and compliments and is impatient of generalities.

When he asked me about my trips through various factories, he wanted detailed reports, department by department, not general judgments as to their operating methods and efficiency. When I asked him about Stalingrad, he developed for me logically not alone its geographical and military importance, but the moral effect on Russia, Germany, and particularly the Middle East, of the successful or unsuccessful defense. He made no predictions as to Russia's ability to hold it and he was quite definite in his assertion that neither love of homeland nor pure bravery could save it. Battles were won or lost primarily by numbers, skill, and matériel.

He told me again and again that his propaganda was deliberately designed to make his people hate the Nazis, but it was obvious that he himself had a certain bitter admiration for the efficiency by which Hitler had transplanted to Germany as much as ninety-four per cent of the working population from some of the conquered Russian territory, and he respected the completely professional training of the German Army, particularly its officers. He discounted, just as Winston Churchill did to me two years before in England, the notion that Hitler was but a tool in the hands of abler men. He did not think we should count upon an early internal collapse in Germany. He said that the way to defeat Germany was to destroy its army. And he believed that one of the most effective methods of destroying faith in Hitler's invincibility throughout Europe was in continuous air-raid bombings of German cities and of German-held docks and factories in the conquered countries.

When we talked of the causes of the war and the economic and political conditions that would face the world after it was over, his comprehension was broad, his detailed information exact, and the cold reality of his thinking apparent. Stalin is a hard man, perhaps even a cruel man, but a very able one. He has few illusions.

His admiration for the effectiveness of American production methods would more than satisfy the National Association of Manufacturers. But he does not understand the indirections and some of the restraints of the democratic methods of waging war. He wondered, for instance, why the democracies should not insist upon using certain bases for war purposes that would be of great value to them, particularly if the nations that owned them were unco-operative and not able to defend them.

Quite contrary to general report, Stalin has great respect for Winston Churchill; he almost said it to me—the respect of one great realist for another.

On the personal side Stalin is a simple man, with no affectations or poses. He does not seek to impress by any artificial mannerisms. His sense of humor is a robust one, and he laughs readily at unsubtle jokes and repartee. Once I was telling him of the Soviet schools and libraries I had seen—how good they seemed to me. And I added, "But if you continue to educate the Russian people, Mr. Stalin, the first thing you know you'll educate yourself out of a job."

He threw his head back and laughed and laughed. Nothing I said to him, or heard anyone else say to him, through two long evenings, seemed to amuse him as much.

Strange as it may seem, Stalin dresses in light pastel shades. His well-known tunic is of finely woven material and is apt to be a soft green or a delicate pink; his trousers a light-tannish yellow or blue. His boots are black and highly polished. Ordinary social pleasantries bother him a little. As I was leaving him after my first talk, I expressed appreciation of the time he had given me, the honor he conferred in talking so candidly. A little embarrassed, he said:

"Mr. Willkie, you know I grew up a Georgian peasant. I am unschooled in pretty talk. All I can say is I like you very much."

Inevitably, Stalin's simple ways have set a fashion of a kind for other Soviet leaders. Especially in Moscow and in Kuibishev, there is an absence of flamboyance about Russian leaders that is remarkable. They all dress simply. They talk little and listen well. A surprising number of them are young, in their thirties. It would be my guess, which I could not prove or document, that Stalin likes a pretty heavy turnover of young people in his immediate entourage in the Kremlin. It is his way, I think, of keeping his ear to the ground.

Among the other leaders I met and talked to at any great length were Viacheslav Molotov, the Foreign Minister, Andrei Vishinsky and Solomon Lozovsky, his assistants, Marshal Voroshilov, the former Commissar of Defense, Anastasia Mikoyan, Commissar of Supply and head of the Soviet foreign-trade apparatus. Each of these is an educated man, interested in the foreign world, completely unlike in manner, appearance, and speech the uncouth, wild Bolshevik of our cartoons.

In Kuibishev, at a dinner given for me by Mr. Vishinsky, who was the chief state prosecutor in all the grim treason trials of four and five years ago, I caught myself studying his white hair, his professor's face, and his quiet, almost studious manner, and wondering if this could possibly be the same man who had purged some of the oldest heroes of the Russian Revolution on charges of murder and betrayal of their country.

Whenever the talk of these men ran to the peace, to what the world must be prepared to do after the war is over, they talked with statesmanship and real understanding.

Since I have returned to the United States, Mr. Stalin has defined the program, as he sees it, of the Anglo-American-Soviet coalition in the European war. These are the goals he calls for:

"Abolition of racial exclusiveness, equality of nations and integrity of their territories, liberation of enslaved nations and restoration of their sovereign rights, the right of every nation to arrange its affairs as it wishes, economic aid to nations that have suffered and assistance to them in attaining their material welfare, restoration of democratic liberties, the destruction of the Hitlerite regime."

We may ask: does Stalin mean what he says? Some will point out that only two years ago Russia was in an alliance of expediency with Germany. I make no defense of expediency, military, political, temporary, or otherwise. For I believe the moral losses of expediency always far outweigh the temporary gains. And I believe that every drop of blood saved through expediency will be paid for by twenty drawn by the sword. But a Russian, feeling that by the German alliance his country was buying time, might well remind the democracies of Munich, and of the seven million tons of the best grade of scrap iron the United States shipped to Japan between 1937 and 1940.

Perhaps we can better measure the good faith of Stalin's statement in the light of the millions of Russians who have already died defending their fatherland and of the sixty million who have become slaves of the Nazis; in those other millions of Russian men and women who are working feverishly sixty-six hours a week in factories and mines to forge and produce instruments of war for the fighters at the front; and in the effort that went into the almost miraculous movement of great factories, hundreds of miles, that they might operate, uninterrupted, beyond Nazi reach. For it is in the attitude of the people that we may find the best interpretation of Stalin's purpose.

Many among the democracies fear and mistrust Soviet Russia. They dread the inroads of an economic order that would be destructive of their own. Such fear is weakness. Russia is neither going to eat us nor seduce us. That is—and this is something for us to think about—that is, unless our democratic institutions and our free economy become so frail through abuse and failure in practice as to make us soft and vulnerable. The best answer to Communism is a living, vibrant, fearless democracy—economic, social, and political. All we need to do is to stand up and perform according to our professed ideals. Then those ideals will be safe.

No, we do not need to fear Russia. We need to learn to work with her against our common enemy, Hitler. We need to learn to work with her in the world after the war. For Russia is a dynamic country, a vital new society, a force that cannot be bypassed in any future world.

V THE REPUBLIC OF YAKUTSK

THE Soviet Union covers an enormous territory, bigger than the United States, Canada, and Central America combined. The people are of many different races and nationalities, speaking many languages.

In a Siberian republic called Yakutsk, I found some answers to some of the questions Americans ask about Russia.

Many of the things I saw in Yakutsk would not hold true for all of Russia. Frontier conditions, a cold climate, endless new land free for the asking, and a pioneering spirit among the people are not to be found all over the Soviet Union. But in spite of these differences, Yakutsk—the story of its past and what I saw of its present—taught me new things about the Russian Revolution.

Yakutsk is a big country. It is twice as big as Alaska. It has not many people, only about 400,000 now, but it has resources enough to support a great many more. The Soviets have begun to develop this country, and what I saw of their efforts seemed to me far more important, to the world and to America, than the political debate which has been carried on, both in Moscow and in New York, for so many years.

First, consider the past history of Yakutsk. The Yakuts were Mongol people who spread north as Genghis Khan moved to the west. Their characteristic high cheekbones, slanting eyes, and black hair still persist. Most of them trapped for furs or picked the earth for gold. They lived in huts, low-ceilinged, dirt-floored, smoky from open fires, with cattle and human beings living under the same roof, breeding places for tuberculosis. In winter, they lived on spoiled fish and roots; disease and frequent famines decimated what was once a hardy people. During the time of the tsars, Yakutsk was famous for syphilis, tuberculosis, and furs.

Russians came into this country slowly, and until recently in no great numbers. The government at St. Petersburg (now Leningrad) sent many of its convicts and political prisoners to Yakutsk. Many writers who had endured its bitter life wrote of it when they were released. And so Yakutsk was known as "the people's prison."

Incidentally, in the waitresses who served us while we were there I found some present-day exiles of the Soviet Union. One Polish woman particularly poured into my ear an account of the Soviet system which hardly accorded with official propaganda.

The first September snow had already coated the airfield when our Liberator bomber landed at Yakutsk, capital city of this republic. We had been flying for hours over the *taiga,* or forestland, which covers the northern part of Siberia as far as the Arctic Circle. The land looks big and cold and empty from the air, with few roads to be seen, and miles upon miles of snow and trees.

A man stepped forward from the small group standing at the edge of the field where our plane stopped.

"My name is Muratov," he said. "I am president of the Council of People's Commissars of the Yakutsk Autonomous Soviet Socialist Republic. I have instructions from Moscow, from Comrade Stalin, to take care of you while you are here, to show you anything you want to see, to answer any questions you may care to ask. Welcome."

It was a short speech, but he gave it everything he had. There were fewer than a dozen men standing on the airfield, but he carried himself with the air of a man flanked by brass bands and guards of honor to welcome a foreign visitor.

I thanked him and explained that we were stopping only briefly as there was still time that day to cover the next thousand-mile lap of our journey.

"You are not going on today, Mr. Willkie," he replied, "nor probably tomorrow. The weather reports are not good and it is part of my instructions to assure your safe arrival at your next stop, or I shall be liquidated."

We drove the five miles or more into the town of Yakutsk in a heavy black Soviet limousine. During the ride Muratov started on the program of selling me his republic, which he never let up on for a moment during the hours I was with him. His enthusiasm knew no subtleties.

"What would you like to see in Yakutsk, Mr. Willkie?" he asked as we neared the town.

"Have you a library?"

"Certainly we have a library."

We went directly to it, and Muratov led us straight to the reading room without stopping for the removal of coats or hats. We were held up at the door, however, by a mild-mannered, slight, studious-looking woman who was completely unabashed by Muratov's obviously official manner. She said politely but firmly, "We are trying to teach the people here not only the habit of reading but the habit of good manners. Please go downstairs and leave your hats and coats in the coatroom." Muratov, a little startled, began to argue, but the best he accomplished was the concession that we might leave our hats and coats in her office. I almost laughed aloud. It was the first and only time in all of Russia that I saw an important Russian official stopped in his stride.

In an old but well-lighted building, clean and well staffed, Yakutsk, a town of 50,000 people, has accumulated 550,000 volumes. The stacks were wooden; the machine for delivering books to the reading room worked like a primitive country well. But the reading room was well occupied. The card catalogues were modern and complete. The records showed that over 100,000 people—many had come from the countryside around—had used books during the past nine months. Special exhibits hung on the walls. Soviet periodicals and reference works were on open shelves. There was an air of great efficiency about the place. This was a library any town of its size might well be proud of.

Our hotel—the only hotel in Yakutsk—was a new building, made of logs, with a Russian stove in every room. It was filled with tough-looking men in leather coats and boots made of reindeer fur. The girls were red-cheeked, with handkerchiefs tied around their heads. They had an amusing way of looking straight at us and laughing their heads off. We were foreigners.

The town itself seemed, in many ways, like a western town in this country a generation ago. In fact, much of this life reminded me of our own early and expanding days—especially the hearty, simple tastes, the not too subtle attitudes of mind, the tremendous vitality. The pavements along the bigger streets were boardwalks, like those I remember in Elwood when I was a boy. The houses had the neat, buttoned-up look of homes in any northern town, with light from the windows and soft smoke coming from the chimneys.

There was plenty to remind us, however, that this was Siberia and not Minnesota or Wisconsin. Most of the houses were built of logs, with felt packed between them, and their façades were covered with the intricate scrollwork of all Siberian houses.

The food was Siberian—a whole roast pig on the table for breakfast, sausages, eggs, cheese, soup, chicken, veal, tomatoes and pickles, wine and a vodka concentrate so strong that even Russians poured water into it. Each meal served to us was as big as the one that preceded it. There was vodka at breakfast, and steaming tea all day long. It is a cold country, and whatever the Yakuts ate outside our hotel, they apparently ate plenty.

I wondered about the amusements of the people.

"Have you a theater?" I asked Muratov.

He had, and we went to it later in the evening. He told me the performance began at nine o'clock. After dinner we drank vodka and talked, and I suddenly realized that it was already after nine.

"What time did you say the show started?" I asked him.

"Mr. Willkie," he answered, "the show starts when I get there."

And so it did. This time nobody stopped him. We walked into our box a half-hour later, sat down, and up went the curtain. We saw a gypsy opera, performed by a Leningrad company on tour. The dancing was excellent, the staging good, the singing fair. The audience liked it noisily, though the theater was not quite filled, this being the ninth consecutive performance of the same opera in that town.

The war was far removed that night from this audience of young people, and so was the ideology of Communism. Love and jealousy and gypsy dances filled the stage, and between the acts the young men with their girls paraded arm in arm around the theater as Russian audiences always do.

But earlier, in the twilight, with the new snow crunching under our feet, we had gone to see the district museum. There we found vivid reminders of the war. The graphs on the walls showing the increase in schools, hospitals, cattle, retail trade, all stopped at June, 1941, as if the country's life had stopped then. And the answer to each of my questions ended with an explanation of how much more could have been done had not the Germans put a temporary end to all normal progress.

Muratov showed me at the museum samples of the real gold which is now the greatest wealth of Yakutsk, and of the "soft gold"—or furs— which is its second most valuable product. Among the sables, foxskins, and bearskins were the soft, small pelts of Arctic hares and white squirrels. These smaller animals, he explained, must be shot through the eye if the skin is not to be spoiled. When I expressed a polite skepticism of the economic possibilities of a profession in which you must shoot squirrels invariably through the eye, Muratov stood his ground. All Yakutsk hunters, he said, when they are mobilized into the Red Army, are so good that they are classified automatically as snipers.

During the day, too, we were aware of the war. Though Yakutsk is three thousand miles from the front, we found simple people, most of whom had never seen a German in their lives or traveled west of the Ural Mountains, talking earnestly of "the war for the fatherland."

I asked Muratov what he was doing about the education of the people.

"Mr. Willkie," he said, "the answer is simple. Before 1917, only two per cent of all the people of Yakutsk were literate; ninety-eight per cent could not read or write. Now the figures are exactly reversed."

"Moreover," he went on, smiling cheerfully at me, "I have now received an order from Moscow to liquidate the two per cent illiteracy before the end of next year."

Once more that term "liquidate." It is constantly used in Russia. It can mean the accomplishment of a set task (the task itself has been liquidated), or it can mean imprisonment, exile, or death for incapacity, failure, or deliberate obstruction. I remembered an item that Joe Barnes had read to me from *Pravda*, about the fate of the manager of a collective farm who had just been sentenced to twenty years' imprisonment because one hundred cows had died on his farm. He had failed to liquidate the causes, so he himself had been liquidated, and the government wanted other farm managers to know.

Muratov showed us with pride Yakutsk's newest motion-picture theater. It was one of the concrete buildings with which he has disproved an old belief that only wooden structures could be built on eternally frozen subsoil.

The most attractive building in town, however, housed the local Communist party headquarters. I had often wondered how in actual practice three million Communist party members—that is all there are in Russia, about one and one-half per cent of the population—could impose their ideas and their control on two hundred million. Here in Yakutsk I began to understand the process.

There was no other organized group in the town; no church, no lodge, no other party. Approximately only 750 people, one and one-half per cent of Yakutsk's 50,000, belong to the Communist party and are members of the town's one club. But these 750 include all the directors of factories, managers of collective farms, the government officials, most of the doctors, superintendents of schools, intellectuals, writers, librarians, and teachers. In other words, in Yakutsk as in most communities in Russia, the best-educated, the most alert, the brightest and ablest men of the community are members of the Communist party. Each of these Communist clubs, all over Russia, is part of a tight-knit national organization, of which Stalin is still Secretary General. One can understand why he still prefers that title to any other which he holds. For this organization keeps the party in power. Its members are the vested-interest group. That is the answer.

Americans would not like that kind of one-party system. But I found in Yakutsk evidence of one of the Soviet Union's greatest achievements and one which the best and most progressive Americans must applaud: its handling of the terrible problem of national and racial minorities.

This town is still largely populated by Yakuts. They made up eighty-two per cent of the population of the republic. As far as I could see, they lived as the Russians lived; they held high office; they wrote their own poetry and had their own theater. Appointive offices filled from Moscow, like Muratov's, were more often held by Russians. Elective offices were usually filled, I was told, by Yakuts. Schools taught both languages. War posters along the streets were captioned in both Russian and Yakut.

How permanent this solution will be it would be hard to predict. Undoubtedly some of its strength lies in the great open spaces of a republic so big that most of it is still unmapped, where more than 100,000 different lakes and streams, Muratov told me, have in the last few years been found and named. I realize that empty space such as we flew over in the republic of Yakutsk for two long days is a great cushion for the conflicts which in Europe have bred prejudice and persecution.

Few things in this Siberian outpost of the Soviet Union interested me more than Muratov himself. If the town of Yakutsk suggested answers to many of my questions, Muratov gave me the key to many others. For he is typical of the new men who are running Russia. And many of his characteristics and much of his career were curiously like those of many Americans I have known.

He is a short, stocky man, with a round, smiling, clean-shaven face. Born in Saratov on the Volga, he was the son of a peasant farmer. Picked from a machine shop in Stalingrad for special schooling because he was bright, he had worked and studied his way through school, through the university, and through the Institute of Red Professors, Moscow's leading graduate school in the social sciences. Two long years ago, he had been sent here close to the Arctic Circle to head the Council of People's Commissars of Yakutsk.

Here he was, thirty-seven years old, educated entirely after the 1917 Revolution, running a republic bigger than any other in the U.S.S.R., more than five times as big as France. I saw a good deal of him for a couple of days. He is a man who would do well in America; in his own country he was doing something more than well.

His way of doing things, like the Soviet way all over Siberia, is rough and tough and often cruel and sometimes mistaken. His comment would be: "But it gets results." When I pressed him for details about the economic development of Yakutsk, he talked like a California real-estate salesman. And once more I was reminded of the robust days of great development in this country, at the beginning of the century, when our own leaders were men chiefly interested in getting things done.

"Why, consider, Mr. Willkie. We set up the Yakutsk Autonomous Soviet Socialist Republic in 1922, when the civil wars were finally won. Stalin was Commissar of Minor Nationalities then. Since that time, we've multiplied the budget of this republic eighty times, and everyone who lives here knows it in his heart and in his stomach.

"Why, Yakutsk used to be just a white spot on all the maps. Now, this month, our gold mines won third place in competing against all the nonferrous mining of Russia. They are ahead of plan." And he filled me with figures.

His power plant had just won first place in a competition of all municipal plants in the Soviet Union, and a red flag from the party for cutting production costs to 6.27 kopecks for each kilowatt hour.

"We've invested more than a billion rubles in Yakutsk in twenty years," he said. "We'll cut nearly 4,000,000 cubic meters of wood this year, against 35,000 in 1911. And we've still got a long way to go before we hit the annual growth, which we figure is 88,000,000 cubic meters."

He had obviously been planning in terms of international trade.

"When this war is over, you in America are going to need wood and wood pulp. And we're going to need machines, all kinds of machines. We're not so far away from you, as soon as we get the Arctic sea route open. Come and get it; we'll be glad to swap."

I saw with my own eyes that his tales were not all salesmanship. Yakutsk is about a thousand miles from a railroad. Only this year they are finishing a hard-surfaced, all-weather highway to tie the republic in with the Trans-Siberian Railroad and Moscow. Until now, they have been dependent for communication on airways and on the Lena River. In summer, steamers and barges move goods up the Lena to Yakutsk from Tikhsi Bay, where the Arctic freighters berth. In winter, the river's frozen surface makes the only hard road the republic has ever known.

Gold and furs are precious goods; they have moved without roads since the beginning of history. But Yakutsk has now been found by Soviet research expeditions to have great wealth in other things: silver, nickel, copper, lead. Oil has been found, and although details of the wells are military secrets, Muratov told me they would be producing commercially before the end of 1943. In fish, lumber, and salt, the country has literally untapped resources. And a sizable ivory industry has been built, curiously enough, on the tusks of mammoths, prehistoric animals which once ranged over this area and have been preserved ever since in Arctic cold storage.

Even in agriculture, Yakutsk has possibilities. At the museum, they showed me samples of the crossbred wheat with which the Russians have been pushing northward the limit of their wheat belt. The growing season is short, but the subsoil is full of water and the sun shines all day and almost all night in summer.

Most of the farms—ninety-seven per cent in September—have been collectivized. Reindeer are still the chief motive power of the republic, but there are now some hundreds of tractors, operated from machine tractor stations which lease them to the farms. The republic even has 160 combines—"Think of it, Mr. Willkie, 160 combines at the Arctic Circle!"—and a small but growing army of specialists determined to make the frozen tundra of the north flower and produce crops.

These people have developed an enthusiasm and a self-confidence which reminded me repeatedly of the romance of our own Western development. I came away from Yakutsk with a powerful curiosity to know what it will look like ten years from now.

When I got home, I found a similar curiosity about all Russia in people's minds and an attitude toward Russia made up of admiration and fear.

What is Russia going to do? Is she going to be the new disturber of the peace? Is she going to demand conditions at the end of the war that will make it impossible to re-establish Europe on a decent peaceful road? Is she going to attempt to infiltrate other countries with her economic and social philosophy?

Frankly, I don't think anyone knows the answers to these questions; I doubt if even Mr. Stalin knows all the answers.

Obviously, it would be ridiculous for me to attempt to say what Russia is going to do. This much, however, I do know to be true: there are 200,000,000 subjects of the U.S.S.R.; they control the largest single land mass in the world under one government; they have almost inexhaustible supplies of timber, iron, coal, oil, which are, practically speaking, unexploited; through elaborate systems of hospitalization and public-health organizations the Russian people are one of the healthiest peoples in the world, living in a vigorous, stimulating climate; in the last twenty-five years, through a widespread, drastic educational system, a large percentage have become literate and tens of thousands technically trained; and from the topmost official to the most insignificant farm or factory worker the Russians are fanatically devoted to Russia and supercharged with the dream of its future development.

I don't know the answers to all the questions about Russia, but there's one other thing I know: that such a force, such a power, such a people cannot be ignored or disposed of with a high hat or a lifting of the skirt. We cannot act as if we were housewives going into an A & P store, picking and choosing among the groceries displayed; taking this, leaving that. The plain fact is: we have no choice in the matter. Russia will be reckoned with. That is the reason why I am constantly telling my fellow Americans: work in ever-closer co-operation with the Russians while we are joined together in the common purpose of defeating a common enemy. Learn all we can about them and let them learn about us.

There's still another thing I know: geographically, from a trade standpoint, in their similarity of approach to many problems, the Russians and the Americans should get along together. The industrialization of Russia will require a limitless amount of American products, and Russia has unlimited natural resources that we need. The Russians, like us, are a hardy, direct people and have great admiration for everything in America, except the capitalistic system. And, frankly, there are many things in Russia that we can admire—its vigor, its vast dreams, its energy, its tenacity of purpose. No one could be more opposed to the Communist doctrine than I am, for I am completely opposed to any system that leads to absolutism. But I have never understood why it should be assumed that in any possible contact between Communism and democracy, democracy should go down.

So let me say once more: I believe it is possible for Russia and America, perhaps the most powerful countries in the world, to work together for the economic welfare and the peace of the world. At least, knowing that there can be no enduring peace, no economic stability, unless the two work together, there is nothing I ever wanted more to believe. And so deep is my faith in the fundamental rightness of our free economic and political institutions that I am convinced they will survive any such working together.

VI CHINA HAS BEEN FIGHTING
FIVE YEARS

IF we are to win a true victory in this world war in which we are now engaged, we must have a clear understanding of the people of the Far East. In our first year of direct fighting, most Americans have come to realize that the war in Asia is no sideshow to the war in Europe. But if we hope to prevent war in the future, we must know what are the forces at work in this vast area of the world. We shall need to know those which are friendly to us, and we shall need to be honest enough to back them, no matter what this may mean to many of our conventional prejudices about the world.

It was because I felt deeply our new involvement with the Far East that I made up my mind to go to China. For a few days after the trip was first discussed in Washington, it seemed that transport difficulties, in view of the President's expressed desire that I should not go to India, might make this extremely hard. But these were cleared up before we left New York.

I lunched in Washington with T. V. Soong, China's Foreign Minister, a few days before I left. He spoke to me openly and frankly about his country's difficulties, both financial and military, and his hopes for a real coalition strategy of the United Nations. Only such a strategy, he thought, could help China, and could make the tremendous potential weight of the democracies effective on the same extensive scale as that on which Hitler and General Tojo make their plans.

I agree with him. But neither my trip to China nor the subsequent history of attempts to forge a real coalition strategy bringing China and Russia into full and unequivocal alliance with Great Britain and America has yet given me any substantial reassurance on this score. The tendency of many of our leaders to let the war fall apart into a

79

first-class war and a second-class war still frightens me. Certainly my
trip to the Far East left no doubt in my own mind about this. Either we
win the war in full partnership with the Chinese in Asia, as with the
British and the Russians and the occupied nations in Europe, or we
shall not have won it.

I know there are many who believe that the way to control the future
is largely through Anglo-American dominance. They expect an eventual
invasion of western Europe by Great Britain and the United States,
when Germany becomes sufficiently softened, and an occupation of the
Middle East by their combined forces. Thus, they figure, Russia's advances and future dominance will be offset by our occupation of western Europe, with the consequent rallying of the conquered peoples to
our standards. They likewise, after Hitler is disposed of, visualize the
United States and Great Britain as jointly, with some help from China,
destroying Japan. They see after the war a China, treated kindly, intact
but weak, and the forces of Asia paternalistically directed for the good
of the East by the Western powers, in the ways that seem best for
future world peace and security. They think of control of the world's
strategic military and trade points as an Anglo-American trusteeship
for East and West alike, guaranteed by superior Anglo-American
strength. Thus the Western cultural and political values will be preserved, peace restored, economic security provided, and all the world
brought to our enlightened standards of democracy and well-being.

It's a persuasive argument. It sounds good—provided you ignore the
noble expressions of the Atlantic Charter which President Roosevelt—
not Prime Minister Churchill—has specifically extended to the peoples
of the Pacific; provided you ignore the preachments of the Four Freedoms with which we have been trying to indoctrinate the world; provided you forget the thinking of about two billion people.

For many years we have lived in ignorance of the true ambitions and
capabilities of Japan and its appeal to the growing aspirations of the
East for a place in the sun. We have underrated the Japanese, as a
result, and disregarded the developing forces in the East. We knew
vaguely that the Japanese were trying to build an empire. We are only
now beginning to realize how great that empire would be if it were
built.

Japan's dreams have at last taken on reality to our eyes, for we have seen the Japanese conquer a great part of the empire they planned. Besides Korea and Manchuria they hold the entire coast of China. They hold most of the Philippines. They have conquered virtually all the East Indies. They have taken half of Burma and cut the Burma Road. They control at least the eastern half of the Indian Ocean and are knocking on the very doors of Calcutta.

They have gone far enough, indeed, for us to grasp a picture of what the world would be like if they should succeed. Suppose, for instance, that India should fall. Suppose that China, cut off from all aid, should be strangled and conquered. I do not believe that these things are going to happen, but to deny them as *possibilities* is simply to repeat the tragic mistakes of the past.

If all this were to come about, we should witness the creation, not merely of a great empire, but of perhaps the biggest empire in history; an empire composed of about a billion people living on approximately fifteen million square miles of land; an empire occupying one third of the earth and including one half of its total population. That is the Japanese dream.

Moreover, this empire would include within itself almost every resource that can be imagined. It would be self-sufficient, whether for peacetime industry or for war. Japan would then have iron from the Philippines, copper from the Philippines and Burma, tin from Malaya, oil from many islands, chrome, manganese, antimony, bauxite for aluminum, and more rubber than she could ever use. Then it would not be the United States that would be known as the bountiful land, but the so-called Greater East Asia Co-Prosperity Sphere.

I have unbounded faith in the courage, the enterprise, and the destiny of the American people. But I believe that if Americans were forced to live hereafter face to face with an empire of such dimensions, our way of life would be little better than an armed camp, and our vaunted freedom would be little more than a fond hope. We should live in continual alarm, in endless war, under crushing armaments which it would be our constant endeavor to increase. Neither peace nor prosperity, neither freedom nor justice, could flourish in such a struggle for existence. And it would not matter in the least how wide or how narrow the Pacific Ocean is.

I believe that we are going to avoid that calamity. I believe we are going to avoid it by striking hard, over and over again, before it is too late. But striking alone will not be enough. We must come to a better understanding of what is happening in the East, of the views of its people, of the changes that have taken place in their ways of thinking, of their loss of faith in Western imperialism, and in the superiority of the white man, and their desires for freedom, according to their standards and ideals. We all say that this is a "war for men's minds," a political war. But too often, as in North Africa and in the East, we perform in terms of old power politics and purely military operations, in terms of expediency and apparent practicalities. We too frequently forget what the war is about and too easily abandon our ideals. We do not keep sufficiently in our active consciousness that it might already be too late to defeat Japan's super-empire either militarily or politically, had it not been for the desperate resistance of the Chinese people through five long, heartbreaking years.

It is not particularly pleasant for Americans to look back across the last five years during which so few realized the importance to our entire civilization of the Chinese resistance. It was not a particularly pleasant thing for me to think about while I was in China, talking to the men who had led and carried out that resistance. While we were absorbed in our bitter quarrels and isolationist delusions, we never took time to understand the heroic role that the Chinese were playing, let alone to send them substantial help. Now we are in a great war to retrieve that error. We must retrieve it.

The Chinese outlook on the future is almost the opposite of that of the Japanese. They do not seek empire. They seek merely to hold and to develop their own vast and lovely homeland. They want to see the new forces that are stirring in the East used for their own freedom and for the freedom of other peoples. Meanwhile the Japanese seek to use the same forces for their imperialistic designs.

China is much larger than the United States, both in area and in population. It contains within its boundaries many rich resources. On the other hand, it is not self-sufficient—and neither are we. This fact does not disturb the Chinese or make them want to conquer the world, any more than it does us. Self-sufficiency is a delusion of the totalitarians. In a truly democratic world, a nation would have no more need

of self-sufficiency than the state of New York has of making itself
independent of the state of Pennsylvania.

We must not expect Chinese ideas of personal liberty and democratic government to be exactly the same as ours. Some of their ideas
may seem to us too radical, others may seem ridiculously archaic. We
should remember that in their eyes some of *our* customs appear ridiculous and even distasteful. We must keep our minds fixed upon the
essential fact that the Chinese want to be free—free in their own way
to govern their lives for the benefit and happiness of their own people.
They want a free Asia.

The recent treaties between the United States and China and between
Great Britain and China, in which extra-territoriality has been given
up by us, are a step toward recognition of China's determination to be
free. No longer will Americans and Englishmen in China be exempt
from Chinese laws and Chinese courts, any more than Chinese in the
United States are exempt from American legal processes. But it must
not be assumed that these treaties solve the problem. The British, for
example, still claim Hong Kong, one of the great ports through which
the people of China must trade with the world. And Hong Kong, like
the claims of Americans and other nationals in the International Settlement at Shanghai, is only a symbol to the Chinese of the foreign rights
and privileges which still bar their way to real freedom.

It is unfortunate that so many Americans still think of China in
terms of great inert masses and not in terms of people, still think of
the death of five million Chinese as something different from and less
costly than the death of five million Westerners. Perhaps the most
significant fact in the world today is the awakening that is going on in
the East. Even if we win this war militarily, this awakening will still
have to be reckoned with. If we are wise, we can direct forces which
are in being throughout the East toward world co-operative effort for
peace and economic security. These same forces, however, if they are
flouted or ignored, will continue to disturb the world.

VII THE OPENING UP OF CHINA'S WEST

I SHALL always be glad that I entered China, on my first visit to that country, not through what used to be called a "treaty port," but through the back door, the vast hinterland of China's northwest. The "treaty ports" on the Pacific—all of which are now held by the Japanese —are symbols to the modern Chinese mind of the generations in which China was regarded by Western nations as a large but primitive country to be converted, exploited, or laughed at. Shanghai, Hong Kong, and Canton may be beautiful cities; but to the Chinese even their names are reminders of the days when, as Sun Yat-sen, founder of the Chinese Republic, put it, "the rest of mankind is the carving knife and the serving dish, while we are the fish and the meat."

Instead, my first stop in China was at Tihwa, called by the Russians Urumchi, capital city of the province of Sinkiang, or Chinese Eastern Turkistan. Our Liberator had flown from Tashkent in Siberia in a single day. Most of the flight had been down the Ili River valley which cuts between some of the highest mountain ranges in the world—the Tien Shan and the Altai Mountains. For hours we flew over empty desert, as strangely beautiful as any landscape I have ever seen, before we came down on the fertile land of grapes and melons which is called by the Chinese Sinkiang, or "New Dominion."

Sinkiang is twice as big as France. It has something less than 5,000,000 inhabitants. It is the largest province of China and may conceivably be the richest. It is not only close to the geographical center of Asia, but also close to its political center, for it is here that Russia and China meet. Over the long pull, what happens in this strange territory, about which many Americans have never heard, may have decisive influence on our history.

Very few foreigners have been there in the last generation. When I was in Tihwa, my Chinese hosts estimated that only a few dozen American or English travelers had flown through Sinkiang on the Chinese-Russian commercial airline which operated between China and Moscow until a year ago. Even these few saw more of Hami, a smaller town with a better airport, than they did of the capital, Tihwa.

The town itself has little to boast of. It is small, sleepy-looking, and incredibly muddy. The street signs are in Russian, the government is Chinese, the people are Turkis, part of the 20,000,000 Moslems who live inside the frontiers of China. It boasts the finest melons in Asia and some small, seedless grapes as good as any I have ever eaten. The mountains around the town are filled with metals. Irrigation gives the province its food; its only export of importance at present is wool, which now goes in substantial quantities to help clothe the Red Army.

Sinkiang is one of the areas in the world where politics and geography combine to make a kind of explosive amalgam full of meaning to those who are curious about what is going to happen to the world. Geography leans Sinkiang toward Russia. The Soviet Turk-Sib Railroad runs a few miles from its frontier. All the consumers' goods we saw in Tihwa came from Russia; the cars we rode in were Russian; the army we saw drove Russian tanks. But politics leans the province back toward China. Chinese have ruled Sinkiang since the Han dynasty. The present governor is Chinese. And now the desperate, hopeful drive in China to open up its own hinterland has blown like a fresh wind through the province. Soviet-Chinese relations will be important to the whole world after this war, and they may be determined in this area.

The Soviet government has always recognized Chinese sovereignty over Sinkiang. There has never been anything like a border clash between the two nations. But the pressure of railroads, markets, commercial credits, Communist ideology, has swung the province steadily into a Soviet orbit during the last ten years, and if the Chinese set up a countervailing pressure by industrializing and developing their northwest provinces, including Sinkiang, it will mean a real test of the strength of two powerful peoples.

I heard tales, both in Moscow and in Chungking, of political difficulties in Sinkiang which bordered on straight fiction. One of the chief actors in the plot, Ma Chung-ying, a Chinese Moslem leader who invaded Sinkiang from the neighboring province of Kansu in 1932, with a Robin Hood reputation and a great way with his fellow Moslems, walked across the frontier in 1934 and is rumored to be in Moscow today, waiting his time to go back. Another chief leader is Sheng Shih-tsai, now Governor of Sinkiang, a Chinese. Since he is a native of China's northeastern provinces of Manchuria, occupied by the Japanese since 1931, he is bitterly anti-Japanese. His brother was found killed in his bed in the Governor's palace last June, and the legends which pass as news in Asia have it that Russians were accused of complicity in his murder.

I could not learn what truth there was in the stories. Probably there was none. I dined with Governor Sheng in Tihwa, and the Soviet Consul General dined with us. We toasted each other and the three countries from which we came in Russian vodka and in Chinese rice wine, and there was no hint of anything but cordial friendship between Russia and China. But the next morning I had a private breakfast, at his suggestion, with the Chinese Governor, who once was sympathetic with the Communists and of late has shifted his allegiance to the Generalissimo. The stories he told me of murder, intrigue, espionage, and counterespionage sounded like a dime thriller and would have been incredible to an American were it not for the evidence all about of suspicion and mystery. Obviously, one of our problems, when the war is over, will be to help China and Russia work out in co-operation the common problems they face in Turkistan, near the roof of the world in Asia. And that is another reason why I urge and urge again the necessity of bringing China and Russia, the United States and Great Britain, in common conference today to learn to work with each other while they fight. For if they do not there is enough explosive powder in Central Asia to blow the lid off the world again when the present fighting is over.

Governor Sheng's dinner was not only the first of a long series of Chinese banquets given for me by what must certainly be the most hospitable people in the world. It was also one of the most interesting. We sat in a long, vaulted room with men facing each other across narrow tables running down both sides of the hall. The walls were covered with inscriptions of welcome to an American, of challenge to our common enemies, of faith in our victory, written in the seventeen languages which pass currency in that crossroads of Asia where one of the oldest caravan routes in the world still links Europe and Asia.

The Governor is a tall man with handsome, black mustaches. He is a Manchurian, Chinese in origin, and has studied in Japan. He has been Governor of Sinkiang for more than ten years and knows the country well, with its intrigue and conflicting forces. I had talked with him in his office in the afternoon, and he had told me of the problems of running a province which is forty-six days' travel from his nation's capital.

In Tihwa, as in every other Chinese city I was to visit, I was given really moving evidence of the good will with which Americans are regarded all over the world. Nothing could have been farther from that banquet hall on that September night than the United States. Even our fellow diners, officials and army officers for the most part, looked at me with curiosity which suggested that many of them were seeing an American for the first time in their lives. Yet there was a warmth and a friendliness in their reception of me which spoke eloquently of their unspoken hope that the United States will continue to be China's friend in the years to come.

Everything about Tihwa reminded us, more vividly than Tashkent or Teheran or Bagdad, of the real vitality and strength of Asia. The next day, the Governor staged a military review for his American visitors. On a big parade ground, we watched the Sinkiang army, or what must have been a very large part of it, file past in dress parade.

It was a fascinating show. The soldiers looked neat, well trained, and healthy. Their equipment was limited in amount, but most of it seemed to be Russian and good. They had mobile artillery, machine guns mounted on motorcycles, scout cars with armor, a few light but fast tanks. There were several contingents of truck-borne infantry. The Russian origin of the equipment became only too clear when one artillery regiment galloped by us with *kachankas,* the Ukrainian farm wagons with machine guns mounted on them which were first developed by guerrillas in the Soviet civil wars and which have now played an important part in holding the Nazis in the Ukraine a second time.

But the climax of the show was strictly local. Several dozen cavalrymen, lithe, wiry Mongols and Kazaks who sat their saddles as if they were part of the horses, charged in turn through a series of assignments, perhaps fifteen, any one of which was enough to take your breath away.

With two-edged sabers they cut through saplings, sliced off a dummy head, picked objects off the ground—all at a dead gallop. It was not hard to understand, after watching them, the terror Genghis Khan inspired in his enemies.

Generalissimo Chiang Kai-shek had sent a formal welcome to me at Tihwa, brought by two of his closest personal friends and aides, who accompanied me all the rest of the time I was in China. They were Dr. Hollington K. Tong, Vice-Minister of Information, and General Chu Shao-liang, commander in chief of the northwest war zone. Before I left China, I had a deep affection for both of them.

"Holly" Tong had been described to me on my way to China by a foreigner whose knowledge of that country and love for it seemed to me as great as any man's, as "one of the Generalissimo's keenest instruments, as faithful as a dog and as clean as a dog's tooth." He is a graduate of Park College, in Missouri, and of the Columbia School of Journalism in New York. After a distinguished career as a Chinese newspaper publisher, he became one of the Generalissimo's closest advisers, helping to run an important ministry and at the same time serving as translator, secretary, and counselor to his chief. He seemed to me, and I came to know him well, the kind of aide any great leader would like to have.

General Chu, unlike "Holly" Tong, whose English is amazingly fluent and idiomatic, spoke not one word that I could understand. He made up for it by one of the most endearing personalities I have ever known. I never sat down to a banquet in China, or finished a speech, or walked out of a conference without seeing him smile at me in the friendliest possible way. He talked little, and held himself with the dignity expected of a distinguished soldier who had fought with the Generalissimo through his hardest and earliest campaigns in unifying China, but he did as much as any man could to make me feel that China was not an alien country, full of strange customs, but a warm-hearted, hospitable land filled with friends of America.

Another Chinese whose warm friendliness is hard to forget had traveled with us all the way from Moscow. He was Major Hsu Huan-sheng, an assistant military attaché in the Chinese Embassy at Kuibishev. On some of the flights we made inside China, he piloted the plane. In 1938, three years before the United States went to war, this young fellow, who still looks like a boy of seventeen, had made himself famous by piloting the first Chinese raid over Japan, dropping pamphlets. I was glad that his trip with us gave him a chance to see his wife and children, on our way to the front near Sian, and I was sorry when he left us in Siberia on our way home, to go back to his job.

These men were in our plane when we left the next morning, September 29, to fly to Lanchow, capital of Kansu province. This five-hour flight was from one point of view the most remarkable lap of our flight around the world. While you are flying through a world at war, trying after each stop to prepare yourself to understand the next one, or to steal a little sleep, scenery inevitably plays a secondary role. But the landscape between Tihwa and Lanchow was one of the most amazing sights of my life, and with utter fascination we watched it unfold beneath us.

For straight beauty, it would be hard to beat. Part of the way was over desert, and part over green, cultivated fields. It was all mountainous, but once we had left the snow-covered Tien Shan range behind us, the mountains were lower and surprisingly fertile. In places, the Chinese have terraced the hills right to the top, and the ground below looked like a gigantic billiard table which had been dented into an irregular, infinitely varied, rolling carpet of green.

As we neared Lanchow, we hit the red loam hills from which the wind and the rivers have carried over centuries the soil which now covers most of northern China. These red hills are unbelievably lovely to look at from the air, but I could not see them without thinking what wealth they represented to a nation determined to open up its west. Irrigation projects, power plants, fertile fields and pastures, whole cities could be built in this region, and all the country lacked to build them, it seemed to me, was people.

I don't know how often I thought of this flight during the weeks I was in China. In the first place, the emptiness of this northwestern region makes a striking contrast with the crowded, teeming lands of southern China. In the second place, every Chinese leader I talked to spoke of the northwest and the present struggle to open its riches with transport, co-operatives, and modern science, as China's most fundamental hope in the war against Japan and in the great task of building a strong, modern nation which will follow the peace.

Finally, and most important, I felt in Tihwa and in Lanchow and in the country between those cities a curious resemblance to our own American West in the days when it was being opened up. The people seemed tall and resourceful, a more rugged type than many we saw in the crowded streets of Chengtu or of Chungking. With the Japanese holding all of the coastal half of China, all the great industrial cities and ports, and much of the rich and fertile agricultural land, the Chinese have no alternative now but to open up their own west. But I was glad to find no attitude of sour grapes in the Chinese who are now pioneering in these areas. Instead, they talk big and a little boastfully and very much like the men of my father's generation in the United States.

In Lanchow I visited some of China's industrial co-operatives. I met there the quiet, sincere New Zealander, Rewi Alley, who has made Indusco an international word and a symbol of what can be done by a people determined to lift itself by its own bootstraps. Alley was having difficulties when I saw him; it is my guess that he will continue to have them. But I have no doubt that he and the Chinese Industrial Co-operative movement I saw in China's northwestern provinces are accomplishing an enormous change in the world's economic geography by opening up the heart of Asia.

This economic struggle in which China is now engaged has been less written about in America than China's military struggle against the Japanese invaders. But everything I saw made me believe that it has been no less heroic. If we Americans were blasted from our seacoasts by a hostile force, we could retire into our great interior and find there the machines and the skilled labor to fight on. But in the vast interior of China there were no such facilities. The Chinese had to carry their factories inland with them; not on freight cars, not on trucks, not even in carts, but on human backs, piece by heavy piece. They carried them up the great river valleys and across the mountain ranges.

They set them down and put them together in the remote highlands, where the whir of machinery had never been heard. From the relatively few factories that could thus be transported, there have now blossomed more than a thousand industrial establishments—small for the most part, and limited in the scope of their manufactures, but each contributing its bit to the foundation of the new China.

Surely we Americans can read the handwriting on the wall. The opening up of this new China compares only, in modern history, with the opening up of our own West. We know the struggle of those people. We know the hope. And in some significant measure we know what the fulfillment can be. The economic aim of the leaders of modern China is to develop their country much as we developed ours. They want to create an industrial foundation with which to raise the standard of living of their people. Many experts believe that the industrialization of China, once started, will proceed even faster than ours did. The new China starts with advanced technologies. Where we had to await the slow development of the locomotive, they can begin with the three-hundred-mile-an-hour airplane.

So far, they have neither airplanes nor locomotives. In Lanchow I saw the terminal of the Russian highway, the one land route into modern China. I wish every American could see it who has wondered whether there was too much salesmanship in the few stories which have been brought back from China of the heroism and the fortitude with which the Chinese people are still fighting back after more than five years of war against the Japanese.

We had flown over stretches of this highway ever since we crossed the Soviet border, east of Alma-Ata. Alma-Ata is a big city, linked by rail and by airlines to the industries and the raw materials of Siberia, of Soviet Central Asia, and of Russia itself. From Alma-Ata, heavy trucks pound eastward along a hard-surfaced road through Tihwa and Hami and up to the western frontier of Kansu province. We flew over these trucks and convinced ourselves that they were as real as they were incongruous on this ancient silk road, perhaps the oldest caravan route in history, along which Marco Polo traveled on his way to ancient Cathay.

The Chinese end of the road, where there is neither roadbed nor gasoline nor trucks, fits much more appropriately the historical traditions of the highway. Instead of trucks, the Chinese use carts, camels, and coolies. Soviet freight, which takes four days from the frontier to the Kansu border, takes seventy more days to reach Lanchow. And still it has not reached a railhead, but must travel days and days farther by the most primitive transport imaginable before it debouches into the heavily populated parts of China where it is so desperately needed.

Outside Lanchow, between the airport and the city, we saw a Chinese caravan being formed for the long haul back toward Russia. It was made up of small, two-wheeled mule carts, rubber-tired—strangely, to my rubber-conscious eyes—and piled high with wool and salt and tea. The mules were standing patiently in a row which must have been some miles long, the coolies next to them, waiting for the order to start. They would be plodding westward for more than two months, I was told, before they could exchange their cargo for the gasoline, airplane parts, engines, and ammunition which the Soviet Union is still shipping to China, largely on credits which have now reached a staggering total.

The road is a shoestring being used to support an enormous weight. If the shoestring breaks, we shall all be the losers. I could get no official figures on the amount of traffic which now travels over the road. But Americans in Lanchow estimated that not more than 2000 tons of freight reach China every month along the 1800-mile highway. This is far below the capacity of the Burma Road, which has been cut by the Japanese. But except for the American airplanes which fly in from India over the Himalayas, and the smuggling which seeps through the entire front against Japan, it is China's only link with the world outside.

Lanchow is on the Yellow River, much nearer its source than Tungkuan, where we were to look across it a week or two later into Japanese encampments. It is a city of roughly half a million people, without a railroad, with no important factory more than six years old, but with a great future. Kansu province, of which it is the capital, is rich land, with enormous possibilities.

It was in Lanchow that General Chu took me to his home to meet his wife. We climbed out of the city up a hill which looks down on the town and the river beyond it. Near the top of the hill is a Chinese temple which serves as headquarters for the military command of the five north-western provinces of China—Shensi, Kansu, Ninghsia, Chinghai, and Sinkiang. Here we sat and drank tea and ate an enormous cake with the general and Mrs. Chu. From a balcony outside the general's work-room, the view fell over the tiled roofs of the temple buildings, across the town itself, to the river with its irrigation works which have been functioning for two thousand years to make the land of Kansu fertile.

That night we had another banquet, given by Governor Ku Cheng-lun of Kansu, in the Officers' Moral Endeavor Association hostel, where we were put up for the night. There were other dignitaries present besides my host: General Yu Fei-peng, Minister of Transport and Supply, and Admiral Shen Hung-lieh, Minister of Agriculture. They talked about the province's forestry, agriculture, and water-conservancy problems, and its fledgling industries, some of which, including a blanket factory, I saw the next morning. I was still some days away from Chungking, China's wartime capital, but I already began to feel the strength from which this amazing nation has drawn its capacity to fight back against the Japanese.

VIII WHAT FREE CHINA FIGHTS WITH

From Lanchow we flew south to Chengtu, then up into the mountains to the capital, Chungking. On the way home from China, we flew north to Sian, then back again to Chengtu to take off on the long flight across north China and the Gobi to Siberia. With shorter flights to visit American headquarters or army camps in Szechwan or Yünnan, we covered a substantial portion of the provinces left in free China still untouched by the Japanese except for bombing raids.

There are ten of these provinces, five in the northwest and five in the southwest. In the northwest, we had seen the future of China. In the southwest, especially in Szechwan province—Chengtu and Chungking—we saw its present at its best.

Here it was not the land but the people that made the strongest impression. It is difficult for anyone to understand fully the inexhaustible human resources of that country. People who know China but have not been there since 1937, when Japan began its present attempt to conquer China, tell me the vitality, the resourcefulness, the courage and devotion to their cause of freedom which distinguish the Chinese people are a constant marvel to them.

After visiting China's cotton mills, its munitions factories, its pottery works and cement plants, after talking with their managers and with hundreds of their workers for many hours. I began really to appreciate the ingenuity and adaptability of Chinese skill in modern industrial methods. And what is generally spoken of as the awakening of China came to mean something actual to me when I had discussed with college professors and grade-school teachers alike the irresistible urge to shake off the past which has caused modern China in a relatively few years to change literacy from the privilege of the few to the right of the masses. Almost 100,000,000 Chinese are now literate. At the universities learn-

ing is no longer measured in terms of pure erudition. Chinese scholars
of today apply China's rich lore to the problems of modern life. No
longer do they seek only the cloisters; they now compete hotly for
better ways to serve society and the state in which they live.

At Chengtu I met and plied with questions the presidents of the
eight universities there. The faculties of six had escaped from Japanese-
occupied areas and were now using the facilities of the two resident universities in shifts which kept the buildings and the libraries and the
laboratories occupied almost twenty-four hours a day.

I shall never forget the impressive scene as I spoke at an early morning hour to the ten thousand students of those universities and heard
their full-throated cheers at every reference to freedom. All over China
I talked with men who were responsible for the little schoolhouses where
the children of Chinese peasants and coolies for the first time in history
have an opportunity to learn.

Where ten years ago there were a hundred newspapers in what is
now free China, today there are a thousand. In almost every sizable
town there are one or more, and the editorials which were translated
for me are pungent and forceful. The Chinese Central News Service in
its professional methods of gathering and distributing the news compares well with our own press services and with British Reuter's.

I arrived in Chungking late in the afternoon, at an airport some miles
from the city. Long before our automobiles had reached the city, the
road on either side was lined with people. Before we reached the middle
of the city, the crowds stood packed from curb to store front. Men,
women, young boys and girls, bearded old gentlemen, Chinese with
fedora hats, others with skullcaps, coolies, porters, students, mothers
nursing their children, well dressed and poorly dressed—they packed
eleven miles of road over which our cars slowly moved on our way
to the guesthouse in which we were to stay. On the other side of the
Yangtze River, they stood and waited. On all the hills of Chungking,
which must be the world's hilliest city, they stood and smiled and
cheered and waved little paper American and Chinese flags.

Any man who has run for President of the United States is used to
crowds. But not to this one. I could discount it in my mind as much as
I wished, but to no avail. The paper flags waved by the people were

all of the same size, suggesting that the hospitable and imaginative Mayor of Chungking, Dr. K. C. Wu, had had a hand in planning this demonstration. It was perfectly clear that not all these people, many of whom were barefoot or dressed in rags, had any clear idea of who I was or why I was there. The firecrackers which were exploding on every street corner, I told myself, are an old Chinese passion, anyway.

But in spite of all my efforts to discount it, this scene moved me profoundly. There was nothing synthetic or fake about the faces I looked at. They were seeing, in me, a representative of America and a tangible hope of friendship and help that might be forthcoming. It was a mass demonstration of good will. And it was an impressive show of the simple strength, in people and in emotions, which is China's greatest national resource.

I had seen a crowd like this one, but a little smaller, on my arrival in Lanchow, far into the northwest. I was later to see another, as impressive as any, which waited for hours in the rain on the streets of Sian, capital of Shensi province, because our plane was late. They never failed to move me deeply. It is impossible in a short trip through a country as big as China to make as many close and personal friendships as one would like, those relationships through which one generally comes to know the spirit and the ideas of a foreign people. But these crowds of Chinese people gave me a sure and lasting feeling that my surface impressions of China were backed by something no one could misread in those thousands of faces.

The Chinese I came to know well were, inevitably, leaders in one field or another. Some of them I will describe later in this account, and in high terms. But I know no praise high enough for the anonymous people of China.

One of them, whom I never met, wrote me a letter while I was in China. He is a student, and he pasted his picture at the end of his letter. His English was the kind that only a student can use who has enormous confidence in himself and in his dictionary.

"Dear Mr. Wendell Willkie," he wrote, "let me assure you that China, one of the bravest and most faithful among the allied countries, has never been daunted or changed her mind while confronting all sorts of hardships; for we perfectly understand that we are fighting for the holy cause of liberty and righteousness, and we firmly believe that a bright future is waiting us ahead, and that God will give us the victory that we ache to get at."

He enclosed a draft plan for the establishment of peace after the war, and it was an interesting plan. But it was the spirit of it which impressed me, like that of the crowds of Chinese I saw everywhere I went. He proposed setting up monuments to make people hate war instead of praising it, and he proposed that the last day of this war should be made a day for public sacrifices all over the world, and be named "Peace, Free, Pleasure Day."

One of the propositions of his plan is called "To increase the affection among human beings." And he suggested that each nation should raise peace funds with which to endow scientific scholarships. Only science, he wrote me, "can solve the pain of human beings, make up the defects of nature, raise the standard of living of human beings, and make the whole human being struggle with nature but not with mankind."

Possibly no other country on our side in this war is so dominated by the personality of one man as China. His name is Chiang Kai-shek, although he is universally referred to in China as "The Generalissimo," sometimes affectionately shortened to "Gissimo."

I had a number of long talks with the Generalissimo, as well as family breakfasts and other meals alone with him and Mme Chiang.

One late afternoon we drove to the Chiangs' country place, high on the steep bank of the Yangtze River. "Holly" Tong was with us. Across the front of the simple frame house was a large porch where we sat looking out to the hills of Chungking. In the river below, a number of small boats moved in the swift current, carrying the Chinese farmer and his produce downstream to market. It had been a hot day in Chungking but here a pleasant breeze was blowing, and as Mme Chiang served us tea, the Generalissimo and I began to talk, Mme Chiang and "Holly" serving alternately as interpreters.

We discussed the past and his administration's aim to change China from an almost exclusively agricultural society into a modern industrial one. He hoped in the change to retain the best of the old traditions and to avoid the social dislocations of large-scale Western industrial development by the establishment of a great number of widely distributed small plants. He was sure that in the teachings of Dr. Sun, the father of the republic, concerning a combined agricultural and industrial society he would find the way. But he was eager to discuss the question with someone from the West and he asked me many questions. I explained to him that the social problems created by mass production in America and the large industrial combinations which he wanted to avoid had not arisen, as he seemed to think, solely because of desire for power and the building of individual fortunes, though these elements undoubtedly contributed. In part, at least, they arose because of economic requirements: mass production greatly lowers costs.

I gave him the illustration of the automobile, which he hoped to see manufactured at low cost in China to fill Chinese roads. I pointed out to him that an automobile manufactured in a small plant would cost five times as much as an automobile manufactured on an assembly line under scientific management in a large plant. That it is impossible to have some of the products that make for a high standard of living at prices within the reach of the great masses of the people, if they must be produced exclusively in small plants. That every thoughtful American knew that in many instances we have created large industrial combinations unnecessarily. That for our social and economic good we should give the utmost encouragement and preference to the small industries. But that in certain industries, in order to maintain our standard of living, it was necessary to have large-scale production. I told him that we recognized the social, economic, and almost non-democratic maladjustments created by the collection of thousands of workers under single factory roofs, with the consequent possibility of unemployment of whole communities at one time. That we regretted the stratification of large groups of our population into a permanent employee class which this system produced, and the reduction of the opportunity for individual men to become owners of their own businesses. I also told the Generalissimo that we had not as yet found all the answers. But we did know that the solution did not consist in breaking up necessary large units into inefficient small ones.

I reminded him that there was an experiment going on much closer to him than any in the Western world, the Communist one in Russia, and that part of its success was due to the mass-production technique of using large groups for the accomplishment of a particular purpose.

He suggested that perhaps he could find the solution in having necessary large units partly owned by government and partly by private capital.

The discussion went on for hours. Then Mme Chiang, who had been acting as interpreter for us, with pleasant but firm feminine authority, said: "It's ten o'clock and you men haven't had anything to eat. Come on now; we must drive into town and get at least a bite. You can finish this some other time."

At other times we did talk more of this, and of many other things. We talked of India, of the whole East, of its aspirations, of its purposes, of how it should fit into a world-wide order, of military strategy, of Japan and its resources, of Pearl Harbor and the fall of Singapore and their profound psychological effect on the attitude of the East toward the West. We talked of the growing spirit of intense, almost fanatical nationalism which I had found developing in the countries of the Middle East, in Russia and now in China, of how such a spirit might upset the possibility of world co-operation. We talked of Russia and of Chiang's relationship to the Communists within China, of Great Britain and her policy in the East, of Franklin Roosevelt and Winston Churchill and Joseph Stalin.

In fact, the six days I was with the Generalissimo were filled with talk.

I can write no account of China without setting down my own conclusion that the Generalissimo, both as a man and as a leader, is bigger even than his legendary reputation. He is a strangely quiet, soft-spoken man. When he is not in military uniform, he wears Chinese dress, and this accentuates the impression he makes of a scholar—almost a clerical scholar—rather than a political leader. He is obviously a trained listener, used to the task of picking other men's brains. He nods his head when he agrees with you, with continuous soft little ya-ya's; it is a subtle form of compliment, and one that disarms the man he is talking to, and wins him in some degree to Chiang's side.

The Generalissimo is reported to spend a part of every day in praying and Bible reading. He has acquired from this, or from some childhood influence, a reflective manner, a quiet poise, and an occasional appearance of thinking out loud. He is undoubtedly sincere and his dignity and personal imperturbability have something almost severe in quality.

The Generalissimo came to power the hard way, a fact of which he is proud. He has known for more than twenty years the toughest problems of the birth of a nation. His loyalty, perhaps as a result of this, both to the extraordinary family into which he married and to the associates of his early years of struggle, is unbreakable and, I should guess, sometimes unreasonable. I could not document this, but no one can stay in Chungking even for a short time without realizing that the young republic, despite its youth, has already developed a sort of "old-school tie" of its own which automatically keeps some men in high position. The chief wearers of this "old-school tie" are the comrades-in-arms of the Generalissimo during the years when he was fighting warlords, and it is China's gain that none of these is yet an old man.

I would not like to suggest that the leaders I met in Chungking were not men of considerable caliber. They were. But they are not all representative men, in the Western sense. Just as the Chinese concept of democracy differs from ours in certain respects, so does the pattern which life imposes on its leaders. The Kuomintang, the party which rules China, includes in its plan for the growth of self-government in China a tutelary stage during which the people are being educated into new habits of living and thinking designed to make them good citizens of a complete democracy, with electoral rights, at a later time.

During this tutelary stage, it is inevitable that China's leaders should be men with considerable training, either in foreign universities or in war and politics, rather than men chosen by the people primarily to represent them. And so it is. I came to believe in China that this was one factor, and an important one, in the feeling of impatience, which can be found especially in foreign circles not unsympathetic with China, at the centralized control of Chinese life which is exercised in Chungking.

China delegated some of its best men to answer my questions and show me its war effort. It would be impossible to list all of those who made a strong impression on me.

General Ho Ying-chin, Minister of War, gave me a luncheon in his house on the top of a hill in Chungking looking down over the river. I talked then to him, to Lieutenant General Joseph W. Stilwell, to

Admiral Chen Shao-kwan, and to other officers of the Chinese Army. Later I had a long discussion with General Pai Chung-hsi, of the Kiangsi triumvirate.

President Lin Sen entertained me formally at his official residence. Dr. H. H. Kung, Vice-President of the Executive Yuan, gave a buffet dinner on the lawn of his home, the finest in Chungking. Dr. Chen Li-fu, Minister of Education, Dr. Wong Wen-hao, Minister of Economics, and Dr. Wang Shih-chieh, at that time Minister of Information, all gave me liberally their time and their services in explaining to me how China was meeting its crisis.

The Generalissimo himself presided at a dinner at the National Military Council, a great hall in the middle of Chungking which had been bombed the year before but was already rebuilt. This was the most appealing public dinner I attended around the world. For it was conducted with the simplicity which one likes to believe exists in high places in these years of necessary sacrifice. The entertainment provided was by musicians playing on instruments of ancient China, many of them one-stringed, and all crude in appearance and construction. But the songs were old Chinese folk songs and the melodies soft.

An episode occurred at this dinner which our party has since remembered with delight. Mike Cowles had been ill the day before, after eating as an experiment some creamed shark's lip. So he was particularly pleased when the dessert at the banquet was good old-fashioned vanilla ice cream. He expressed his pleasure to the Mayor of Chungking, who explained: In April the medical authorities had feared that China would be swept by a cholera epidemic. Since they had no anticholera serum, and since cholera was being spread by milk, they passed a municipal ordinance making it a criminal offense to serve ice cream.

"But," he added, "yesterday I decided that ice cream is such a delicacy and we are so pleased that Mr. Willkie came to Chungking, I just repealed the ordinance for one day so we could serve you ice cream tonight."

For the next few days we waited anxiously to see if our anticholera inoculations were really any good.

There were a great many other Chinese whom I saw in the intervals of time left over by my hospitable hosts, ostensibly for rest. Dr. Soong's home was a convenient meeting place. My curiosity was enormous.

The willingness of Chinese to come and be interviewed was without limit.

For instance, it was there that I talked, at leisure, alone and uninterrupted, with Chou En-lai, one of the leaders of the Chinese Communist party. This excellent, sober, and sincere man won my respect as a man of obvious ability. He lives in Chungking, where he helps to edit a Communist newspaper, the *Hsin Hua Jih Pao,* and takes his full part in the meetings of the People's Political Council, China's closest approximation at present to a representative legislative body, of which both he and his wife are members.

I saw General Chou again—he won the rank of general in the civil wars fighting against the Generalissimo on the side of the Communists —at Dr. Kung's dinner party, to which he was invited with his wife, at my suggestion. I was later told that it was the first time he had been entertained by the official family of China. It was interesting to see him greeted in a pleasant but somewhat cautious manner by men he had fought against, and with obvious respect by General Stilwell, who had known him in Hankow ten years ago.

General Chou wears a blue denim suit which suggests traditional Chinese garb and at the same time looks like the dress of any skilled worker. He has an open face, with wide-spaced, serious eyes. He talks English slowly. He defined to me the nature of the compromises on both sides on which China's wartime united front has been built. He admitted impatience with what he regarded as the slowness of domestic reform in China, but assured me that the united front would last certainly until Japan was defeated. When I asked him if he thought it would survive the strain of the old Kuomintang-Communist enmity after the war, he frankly was not willing to make predictions. However, he had undoubted respect for and faith in the selfless devotion of the Generalissimo to China. He was not so sure of some of her other leaders. He left me with the feeling that if all Chinese Communists are like himself, their movement is more a national and agrarian awakening than an international or proletarian conspiracy.

Another man who impressed me deeply was Dr. Chang Po-ling. He is an enormous man, with the grave, deliberate manner of a scholar but a fine, warm sense of humor. He is the head of Nankai, one of the leading schools of China, and also a member of the People's Political

Council. Whether we talked of India, or the war, or American universities, he spoke with a background and a judgment which would be hard to equal in the United States.

There were two other men in Chungking who illustrated for me the new China not to be found in any of the books I had read about traditional Chinese life. One was Li Wei-kuo, private secretary to the Generalissimo. He is young, wise beyond his years, and able in the sense that a great leader needs ability in his secretaries. The other was General J. L. Huang, Secretary General of the Officers' Moral Endeavor Association. The general is as big and robust as his laugh, which is very big. It would be easy to describe him as an exceptionally talented host and manager. One of his jobs is to organize the hostels in which American fliers live in China, and he does it superbly. But underneath his jovial manner and his social skills, I found a thoughtful, patient, untiring fighter for China's victory and a better world.

China has no lack of good men for the top jobs in Chungking. But no matter how high the standard they set, the Soong family is in a class by itself in Chinese life. Three brothers and three sisters, all trained by Methodist missionaries and in American colleges, have given China an aristocracy of talent, political skill, great wealth, and unswerving devotion to the cause of the young republic. They make up one of the most remarkable families in the world.

I had known T. V. Soong in Washington. He is China's Foreign Minister, and one of the great statesmen of the United Nations. His three sisters I met in China. One is the wife of the Generalissimo. Another is the wife of H. H. Kung, who runs China's finances. The third is the widow of Dr. Sun Yat-sen, founder of the Chinese Republic.

At the dinner party given for me by Dr. Kung, served on the lawn, I was placed at the head table between Madame Sun and Madame Chiang. The conversation was lively, and I had a great time. Both ladies speak excellent English and are full of information and wit.

When the dinner was over, Madame Chiang took me by the arm. "I want you to meet my other sister. She has neuralgia and couldn't come outdoors for the party." Indoors, we found Madame Kung with her arm in a sling, eager to hear about America, where she had lived as a girl. The three of us talked and had such a good time we forgot about the hour and the people outdoors.

About eleven o'clock, Dr. Kung came in and gently scolded Madame Chiang and me for our failure to return to the party, which by then had broken up. Then he sat down, and the four of us set out to solve the problems of the universe.

We talked about the revolution of ideas that is sweeping the East—a subject that came up wherever I went—of India and Nehru, of China and Chiang, of the overpowering surge toward freedom of Asia's hundreds of millions, of their demands for education and better living and, above all, for the right to their own governments, independent of the West.

To me, it was fascinating. All three of them knew their facts. All three held strong opinions and each contributed much to the conversation, especially Madame Chiang. Finally, just before we were to leave, Madame Chiang said to Dr. and Madame Kung: "Last night at dinner Mr. Willkie suggested that I should go to America on a good-will tour." The Kungs looked at me as if questioning. I said: "That is correct, and I know I am right in suggesting it."

Then Dr. Kung spoke, seriously. "Mr. Willkie, do you really mean that, and, if so, why?"

I said to him, "Dr. Kung, you know from our conversation how strongly I believe that it is vital for my fellow countrymen to understand the problems of Asia and the viewpoint of its people, how sure I am that the future peace of the world probably lies in a just solution of the problems of the Orient after the war.

"Someone from this section with brains and persuasiveness and moral force must help educate us about China and India and their peoples. Madame would be the perfect ambassador. Her great ability—and I know she will excuse me for speaking so personally—her great devotion to China, are well known in the United States. She would find herself not only beloved, but immensely effective. We would listen to her as to no one else. With wit and charm, a generous and understanding heart, a gracious and beautiful manner and appearance, and a burning conviction, she is just what we need as a visitor."

She has now come to America, and ever since her moving address to Congress and her charming but pointed reminder to the President that the Lord helps those who help themselves America has applauded her gallantry and her cause.

Brigadier General Claire L. Chennault, commander of the China Air Task Force of the United States Army Air Forces, is a hard man to forget once you have talked with him. He is tall, swarthy, lean, and rangy, and there is something hard about his jaw and his eyes which contrasts curiously with his Louisiana drawl. He first went to China as an individual fighter and aerial strategist, to help train the Chinese air force. Later he organized the American Volunteer Group which covered itself with glory both in China and in Burma. He is in the Army now, and the Army is lucky to have him.

The story is now well known of what he and his men have done. They have shot down Japanese planes in combat with a loss ratio ranging from twelve to one to twenty to one. When I was in Chungking, the Chinese records showed his forces to have won more than seventy consecutive air battles against the Japanese without a single loss, in spite of the fact that the Americans were outnumbered in each battle. According to Colonel Merian C. Cooper, his chief of staff, who came to lunch with me in Chungking one day and told me stories his commander would have blushed to hear, the general combines orthodox strategy in the air with fantastically unorthodox tactics, and the result is something the Japanese have clearly shown they do not like. And Major Kight, our own pilot, told me that General Chennault's system of information about weather, aerial operating conditions, and geography, in view of the facilities he had, was absolutely amazing. For there are no well-established meteorological stations in China to give information to aviators. General Chennault's men depend largely on information relayed over large areas by Chinese couriers and the grapevine route.

I learned for myself that General Chennault has no rival in popularity among the Chinese. A schoolteacher in Chengtu told me without a second's hesitation, when I asked who was the American best known and most liked by her students, "General Chennault." I also heard him discussed at length by the most important leaders of China, and always with enormous respect and affection.

I had several engagements to meet and talk with General Chennault, but each time they failed to come off. Finally, I flew out to his headquarters near Chungking in order to see him. When I found him on his own airfield, standing against a line of his P40 fighter planes, each of them painted to look like a giant shark, I understood why he found it hard to keep an engagement in Chungking.

He was running, by direct and personal command, one of the busiest and most exciting bases I have ever seen. His assignment includes defense not only of the sky over Chungking and Kunming, capital of Yünnan province, but also defense of the all-important air route over Burma from India. In addition to this, he has taken on a side job of bombing the Japanese in Canton, in Hong Kong, as far north as the Kailan mines near the Great Wall in the north of China. His air-raid detection service was one of the most ingenious and effective I have ever heard of. His men, nearly all of them southerners and a frightening number of them from Texas, swore by him and performed miracles for him.

I was shocked at only one thing I saw: the paucity of the material he had to work with. What he had done became even more incredible when one saw the limited force under his command. General Chennault belongs in the great tradition of American fighting men, and the fliers who serve under him deserve the best that we can give them and as much of it as we can give them.

What he asks for is amazingly little; and what we have sent him falls far short of even that little. General Chennault speaks quietly but with great conviction of what could be done to harass the Japanese in China, to cut their supply lines through the China Sea, to give help to the great Chinese armies which could move forward across the plains of eastern China if they had an air cover of any sort. He told me that a limited air offensive in China could be maintained by transporting gasoline, oil, spare parts, and replacements over the Himalayas by the present air route.

He has a sense of bafflement at the failure of officials back home to see what to him is so clear.

For an offensive here would have more than military consequences. It would give new confidence to the Chinese armies, and it would give heart to the Chinese people. I came home from China convinced that we must avoid at all costs giving the Chinese the idea that we are

going to disregard them for another year and concentrate our fighting
in other theaters of war. Regardless of what this might do to Chinese
resistance, it would complicate a morale problem already made dangerous by inflation, and it would imperil all our chances of a solid basis
of understanding with China on which to build the peace and the post-
war world.

I was conscious every day I was in China of the fact that China has
been at war with Japan for more than five long years. I saw it in the
incredible caves dug into the hills of Chungking, where the entire population of the city takes refuge when the Japanese bombing planes come
over the city. I saw it in the skill and fortitude with which again and
again the Chinese emerged from those caves, after the raids were over,
to rebuild their devastated city and continue fighting back.

I did not see it, but heard about it, in the amazing tales which can be
double-checked and riveted with proof in Chungking of the heroic
civilian resistance which goes on behind the Japanese lines in China.
While I was in Chungking, footsore but happy Englishmen and Americans were still arriving from the Japanese-conquered cities of Shanghai,
Hong Kong, and Peking. They had been passed on across half a continent from band to band of guerrilla fighters, Chinese who formed a
living chain of resistance deep into Japanese territory. All the farmers
of China are showing by daily acts of heroism their stake in freedom
and their eagerness to fight for it.

I also saw evidence that China had been fighting a long time in a
Chinese military organization, which was news to me and, I found
later, to many Chinese themselves. The picture many Americans still
have of a Chinese army as a band of professional ruffians whose generals are experts at dickering with the enemy was probably never anything more than a caricature of military affairs in a disunited, technically backward country. Today, it is not even a caricature. Military
China is united; its leaders are trained and able generals; its new
armies are tough, fighting organizations of men who know both what
they are fighting for and how to fight for it, even though they markedly
lack any quantity of modern fighting equipment. In China, just as in
Russia, this is truly a people's war. Even the sons of those of high estate
enlist as privates in the army, an unthinkable act in China a generation

ago, when service in the army was for hired and ignorant mercenaries.

I stood one afternoon outside Chengtu on a narrow bridge across a muddy but fast-running river. In front of me smoke rose in a heavy, blinding wall along the bank of the river. Through it could be seen flashes of machine-gun fire. Mortars were pounding in the fields behind me. The river was full of young Chinese, swimming desperately against the heavy current, some carrying rifles above their heads, others carrying ropes attached to a pontoon bridge.

They took the bridge across the river, although at one time when the current caught it full I would have given heavy odds that they could never make it. Then suddenly hundreds of other soldiers rose from the fields behind me, their helmets and uniforms so carefully camouflaged that I had never seen them. They ran across the pontoon bridge, scrambled up the other bank, and deployed for an attack on a village perhaps a mile away.

They took the village, but not until they had cut their way through barbed wire, threaded through a mine field which lifted heavy columns of smoke into the air whenever a mine was touched off, and finally wormed their way on their bellies across an open field with no cover. They entered the village with full equipment, hot and tired and dirty and proud of their newly won knowledge of how to carry out a complicated operation in the field.

For this had been a maneuver, a training exercise, at the Chengtu Military Academy, the largest in China. It had been organized by a Chinese graduate of West Point, who stood beside me and explained the rules of the exercise while it was going on. At least a large part of the 10,000 students regularly in training there to become officers in the new Chinese Army had taken part in it. It had been an exciting show, as professional as any similar exercise anywhere in the world. For me, what I saw that afternoon and was to see again and again in China marked the end of an era—the era in which 400,000,000 Chinese could be kicked around by any army, Japanese or English or American, for that matter.

I saw evidence of the fact that China had been fighting for five years again the next day at the Air Corps training school also at Chengtu. Here I saw hundreds of Chinese cadets—the men of whom it was thought charitable to say only a few years ago that they were "not a fighting race"—slash and hammer each other with heavy sticks, in the Japanese style, shouting and screaming while they belabored each other, in the toughest personal combat training I had ever watched. Here, too, I saw Chinese Boy Scouts, some as young as eight years old, going through the full discipline and training of army life in preparation for careers as professional soldiers.

I told "Holly" Tong that I wanted to see the Chinese front at some sector. At first, it seemed impossible. It was only later that I learned that the Generalissimo's solicitude for my safety while I was in China had had to be overcome, and that "Holly" had required time to accomplish this. Finally a trip was arranged, and although we were to find less physical danger than we expected, we were to have another lesson in how much the Chinese have learned in their five years of all-out war.

We flew to Sian, one of the ancient capitals of China, near the great bend in the Yellow River where it starts to flow eastward to the sea. We drove miles outside the city and climbed, by the light of Chinese lanterns strung along a mountain path, up to another military academy, this one the school where Chiang Kai-shek was living just before his famous kidnaping at Sian in 1936. That evening we set out for the front, incongruously enough, in luxurious sleeping cars on one of the few railroads left in free China.

We left the train at dawn the next morning, and rode another fifteen miles on handcars. A few miles from the river, which at this sector is the front, one of the generals with us decided we looked too much like sitting pigeons to the Japanese across the river, and we took to our own legs, walking the last few miles along a road cut, like a trench, deep into the red loam of central China.

The front turned out to be a village surrounded by a network of trenches. The river is 1200 yards across at this point, but through artillery telescopes in the forward observation posts we could look down the muzzles of Japanese guns pointed at us and see the Japanese soldiers in their own encampments. It was quiet while we were there, but it was clear that it was not always quiet; in fact, there had been a bombardment just before our arrival.

It was at this front that I met Captain Chiang Wei-kao, son of the Generalissimo by an earlier marriage. Captain Chiang, who speaks perfect English, showed us in a long day the reasons why the Japanese had been unable to push across the river here, where there is a gap in the mountains, the traditional invasion route of south China.

We saw artillery and infantry and armored cars and fortresses built into the hills so deep that Japanese would have to blast them out. We saw a review of the 208th Division, one of the Generalissimo's crack units, well trained, well uniformed, and equipped with good, modern weapons. I talked to these soldiers, some 9000 of them standing in the blazing sun. They looked up at the little wooden platform which had been given me to stand on, and it seemed to me that not one man wavered in his attention until I had finished, although I was speaking in English. When what I said had been translated, they cheered so loudly that the Japanese must have heard them and wondered what the excitement was all about.

Back in our train again, where we sat down to dinner, Captain Chiang demonstrated conclusively to me that the front I had just seen was more than a showplace. He walked into the dining car with his arms full of Japanese cavalry swords, as presents for my party, and excellent French wine. Both had been captured by raiding parties which crossed the river at night, struck swiftly behind the Japanese lines, and returned with booty like this and more important trophies, including prisoners and military plans. Sometimes, Captain Chiang told me, such raiding parties stay for weeks inside the enemy lines, cutting communications and organizing sabotage, before returning to their own headquarters on the west bank of the river.

IX SOME NOTES ON CHINESE
INFLATION

I LEFT China somewhat baffled by its present economic and inflationary problems. Obviously its inflation would have long since been disastrous, measured in terms of a money economy, and yet financial disaster never quite comes to China. One has a feeling, however, that it's just around the proverbial corner and has been for a long while.

Price indices in China are not everything an American banker would want before deciding on an answer to an inflationary situation. Prices were markedly different in the several cities we visited. And it was made clear to me every day that enormous numbers of Chinese live largely outside the money economy of their country and are independent of prices, except for scant clothing needs and a few essential manufactured goods. But even admitting these qualifications, the signs of inflation around us were disturbing in the extreme to an American.

In Chungking, I was told, wholesale prices have risen to at least fifty times their prewar level. Retail prices are in many cases sixty times higher than they were. During the few months before my arrival in October, the rate of increase was about ten per cent a month. For whole groups of the population, and especially those who live on fixed incomes, this has meant that many articles formerly consumed are now all but unattainable.

In Chengtu, two young women teachers helped me out with interpreting on a busy day. They were both educated women, who spoke good English. They were obviously the best type of citizen in a young republic still desperately short of trained personnel. They told me that living costs had risen so sharply, however, that they could no longer afford to eat as well as, for example, the most humble freight-carrying coolies, who live not on fixed salaries but on wages which have also reflected the inflation.

In the same city, where I discussed the problems of Chinese education with the heads of most of China's great universities, I found that the universities' income had in many cases held steady or actually increased. United China Relief had helped enormously to keep university budgets close to their prewar figures. But against prices that have multiplied fifty times, the value of American currency in terms of Chinese money has risen only about three times. As a result, the universities face the same crisis now as their teachers and their students.

There are several reasons, as I saw it, for this inflation. The first is that China has been forced to finance the war by the issue of paper money. In 1942, only about one quarter of the expenses of the government were covered by taxation. New government monopolies, which now include salt, sugar, matches, tobacco, tea, and wine, have helped to increase revenue, but not nearly enough. There is almost no public saving in China, to absorb government loans. So, to continue the war, the government has been forced to continue to use the printing presses. Much of the cargo flown over the Himalayas, I learned from pilots on the run, is paper money to meet the steadily growing costs of fighting the war.

This is in part due to the failure of the government itself to adopt a sound fiscal policy, a system of monetary and price control, and a method of adequate income and other taxation that would drain off the increased profits and incomes among some groups created by the inflation itself. The government has also failed rigidly to enforce its directives against speculation in basic commodities. Some of the independent editors in China insisted to me that speculation was indulged in even by government officials themselves. Everyone told me that the Generalissimo was using his utmost efforts to stamp out the irregularities, to bring about some financial order, and to eliminate any corrupt elements. But the Generalissimo is not a man schooled in finance or the intricacies of a fiscal policy. His training and his bent are in other directions.

Another reason for this inflationary development is the acute shortage of goods in free China, which is in part created by our own failure to send goods to China, and in part by the Japanese conquest of most of China's earlier-developed industrial regions and the cutting off of China's access to the world except through Russia and over the Himalayas. China needs both raw materials and certain essential machinery for any large-scale production inside the limits of free China. Both of these are now extremely difficult to secure.

Judging by what I saw myself, the Chinese have done miracles to meet this problem, but miracles have not been enough. Dr. Wong Wen-hao, Minister of Economics, showed me on one exciting day in Chungking a cotton mill which had been moved to Szechwan from Honan province, and a paper mill which had been moved from Shanghai in 1938. In all, he told me, the government had succeeded in transporting close to 120,000 tons of equipment inland, most of it concentrated in the iron and steel and spinning and weaving industries.

Both mills were fair-sized, efficient-looking plants. The paper mill, by the way, was about to begin the manufacture of bank-note paper. Its present capacity is from five to nine tons of such paper a day, Dr. Wong told me, and the comparison of that figure with the needs of 100,000,000 people living in free China was illustration enough of the grave problem which China faces in trying to build a new economic base in the middle of a war.

The Chinese Industrial Co-operatives, which I saw in Lanchow, have helped to meet the problem, but they have had difficulties growing out of disagreement over who should control them. It is the belief of those who operate them that there are certain financial and industrial forces in China seeking to destroy them. But they have in the Generalissimo, with whom I discussed their problems in detail, a firm and steadfast friend. It would be hard for them in any case to meet in the immediate future the demands of the war on production without a heavy-industry base, and without anything like adequate transport. Free China has left something less than a thousand miles of railroad. The Russian highway, as I pointed out before, is the only open land route over which exports and imports can move, and the capacity of the Himalaya air route and of the smuggling routes through the Japanese lines is strictly limited.

This is the problem, then, and the best minds I found in China, both Chinese and foreign, were looking for a solution. What this solution will be I could not say without a great deal more study of the problem. But I am sure that one of its chief features must be a loosening of the tight controls over Chinese economic life and of hereditary property and a mobilization of the enormous human resources of the country for the production of goods and services on a far larger scale than at present.

Members of the government were inclined, I thought, to take a far less serious view of inflation than many Americans I talked with. They pointed out to me that only the Chinese middle class has fixed incomes so low that their living standard is jeopardized by inflation, and that this middle class consists of a very small number of people. They claimed that coolies, manual labor in general, and many farmers who had no fixed income but were getting high prices for their products were actually profiting from the inflation.

There is this to be said for that viewpoint: that one who attempts to measure the inflationary problems of China in the light of similar problems in an economy such as ours may well come to some shockingly erroneous conclusions. One of the best students of Chinese economics I met estimated to me that eighty per cent of the Chinese people grow their own food and have little need for money. Their money purchasing power has always been almost insignificant.

But this argument cannot be carried too far. Although it made the present situation seem less desperate, it held out little hope for the future. Governor Chang Chun of Szechwan province, one of the most skilled and thoughtful administrators I met in China, told me that seventy per cent of the men actually raising crops in his province were either full or part tenants of the land they tilled. These men paid their rents, he said, in kind and not in cash, and therefore any rise in the price of food would benefit them only slightly, while a corresponding rise in the cost of even the few things they were required to buy might well eat up the thin margin of subsistence on which most Chinese farmers live.

Most important of all, however, was the ugly fact that Chinese economy is still poor, desperately poor. It must have, to finance the war or to finance the reconstruction which must follow the war, immensely greater productive organization of its natural resources. No one can doubt this fact who has seen the resources, both in human and raw-material terms, and who has sensed the deep, driving determination of the Chinese people themselves to mobilize these resources.

A greater flow of goods and services, scaled up to what China is capable of in technical terms, would be probably the best solution, it seemed to me, for inflation in China. It is up to the Chinese people to decide how they want to organize the finance that greater flow and production of goods and services. More widespread ownership of the land than I found anywhere in China would help. So would a greater degree of decentralization of financial control, I thought, after I had talked with young Chinese bankers and factory managers in Sian and Lanchow. The government will inevitably play an important part; it seemed to me it might be wise to cut the people in on it to a large extent. But these are questions for the Chinese to decide.

Meanwhile there is much that America can do to help. First, I am convinced, we must make our friendship for the Chinese, who are fighting on our side, more real and tangible. We must send them, through Russia, over the Himalayas, or by reconquering Burma, or by all three routes, machines and airplanes and ammunition and the raw materials they need.

But we must also think out this alliance for ourselves, and decide what it really means to us. We must decide whether or not we can ever find a better ally in eastern Asia than the Chinese, and if the answer is negative, as I predict it will be, then we must be prepared to fulfill the obligations of an ally. These obligations will include economic co-operation and present military help. But they also include the obligation to understand the Chinese and their problems. Chinese faith in noble phrases and protestations is wearing a little thin.

X OUR RESERVOIR OF GOOD WILL

WE left Chengtu on October 9, traveled almost a thousand miles in China, crossed the vast expanse of the Gobi and the Mongolian Republic, crossed thousands of miles of Siberia, crossed the Bering Sea, the full length of Alaska and the full width of Canada, and arrived in the United States on October 13. We had gained a day by crossing the international date line.

When you fly around the world in forty-nine days, you learn that the world has become small not only on the map, but also in the minds of men. All around the world, there are some ideas which millions and millions of men hold in common, almost as much as if they lived in the same town. One of these ideas, and one which I can report without hesitation, has tremendous significance for us in America; it is the mixture of respect and hope with which the world looks to this country.

Whether I was talking to a resident of Belém or Natal in Brazil, or one toting his burden on his head in Nigeria, or a prime minister or a king in Egypt, or a veiled woman in ancient Bagdad, or a shah or a weaver of carpets in legendary Persia, now known as Iran, or a follower of Ataturk in those streets of Ankara which look so like the streets of our Middle Western cities, or to a strong-limbed, resolute factory worker in Russia, or to Stalin himself, or the enchanting wife of the great Generalissimo of China, or a Chinese soldier at the front, or a fur-capped hunter on the edge of the trackless forests of Siberia—whether I was talking to any of these people, or to any others, I found that they all have one common bond, and that is their deep friendship for the United States.

They, each and every one, turn to the United States with a friendliness that is often akin to genuine affection. I came home certain of one clear and significant fact: that there exists in the world today a gigantic reservoir of good will toward us, the American people.

Many things have created this enormous reservoir. At the top of the list go the hospitals, schools, and colleges which Americans—missionaries, teachers, and doctors—have founded in the far corners of the world. Many of the new leaders of old countries—men who are today running Iraq or Turkey or China—have studied under American teachers whose only interest has been to spread knowledge. Now, in our time of crisis, we owe a great debt to these men and women who have made friends for us.

Good will has also been stored up for us, like credit in a bank account, by those Americans who have pioneered in the opening of new roads, new airways, new shipping lines. Because of them, the peoples of the world think of us as a people who move goods, and ideas, and move them fast. They like us for this, and they respect us.

Our motion pictures have played an important role in building up this reservoir of friendliness. They are shown all over the world. People of every country can see with their own eyes what we look like, can hear our voices. From Natal to Chungking I was plied with questions about American motion-picture stars—questions asked eagerly by shopgirls and those who served me coffee, and just as eagerly by the wives of prime ministers and kings.

There are still other reasons for our reserve of good will abroad. The people of every land, whether industrialized or not, admire the aspirations and accomplishments of American labor, which they have heard about, and which they long to emulate. Also they are impressed by American methods of agriculture, business, and industry. In nearly every country I went to, there is some great dam or irrigation project, some harbor or factory, which has been built by Americans. People like our works, I found, not only because they help to make life easier and richer, but also because we have shown that American business enterprise does not necessarily lead to attempts at political control.

I found this dread of foreign control everywhere. The fact that we are not associated with it in men's minds has caused people to go much farther in their approval of us than I had dared to imagine. I was amazed to discover how keenly the world is aware of the fact that we do not seek—anywhere, in any region—to impose our rule upon others or to exact special privileges.

All the people of the earth know that we have no sinister designs upon them, that even when we have in the past withdrawn from international affairs into a false self-sufficiency, it was without sinister purpose. And they know that, now we are in this war, we are not fighting for profit, or loot, or territory, or mandatory power over the lives or the governments of other people. That, I think, is the single most important reason for the existence of our reservoir of good will around the world.

Everywhere I went around the world, and I mean literally everywhere, I found officers and men of the United States Army. Sometimes they were in very small units; in other places they filled enormous army camps which covered acres of some foreign country. In every situation in which I found them, they were adding to the good will foreign peoples hold toward America.

A striking example of this was the crew of our C-87 army plane. None of its officers or enlisted men had ever been abroad before except on a fighting assignment. They were not trained diplomats. Most of them spoke no foreign language. But everywhere we landed, they made friends for America. I shall remember for a long time the sight of the Shah of Iran, just after we had given him the first airplane ride of his life, shaking hands with Major Richard Kight, our pilot, and looking at him with what I can only describe as a mixture of admiration and envy.

I was proud of American soldiers everywhere I saw them. I felt a confidence that our citizens' army, uninterested in entrenching themselves as professional army men, would automatically help to preserve the reservoir of good will which our generation inherits, and would at the same time find out, through firsthand experience, why this is America's war.

For, as I see it, the existence of this reservoir is the biggest political fact of our time. No other Western nation has such a reservoir. Ours must be used to unify the peoples of the earth in the human quest for freedom and justice. It must be maintained so that, with confidence, they may fight and work with us against the gigantic evil forces that are seeking to destroy all that we stand for, all that they hope for. The preservation of this reservoir of good will is a sacred responsibility, not alone toward the aspiring peoples of the earth, but toward our own sons who are fighting this battle on every continent. For the water in this reservoir is the clean, invigorating water of freedom.

Neither Hitler nor Mussolini nor Hirohito, with their propaganda or by their arms, can take from us the unifying force of this good will—and there is no other such unifying force in the world—or divide us among ourselves or from our allies, as long as we do not make a mockery of our protestations of the ideals for which we have proclaimed we fight. A policy of expediency will prove inexpedient. For it will lose us the invaluable spiritual and practical assets that come from the faith of the people of the world in both our ideals and our methods.

If we permit ourselves to become involved in the machinations of Old World intrigue and religious, nationalistic and racial blocs, we will find ourselves amateurs indeed. If we stand true to our basic principles, then we shall find ourselves professionals of the kind of world toward which men in every part of it are aspiring.

XI WHAT WE ARE FIGHTING FOR

IT has become banal to say that this war is a revolution, in men's think-ing, in their way of living, all over the world. It is not banal to see that revolution taking place, and that is what I saw. It is exciting and a little frightening. It is exciting because it is fresh proof of the enormous power within human beings to change their environment, to fight for freedom with an instinctive, awakened confidence that with freedom they can achieve anything. It is frightening because the different peo-ples of the United Nations, let alone their leaders, have by no means reached common agreement as to what they are fighting for, the ideas with which we must arm our fighting men.

For, however important the role of bayonets and guns may have been in the development of mankind, the role of ideas has been vastly more important—and, in the long run, more conclusive. In historical times, at any rate, men have not often fought merely for the joy of killing each other. They have fought for a purpose. Sometimes that purpose has not been very inspiring. Sometimes it has been quite selfish. But a war won without a purpose is a war won without victory.

A most outstanding example of a war fought with a purpose was our own American Revolution. We did not fight the Revolution because we hated Englishmen and wanted to kill them, but because we loved freedom and wanted to establish it. I think it is fair to say, in the light of what that freedom has meant to the world, that the victory won at Yorktown was the greatest victory ever won by force of arms. But this was not because our army was large and formidable. It was because our purpose was so clear, so lofty, and so well defined.

Unhappily this cannot be said of the war of 1914-18. It has become almost a historical truism that that was a war without victory. Of course, it is true that, while we were engaged in it, we thought, or said, that we were fighting for a high purpose. Woodrow Wilson, our Commander in Chief, stated our purpose in eloquent terms. We were fighting to make the world safe for democracy—to make it safe, not just with a slogan, but by accepting a set of principles known as the Fourteen Points, and by setting up a full-fledged international structure to be known as the League of Nations. That was a high purpose, surely. But when the time came to execute it in a peace treaty, a fatal flaw was discovered. We found that we and our allies were not really agreed upon that purpose. On the one hand, some of our allies had entangled themselves in secret treaties; and they were more intent upon carrying out those treaties, and upon pursuing traditional power diplomacy, than upon opening up the new vista that Mr. Wilson had sought to define. And, on the other hand, we ourselves were not so deeply dedicated to our declared purposes as we had led the world to believe. The net result was the abandonment of most of the purposes for which the war had supposedly been fought. Because those purposes were abandoned, that war was denounced by our generation as an enormous and futile slaughter. Millions had lost their lives. But no new idea, no new goal, rose from the ashes of their sacrifice.

Now I think that these considerations lead us inescapably to one conclusion. I think we must conclude that, generally speaking, nothing of importance can be won in peace which has not already been won in the war itself. I say nothing of importance. It is quite true, of course, that many details must be worked out at the peace table and at conferences succeeding the peace table—details which cannot be judiciously worked out under the pressure of war. We—we and our allies, of course —cannot, for instance, stop fighting the Japanese to make a detailed plan of what we intend to do about Burma when victory is won. Nor can we relent in our pressure against Hitler to decide the detailed future of Poland now.

What we must win now, during the war, are the principles. We must know what our line of solution will be. Again, let me use the American Revolution as an example. When we fought that war, we had no inkling of the actual structure of the United States of America. No one had ever heard of the Constitution. The federal system, the three branches of government, the brilliant bicameral compromise by which the small states were induced to come into the Union—all these innovations lay as yet in the future, nourished only by the brains of a few great political thinkers—who, themselves, were not entirely clear. And yet the basic principles of that great political structure that was to become the United States of America were, surely, contained in the Declaration of Independence, in the songs and speeches of that day, in after-dinner discussions and private arguments around soldiers' campfires and everywhere along the Atlantic Coast. Even though the great states of Massachusetts and Virginia were held together by the vaguest pronouncements and the flimsiest of political contraptions (the Continental Congress), their citizens were in substantial agreement as to the cause they were fighting for and the goal they wished to achieve.

Had they not agreed during the war, Massachusetts and Virginia, surely, would have failed to agree concerning the principles of the peace. They won in the peace exactly what they won in the war—no more and no less. This truth, if it were not self-evident, could be proved by citing one calamity. The people of those states did fail to agree concerning the freedom or slavery of the Negro. The result was that there grew up around the enslaved Negro in the South an entirely different economy from that which grew up in the North. And this resulted in another, and far bloodier, war.

Can we not learn from this simple lesson, and from similar lessons of history, what our task is today? We must learn. We must know that we shall win in the future peace only what we are now winning in the war—no more and no less.

First, to determine what we want to win, it is clearly necessary to reach substantial agreement with our allies. Here, as in our own Revolution, agreement in detail is not necessary, or even desirable. But unless we are to repeat the unhappy history of the last war, agreement in principle must be won. Moreover, it must exist not just among the leaders of the allies. The basic agreement I am thinking of must be established among the allied peoples themselves. We must make sure that we are all fighting for essentially the same thing.

Now what does this mean? It means that every one of us has the obligation to speak out, to exchange ideas, freely and frankly, across the Pacific, across the Atlantic, and here at home. Unless the British people know the way we are thinking in America, and take it to heart, and unless we have a similar idea of what they are thinking in England and in the Commonwealth, there can be no hope of agreement. We must know what the people of Russia and China aim for and we must let them know our aims.

It is the utmost folly—it is just short of suicide—to take the position that citizens of any country should hold their tongues for fear of causing distress to the immediate and sometimes tortuous policies of their leaders.

We have been told, for example, that private citizens, particularly those not expert in military affairs or those unconnected with government, should refrain from making suggestions about the conduct of the war—military, industrial, economic, or political. It is said that we must remain silent and allow our leaders and the experts to solve these problems unmolested.

This position threatens, I believe, to become a tight wall which will keep the truth out and lock misrepresentation and false security within. I reported to the American people when I returned last fall that in many important respects we were not doing a good job; that we were on the road to winning the war, but that we ran a heavy risk of spending far more in men and materials than we need to spend. That report was based on facts. Such facts should not be censored. They should be given to us all. For unless we recognize and correct our mistakes, we may lose the friendship of half our allies before the war is over and then lose the peace.

It is plain that to win this war we must make it our war, the war of all of us. In order to do this we must all know as much about it as possible, subject only to the needs of military security. A misdirected censorship will not accomplish this.

France had a military leader by the name of Maginot. When a farsighted citizen of France occasionally suggested that perhaps conditions of modern warfare were such that fortresses built underground would not be adequate against airplanes and tanks, he was reminded that he should leave such matters to the experts.

The record of this war to date is not such as to inspire in us any sublime faith in the infallibility of our political, military, and naval experts. Military experts, as well as our leaders, must be constantly exposed to democracy's greatest driving power—the whiplash of public opinion, developed from honest, free discussion.

For instance, it was public criticism of the constant failures in North Africa at the time of Rommel's great victory that brought about a change of command there. When I was in Egypt, that new command stopped Rommel. It has since driven him three-quarters of the way across Africa. I think some of the credit for that victory should be chalked up to British public opinion.

People in the United States are apt to conclude that there is no such thing as public opinion or the operation of its power in countries under absolute forms of government. As a matter of fact, in every absolutely governed country I visited, the government had elaborate methods of determining what the people were thinking. Even Stalin has his form of "Gallup poll," and it is recorded that Napoleon at the height of his power, as he sat astride his white horse amid the smoldering ruins of Moscow, anxiously waited for his daily courier's report of what the mobs in Paris were thinking.

In every country I saw around the world, I found some kind of public opinion operating powerfully both on the course of the war and on the slowly emerging ideas of peace. In Bagdad I found it in the conversation in every coffeehouse, and there are a multitude of them. In Russia, it was expressed in great factory meetings and in the talk of Russians everywhere, who, however contrary it may seem to our notion of Soviet Russia, exchange ideas in private conversation almost as freely as we do. In China, newspapers, though not as unrestricted as ours, nevertheless with a surprising freedom reflect and lead public opinion. No man I talked to in China, whether he was the leader of the Communist party, a factory worker, a college professor, or a soldier seemed to have any hesitancy about expressing his views, and many of the views were in conflict with some of the policies of the government.

In every country I found worry and doubt in the hearts and minds of people behind the fighting fronts. They were searching for a common purpose. This was plain in the questions they asked about America after the war, about Great Britain, and, when I was in China, about Russia. The whole world seemed to me in an eager, demanding, hungry, ambitious mood ready for incredible sacrifices if only they could see some hope that those sacrifices would prove worth while.

Europe in 1917 was probably in much the same mood. It is an inevitable corollary of blood and war weariness. Then, in 1917, Lenin gave the world one set of answers. A little later Wilson gave it another. Neither set of answers ever became blood-and-bone part of the war, but were superimposed on it, in the various treaties of peace. So neither set of answers redeemed the war or made it anything more than a costly fight for power. It ended with an armistice, not a real peace.

I do not believe this war need be the same. There are now, during the war, common purposes in the minds of men living as far apart as the citizens of Great Britain and the Free Commonwealth of Nations, the Americans, the Russians, and the Chinese. But we shall have to make articulate and real our common purposes.

The people must define their purposes during the war. I have quite deliberately tried to provoke discussion of those purposes among the peoples of the various countries of the world. For I live in a constant dread that this war may end before the people of the world have come to a common understanding of what they fight for and what they hope for after the war is over. I was a soldier in the last war and after that war was over, I saw our bright dreams disappear, our stirring slogans become the jests of the cynical, and all because the fighting peoples did not arrive at any common postwar purposes while they fought. It must be our resolve to see that that does not happen again.

Millions have already died in this war and many thousands more will go before it is over. Unless Britons and Canadians and Russians and Chinese and Americans and all our fighting allies, in the common co-operation of war, find the instrumentalities and the methods of co-operative effort after the war, we, the people, have failed our time and our generation.

Our leaders, jointly and singly, have expressed some of our common aspirations. One of the finest expressions came from Chiang Kai-shek in a message to the Western world, delivered through the *New York Herald Tribune* Forum on Current Events in New York City last November. He concluded:

China has no desire to replace Western imperialism in Asia with an Oriental imperialism or isolationism of its own or of anyone else. We hold that we must advance from the narrow idea of exclusive alliances and regional blocs, which in the end make for bigger and better wars, to effective organization of world unity. Unless real world co-operation replaces both isolationism and imperialism of whatever form in the new interdependent world of free nations, there will be no lasting security for you or for us.

Add to this Stalin's statement of purpose, which I quoted earlier, a statement on November 6, 1942, on the occasion of the twenty-fifth anniversary of the October Revolution. It is a singularly explicit and exact statement:

Abolition of racial exclusiveness, equality of nations and integrity of their territories, liberation of enslaved nations and restoration of their sovereign rights, the right of every nation to arrange its affairs as it wishes, economic aid to nations that have suffered and assistance to them in attaining their material welfare, restoration of democratic liberties, the destruction of the Hitlerite regime.

Franklin Roosevelt has proclaimed the Four Freedoms and Winston Churchill, with Franklin Roosevelt, has announced to the world the pact of the Atlantic Charter.

The statement of Mr. Stalin and the Atlantic Charter seem to me to have a common fallacy. They forecast the re-creation of western Europe in its old divisions of small nations, each with its own individual political, economic, and military sovereignty. It was this outmoded system that caused millions in Europe to be captivated by Hitler's proposed new order. For even with Hitler tyranny they at least saw the hope of the creation of an area large enough so that the economics of the modern world could successfully function. They had come to realize through bitter experience that the restricted areas of trade imposed by the high walls of a multitude of individual nationalisms, with the consequent manipulations of power politics, made impoverishment and war inevitable.

The re-creation of the small countries of Europe as political units, *yes;* their re-creation as economic and military units, *no,* if we really hope to bring stabilization to western Europe both for its own benefit and for the peace and economic security of the world.

The statement of the Generalissimo, the declaration of Mr. Stalin, the provisions of the Atlantic Charter, and the enunciation of the Four Freedoms are nevertheless each and all signs of great progress and have aroused high hopes around the world.

If the performance, however, does not measure up to the professions or if individual aspirations of nations that make the performance impossible are interposed, the peoples of the world will turn to a corrosive cynicism that will destroy every chance of world order.

People everywhere, articulate and inarticulate people, are watching to see whether the leaders who proclaimed the principles of these documents really meant what they said.

Before I started on my trip, Mr. Winston Churchill had made two statements about the Atlantic Charter: (1) that its authors had 'in mind primarily the restoration of the sovereignty, self-government, and national life of the states and nations of Europe now under the Nazi yoke"; and (2) that the provisions of the Charter did "not qualify in any way the various statements of policy which have been made from time to time about the development of constitutional government in India, Burma, or other parts of the British Empire." Practically every Prime Minister and Foreign Minister in every country I visited, as well as numberless people, asked me whether this meant that the Atlantic Charter was to be applied only to western Europe. I told them that I of course did not know what Mr. Churchill meant, but that obviously when Mr. Churchill said its authors had in mind primarily the countries of Europe, he did not necessarily exclude other countries. My auditors, without fail, brushed my answer aside with impatience as legalistic and trivial. That was one of the reasons why I was so greatly distressed when Mr. Churchill subsequently made his world-disturbing remark, "We mean to hold our own. I did not become His Majesty's first minister in order to preside over the liquidation of the British Empire." I have been cheered since, however, by discussion with many British now resident in the United States, by following the British press, and by an amazingly large and steadily continuing correspondence from people in England and all over the British Empire, to find that British public opinion on these matters is even ahead of opinion in the United States. The British have no doubt—and, so far as I can see, little regret—that the old imperialism must pass and that the principles of the British Free Commonwealth of Nations must be extended at a rapidly accelerating pace to all corners of the British Empire.

It is because also the performance of our leaders, in the light of their statements, is under test that our own policy in North Africa has seemed to me such a tragedy. It began when the President, in his proclamation of the triumphant entry of American forces into North Africa, instead of giving a candid reason for our entrance, gave as a reason the same age-old worn-out diplomatic formula that has never fooled anyone, certainly not Belgium and Holland when Hitler entered their territories and gave a similar reason: "In order to forestall an invasion of Africa by Germany and Italy, which if successful would constitute a direct threat to America across the comparatively narrow sea from western Africa, a powerful American force . . . is today landing on the Mediterranean and Atlantic coasts of the French colonies in Africa."

There followed the dealings with Darlan, the very symbol of all that free people had been taught to despise, on the ground of "temporary military expediency," an explanation which rendered it difficult to criticize without seeming to be disloyal to a fine military commander who had just accomplished, in conjunction with the British fleet, a brilliant piece of organizational strategy. The explanation, however, failed to satisfy many who did not believe that the soldier's mind conceived the deal, and felt they saw diplomacy once more, in devious ways, trading away the principles which we had proclaimed to the world.

The subsequent appointment of Peyrouton confirmed their forebodings. Those of us who are troubled hope that something better than seems apparent will unfold. But even if that happens it is sure that had not America's reservoir of good will been so great, it could not have withstood this heavy draft on it. For the people of Russia and Great Britain and the conquered countries of Europe felt betrayed and baffled. Even in faraway China it was one more blow to a faith that had already been shocked by our arbitrary promise to return Indo-China to the French Empire. And at home it has done much to cause in the minds of those people who sincerely believed that we were fighting only a war of defense, a revival of the feeling that when the war is over we should withdraw again into our own borders.

Winston Churchill and Franklin Roosevelt are not the only leaders whose words and activities in the light of their proclamations are being watched. The failure of Mr. Stalin to announce to a worried world Russia's specific aspirations with reference to eastern Europe weighs the scales once more against the proclaimed purposes of leaders.

Neither the proclamations of leaders nor the opinion of the people of the world, however articulate, can accomplish anything unless we plan while we fight and unless we give our plans reality.

When the United Nations pact was announced, hundreds of millions of men and women in South America, in Africa, in Russia, in China, in the British Commonwealth, in the United States, in the conquered countries of Europe, perhaps even deep in Germany and Italy, thought they saw a vision of the nations signatory to that pact joining as partners in a common struggle to work together to free mankind. They thought that those nations would, during the war, sit in common council of strategy, of economic warfare, of planning for the future. For they knew that thus the war would be brought to a speedier end. They also knew that to learn to work together now would be the best insurance that the nations would learn to live together in the future.

More than a year has passed since the signing of the pact. Today the United Nations is a great symbol and a treaty of alliance. But we must face the fact that if hopeful billions of human beings are not to be disappointed, if the world of which we dream is to be achieved, even in part, then today, not tomorrow, the United Nations must become a common council, not only for the winning of the war but for the future welfare of mankind.

While we fight, we must develop a mechanism of working together that will survive after the fighting is over. Successful instruments of either national or international government are the result of growth. They cannot be created in a day. Nor is there much hope of their being created amid the reawakened nationalistic impulses, the self-seeking, the moral degenerations, and the economic and social dislocations that are always incident to a postwar period. They must be created now under the cementing force of common danger. They must be made workable and smooth-running, under the emery of day-to-day effort in the solution of common problems.

It is idle to talk about creating after the war is over a machinery for preventing economic warfare and promoting peace between nations, unless the parts of that machinery have been assembled under the unifying effort and common purpose of seeking to defeat the enemy. It is a mere dream to talk of full employment dependent upon international trade and development after the war, unless now while we fight together we learn to work together in accord, respect, and understanding. Can we, as some of our leaders have forecast, develop enormous trade rela-tions with China and the Far East, unless today we are able to develop a joint military strategy with China? Can we hope to bring Russia, with its almost startling potentialities, within the orbit of a future co-ordinated economic world unless we have learned to work with her military strategists and her political leaders in common council?

What we need is a council today of the United Nations—a common council in which all plan together, not a council of a few, who direct or merely aid others, as they think wise. We must have a council of grand military strategy on which all nations that are bearing the brunt of the fighting are represented. Perhaps we might even learn something from the Chinese, who with so little have fought so well, so long. Or from the Russians who have recently seemed to know something about the art of war.

We must have a common council to amalgamate the economic strength of the United Nations toward total war production and to study jointly the possibilities of future economic co-operation.

And most important of all, as United Nations, we must formulate now the principles which will govern our actions as we move step by step to the freeing of the conquered countries. And we must set up a joint machinery to deal with the multiple problems that will accompany every forward step of our victorious armies. Otherwise we will find our-selves moving from one expediency to another, sowing the seeds of future discontents—racial, religious, political—not alone among the peoples we seek to free, but even among the United Nations themselves. It is such discontents that have wrecked the hopes of men of good will throughout the ages.

XII THIS IS A WAR OF LIBERATION

THIS war that I saw going on all around the world is, in Mr. Stalin's phrase, a war of liberation. It is to liberate some nations from the Nazi or the Japanese Army, and to liberate others from the threat of those armies. On this much we are all agreed. Are we yet agreed that liberation means more than this? Specifically, are the thirty-one United Nations now fighting together agreed that our common job of liberation includes giving to *all* peoples freedom to govern themselves as soon as they are able, and the economic freedom on which all lasting self-government inevitably rests?

It is these two aspects of freedom, I believe, which form the touchstone of our good faith in this war. I believe we must include them both in our idea of the freedom we are fighting for. Otherwise, I am certain we shall not win the peace, and I am not sure we can win the war.

In Chungking, on October 7, 1942, I made a statement to the Chinese and foreign press in which I tried to state some of the conclusions I had reached on my trip around the world. In part, this is what I said:

I have traveled through thirteen countries. I have seen kingdoms, soviets, republics, mandated areas, colonies, and dependencies. I have seen an almost bewildering variety of ways of living and ways of ruling and of being ruled. But I have found certain things common to all the countries I have visited and to all the ordinary people in those countries with whom I have talked:

They all want the United Nations to win the war.

They all want a chance at the end of the war to live in liberty and independence.

They all doubt, in varying degree, the readiness of the leading democracies of the world to stand up and be counted for freedom for others after the war is over. This doubt kills their enthusiastic participation on our side.

Now, without the real support of these common people, the winning of the war will be enormously difficult. The winning of the peace will be nearly impossible. This war is not a simple, technical problem for task forces. It is also a war for men's minds. We must organize on our side not simply the sympathies but the active, aggressive, offensive spirit of nearly three fourths of the people of the world who live in South America, Africa, eastern Europe, and Asia. We have not done this, and at present are not doing this. We have got to do it. . . .

Men need more than arms with which to fight and win this kind of war. They need enthusiasm for the future and a conviction that the flags they fight under are in bright, clean colors. The truth is that we as a nation have not made up our minds what kind of world we want to speak for when victory comes.

Especially here in Asia the common people feel that we have asked them to join us for no better reason than that Japanese rule would be even worse than Western imperialism. This is a continent where the record of the Western democracies has been long and mixed, but where people—and remember there are a billion of them—are determined no longer to live under foreign control. Freedom and opportunity are the words which have modern magic for the people of Asia, and we have let the Japanese—the most cruel imperialists the modern world has known —steal these words from us and corrupt them to their own uses.

Most of the people in Asia have never known democracy. They may or may not want *our* type of democracy. Obviously all of them are not ready to have democracy handed to them next Tuesday on a silver platter. But they are determined to work out their own destiny under governments selected by themselves.

Even the name of the Atlantic Charter disturbs thoughtful men and women I have been talking to. Do all of those who signed it, these people ask, agree that it applies to the Pacific? We must answer this question with a clear and simple statement of where we stand. And we must begin to sweat over our common problem of translating such a statement into plans which will be concrete and meaningful to the lives of these millions of people who are our allies.

Some of the plans to which such a statement would lead are already clear, I deeply believe, to most Americans:

We believe this war must mean an end to the empire of nations over other nations. No foot of Chinese soil, for example, should be or can be ruled from now on except by the people who live on it. And we must say so *now*, not after the war.

We believe it is the world's job to find some system for helping colonial peoples who join the United Nations' cause to become free and independent nations. We must set up firm timetables under which they can work out and train governments of their own choosing, and we must establish ironclad guarantees, administered by all the United Nations jointly, that they shall not slip back into colonial status.

Some say these subjects should be hushed until victory is won. Exactly the reverse is true. Sincere efforts to find progressive solutions now will bring strength to our cause. Remember, opponents of social change always urge delay because of some present crisis. After the war, the changes may be too little and too late.

We must develop between nations trade and trade routes strong enough to give all peoples the same vested interest in peace which we in America have had.

In the United States, we are being asked to give up temporarily our individual freedom and economic liberty in order to crush the Axis. We must recover this freedom and this liberty after the war. The way to make certain we do recover our traditional American way of life with a rising standard of living for all is to create a world in which all men everywhere can be free.

This statement caused a good deal of comment. Some of it was angry, but for the most part the reaction cheered me greatly. For it confirmed my feeling that the deep drift of public opinion, which works quietly but powerfully, has already moved ahead of many of our leaders on these questions and that it will, before long, push us into the open acknowledgment, before the world, of the beliefs we hold most firmly.

The temptation is great, in all of us, to limit the objectives of a war. Cynically, we may hope that the big words we have used will become smaller at the peace table, that we can avoid the costly and difficult readjustments which will be required to establish and defend real freedom for all peoples.

Many men and women I have talked with from Africa to Alaska asked me the question which has become almost a symbol all through Asia: what about India? Now I did not go to India. I do not propose to discuss that tangled question. But it has one aspect, in the East, which I should report. From Cairo on, it confronted me at every turn. The wisest man in China said to me: "When the aspiration of India for freedom was put aside to some future date, it was not Great Britain that suffered in public esteem in the Far East. It was the United States."

This wise man was not quarreling with British imperialism in India when he said this—a benevolent imperialism, if you like. He does not happen to believe in it, but he was not even talking about it. He was telling me that by our silence on India we have already drawn heavily on our reservoir of good will in the East. People of the East who would like to count on us are doubtful. They cannot ascertain from our attitude toward the problem of India what we are likely to feel at the end of the war about all the other hundreds of millions of Eastern peoples. They cannot tell from our vague and vacillating talk whether or not we really do stand for freedom, or what we mean by freedom.

In China, students who were refugees a thousand miles from their homes asked me if we were going to try to take back Shanghai after the war. In Beirut, Lebanese asked me if their relatives in Brooklyn—one third of all the Lebanese in the world live in the United States—would help to persuade the British and French occupying forces to leave Syria and the Lebanon after the war and let them run their own country.

In Africa, in the Middle East, throughout the Arab world, as well as in China and the whole Far East, freedom means the orderly but scheduled abolition of the colonial system. Whether we like it or not, this is true.

The British Commonwealth of Free Nations is the world's most spectacular example of such an orderly process. And the success of that great experiment should be immensely encouraging to the United Nations in working out the problems of self-government that lie ahead. For large sections of the world are still governed by the colonial system. Despite the Commonwealth, Great Britain still has numerous colonies, remnants of empire, with little or no self-rule, though the English people, millions of them, at home and throughout the Commonwealth, are working selflessly and with great skill toward reducing these remnants, toward extending the Commonwealth in place of the colonial system.

The English are by no means the only colonial rulers. The French still claim empire in Africa, in Indo-China, in South America, and in islands throughout the world. The Dutch still regard themselves as rulers of large parts of the East Indies and of territories in the West. The Portuguese, the Belgians, and others nations have colonial possessions. And we ourselves have not yet promised complete freedom to all the peoples in the West Indies for whom we have assumed responsibility. Furthermore, we have our domestic imperialisms.

But the world is awake, at last, to the knowledge that the rule of people by other peoples is not freedom, and not what we must fight to preserve.

There will be lots of tough problems ahead. And they will differ in different mandates and different colonies. Not all the peoples of the world are ready for freedom, or can defend it, the day after tomorrow. But today they all want some date to work toward, some assurance that the date will be kept. For the future, they do not ask that we solve their problems for them. They are neither so foolish nor so faint-hearted. They ask only for the chance to solve their own problems with economic as well as political co-operation. For the peoples of the world intend to be free not only for their political satisfaction, but also for their economic advancement.

XIII OUR IMPERIALISMS AT HOME

I mentioned among the imperialisms of the world our own domestic imperialisms. This war has opened for us new horizons—new geographical horizons, new mental horizons. We have been a people devoted largely to home enterprise. We have become a people whose first interests are beyond the seas. The names of Russian, Burmese, Tunisian, or Chinese towns command primary attention in our newspapers. The most eagerly seized letters coming into our homes are from our young men in Australia, New Guinea, Guadalcanal, Ireland, or North Africa. Our interests go with their interests, and we may feel certain that when they have battled over the world, they will not return home as provincial Americans. Nor will they find us so. What does all this mean? It means that though we began to grow up with the earlier World War, we are only now changing completely from a young nation of domestic concerns to an adult nation of international interests and world outlook.

A true world outlook is incompatible with a foreign imperialism, no matter how high-minded the governing country. It is equally incompatible with the kind of imperialism which can develop inside any nation. Freedom is an indivisible word. If we want to enjoy it, and fight for it, we must be prepared to extend it to everyone, whether they are rich or poor, whether they agree with us or not, no matter what their race or the color of their skin. We cannot, with good conscience, expect the British to set up an orderly schedule for the liberation of India before we have decided for ourselves to make all who live in America free.

In this war we are allied with four hundred million people of China and we count as our friends three hundred million people of India. Fighting with us are the Filipinos and the natives of Java and the East Indies and of South Africa. Together, these peoples comprise almost half of the world's population. With none of them have the majority of Americans any ties of race. But we are learning in this war that it is not racial classifications nor ethnological considerations which bind men together; it is shared concepts and kindred objectives.

We are learning that the test of a people is their aim and not their color. Even Hitler's high racial wall has been breached by the recognition of a common purpose with those "honorary Aryans," the Japanese. We, too, have our natural allies. We must, now and hereafter, cast our lot as a nation with all those other peoples, whatever their race or color, who prize liberty as an innate right, both for themselves and for others. We must, now and hereafter, together with those peoples, reject the doctrine of imperialism which condemns the world to endless war.

Let me emphasize once more that race and color do not determine what people are allies and what people are enemies in this struggle. In the East, we have a plain example. Japan is our enemy because of her wanton and barbaric aggression upon weaker nations and because of the imperialistic doctrine by which she seeks to rule and enslave the world. Japan is our enemy because of the treacherous and unprovoked attacks by which she has launched each of her assaults in carrying forward her scheme of conquest.

China is our friend because like us she nourishes no dream of conquest and because she values liberty. She is our ally because, first among the nations, she resisted aggression and enslavement.

Here are two Oriental peoples. One is our enemy; one is our friend. Race and color have nothing to do with what we are fighting for today. Race and color do not determine at whose side we shall fight. These are things the white race is learning through this war. These are things we needed to learn.

Even our enemy, Japan, has been able to shock our racial complacency. She has rudely awakened us to the fact that the white race is not a select race and enjoys no superior rights in combat merely because of past progress and ascendancy. Whereas, a year and a half ago, we were generally contemptuous of Japan as a possible enemy, we now recognize that we have encountered a formidable foe, against whom we must marshal our full strength.

Our ally, China, has by the same token taught us a new and healthy humility. For we have seen her for more than five years, alone, with none of the equipment of modern warfare, defy that same formidable foe. And today her people still resist while we are still making ready to take our full share in the struggle. The moral atmosphere in which the white race lives is changing. It is changing not only in our attitude toward the people of the Far East. It is changing here at home.

It has been a long while since the United States had any imperialistic designs toward the outside world. But we have practiced within our own boundaries something that amounts to race imperialism. The attitude of the white citizens of this country toward the Negroes has undeniably had some of the unlovely characteristics of an alien imperialism—a smug racial superiority, a willingness to exploit an unprotected people. We have justified it by telling ourselves that its end is benevolent. And sometimes it has been. But so sometimes have been the ends of imperialism. And the moral atmosphere in which it has existed is identical with that in which men—well-meaning men—talk of "the white man's burden."

But that atmosphere is changing. Today it is becoming increasingly apparent to thoughtful Americans that we cannot fight the forces and ideas of imperialism abroad and maintain any form of imperialism at home. The war has done this to our thinking.

Emancipation came to the colored race in America as a war measure. It was an act of military necessity. Manifestly it would have come without war, in the slower process of humanitarian reform and social enlightenment. But it required a disastrous, internecine war to bring this question of human freedom to a crisis, and the process of striking the shackles from the slave was accomplished in a single hour. We are finding under the pressures of this present conflict that long-standing barriers and prejudices are breaking down. The defense of our democracy against the forces that threaten it from without has made some of its failures to function at home glaringly apparent.

Our very proclamations of what we are fighting for have rendered our own inequities self-evident. When we talk of freedom and opportunity for all nations, the mocking paradoxes in our own society become so clear they can no longer be ignored. If we want to talk about freedom, we must mean freedom for others as well as ourselves, and we must mean freedom for everyone inside our frontiers as well as outside. During a war, this is especially important.

The threat to racial and religious, even to political, minority groups springs in wartime from two things—an overzealous mass insistence upon general conformity to majority standards, and the revival under emotional strains of age-old racial and religious distrusts. Minorities then are apt to be charged with responsibility for the war itself, and all the dislocations and discomforts arising from it. They are jealously subjected to scrutiny to determine if they are the recipients of special advantages.

We are all familiar with the process by which, in a war psychology, the unusual is distrusted and anything unorthodox is associated by some people with enemy intriguing. Chauvinists are likely to spring up in any community. There is the instance in our War of 1812 of a young man arrested and held for espionage on the suspicious circumstances that "he carried a long whip and wore an unusual number of buttons on his pantaloons." When affairs go wrong the public, by ancient custom, demands a scapegoat, and the first place to seek one is from a minority.

All this would appear ridiculous in our modern age were it not for the examples of bigotry and persecution we see in countries once presumed to be enlightened, and, even more seriously, were it not for the fact that we are already witnessing a crawling, insidious anti-Semitism in our own country. It will be well to bear in mind continuously that we are fighting today against intolerance and oppression, and that we shall get them in abundance if we lose. If we allow them to develop at home while we are engaging the enemy abroad, we shall have immeasurably weakened our fighting arm.

Our nation is composed of no one race, faith, or cultural heritage. It is a grouping of some thirty peoples possessing varying religious concepts, philosophies, and historical backgrounds. They are linked together by their confidence in our democratic institutions as expressed in the Declaration of Independence and guaranteed by the Constitution for themselves and for their children.

The keystone of our union of states is freedom—freedom for the individual to worship as he chooses, to work as he chooses, and to live and rear his children as he chooses. Liberty, if it is to be for all, must be protected by basic safeguards intended to give it the most general diffusion attainable, and none can expect privileges which encroach upon the rights of others. Despite the functionings of our mischievous bureaucracies, and our sometimes excessively enterprising legislatures, and—in deplorable but fortunately isolated instances—the flaring of mob law, we have obtained here in America, in the course of little more than a century and a half of experience and adjustment, the most reasonable expression of freedom that has yet existed in history.

Our success thus far as a nation is not because we have built great cities and big factories and cultivated vast areas, but because we have promoted this fundamental assurance of freedom upon which all our material development has depended, and have tolerated, and learned to use, our diversities.

We remain a relatively new nation. As recently as fifty years ago, more than half our mining and a third of our total manufacturing were carried on by immigrants. More than half of the farm population of some of our leading agricultural states was alien-born. In the formative period of the nation, between 1820 and 1890, more than 15,000,000 newcomers reached our shores, and a still greater number were yet to arrive in the twenty-four years preceding the outbreak of the last war. In other words, we have had two hundred years of reinvigorating immigration which has brought us new blood, new experiences, new ideas. Here was a vast assembly of minority groups which have gone into the welding of a nation. We have created a strong nation because these new arrivals did not have the distractions, under our form of government, of continually opposing and battling one another, but entered as partners into the general upbuilding and consolidation. The height of our civilization, it seems to me, has been reached not by our assembly lines, our inventions, or any of our great factitious development, but by the ability of peoples of varying beliefs and of different racial extractions to live side by side here in the United States with common understanding, respect, and helpfulness.

If we want to see the opposite of this American system, we have merely to look at the military despotism of Hitler and the autocracy of Japan, and the fading dictatorship of Fascist Italy. The story of Germany for the last ten years has been one of racial and religious intolerance that provided a mask behind which a peace-professing dictator lured the people first to minority persecution, then to war. This intolerance gave the German nation the momentary strength of complete regimentation. Actually, it has undermined and weakened the social structure so that when the tide of war turns, collapse is likely to be sudden and complete.

It has always impressed me that, quite apart from any reasons of humanitarianism or justice or any sentiment regarding the protection of the weak by the strong, it is only common sense to safeguard jealously the rights of minorities. For minorities are rich assets of a democracy, assets which no totalitarian government can afford. Dictatorships must, of necessity, fear and suppress them. But within the tolerance of a democracy, minorities are the constant spring of new ideas, stimulating new thought and action, the constant source of new vigor.

To suppress minority thinking and minority expression would tend to freeze society and prevent progress. For the majority itself is stimulated by the existence of minority groups. The human mind requires contrary expressions against which to test itself.

For now more than ever, we must keep in the forefront of our minds the fact that whenever we take away the liberties of those whom we hate, we are opening the way to loss of liberty for those we love.

Our way of living together in America is a strong but delicate fabric. It is made up of many threads. It has been woven over many centuries by the patience and sacrifice of countless liberty-loving men and women. It serves as a cloak for the protection of poor and rich, of black and white, of Jew and gentile, of foreign- and native-born.

Let us not tear it asunder. For no man knows, once it is destroyed, where or when man will find its protective warmth again.

XIV ONE WORLD

IT was only a short time ago—less than a quarter of a century—that the allied nations gained an outstanding victory over the forces of conquest and aggression then led by imperial Germany.

But the peace that should have followed that war failed primarily because no joint objectives upon which it could be based had been arrived at in the minds of the people, and therefore no world peace was possible. The League of Nations was created full-blown; and men and women, having developed no joint purpose, except to defeat a common enemy, fell into capricious arguments about its structural form. Likewise, it failed because it was primarily an Anglo-French-American solution, retaining the old colonial imperialisms under new and fancy terms. It took inadequate account of the pressing needs of the Far East, nor did it sufficiently seek solution of the economic problems of the world. Its attempts to solve the world's problems were primarily political. But political internationalism without economic internationalism is a house built upon sand. For no nation can reach its fullest development alone.

Our own history furnishes, I believe, another clue to our failure. One of our most obvious weaknesses, in the light of what is going on today, is the lack of any continuity in our foreign policy. Neither major party can claim to have pursued a stable or consistent program of international co-operation even during the relatively brief period of the last forty-five years. Each has had its season of world outlook—sometimes an imperialistic one—and each its season of strict isolationism, the Congressional leadership of the party out of power usually, according to accepted American political practice, opposing the program of the party in power, whatever it might be.

For years many in both parties have recognized that if peace, economic prosperity, and liberty itself were to continue in this world, the nations of the world must find a method of economic stabilization and co-operative effort.

These aspirations at the end of the First World War, under the presidency of Woodrow Wilson, produced a program of international co-operation intended to safeguard all nations against military aggression, to protect racial minorities, and to give the oncoming generation some confidence that it could go about its affairs without a return of the disrupting and blighting scourge of war. Whatever we may think about the details of that program, it was definite, affirmative action for world peace. We cannot state positively just how effective it might have proved had the United States extended to it support, influence, and active participation.

But we do know that we tried the opposite course and found it altogether futile. We entered into an era of strictest detachment from world affairs. Many of our public leaders, Democratic and Republican, went about the country proclaiming that we had been tricked into the last war, that our ideals had been betrayed, that never again should we allow ourselves to become entangled in world politics which would inevitably bring about another armed outbreak. We were blessed with natural barriers, they maintained, and need not concern ourselves with the complicated and unsavory affairs of an old world beyond our borders.

We shut ourselves away from world trade by excessive tariff barriers. We washed our hands of the continent of Europe and displayed no interest in its fate while Germany rearmed. We torpedoed the London Economic Conference when the European democracies, with France lagging in the rear, were just beginning to recover from the economic depression that had sapped their vitality, and when the instability of foreign exchange remained the principal obstacle to full revival. And in so doing, we sacrificed a magnificent opportunity for leadership in strengthening and rehabilitating the democratic nations, in fortifying them against assault by the forces of aggression which at that very moment were beginning to gather.

The responsibility for this does not attack solely to any political party. For neither major party stood consistently and conclusively before the American public as either the party of world outlook or the party of isolation. If we were to say that Republican leadership destroyed the

League of Nations in 1920, we must add that it was Democratic leadership that broke up the London Economic Conference in 1933.

I was a believer in the League. Without, at this time, however, arguing either for or against the provisions of the League plans, I should like to point out the steps leading to its defeat here in the United States. For that fight furnishes a perfect example of the type of leadership we must avoid in this country if we are ever going to fulfill our responsibilities as a nation that believes in a free world, a just world, a world at peace.

President Wilson negotiated the peace proposals at Versailles, including the covenant of the League, without consultation with or the participation of the Republican leadership in the Senate. He monopolized the issue for the Democratic party and thereby strategically caused many Republicans—even international-minded Republicans—to take the opposite position. Upon his return the treaty and the covenant were submitted to the United States Senate for ratification. And there arose one of the most dramatic episodes in American history. I cannot here trace the details of that fight which resulted in rejection on the part of the United States of world leadership. It is important for us today, however, to remember the broad outlines of the picture.

First, as to the Senate group, the so-called "battalion of death," the "irreconcilables," or the "bitter-enders." Here was a group that had no party complexion. In its leadership the name of the Democratic orator, James A. Reed, occupies as conspicuous a position as that of the Republican, Borah. At the other extreme was the uncompromising war President, Woodrow Wilson, who insisted on the treaty with every i dotted and every t crossed. Between them were the reservationists, of various complexions and opinions, and of both Republican and Democratic affiliation.

We do not know today, and perhaps we never shall know, whether the man who was then Republican leader of the Senate, Henry Cabot Lodge, whose name we now associate with the defeat of the League, truly wanted the League adopted with safeguarding reservations or whether he employed the reservations to kill the League. Even his close friends and members of his family have reported contrary opinions on the subject.

But we do know that when this question passed from the Senate to the two great political conventions of 1920, neither of them stood altogether for, or altogether against, the treaty as it had been brought home by the President. The Democratic Convention in its platform did not oppose reservations. The Republican platform adopted a compromise plank which was broad enough to accommodate the firm supporters of the League in the Republican ranks. The anti-League delegates found safe footing there too.

Both platforms were ambiguous; the parties had no consistent historical position about the co-operation of the United States with other nations. The confusion was doubled by the attitude of the Republican candidate, Warren Harding, an amiable, pleasant man of no firm convictions. There was no doubt that Cox's position on the Democratic ticket was a fairly definite support of the Wilson treaty, though his party platform left open the possibility of reservations and many of the Democratic leaders were strongly in opposition. But no one was certain whether Harding was merely pulling his punches against the League or whether he intended to support it upon election, in a modified form. All that was clear was that he felt he had to make some opposition to the League since it had been made a political issue by the Democrats. In private conversation, he gave each man the answer he wanted. It was not until after the election returns were in that Harding spoke frankly of the League as "now deceased."

The election, ironically, had turned primarily on different questions. The great cause of America's co-operation with the world was put to the test of an election dominated by local issues through the fault of both parties. The Democratic party and its leaders unwisely sought to monopolize the international position and the Republican party equally unwisely allowed itself to be pushed strategically in the opposite direction. The time is approaching when we must once more determine whether America will assume its proper position in world affairs, and we must not let that determination be again decided by mere party strategy.

I am satisfied that the American people never deliberately and intentionally turned their backs on a program for international co-operation. Possibly they would have preferred changes in the precise Versailles covenant, but not complete aloofness from the efforts of other nations. They were betrayed by leaders without convictions who were thinking in terms of group vote catching and partisan advantage.

If our withdrawal from world affairs after the last war was a contributing factor to the present war and to the economic instability of the past twenty years—and it seems plain that it was—a withdrawal from the problems and responsibilities of the world after this war would be sheer disaster. Even our relative geographical isolation no longer exists.

At the end of the last war, not a single plane had flown across the Atlantic. Today that ocean is a mere ribbon, with airplanes making regular scheduled flights. The Pacific is only a slightly wider ribbon in the ocean of the air, and Europe and Asia are at our very doorstep.

America must choose one of three courses after this war: narrow nationalism, which inevitably means the ultimate loss of our own liberty; international imperialism, which means the sacrifice of some other nation's liberty; or the creation of a world in which there shall be an equality of opportunity for every race and every nation. I am convinced the American people will choose, by overwhelming majority, the last of these courses. To make this choice effective, we must win not only the war, but also the peace, and we must start winning it now.

To win this peace three things seem to me necessary—first, we must plan now for peace on a world basis; second, the world must be free, politically and economically, for nations and for men, that peace may exist in it; third, America must play an active, constructive part in freeing it and keeping its peace.

When I say that peace must be planned on a world basis, I mean quite literally that it must embrace the earth. Continents and oceans are plainly only parts of a whole, seen, as I have seen them, from the air. England and America are parts. Russia and China, Egypt, Syria and Turkey, Iraq and Iran are also parts. And it is inescapable that there can be no peace for any part of the world unless the foundations of peace are made secure throughout all parts of the world.

This cannot be accomplished by mere declarations of our leaders, as in an Atlantic Charter. Its accomplishment depends primarily upon acceptance by the peoples of the world. For if the failure to reach international understanding after the last war taught us anything it taught us this: even if war leaders apparently agree upon generalized principles and slogans while the war is being fought, when they come to the peace table they make their own interpretations of their previous declarations. So unless today, while the war is being fought, the people of the United States and of Great Britain, of Russia and of China, and of all the other

United Nations, fundamentally agree on their purposes, fine and ideal-istic expressions of hope such as those of the Atlantic Charter will live merely to mock us as have Mr. Wilson's Fourteen Points. The Four Freedoms will not be accomplished by the declarations of those momen-tarily in power. They will become real only if the people of the world forge them into actuality.

When I say that in order to have peace this world must be free, I am only reporting that a great process has started which no man—certainly not Hitler—can stop. Men and women all over the world are on the march, physically, intellectually, and spiritually. After centuries of ignorant and dull compliance, hundreds of millions of people in eastern Europe and Asia have opened the books. Old fears no longer frighten them. They are no longer willing to be Eastern slaves for Western profits. They are beginning to know that men's welfare throughout the world is interdependent. They are resolved, as we must be, that there is no more place for imperialism within their own society than in the society of nations. The big house on the hill surrounded by mud huts has lost its awesome charm.

Our Western world and our presumed supremacy are now on trial. Our boasting and our big talk leave Asia cold. Men and women in Russia and China and in the Middle East are conscious now of their own potential strength. They are coming to know that many of the de-cisions about the future of the world lie in their hands. And they intend that these decisions shall leave the peoples of each nation free from foreign domination, free for economic, social, and spiritual growth.

Economic freedom is as important as political freedom. Not only must people have access to what other peoples produce, but their own products must in turn have some chance of reaching men all over the world. There will be no peace, there will be no real development, there will be no eco-nomic stability, unless we find the method by which we can begin to break down the unnecessary trade barriers hampering the flow of goods. Obviously, the sudden and uncompromising abolition of tariffs after the war could only result in disaster. But obviously, also, one of the free-doms we are fighting for is freedom to trade. I know there are many men, particularly in America, where our standard of living exceeds the standard of living in the rest of the world, who are genuinely alarmed at such a prospect, who believe that any such process will only lessen our own standard of living. The reverse of this is true.

Many reasons may be assigned for the amazing economic development of the United States. The abundance of our national resources, the freedom of our political institutions, and the character of our population have all undoubtedly contributed. But in my judgment the greatest factor has been the fact that by the happenstance of good fortune there was created here in America the largest area in the world in which there were no barriers to the exchange of goods and ideas.

And I should like to point out to those who are fearful one inescapable fact. In view of the astronomical figures our national debt will assume by the end of this war, and in a world reduced in size by industrial and transportation developments, even our present standard of living in America cannot be maintained unless the exchange of goods flows more freely over the whole world. It is also inescapably true that to raise the standard of living of any man anywhere in the world is to raise the standard of living by some slight degree of every man everywhere in the world.

Finally, when I say that this world demands the full participation of a self-confident America, I am only passing on an invitation which the peoples of the East have given us. They would like the United States and the other United Nations to be partners with them in this grand adventure. They want us to join them in creating a new society of independent nations, free alike of the economic injustices of the West and the political malpractices of the East. But as partners in that great new combination they want us neither hesitant, incompetent, nor afraid. They want partners who will not hesitate to speak out for the correction of injustice anywhere in the world.

Our allies in the East know that we intend to pour out our resources in this war. But they expect us now—not after the war—to use the enormous power of our giving to promote liberty and justice. Other peoples, not yet fighting, are waiting no less eagerly for us to accept the most challenging opportunity of all history—the chance to help create a new society in which men and women the world around can live and grow invigorated by independence and freedom.

The Problems
of Lasting Peace

BY HERBERT HOOVER

AND HUGH GIBSON

PREFACE

THE AUTHORS wish to make acknowledgment to the number of persons to whom this manuscript has been submitted and from whom they have received most valuable suggestions.

They also wish to make acknowledgment to the research staff at the Stanford University Library on War, Revolution, and Peace, and to the Henry M. Robinson Research Fund of that library.

In order to make the book as convenient as possible for the reader, it has been divided into three parts.

Part One
  Chapter I: Description of the seven dynamic forces which make for war and peace.
  Chapters II to IV: The movement of these forces from the Renaissance until the first World War in 1914.

Part Two
  Chapters V to IX: The movement of these forces from the beginning of the first World War to the beginning of the second World War in 1939. Included is an analysis of the Treaty of Versailles, the League of Nations, and other peace efforts.

Part Three
  Chapters X to XIV: Conclusions as to the essential foundations of peace and the various plans and proposals to maintain the peace when the foundations are so laid.

INTRODUCTION

OUR country is now engaged in the greatest struggle of its existence. All Americans, regardless of their past views, are now united in a single purpose. That purpose is to achieve victory and thereafter build a world where we can hope to live in peace and security.

There lie before us two great campaigns. The first is the military campaign to defeat the enemy.

But the second and equally difficult undertaking is to win a lasting peace for the world. Military victory alone will not give us peace. That was proved in 1918. Victory, however essential, is chiefly important for the privilege it gives of shaping an era of peace for the world.

There must sometime be a cessation of hostilities, following which some method will be arrived at for making and preserving peace. It may be by mandates of the leading victors, or by a great conference, or by stages of settlement. For purposes of this discussion, we shall refer to these processes as the peace table.

And we must assume that if democracy is to live, these settlements will be submitted to the representatives of peoples in congresses or legislatures or parliaments, for ratification by each.

This essay is based upon victory and an American point of view. There are, however, reservations on any proposed American principles of peace that should not be forgotten.

In the first place, we must recognize that our allies in this war—Britain, Russia, China, and the others—will look upon the problems of peace through different eyes. We cannot know their conclusions at this stage. In the second place, we cannot foresee the kaleidoscopic shifts in the relation of nations which will probably take place during this war.

But whatever the fortunes of war may be, we feel that exploration of the past and the complexities of the future will demonstrate that it is essential that the principles and the methods of peace be threshed out and clarified in our own minds.

The men who gather at the peace table will have but a fleeting opportunity to make secure the foundations of lasting peace. Nations can blunder into war. They cannot blunder into peace. The wisdom and courage exercised in making the next peace will determine the fate of humanity for long years to come.

When the day of the armistice or any other end to military action comes, nations will be exhausted and many of them starving. The demobilization of armies, navies, and the workers in war industries will bring great economic and governmental problems to the victors as well as to the vanquished. Political stability cannot be founded, boundaries settled, armies demobilized, peaceful production started, hunger ended, reconstruction begun until peace is proclaimed. The whole world will be crying for haste. There will be little time then to think out the forces of lasting peace. That must begin now.

We were told in the last war: "Destroy the Kaiser first. Discuss peace afterwards." Today, again, it is "Hitler, Mussolini, and Tojo must be first destroyed; we cannot discuss peace until that is done."

We went to the peace conference in 1919 animated by the loftiest and most disinterested ideals, but we were totally unprepared for the specific problems that had to be met at the peace table. We secured neither peace, freedom, nor prosperity.

There must be just as much preparedness for peace-making as there is for war. And in many ways the preparations for peace are a more difficult task. Preparedness for war deals mostly with tangibles—men, guns, ships, planes, money—and with tactics and strategy. Preparedness for peace deals largely with intangibles—the setting up of moral, intellectual, economic, and political forces over the whole world which will produce and hold peace.

And lasting peace cannot be made simply of lofty expressions of aims and ideals. Such ideals are necessary. We must have aims. But that is only the starting point of the job of making lasting peace. Any peace consists of a realistic definition of territorial, economic, political, military, and other settlements, with terms, methods, and machinery for carrying it out. The "aims" and "ideals" are not part of the binding words of a peace. They are only background to be expressed in under-takings of concrete character.

The difference between "aims" and peace treaties is the same differ-ence as that between the Declaration of Independence and the Constitu-tion of the United States. It takes little effort of the imagination to pic-ture the results if, instead of elaborating a Constitution, the Founding Fathers and their descendants had endeavored to govern this country under the terms of the Declaration of Independence.

The vital question in the peace is how our aims and ideals are to be made to work. That is, by what means, what powers, what machinery, is peace to be made to prevail?

If we are to make a better job of the peace this time than last, it will be because intelligent public interest and discussion succeed in develop-ing more ideas and better ideas. And it will be because of better under-standing of the causes of failure in the past and the experience that can be drawn from mankind's many efforts in the prevention of war. And finally, if constructive plans for peace and justice could be de-veloped, they might even help bring the war to an earlier victorious end. For today, great masses of people in the enemy countries are yearn-ing for any peace which brings legitimate hope for the future.

There is no doubt that the tribulations of the world today are in large measure due to the acceptance of materialism and loss of spiritual standards. Without these developments there would have been no room for the growth of regimes based on brutality, the arbitrary use of force, and disregard of all the spiritual values which make life tolerable. If the authors do not labor this view it is because it is so staggeringly obvious that it can be taken for granted in an essay devoted to analysis of political problems.

However, for the sake of clarity it must be said that no political solutions, however realistic, will suffice to give us a peaceful world unless they are accompanied by a return to something better than a belief in material well-being—a return to faith in higher things.

This book is offered as a sort of preface to peacemaking. It does not attempt to write the inevitable treaty of peace. But there are certain dynamic forces among men which make for peace and war. The world has had vast and bitter experience in peacemaking. This book seeks to draw from the experience of the past some principles, some methods of action, which allay those forces that make for war and strengthen those that make for peace. We have sought to distill some conclusions from the failures and successes of the past.

And there must be some organization, some machinery for the preservation of the peace when it is made. Again, the world has had experience and many experiments from which some guidance can be deduced.

There are indeed many plans now under discussion to preserve the peace. Some are Utopian. But there is no reason to scoff at Utopian ideas, for they stimulate thought, imagination, and discussion. Without dreamers, mankind might never have emerged from savagery. But again, there is great need to apply the tests of experience and to weigh such plans in the scales of the dynamic forces which will continue to work for peace or war.

Therefore, there are certain fundamentals upon which this essay is based:

First, that a satisfactory and durable peace must be founded on victory. Many of its essentials would crumble with compromise.

Second, that lasting peace can come only if the settlements take account realistically of the underlying dynamic forces in civilization that make for war and peace.

Third, that the new peace must provide for some organization, some machinery for international co-operation to preserve the peace once it has been made.

Fourth, that the American people must begin to think of the problems of peace. And they must think in a far larger frame than ever before.

Our hope is that we may here aid to stimulate American discussion and to clarify thinking. The authors' justification for venturing upon this subject is that both of them have had to deal actively with these problems for the past thirty years.

With a limited canvas for the portrayal of such a broad sweep of history as it bears upon war and peace, they have endeavored not to burden the reader's mind with detail that does not bear directly upon this major purpose.

We are in a gigantic war. Our first task is to win it. Having set our hand to the task, we cannot stop until lasting peace has been made. Only from a lasting peace can we hope to save our civilization.

To contribute to that end is the purpose of this book.

Part One

I THE DYNAMIC FORCES
WHICH MAKE FOR PEACE AND WAR

WE have now had a generation of almost continuous wars, revolutions, and social and economic disorder, and the end is not yet. The world has seen such periods of explosion and degeneration before, separated by varying periods of more or less peace and human progress.

Boundary lines between periods of history are not always clear-cut, but they can be sketched with a broad brush.

If we scan the history of modern Western civilization, we can see the dim shapes of three great periods of new ideas and rising forces, each of which culminated in long world wars, tumults, and world disorder.

There have been three of these major widespread upheavals since the Renaissance. First was the Thirty Years' War, ending with the Peace of Westphalia in 1648; second, the forty years of war following the American and French revolutions, ending with the Congress of Vienna in 1815; and third, the world-wide wars beginning in 1914 and still raging.

In each of these periods, civilization took on new impulses, new forms, and new directions. Today we are probably in the presence of a third period of great change.

It is too easy to attribute our present wars to individuals or groups of individuals or even to perverse nations. It is easy to assume that lasting peace will come when these individuals or nations are punished as a flaming notice to future evildoers.

But great explosions in civilization do not have their origins in single men or a perverse nation. Such evil persons or peoples are themselves the product of deep-seated forces which must be stopped, allayed, or controlled if there is to be lasting peace. Those men or groups only light the match to a train of powder which has been laid over the years before.

Whatever may be done in making plans for the future or in writing the documents of peace will have no value unless account is taken of the evolving forces which have their birth in the years behind us. To gain some comprehension of these gigantic issues, we must reach into the dynamic forces that have been building this crisis—and must seek solutions that will ease the strains of the period to follow. And unless we are prepared to inquire objectively into and accept these forces as revealing the real problems of peacemaking, this war will be but the prelude to still another.

We must set aside our preconceived ideas on measures for making and keeping peace—that is, until we can establish whether they reach essential ills. The surgeon does not succeed in diagnosis by looking at the outside of his patient. He explores the action of the nervous system, the circulatory system, the digestive system, the cell structure, the pains, and the will to recovery in his patient. And this is a sick world— a very sick world.

The Seven Dynamic Forces

There are many of these dynamic forces that make for peace and war. They have been in operation unceasingly, though in varying degrees, ever since the dawn of recorded civilization. These forces can, for diagnosis, be separated into:

1. Ideologies
2. Economic pressures
3. Nationalism
4. Militarism
5. Imperialism
6. The complexes of fear, hate, and revenge
7. The will to peace

These forces are not arranged in order of their importance. That varies in different periods. They overlap and are interwoven into the whole fabric of civilization. Other students may prefer different divisions and different designations for these parts of world anatomy. We have reached the conclusion, however, that these divisions and separations most nearly represent not only these dominant world movements, but are historically the more conclusive basis, and they furnish a new approach in discussion of these problems.

The history of peace and war is largely a recitation of the operation of these forces and the failures of men to comprehend and control them. Much of it is mistakenly written into terms of personalities, both good and bad. Now is the time when the problems of this peace must be studied in far larger patterns than ever before.

Ideological Forces

The importance of religious faith, of social, economic, political, artistic, and scientific ideas, in shaping the form of the world and the making of its wars and peace is not to be estimated as less than that of other forces. Over the long range of history, they are the determining factors in civilization.

One thing is certain: that is, the ideas which involve human belief and faith contain a militant crusading spirit. Within them is inherent aggressiveness. Great and revolutionary ideas have within them at least a period where they are borne aloft by military action. Christianity, Mohammedanism, the Divine Right of Kings, the Protestant Reformation, and Liberalism have all in their time marched with the sword. Now, new ideologies—Communism, Fascism, and Nazism—are on the warpath. And ideological wars, whether religious or temporal, are more cruel and more bitter than were wars of mere conquest or exploitation. While the ideology of personal liberty is today less aggressive than the ideologies of collectivism, yet it can rise to crusading heights.

Ideologies can also make for peace. For these nineteen centuries Christianity has been unique among religious faiths in its preaching of peace and compassion. Personal liberty and representative government as a political concept have also preached the gospel of peace. Both, at times, have sought to impose their beliefs with the sword. But their final purpose is peace. And as long as men have beliefs, they will strive to protect and expand them.

Economic Forces

While we have no faith in theories of complete economic determinism in history, yet it occupies a large place among these seven forces.

Since men must have food and living, the striving for them creates eternal economic forces and pressures. Certainly, through the history of modern civilization, economic forces have played a large part. It was the wealth of the Indies which stimulated the great explorations and conquests of the fifteenth and sixteenth centuries. Pressures of overpopulation to find outlets for men and goods play a striking part on the world stage today. The cravings for security of supply of raw materials and places to sell surplus products have led to incessant friction, hate, fear, and war. Insistence that "trade follows the flag" has cost rivers of blood and untold sorrow. All these are part of the incentives to imperialism.

Whatever may have been the weight of economic pressures in creating the World War of 1914, the economic aftermaths of that war were among the primary causes of the collapse of the world into this second World War. War's disruption of economic life has been burned into the consciousness of nations, yet not so deeply as was hoped by some observers. But economic forces have also at times and under other circumstances acted as a restraint on war.

Nationalism

Nationalism has developed from the deepest of primitive instincts and emotional forces in mankind.

It gathers from a thousand springs of common race with its common language, religion, folklore, traditions, literature, art, music, beliefs, habits, modes of expression, hates, fears, ideals, and tribal loyalties. It expresses itself in patriotism, which is itself built from the fundamentals of love of family, love of country, pride in racial accomplishments. Men fight for their hearths and their homes. They fight for their flag.

From all these racial instincts and mores rises the eternal yearning for independence from foreign subjection or domination. Thus, the subjection of races is one of the most potent of all causes of war. Nations are eternally striving for independence—self-determination. The oppressions which they suffer harden their souls and invigorate their resistance. All the thousands of years of human history are punctuated by wars of independence.

Who can even recite the repeated wars for independence of the Greeks, the Germans, the Spanish, the French, the Romans, and their successors, the Italians?

Nationalism will not be stilled by battle or defeat. It is fired to greater heat by every war and every peacemaking. A fiercer nationalism flares out of every defeat and every victory.

Victorious peoples who have marched to the defense of their homes and country to the stirring words of their national songs, who have followed their flags on the battlefield, who have sacrificed their sons and their wealth are little inclined to accept abrogation of their independence of action or of their sovereignty.

Nationalism can be both a cause of war or a bulwark of peace and progress. The values of nationalism cannot be ignored because of its secondary evils.

Where it is an impulse to strive for independence from oppression, for defense against aggression, it makes for war. But independence and spiritual unity, pride of country, constructive rivalry, the building of national cultures out of cohesive mores, the better conduct of government in areas of unity of thought and purpose bring more flowering of progress and the expansion of cultural institutions, scientific research, art, music, and literature. Nationalism in the best sense is a satisfaction, a fulfillment.

Extreme nationalism does have liabilities to peace and progress. As among individuals, there are ambitions in races for glory and for power of the race. Dignity, honor, and aggrandizement of his country is a satisfaction to the individual. To gain a place in the sun is an inspiring call.

Nationalism can readily expand into dangerous forms—greed in exploitation of the resources and foreign trade of other peoples and in aggression which quickly turns into imperialism.

There are about sixty separate nations in the world. And in the deep currents of human emotion, the primary interest of every citizen of them is his own country first and foremost.

Nationalism, with all its emotions, will continue as long as man inhabits this earth and will have to be embraced in any plan to preserve the peace.

Militarism

Man is a combative animal. He loves contest. He hates easily. He is an egoistic animal, and in the mass becomes more egoistic. His beliefs in superiority are quickly transformed into arrogance. And that is one of the stimulants of aggression.

The pomp and glory of war have an appeal to man. He loves adventure, and to great numbers of people war becomes a wholesale relief from the dull routines of life.

Common defense is an age-old instinct. It started with the defense of the family and spread to the tribe and finally to the nation. By reason of this need of defense, every nation must have some degree of military organization, even among the most peaceful peoples. The possession of armament, however, no matter how necessary, breeds suspicion, fear, counterarmament, and hate.

And out of military organization there often comes a military caste. Its hope of renown lies in war, not in peace. And its voice in government is more often for settlement of grievances by war than by the processes of peace.

The militarism we describe is an aggressive force. It always makes for war.

But military organization can have two quite different spirits. The one defense, the other aggression.

Like individuals, some peoples are naturally pacific and some, naturally aggressive. China has been outstandingly the most pacific of all nations. So pacific has she been that in 3,000 years she has been conquered and ruled by foreign dynasties in all but two comparatively short periods.

Moreover, there is in some races a definite aggressive warrior strain. It grows in an aggressive race to a glorification of war for war's sake. The "reinvigoration" of the race through war has long been preached in Germany, Italy, and Japan. The "warrior concept" is deeply rooted in Germany, particularly in Prussia. This may be because of the constant threat of invasion. On the other hand, it has been argued that the trouble with the Germans is that, unlike the French and the Britons, they were never conquered by the Romans and given the advantages of that form of education. Tacitus was eloquent on the subject of Germany nearly 2,000 years ago. The order of Teutonic Knights carried their thirteenth-century ideas with fire and sword. Their ideas of an aggressive military caste have come down through the centuries, with periodic modernizations, through Frederick the Great to Bismarck, with his "blood and iron," to Hitler with his "master race," his "guns instead of butter."

The same could be said of the Japanese. Their two feudal military clans—the Choshu and the Satsuma—are represented today in the control of the Army and Navy respectively.

Probably 80 per cent of the German and Japanese people are no more militaristic than any other. But, by their very docility, they are constantly overridden by the warrior groups.

And we must not overlook the Pied Pipers, consumed with ambition, who call their countrymen to glory and conquest. These men, seeking power on earth and a place in the eternity of history, are the apotheoses of militarism and aggression. They are the Alexander the Greats, the Genghis Khans, the Julius Caesars, the Charlemagnes, the Gustavus Adolphuses, the Napoleons, the Kaiser Wilhelms, and the current exhibits.

Imperialism

Another of the larger forces moving in all history is imperialism. It may, for our purposes, be defined as the movement of races over their racial borders.

It is part cause, part effect. It springs from excessive nationalism, militarism, thirst for power, and economic pressures. They all feed upon one another. Old as the Chaldeans and as modern as this morning, its purpose has not changed, although its form has altered. At one time, part of the motivation of imperialism was dynastic or racial glory; at another, zeal to spread religious faith—for instance, Mohammedanism or Christianity. But in modern civilization its motivation has been chiefly economic.

Modern imperialism has developed into three varieties, of which one is justified by modern moral standards, the second may be justified, and the third has no justification in morals or hope of peace. The first variety is expansion of races into the settlement and development of areas mostly unpopulated; the second, into areas of uncivilized races incapable of self-government; the third, sheer conquest of civilized races. The last two have always embodied one purpose—that is, to secure superior living by exploiting other races and their resources.

Whether its impelling force be glory, prestige, spread of religion, ideology, development of backward races, or exploitation of labor and resources, imperialism is not essentially an appendage of the Divine Right of Kings or the attribute of dictators. Democracies have been no less imperialistic than kings, emperors, or dictators. Rome was imperialistic before the Emperor was invented. Britain and France and the United States have expanded steadily. But wherever imperialism has been successful over long periods, it has always rested upon class government.

There can be no doubt that domination and exploitation of other races is one of the eternal causes of war. We know of no case where it has made for durable peace. Even in the phase of expansion over backward races or into open spaces, the rivalries between imperialisms have made for war. In the spread of civilization, it has compensations. But as a method of advancing peace, it cannot be given a great deal of credit. Much can be said for a satiated empire like Britain, which has arrived at a point where it becomes a stabilizing force. More especially that Empire, being liberal in instinct, makes for representative government among its components.

But imperialism as a theory of maintaining peace in the modern world has the disturbing consequences of setting up a dozen rival forms of Pax Romana to fight one another.

Imperialism has been present at every peacemaking, and it will be there next time.

The Forces of Fear, Hate, and Revenge

Fear, hate, and revenge play a large part in the causes of war. The greatest of these is fear. Hate and revenge often spring from it. Fear of invasion, fear of starvation by blockade in war, fear of economic disadvantage; age-old hates from wrong, from rivalries, from oppression; yearnings for revenge for past wrongs and defeats—all press toward violence.

These great forces of violence lie deep in the recesses of racial consciousness and racial experience. These emotions are the inheritance from all previous wars. Wrongs live for centuries in the minds of a people. There are traditional age-old hates between nations which are burned into their souls. From these emotions, wars have bred new wars. They have seldom settled anything. Fear of stronger races by their weaker neighbors born of invasions and defeat keeps them in constant sacrifice for the burdens of defense.

It keeps them in constant agitation, seeking diplomatic action, seeking support and military alliances. And the humiliations and privations of defeat and punishment create an undying demand for revenge.

The defeated are always humiliated. They are always impoverished. Either in reality or belief, the national pride, the national hopes, the national economy, or the national dignity of the vanquished have suffered. No nation ever recognizes or admits that it is wrong. No leader of that nation would dare suggest such a thing. Hate lives on, and it becomes entrenched in the mores of a people.

These emotions are eternal inheritances and causes of war. They, too, will sit at every peace table.

The Will to Peace

Against all the forces which make for war stands the will to peace. Ever in the background of men's minds is the infinite suffering of war. It kills or maims the best of the race. It brings the deepest of all griefs to every home. It brings poverty and moral degeneration. It brings these poignant ills to victor and vanquished alike.

The Sermon on the Mount launched the transcendent concept of compassion, of peace and good will among men as a fundamental of the Christian faith. "Blessed are the peacemakers, for they shall be called the children of God" epitomizes man's noblest hope. And despite all his violation of these spiritual concepts, man has received from them an undying inspiration to strive for peace.

The search over centuries by men of good will for methods of lasting peace testifies to the yearning of peoples for relief from the world's greatest scourge. The multitude of peace treaties, the establishment of embassies and legations, the Holy Alliance, the Concert of Europe, the balance of power, the Hague Tribunal, the processes of settlement of controversy by negotiation, by mediation, by arbitration, the League of Nations, and the World Court are all exhibits of the impelling will to peace.

And indeed, the spiritual concepts of peace have brought it to pass that every war must be justified by its leaders as a war of defense and for the one purpose of securing peace. And the end of every war is received with joy and the ringing of church bells.

Conclusion

These seven dynamic forces—ideologies; economic pressures; nationalism; imperialism; militarism; fear, with its consequences hate and revenge; and the will to peace—have largely shaped the history of the world. The shapes have been different in different periods of history, for these forces have varied in their relative potency. They will continue to shape the world; they will haunt the halls of the next peacemaking. It will not be a new world after this war. It will be a different world.

We must not overlook the part which individuals may play. When great crises arise from these forces, they must be dealt with by statesmen. No student of history can ignore the part such men have played in the crises of war and peace. When these great pressures are met successfully, it means peace; when there is failure, it means war or the seeds of war. The leaders in times of crisis may be men of ability, character, courage, and vision. Or they may be men of ignorance, incompetence, consuming vanity, egotism, ambition, or corruption. They may be Utopian dreamers. They may be a mixture of these characteristics, good and bad. We agree that they have an immense responsibility. But the character of men should not obscure the fact that the fundamental approach to the problems of peace and war lies in recognition of the great forces in motion. The influence of statesmanship upon these forces holds a secondary place.

Whatever the weight of the individual may be, we are confronted with these dynamic forces and total world disorder now. And therefore, some recognition of these forces, some exploration of their impact upon peace and war in the past, some estimate of how they can be controlled in the future are vital if we are to be prepared to overcome the evil and promote the good by peace-making.

II FORMER GREAT CRISES IN THE MODERN WORLD

I<small>T</small> is our purpose to explore the movement of these seven dynamic forces in the present world upheaval and their relationship to future peace. For the problems of today, the largest importance lies in the period of 165 years since the American and French revolutions. We shall in subsequent chapters divide that discussion into the periods:

From the American and French revolutions during 140 years to the World War of 1914.

During the four years of the first World War, from 1914 to 1918.

During the Armistice and the peace conference of 1919.

During the twenty years from 1919 to the resumption of World War in 1939.

As we have said, boundary lines between periods of history are not precise, but they can be sketched with a broad brush.

Our present gigantic crisis has sources in all history. And before we discuss the movement of forces in the periods named above, we will in this chapter shortly review some of the previous upheavals of modern Western civilizations. They have a bearing upon the problem as has also the early development of ideas for the preservation of peace.

The First Modern Crisis

The first of these great crises may be said to have been born in the rise of cultural, political, and religious ideas which gave impulse to the Renaissance and the Protestant Reformation and marked the emergence from the Dark Ages.

The period of gestation of these revolution-bearing ideas extended from the middle of the fifteenth to the middle of the sixteenth century. In this period, the movement of ideas and the spread of conflict was greatly stimulated by the expansion of the art of printing. The method of warfare was transformed by greater perfection in firearms. And in this time world-wide free economic enterprise found its beginnings.

In this period also can be seen the beginnings of a shift in civilization from the dominantly religious and spiritual basis prior to the Renaissance, to the dominantly materialistic basis that was to follow.

From all these enlivening ferments came the great era of world exploration which added the Western Hemisphere to European concerns, the discovery of the sea routes to the Indian Ocean via the Cape of Good Hope, and to the Pacific via Cape Horn.

Nationalism, imperialism and militarism were not idle. And wars which had been chiefly religious and dynastic in character gave way to wars for conquest.

Finally, the strains in these forces rose to the Thirty Years' War, involving every nation in Europe. One third of the population of Europe is said to have died in that war and from famine and pestilence after the Treaty of Westphalia in 1648.

The Second Modern Crisis

During the next 130 years, from the Thirty Years' War to the American Revolution, many different religious, dynastic, and imperialistic wars raged over parts of Europe. They did not, however, become universal in character. Some countries remained isolated from war in long-enough intervals for cultural ideas and economic life to make progress, stimulated by colonial expansion and overseas trade.

But in the latter part of this period—the end of the eighteenth century—a new world crisis was fermenting. Gradually, nearly 2,000 years after free Greece and early Rome, there came a resurgence of the idea of the rights of the individual man. This resurgence of the freedom of men is amply indicated at Runnymede, in the Puritan Revolution, in the Declaration of Rights, in the emigrations to America, in the work of the French Encyclopedists. But it is not our purpose to discuss its growth in detail.

Along with these dynamic ideas were again economic and nationalistic pressures, imperial and militaristic growths, and a generous seasoning of fear, hate, and revenge. The conflict and pressures of these forces finally began to explode in the American and French revolutions.

There followed forty years of wars, revolution, and disorder involving, at one time or another, all the Western World. The outstanding militaristic figure of this period was Napoleon. Peace was made at the Congress of Vienna in 1815.

The century which followed was marked by growing recognition of the rights of the individual man and the rapid expansion of representative government, by the Industrial Revolution, by vast expansion in science and invention and the arts. Within this period there were great pressures from the seven dynamic forces which, with the failures of statesmanship in attempting to allay them, led to the explosion of 1914.

Early Efforts to Preserve Peace

During all the history of man there have been strivings to find methods for preserving peace. In our discussions nowadays, we are inclined to assume that our own generation is the first to see the light and that we have brought to bear on the age-old problems of war and peace a new vision and a new intelligence. A study of the past is always a wholesome corrective for this assumption of superiority.

From time immemorial, nations have marked the end of their wars by the signature of treaties of "perpetual peace" and solemnly promised its continuance. We are, however, at this point interested not in promises, but only in methods for preserving peace. Aside from the ancient Chinese proposals of arbitration and some settlement of controversies among the early Greek states, the first workable scheme for the preservation of peace was the Pax Romana.

In giving a short account of these early movements we have not attempted exhaustive treatment. We have done no more than discuss those which made a special impression upon their times and gave some lasting impulse. There were thousands of other writings and millions of preachers of peace and good will. And always the greatest of all contributions to the building of moral and spiritual foundation of peace began with the Sermon on the Mount. These teachings of Christ have thundered down over these 1900 years.

Governmental action to preserve peace began perhaps with that first unknown treaty at the end of some now-forgotten war which bore the startling designation of a "treaty of perpetual peace."

Pax Romana

The Pax Romana is proverbial and the model of various later systems which have not always admitted the resemblance.

Its short description would be the enforcement of peace by a dominant military power, with recognition of the rights of the defeated. The analogy with some modern proposals is more than superficial.

With the triumph of the Roman Empire at the beginning of the Christian era came a period of peace which lasted for more than three centuries. That is to say, there was peace within the Empire, although there was constant fighting on its frontiers.

It was possible to keep the peace during this period because Rome alone had a high degree of military and administrative efficiency and, on the other hand, was threatened by no redoubtable neighbor. For the most part, her immediate neighbors were barbarians. These could be dealt with by the use of police forces. Parthia, the only serious rival, was far away and hardly offered a threat of invasion.

The maintenance of peace was not an end in itself. Rome was like the Britain of our day in that she was dependent on food from overseas. To keep the sea lanes open, it was necessary to suppress piracy and other naval Powers on the high seas. Under this regime of freedom of the seas, trade with India was developed in order to avoid payment of the ruinous Parthian tolls on the overland route.

The strength of the Empire within its borders was not due entirely to fear inspired by the Roman Eagles, but perhaps more by developments in the outlying regions of the Empire; local government, roads, aqueducts, the fostering and protection of agriculture, and, above all, the benefits of Roman law.

Like all methods for maintaining the peace by force, the Pax Romana came to a disastrous end. It came to an end from forces within the Empire. Military attacks from beyond the frontiers were only contributing factors. The stamina of the peoples of Italy and Greece was sapped by the spread of malaria, and the peasantry was wiped out by the growth of slavery and the development of huge landed properties. Finally, in desperation, a sort of "managed economy" was introduced by Diocletian. The growth of centralized power and dependence on the

Legions for order and protection left no fund of local strength or of public spirit for defense upon which to fall back.

Hitler's "New Order" is often compared to the Pax Romana, but there is an essential difference. The Pax Romana was established as the only alternative to barbarian violence and chaos, from which it emerged. Hitler has imposed and substituted his system by force after destroying an established regime of law and order.

Role of the Papacy

In a brief study of this sort we cannot hope even to outline the important role of the Papacy in the struggle for peace. A separate volume could be profitably devoted to this phase of the Church's activities during nearly two thousand years.

In an age of unbridled cruelty the Church took the first steps toward regulation and restraint of warfare. A notable instance of this was the "Peace of God"—a tenth-century attempt to do away with private warfare. This was an early effort to compel those accustomed to bear arms to agree not to use them and to submit their conflicts to the judgment of tribunals. These judgments were sanctioned by spiritual penalties. The scheme was not successful partly because the nobles were unwilling to forego the use of arms or to accept the decisions of the tribunals. The Peace of God was later (in the eleventh century) supplemented by the Truce of God, designed to regulate what could not be suppressed. It prescribed that there should be no private warfare during certain seasons and on certain days. The seasons included the time from Advent to Epiphany and from Septuagesima to one week after Pentecost. Throughout the rest of the year hostilities were forbidden from sunset on Wednesday until Monday morning and on all saints' days. By the end of the eleventh century private warfare was forbidden on all but some eighty days in the year. Sometimes the national sovereign supported the decrees of the Church, which thus became law of the land.

During many centuries the temporal sovereigns recognized the primacy of the Pope, not only in spiritual matters, but also in matters of government, war, and peace as well. Throughout this period the Church exercised a powerful restraining influence rendered doubly necessary by the standards of the times. Some of the solutions were of a character that could be imposed by a clearly recognized authority, as when Pope Alexander VI drew a line on the map and divided the overseas world between the great colonizing powers, Spain and Portugal. The penalties were of a spiritual character, culminating in the dread sanction of excommunication.

The influence of the Church was effective in averting warfare and contributed materially to the growth of higher standards of international conduct.

The Protestant Reformation brought a cleavage in authority, but in spite of this the voice of successive Popes has been raised in the cause of peace. The loss of temporal power in no sense lessened the moral authority of the Papacy, and the pronouncements of the present Pontiff command the respect of Catholic and non-Catholic alike.

The Protestant churches have been no less vigorous in teaching the moral foundations of peace. In our own time the organizations of Protestant churches have devoted systematic effort to this subject and have made a precious contribution to stimulating thought and awakening our people to the need for grappling with the problems of peace.

The Development of Peace Plans

From the Middle Ages down to the second great crisis, culminating in the explosions of the American and French revolutions, there was a wealth of plans for averting war and keeping the peace. Allowing for the differing conditions, they are strikingly like the plans of our own day. There are plans for a League of Nations. There are plans for federations. We find supergovernment and an international force to impose its rulings, collective security, mutual assistance, sanctions against an aggressor—even the radical idea of applying undiluted Christian morality to international affairs.

The Proposals of Gerohus

Gerohus of Regensburg, about the time of the Third Crusade (1190), advanced a plan for abolishing war. Gerohus saw the problem in simple terms. In his view, it would suffice for the Pope to forbid all war—an early version of the outlawry of war. He proposed that once this was done, all conflicts between princes should be referred to Rome for decision—here we have compulsory arbitration. And finally, any prince

rejecting the arbitral award should be excommunicated and deposed—
sanctions with a vengeance.

The Plan of Pierre Dubois

A plan for a League of Nations appeared in the fourteenth century.
In a document entitled *On the Recovery of the Holy Land,* Pierre
Dubois of Normandy, an adviser of Philip the Fair, advocated a federation of Christian sovereign states. There was to be a Council of the
Nations to arbitrate all quarrels. There was a catch in this scheme,
however, as in many later ones, in that it was prescribed that France
should be dominant in Europe and that the Council of the Nations
should concentrate its efforts on subjugation of the infidel.

The Proposals of Dante

Even Dante, in his *De Monarchia,* tried his hand at designing a brave
new world. He was primarily concerned with arguing the case for the
Emperor against the Pope. The Empire had existed, he said, before the
Church, and as Aeneas was the ancestor of the Romans, they were of a
superior race and thus qualified to govern lesser breeds. Already, in the
fourteenth century, Dante had his version of Aryan superiority.

In discussing controversial matters in his dangerous times, it was
prudent to seek safety in allegory, and Dante's argument is sometimes
cryptic in the extreme. But he did put forward the idea that human
happiness must come from the reign of law. He did not advocate the
supremacy of one state over another, but the supremacy of law over
all, so that national passions might be held in check—in other words,
international law for arbitration of disputes. There would be a supreme
power under "the ideal prince" to give needed guidance. He desired
that Italy should be "an angel of light among the nations," but he did
not desire her to be dominant.

Rather, she was to become a member of a world state guided by a
Supreme Court of Justice.

The Great Design of Henry of Navarre

Henry of Navarre (1553–1610) and his adviser, the Duc de Sully,
produced a more specific and detailed plan, the Great Design.

According to Sully the plan seems to have arisen from Henry's conviction that the humiliation of the House of Austria was essential to his own safety. But after this was achieved it was desirable to set up a regime in Europe that would keep the peace.

Austria having been destroyed, Europe was to be redivided among fifteen Powers in such equal portions as would prevent any future uneven balance of power—a drastic and original method.

Having redrawn the frontiers of Europe, Henry set up—on paper— his League of Nations. The fifteen Powers were to be represented in a Great Council, whose members would be subject to re-election every three years. The expenses of the Council were to be paid by proportional contributions from the member states. It would be the duty of the Great Council to settle disputes of all sorts among the states and to deal with current affairs.

Thus far, Henry kept closely to the lines of the future League of Nations. But he further proposed an international army and navy to enforce the decisions of the Great Council.

While the Great Design was to do away with war among the fifteen member states, yet it was not so radical as to forbid aggression against outsiders. Territories conquered in this way would be formed into new kingdoms, which would be given to princes put out of work by the reorganization of Europe—and these new kingdoms would be admitted to the Christian Republic.

It was prescribed that the Council should adopt "to the contentment of all parties" such laws as were calculated to cement the union of all states and to maintain order, freedom of trade, etc. And it was prescribed that the Council should undertake reforms which would from time to time be necessary. This was a wise and farsighted regulation by which Henry of Navarre proposed the peaceful revision of treaties.

Henry's plan was never put into operation, although Sully tells us it was on the eve of being tried "when it pleased God to call him too soon for the happiness of the world." But it has been a mine of precedent and ideas for every subsequent plan for international government. It is the first balanced plan of federal partnership among sovereign states, with machinery for the peaceful settlement of international disputes and an international force to apply sanctions.

The Proposals of Emeric Crucé

Emeric Crucé produced his *Nouveau Cynée* some twenty years after the Grand Design of Henry of Navarre. He went further in two particulars. He advocated that membership in the League of States should be open to non-Christian as well as Christian states—which thus opened the door to world federation. He further proposed that war should be done away with by the adoption of a comprehensive system of arbitration.

The Plan of William Penn

William Penn advanced in his *Essay towards the Present and Future Peace of Europe* (1693) a scheme for the future organizing of the world which he hoped would create tremendous benefits. By stopping war, he hoped to avoid bloodshed, save money, strengthen Christianity's reputation, increase trade and commerce—and make it possible for princes to marry for love, not power. A permanent International Tribunal was to be set up by the sovereigns of Europe, consisting of ninety representatives, chosen by a system of proportional representation, meeting every year to discuss and settle all international differences not settled by diplomatic means. Decisions were to be made by ballot, with a minimum majority of three quarters of the votes. Business was to be done in Latin or French, records to be circulated to each sovereign.

There is a general impression that Penn avoided the question of the use of force to compel a state to abide by an arbitral award. It is assumed that it would have run counter to his faith to provide sanctions. As a matter of fact, he recognized the need for sanctions in clearly providing for common action against an offender in the following terms:

If any of the sovereignties that constitute these imperial states shall refuse to submit their claim or pretensions to them, or to abide or perform the judgment thereof, and seek remedy by arms, or delay their compliance beyond the time prefixed in their resolutions, all the other sovereignties, united as one strength, shall compel the submission and performance of the sentence, with damages to the suffering party, and charges to the sovereignties that obliged their submission.

In other words, he prescribed common action involving the use of sanctions of more violent order than those of the League of Nations.

The Plan of Saint-Pierre

Charles Irénée Castel, Abbé in Saint-Pierre's *Project for Settling Perpetual Peace in Europe* (1713) was prompted by the sordid bargaining that went on at the peace negotiations at Utrecht at the end of the War of the Spanish Succession. It shows the inspiration of Henry of Navarre.

Saint-Pierre proposed: a League of Sovereign States in a permanent Congress of Representatives; a code of Articles of Commerce; arbitration of disputes by a permanent Senate; combined military sanctions against a rebellious state; reduction of peacetime armies in all states to 6,000 men; weights, measures, and coinage to be standardized throughout Europe; creation of a similar self-contained Asiatic League.

The Plan of Jean Jacques Rousseau

Jean Jacques Rousseau's *Judgment on a Plan for Perpetual Peace* (1761) sought to improve on Saint-Pierre's plan by guaranteeing the existing *status quo* and rendering it subject to modification by arbitration only. He provided for the drafting of a Code of International Law and its amendment by unanimous vote of the Diet or Congress of Representatives.

Perhaps the most serious defect in his plan was the principle that sovereigns should be guaranteed against rebellions among their subjects—a cornerstone of the Holy Alliance in 1815.

The Plan of Jeremy Bentham

Jeremy Bentham, in *Fragment of an Essay on International Law* (1786–89), devised a plan to avert future wars comprising four fundamentals: reduction of armaments; "Permanent Court of Judicature" with powers of arbitration backed by sanctions of force; codification of international law; emancipation of all colonies.

The Plan of Immanuel Kant

Kant's *Zum Ewigen Frieden* (*Perpetual Peace*) (1795) contained an examination of reforms to be undertaken while war still existed, in order to create a public opinion favorable to the abolition of war, and suggestions for final organization of perpetual peace.

He contended that man was by nature selfish and base, but that mankind had risen to a high state of civilization through competition and mutual antagonisms of individuals in society, which had not only produced social chaos, but had also brought out all man's latent powers until the chaos had been resolved by the formation of the state. He foreshadowed an analogous development among states themselves, culminating in a "federation of free republics," meaning by "republic" any form of government embodying the liberty and equality of its subjects. Federation would involve surrender of a portion of power in return for participation in a wider, richer, more abundant life.

His practical measures concentrated on non-intervention in wars of other nations and the gradual abolition of standing armies. He made no detailed provisions for an international tribunal.

Kant's enduring contribution to the problem was that he lifted the discussion of war and peace above the level of politics and exalted it into a question of ethics and social conscience.

In the period before the American and French revolutions, there were other plans and proposals for maintaining peace. But these references will at least indicate the antiquity of peace yearnings.

This survey of these early methods of preserving peace shows that they are, dominantly, to keep it by military force. Such were the Pax Romana, the Great Design of Henry of Navarre, and some parts of the less belligerent plans. But in this early period there arose also some proposals for preserving peace by moral force, reason, good will, and international co-operation. Such were early agreements between cities, and much of the proposals of Gerohus, of Pierre Dubois, Dante, Emeric Cruce, William Penn, Saint-Pierre, J. J. Rousseau, Jeremy Bentham, and Immanuel Kant.

III MOVEMENT OF THE SEVEN DYNAMIC FORCES IN THE 140 YEARS BEFORE 1914

WE are not here concerned with military campaigns or battles. Therefore, we do not delay our readers with an account of the forty years of world-wide wars beginning with the American Revolution and ending with the defeat of Napoleon and the treaty of peace at the Congress of Vienna in 1815. Our concern is to follow as far as may be essential the movement of the seven dynamic forces over the 140 years up to the explosion of 1914. For, as we have said, it is from analysis of these forces and the manner in which statesmen dealt with them that we can gain both negative and positive experience in making and in preserving peace. We shall first briefly describe the movement of the pressures of ideologies; economic pressures; nationalism; imperialism; militarism; fear and its satellites, hate and revenge; together with the will to peace during this period and then will sum up their relation to the world explosion in 1914.

The Ideological Forces [1]

Early in this period of 140 years ending in 1914 emerged the world-wide conflict of two fundamental and irreconcilable ideologies. On the one hand was the ideology of personal liberty [2] and representative government—and on the other, advocacy of various degrees of subjection or enslavement of the individual, whether by actual slavery, serfdom, or oppression by class, monarch, or state. Neither ideology is capable

---

[1] For outline of these forces, see p. 159.

[2] We have generally adopted the expression "personal liberty" and "representative government" or "free nations" rather than the terms "Liberalism" or "democracy." These latter terms have come to be used for many purposes far from their original meanings and have often been adopted by advocates of other systems.

of precise definition, but it is necessary to introduce some definition in order to follow the conflict and its relation to war and peace.

The definition of personal liberty varies from time to time and from race to race, for it is modified by the whole racial history of peoples. But there are two essential common denominators.

The first common denominator is the concept of the dignity of man and his personal rights. And, included in this concept, is that these rights are an endowment by the Creator and are inalienable by the state or any other domination. This concept came from two urges. One was from the demand of men for intellectual and spiritual freedom— free speech and free worship; the second, equally potent, was the demand of men for an economic freedom in which they might choose their own callings, bargain for their own labor, and reap and hold the rewards from their own enterprise and efforts.

The second common denominator is the political foundation of government upon laws made by the peoples' freely chosen representatives and not by any arbitrary power.

This ideology of personal liberty based its faith of progress in spiritual, intellectual, and economic life upon the sum of individual accomplishment, not of governmental action.

The formulation of the American representative government was greatly influenced by the insistence of Locke, Montesquieu, and Rousseau that sovereign power must rest in the people, that they could delegate these powers to their representatives in legislative bodies, that legislative bodies could in turn entrust administration to executive officers, but that these executive officers are trustees who must not dictate policies or improperly influence the people's representatives, or that again would be autocratic government, dissolving the Social Contract.

While the functioning of representative government requires rule by the majority, yet it is not tyranny by the majority, as is so often stated. The primary foundation of representative government lies in the inalienable rights of the individual. And protest at the invasions of those rights swiftly turns the minority into a majority.

These protective ideas were even further reinforced by the Founding Fathers in America through the genius of their separation of judicial, legislative and executive powers and their Bill of Rights.

The ideology of subjection of the individual is even more difficult to define, for it has had a score of shapes and has changed them with the times. Its mildest common denominator is the idea that the purposes of the state take precedence over all personal liberties. Its more oppressive forms embrace all degrees of slavery, serfdom, or peonage. And this subjection of individual freedom is expressed in political organization not only based upon the Divine Right of Kings or dictators, but also by class government, whether military, aristocratic, landowning, ecclesiastic, or labor, or by a single political party.

No one can doubt the challenge of liberty to all peoples during the 140 years prior to the first World War. The success of the United States stimulated and inspired the entire world with the principles of representative government and inalienable rights. The forms of representative government spread over the whole Western Hemisphere. Britain, France, the Scandinavian states, the Low Countries, Switzerland, and Italy successfully developed it. Germany and Austria had made concessions to it. The ferment was active even in Russia, and the Czar had been compelled to yield to a Duma sporadic checks on arbitrary power. Japan and China were moving into this current. It rumbled in India, in Egypt and Turkey, and among the tribal Negroes of South Africa. Class government and aristocratic privilege were weakening everywhere.

Some degree of economic freedom long preceded the spread of spiritual and intellectual freedom and, indeed, was one of the greatest impulses to them. With increased production and wealth came the rise of the middle class, and this class was ceaselessly pushing for more intellectual and spiritual freedom and more political liberty.

The penetration of the concept of personal liberty over that period can also be measured in other terms. Slavery first fell into disrepute and then practically disappeared on the earth. Serfdom and peonage lived on only in a few still backward areas. Religious and intellectual freedom made wide progress even in the more reactionary nations.

Nevertheless, the old concepts held in central and eastern Europe and in Asia but were modified by time, and, finally, in the period we are discussing, prior to the first World War, for the most part simmered down to the subjection of the individual to class. Class government expressed itself in various forms: aristocratic, militaristic, or landowning.

Even in some liberal states, the catechism still carries the admonition to be content in the station in life to which it has pleased God to call us.

Individual liberty itself was modified by the Industrial Revolution from extreme *laissez faire* to a degree of intervention of the state to prevent economic abuse. That we shall discuss later. It can be said generally that in the clash between these two ideologies there was constant swing in the center of gravity between the authority of the state and the "inalienable" rights of the individual.

The important thing in great ideological changes is the direction in which they are moving. Certainly, personal liberty and representative government were moving forward over the whole world in this period prior to 1914.

We discuss the contribution of the systems of personal liberty and representative government to lasting peace later on. But here it may be said that this philosophic basis of life can flourish only in peace. The price of war to democracy is immediate surrender of personal freedom, with grave uncertainties as to its recovery after war. One purpose of this form of life is economic prosperity, and the consequence of war is its antithesis, impoverishment. Its foundation is the family, and the consequence of war is the sacrifice of its sons and brothers. From instinctive caution against these sacrifices there is inherent in representative government the live opposition to war. And in representative government there is opportunity for opposition and thus for placing a brake upon warmakers.

The alarm of the other concepts and this rising tide of liberalism had no little part in the forces which led to the explosion of 1914.

Economic Forces [3]

The most important economic pressure bearing on peace and war during this period was the Industrial Revolution. Early in the century, the mercantile system had begun to yield to wider freedom of enterprise—from the combined pressures of the ideals of freedom, the invention of the steam engine, and from the philosophies of Adam Smith and his contemporaries.

[3] For outline of these forces, see p. 159.

Yet the revolutions which won the freedom of men had formulated their governmental framework to protect personal and political liberty. These governments were instituted in a climate of comparatively simple economic life. But from the very freedoms of mind and economic life which they provided came a second revolution. Out of free minds sprang a great flowering of scientific research and widening of knowledge of fundamental laws of nature. With the impulses of economic freedom, these discoveries and inventions were turned into huge tools of production, transportation, and communication. And with them came gigantic aggregations of capital and finance—the rise of modern capitalism. From these developments of technology and of mechanical power came a vast increase in the productivity of man, an unparalleled rise in the standard of living and comfort among all civilized races. And in turn, from these resources came an expansion of the humanities. Art and music were made accessible to all; literature flourished; science developed rapidly; education was widespread; public health was studied and improved; and there were a thousand lesser manifestations of this trend. This progress and the constantly wider spread of intellectual, spiritual, and political freedom filled the hearts of men with hope and confidence. Men moved almost everywhere over the earth without fear or passports. Indeed, the last quarter of a century before the first World War may have been the golden age of good living. Certainly, despite the turn toward materialism, it was an age of confidence and hope.

In the light of experience of the past thirty years, however, we can see more clearly certain forces and clashes rising in the economic system that were to contribute to the great explosion of 1914. They were in the making before and in the golden age itself.

With the Industrial Revolution, civilization did turn dominantly to the materialistic side. The predominantly religious and spiritual character of the previous period greatly weakened.

The economic machine became infinitely more complicated and delicately balanced. International transportation and communications, finance, and trade brought enormous interchange and dependency among nations. A disruption anywhere in the world brought repercussions in stagnated markets and shocks in the flow of credit and capital, and finally, widespread unemployment.

Out of the economic system so intensified by the Machine Age grew a sort of rhythm of production and consumption, partly affected by credit movements and speculation, all of which brought periodic booms and slumps. In the boom, greed, speculation, and waste were rampant; and in the slump, the worker took the brunt in unemployment and misery, the farmer in inability to sell his products so vitally needed by the worker.

As we have said, the Industrial Revolution was superimposed upon the earlier revolution of political and personal liberty and its simpler economic frame. The two revolutions developed into sharp clashes over personal liberty. Out of the Machine Age grew forms of organization outside government which at times dominated the freedom of men. Pressure groups of labor, farmers, and business sprang up which interfered with government for their own selfish interest. The units of big business and big production and the groupings of finance around them penetrated into and dominated government. They were unfair in their treatment of and sharing with labor. Huge concentrations of finance and credit which were necessary to finance the advantageously huge industrial units brought their own train of evils. The control of finance and credit came to dominate free industry instead of merely serving as its lubricant. And the making of profit from sheer financial manipulation instead of production of commodities rose to a point of shrieking evil equally in the financial markets of London, Berlin, Paris, Petrograd, New York, Chicago, and a hundred lesser centers. Trade-union organization, a very necessary resistance by the workers to the domination of their lives and livelihoods by huge industrial units, in itself established dominations over freedom of men and made for inflexibilities and waste in the economic system.

Before the World War of 1914, the American people were slowly awakening to the necessity to correct these abuses and to become masters in their own house. That sort of *laissez faire* which struck at the freedom of men was not part of true liberty. However, abuses were being slowly corrected through regulation by specific law. Credit was being organized to modify the swing of the economic cycle. The growth of ethical concepts within most economic groupings was maturing. But before these problems could be solved, the first World War threw terrific shocks into these delicate balances of world economy and the movements of reform.

These weaknesses and clashes in the economic system had less consequence in producing the first World War than in the degeneration which followed it. But other economic pressures had very direct effect in bringing on the war of 1914. They came from the pressures of intensified populations in manufacturing countries for elbow room and markets. This contributed in turn to vast increases of armament and military rivalry. Especially in Britain, Germany, Italy, and Japan, industrialization made the people dependent upon imports for food and raw materials. The consequence was an enormous growth and rivalry in navies with which to safeguard the flow of supplies. This dependence upon imports and exports and the desire for elbow room greatly stimulated imperialism in the direction of control of colonial areas so as to secure independent sources of supplies and outlets for population. It stimulated economic and intellectual penetration into countries politically independent while possessed of sources of supplies and materials in an effort to keep them friendly and co-operative. Thus, it intensified the drive of power politics into every corner of the world.

The Beginnings of Ideologies Hostile to Personal Liberty and Representative Government. Into this scene, while representative government was freeing the world from the overhang of medieval reactionary ideas of absolutism, militarist dictatorship, and domination of the state or class, a new shape of hostile ideology was to come into being. Karl Marx's *Das Kapital* had its immediate practical impulse from the Industrial Revolution and its theoretical basis in Hegel's philosophic glorification of the state. The ideology was not new in history, indeed it was very old, but it was largely formalized by Marx and his followers. And in furtherance of it, we witnessed the birth of a blood brother, Communism. The major distinction between the Socialists and the Communists was that Socialism was to be applied by parliamentary action, whereas Communism was to be applied by revolution and "dictatorship of the proletariat."

They both gave a beautiful blueprint of Utopia to the masses suffering from the hard masters of European industrialism and the pull and haul of the economic system. And inherent in these ideas was again the subjection of the individual to the state—again the apparition of the Middle Ages. These systems were basically more materialistic than the systems of liberty, because their whole thesis was to make a god of economic equality and to lessen intellectual and spiritual liberty. Socialism and Communism were to guarantee security without risk and all human blessings without that striving which the Lord laid upon Adam.

In the rapid growth of wealth and comfort, the condition of the worker did not sink as Marx prophesied. It rose. However, these ideas secured a hold on limited groups of theoretical intellectuals throughout the world, and the influence of their preachings did confuse liberal thought and add to the difficulties of representative government striving to solve the clashes within its own house. They, in some places, infected liberty by introducing government into the operation of and dictation to economic life, instead of regulating abuses by law. And thus freedom began the surrender to the state.

Nationalism [4]

After the first World War, these ideologies were to take a high place in disruption of the world and to play a huge part in deepening this crisis of civilization.

The 140 years prior to 1914 mark the period of greatest growth of nationalistic spirit in all history. The Renaissance, the Reformation, the growth of liberty and economic progress all contributed to a revival in racial interests and a yearning for self-government. And that desire was well stimulated by the hard heel of oppression.

In the Western Hemisphere during this 140 years, independence came to the United States, Argentina, Brazil, Uruguay, Paraguay, Bolivia, Peru, Chile, Ecuador, Colombia, Venezuela, Costa Rica, Panama, Nicaragua, Honduras, Guatemala, Haiti, Santo Domingo, El Salvador, Cuba, and Mexico. In the Eastern Hemisphere, Belgium, Greece, Rumania, Bulgaria, Serbia, and Montenegro gained their independence. Other races rebelled and failed. Such was the fate of Poland, Finland, and Hungary. Later, it is true, Hungary was joined to Austria by a personal union and, in some respects, was the dominant partner in the Dual Empire. Altogether, some twenty-seven new nations emerged in this period, prior to 1914. Germany and Italy achieved

[4] For outline of this force, see p. 160.

national unity. Almost all of these changes were the result of wars, and the very privations of the struggle solidified the nationalist spirit of the liberated countries.

Of the more capable submerged races, the Irish, the Finns, the Estonians, the Latvians, the Lithuanians, the Poles, the Czechs, the Slovaks the Slovenes, the Croats, the Dalmatians, the Georgians, the Azerbaijanese, the Armenians, the Arabs, the Egyptians and the peoples of India and Malaysia were still subject to foreign rule. And in some cases, their oppression not only took the form of exploitation, but also bitter restriction of racial cultures. In the desire of the conquerors of many of them to break down rising nationalism among them, their native language, literature, education, and all national manifestations were suppressed with a heavy hand. These very oppressions hardened them not only for physical rebellion, but for intellectual resistance.

And the racial yearnings for independence produced action upon still another stage. Over Europe there were many areas where the races were mixed—the "irredentas." Fragments of the French, the Poles, and the Danes were under Germany; Greeks under Turkey and Bulgaria; Serbians and Rumanians under Austria-Hungary; and so on. Any boundaries athwart the areas of mixed population leave great masses of people separated from their homelands. The dominating governments on both sides of such boundaries invariably endeavor to minimize or extinguish these alien cultures and institutions and to absorb them into the dominant race. Their homelands are stirred in sympathy and hate.

These were all areas of ferment for freedom. And these racial frictions extended even further. There were racial groupings, such as the Slavs, for whom Russia professed a guardianship as far afield as the Adriatic. Germany professed to take foreign groups of Germanic origins under her protection.

Within the pressures of these nationalistic forces and their strivings were huge stores of powder ready for the great explosion of 1914.

Imperialism [5]

The movement of imperialism in the 140 years prior to the World War of 1914 and the clashes it produced were to bring portentous con-

[5] For outline of this force, see p. 163.

sequences in war and peace. Within it were the old urges to power, glory, and exploitation of other races. But the Industrial Revolution added still further urges. Modern education, periodicals, movies, quicker modes of travel and communication, closer contact with neighbors all stimulated knowledge of higher standards of living elsewhere. The Industrial Revolution immensely stimulated the growth of populations, created an urge for more elbow room. As we have said, it brought great pressures for outlets of surplus goods and an assurance of overseas supplies of raw materials. Surplus capital sought areas to develop.

All these hopes and purposes were advanced by expansion in conquest of colonies or the occupation of backward races and vacant spaces.

The imperial movement in these 140 years was the greatest of all history. Beyond the coastal settlements in North America, Australasia, and Africa there were either open spaces or lands held by backward races waiting to be occupied and divided. India, the East Indies, and parts of China were open to be taken by conquest.

Under the varied pressures of rivalry, weakness, and expansive energy, vast empires were to rise and fall. The part this development of empire played in war and peace and its continuing pressure can be indicated from a short review of these imperial growths and decays.

Within this period, the Spanish Empire almost disappeared. At the beginning, it embraced all of South America with the exception of Brazil; all Central America, Mexico, Texas, and a great sweep of territory westward to include California; and Florida to the east. It included Cuba, Puerto Rico, Guam, and the Philippines—a vast empire of well over six million square miles. At the end of this period, Spain held but a scrap of a great empire. Her incapacity in colonial government, her hard exploitation of the people, and rising demand for liberty cost her all her holdings in North, Central, and South America by revolutions for independence. The United States took Florida from her by annexation in 1819; Cuba, Puerto Rico, Guam' and the Philippines by war in 1898. There remained to her only the minor appendages of Spanish Morocco, Rio de Oro and Fernando Po, Cape Juby, and Spanish Guinea. Territorially, the greatest empire in history had gone out of business.

The Portuguese Empire, which had once shared the world with Spain under a ruling from the Pope, began this period with vast possessions, including the Azores, Portuguese East and West Africa, Brazil, and various holdings in the Far East. During these years it saw the shrinkage of these holdings, and in 1822 Brazil set up its independent existence. At the end of the period, however, Portugal still remained an empire of 838,000 square miles, with 14,500,000 people, including the important territories of Angola and Mozambique and various small outposts in India, China, and Malaya.

The Dutch had long rivaled the English as a sea power. But in this period they lost Penang, Singapore, Malacca, Ceylon, Cape Colony, and part of Borneo to the British. They, however, even as the weaker sea power, managed to keep a very considerable empire, including the Netherlands Indies, composed of Java, Sumatra, Celebes, part of Borneo, and a host of islands, as well as Dutch Guiana and Curaçao in the Western Hemisphere. Altogether, the Dutch Empire in 1914 comprised some 800,000 square miles, with 41,000,000 people.

Belgium was a late-comer in the imperial class when, in 1885, she set up the Congo Free State, an important territory of over 900,000 square miles, giving her a total population of 17,000,000 people.

Italy, during the early part of this period, was engaged in the process of national unification of the Italian states. She ventured into overseas imperialism by an attempted expansion in Abyssinia, which failed (1885–89), and the conquest of Eritrea, Tripoli, and Italian Somaliland, which succeeded.

During this period, Russia was in steady growth. She gained what were later called Estonia, Latvia, Lithuania, Finland, and a large part of Poland, the Crimea, the Caucasus, and Bessarabia by conquest. She expanded across Siberia to the Pacific. In the relatively short period from 1850 to 1914, Russia, despite some losses to Japan, had acquired an area of 3,250,000 square miles, and in 1914 governed 170,000,000 people.

Turkey began the period as a large, if unwieldy and loosely knit empire holding Rumania, Bulgaria, Serbia, Montenegro, Albania, Macedonia, Arabia, Egypt, Armenia, Greece, Crete, Smyrna, Cyprus, Syria, Palestine, Mesopotamia, Algeria, and Tunisia. She lost Algeria and Tunisia to the French; Tripoli to the Italians; and Egypt to the British. Revolutions for independence cost her Rumania, Serbia,

Montenegro, Bulgaria, and Greece. In spite of all these losses, Turkey arrived at the first World War as a considerable imperial power, holding Syria, Smyrna and Arabia, Palestine, and part of Armenia.

Japan was one of the last Powers to begin an imperial career. She seized Korea. She won Dairen and half of Sakhalin from the Russians and parts of Manchuria, Shantung, Formosa, and the Pescadores from China. In 1914 her imperialism was burning brightly.

The French Empire underwent many changes. Shortly before this period began, France lost to Great Britain almost the whole of her great colonial empire in North America as well as in the West Indies and India. During this period, she sold the Louisiana Territory to the United States. These losses were partly compensated by the successive acquisition of Algeria, French Equatorial Africa, Cochin China, Cambodia, Annam, Dahomey, Tunis, Tonkin, Madagascar, and many lesser possessions. She ended the period with 4,000,000 square miles of colonial territory.

The Austro-Hungarian Empire emerged from the Napoleonic Wars with Austria, Hungary, Bohemia, Slovakia, Galicia, Croatia, Slovenia, Transylvania, Dalmatia, and broad stretches of Italian territory. It lost the Italian provinces in the unification of Italy but managed to hold the rest and later annexed Bosnia and Herzegovina. Austria did not endeavor to become an overseas empire.

Germany confined her imperialistic energies to the continent of Europe in the earlier part of the period. She united all the chief German areas except Austria and the Sudetenland. She obtained part of Poland, Alsace-Lorraine, and a bit of Denmark by various wars. In 1884, she annexed German East Africa and German Southwest Africa; also Togoland, the Cameroons, and German New Guinea. Kiaochow was taken by Germany from the Chinese in 1898. In 1914, German imperialism was clearly on the march.

Great Britain shows the greatest of all imperial expansions in this period of 140 years prior to the World War of 1914. Before that time she possessed, aside from the rebellious American colonies, the greater part of Canada and most of her West Indies possessions. She held a minor part of India. By successive conquests she acquired Ceylon, Hong Kong, Natal, Cape Colony, part of Borneo, the Straits Settlements, the Falkland islands, the Transvaal, Orange Free State, Trinidad, Egypt, the Sudan, Ashanti, Burma, and the Shan States. She occupied Australasia, British West Africa, Nigeria, Somaliland, Rhodesia, Uganda, Nyasaland. She expanded over western Canada, almost the whole of India, and the Malay States. She acquired numbers of islands and military bases. At the end of the period she occupied about 12,000,000 square miles with a population of 475,000,000. And she had demonstrated the greatest capacity for colonial administration in history.

Our own American territorial growth should not be overlooked. By the Louisiana Purchase we acquired the vast Midwest and part of the Mountain States, extending from Canada to the Gulf of Mexico. We seized Florida, Puerto Rico, Guam, and the Philippine Islands from Spain, and New Mexico, Arizona, Nevada, and California from Mexico. Texas was admitted to the Union. We expanded over Oregon and Washington and some Pacific islands. We purchased Alaska, and Hawaii joined us voluntarily.

American expansion overseas, as events have shown, can hardly be called imperialism. We took Cuba and gave it independence. Far from exploiting the Philippines, we poured money into them for more than forty years. We brought up successive generations on the Declaration of Independence, "Give me liberty or give me death," and the rights of the individual. The inevitable result was the demand for independence, to which we agreed. And now we have seen Filipino troops fighting side by side with our own.

Thus we see that in this period Spain decayed as an imperial Power; Portugal and Turkey lost ground; the Netherlands, Russia, France, Germany, Japan, Britain, and the United States expanded in varying degrees.

There is no doubt that imperialism was a gigantic force in world affairs during this period. Its frictions and pressures nowhere made for peace. And these pressures of imperialism had much to do with the explosion of 1914.

Militarism [6]

As stated in defining the force of militarism, we are here considering only the spirit of military organization as a force in itself. The neces-

[6] For outline of this force, see p. 161.

sity of organization for defense in a world swarming with aggressive races needs no justification. But it must not be overlooked that even such defense organization often develops a military caste whose sole life outlet is war. In order to reduce this danger, the representative governments have always insisted upon the subjection of the military to the civilian arm of the government and its exclusion from policy making. But not so under non-representative forms of government.

In the period under discussion, two profound examples of militarism developed, the one in France, the other in Germany. There can be no doubt of the sheer militarism in Napoleon. His very phrases burst with war and the glory of war. Militarism developed in the German race partly as the repercussion of repeated French invasions and was successfully organized under Frederick the Great. He was the warlord as well as the head of the state. And his successors perpetuated this idea. There also arose a group of German philosophers who extolled military service as a foundation of moral development and iron discipline as a part of "culture." They eulogized military action as the highest expression of race.

None of this was new in history. Sparta had brought ruin upon liberal Greece by just such philosophy and organization.

Europe became a network of military alliances glaring at one another. The Triple Alliance of Germany, Austria, and Italy was constantly rattling its swords. Counter to them grew up an alliance between Russia and France with British support. And the Balkans allied and counter-allied themselves under inspirations from the greater alliances. During the century after the demobilization following the Congress of Vienna in 1814, the armies and navies of the world increased far more rapidly than the growth of population.

The greatest growth of military establishments took place in Germany, Russia, Austria, and France. Japan was at this time somewhat less aggressive, although here the military held authority equal to the civil authority, on which they gradually encroached.

The chips on all these shoulder-straps and the stupid, arrogant, and aggressive minds that flaunted them gave warning that powder trains were being laid for the gigantic explosion of 1914.

Hate, Fear, and Revenge [7]

Hate and its kinsman, fear and revenge, were not inactive forces in international life during these 140 years. Our own feeling of hostility for the British, born with the Revolution, stimulated by the War of 1812, did not fade until after the Spanish-American War. After that it lingered on in suspicion and constantly kept alive our naval building.

A combined hate-fear-and-revenge complex against Germany dominated all French policies after the humiliation of the Franco-Prussian War of 1870 and the seizure of Alsace-Lorraine. These emotions bred the alliance with Russia and the entente with Britain. Frequent wars between France and Britain over 300 years had built a hate that only faded because of the common menace of Germany.

Russia generated a profound dislike of Austria for her designs upon the Slav races, for which Russia considered herself the protector.

Italian hate and fear of France, because of her intrigues to prevent unification of Italy and the thwarting of Italian African colonial ambitions, kept Italy's suspicions aflame and eventually threw her into military alliance with Germany and Austria.

The Germans generated a hate for Britain and British supremacy in empire and trade which gave birth to the expression "der Tag." Germany and Austria entered into military alliance largely out of fear of Russia.

The very rise and decay of the great empires produced constant hates and suspicions.

There were lesser hates: Hungary against Rumania; Greece against Serbia; Greece, Bulgaria, and Rumania against Turkey; the Poles against Germans, Russians, and Austrians. Generally, there were hates toward their oppressors in all the submerged states and racial minorities. And we were to see in this period the growth of another great fear—the fear of interruption of overseas food supplies and raw materials and markets among the industrial nations—and this fear found rest only in expanding the rival navies.

All these emotions profoundly affected international relations and were ready to explode with any lighted match.

[7] For outline of these forces, see p. 164.

IV MOVEMENT OF THE SEVEN DYNAMIC FORCES IN THE 140 YEARS BEFORE 1914 (*Continued*)

THE WILL TO PEACE[1]

THE will to peace found great development in the century from the Congress of Vienna to 1914. But the efforts at definite organization to preserve peace present a tangled skein of gradually evolving concepts. And again they could be classified, on one hand, into those based on military force, and those relying upon pacific means of law, morals, and reason.

Among the developments of a more positive order during this period, aside from the balance of power, were the Holy Alliance and the Quadruple Alliance of 1815, the Monroe Doctrine of 1823, the Hague Conferences, the broader concept of the Concert of Europe, and various military alliances. With the spread of personal liberty and representative government, there followed a fruitful period in the development of international law, of international co-operation, and the creation of methods of settling controversy by peaceful means.

The Holy Alliance

The Congress of Vienna met in 1814 to put an end to the forty years of world wars bred by the ideas emerging from the American and French revolutions. Its general principle was the restoration, so far as possible, of the situation prior to those wars. The general philosophy was the *status quo ante* and Talleyrand's Legitimist Restoration—that is, the Divine Right of legitimate emperors and kings. The concepts of liberty, with their principles of the right of self-determination of na-

[1] For outline of this force, see p. 165.

tions and of rights of nationalism to all peoples, were hotly repudiated. Metternich believed peace could best be maintained by "the vigilant benevolence of the allied sovereigns."

History stated in the usual terms of military victory and defeat is often entirely misleading. The Congress of Vienna marked a decisive Allied victory over revolutionary France, and this victory was intended to set the clock back and restore conditions as they were before the world was troubled by disturbing thoughts of human freedom. The victory was clear and the treaty was clear, but there is no escaping the fact that the very ideas of liberty, which had supposedly been defeated, largely dominated Europe during the next century in complete disregard of what had been signed and sealed.

Out of this conference came the Holy Alliance, which was a shortlived attempt to maintain peace and order upon certain high principles. The great sovereigns agreed to "remain united by the bonds of a true and indissoluble fraternity, . . . they will, on all occasions and in all places, lend each other aid and assistance . . . to protect Religion, Peace, and Justice."

They further "solemnly declared . . . in their political relations with every other government, to take for their sole guide the precepts of that holy religion, namely, the Precepts of Justice, Christian Charity, and Peace. . . ."

The pact concluded with an invitation to all Powers who might "choose solemnly to avow the sacred principles which have dictated this act" to become members of "this Holy Alliance." It was a sort of 1815 version of the Kellogg-Briand Pact of a strictly personal character between three absolute sovereigns.

The signatories can hardly be accused of having followed these principles. Alexander of Russia alone seems to have taken it at all seriously. There is no reason to doubt the sincerity of this mystic. The Emperor of Austria signed in a scoffing mood after remarking that "if it was a question of politics, he must refer it to his chancellor, if of religion, to his confessor." Metternich's approval was limited to calling it a "loud-sounding nothing." Castlereagh was kinder in referring to it as "a piece of sublime mysticism and nonsense." Although the King was restored in France, from the start the French Government treated the Holy Alliance with contempt.

The Alliance was in fact a sort of personal league of sovereigns with no definite plan or procedure, and its real purpose was to justify foreign intervention in the affairs of any state threatened with revolution.

The actual achievements of the Holy Alliance were not great. The Emperor of Russia did intervene to help the Greek rebels against the Ottoman Empire, and as late as 1848 he sent an army to Hungary to suppress Kossuth. But the policy of intervention split with British opposition and upon the rock of the American Monroe Doctrine. As an effective force it lasted a very short time.

The Quadruple Alliance (1815)

Out of the Holy Alliance, however, the practical gentlemen a few months later produced the Quadruple Alliance.

This agreement is sometimes confused with the Holy Alliance. The latter was merely a statement of high aims and motives, whereas the Quadruple Alliance was a working arrangement for dealing with European problems. It was signed on November 20, 1815, by Austria, Great Britain, Prussia, and Russia. It was responsible for calling the four great European congresses which dealt with the troubled situation from the Congress of Vienna until 1822. These were the congresses at Aix-la-Chapelle (1818), Troppau (1820), Laibach (1821), and Verona (1822). The Quadruple Alliance had clear and obvious aims. It existed primarily to hold the *status quo* and bolster up the doctrine of legitimacy which had been seriously undermined by the upheavals of the revolutionary period. To this end it directed considerable energy to the suppression of growing Liberalism and nationalism.

These methods were carried to such an extreme that the British Government could not accept the protocol of Troppau providing that, "States which have undergone a change of government due to revolution, the results of which threaten other States, *ipso facto* cease to be members of the European Alliance, and remain excluded from it until their situation gives guarantees for legal order and stability. If, owing to such alterations, immediate danger threatens other States, the Powers bind themselves, by peaceful means, or if need be by arms, to bring back the guilty State into the bosom of the Great Alliance."

The Balance of Power

These plans growing out of the Congress of Vienna were, however, ultimately absorbed into the balance of power and the Concert of Europe.

The origins of the principle of the balance of power are lost in the mists of history. Grotius formulated the idea clearly as a fundamental principle. According to him, it was in the common interest and it was the right and duty of all nations to go to war if the balance of power was menaced.

The balance of power is not a principle of law, but rather a principle of action with the claim that it was a law of nature. Its essential base is to maintain a situation where nations modify their aggressiveness by fear of defeat. Fear of defeat always modifies aggressiveness—even in the jungle.

We must remember that the theory of the balance of power recognized the collective right of Europe to peace and freedom from territorial aggression. It recognized a collective interest in preventing undue expansion by any nation. It has often been said that the system had not often been called into operation to resist military invasions. This is perhaps true, but the fear of its operation gives it a long record of successful retarding of such aggression.

The practice of the balance of power fundamentally rested on groupings and periodic regroupings to hold three most important aggressive centers in restraint. They were France, the German-dominated Central Empires, and Russia. The minor states revolved mostly around these suns.

Britain played a major but outside part in these affairs. And she was the determining weight in the balance of power. Her empire and her life are curiously exposed in a military sense, and she must depend very largely upon sea power and upon diplomacy—power politics—for her protection. Her face has always been turned toward the seven seas and her colonial activities far from Europe. But she is only twenty miles away from the Continent, and her safety requires that the shores of the channel and the North Sea remain in friendly hands. Furthermore, her prosperity is closely interwoven with peace on the Continent. Thus, economic and political dangers have periodically thrust her back into continental action, little as she may have liked it.

Her major method has, for centuries, been to maintain a dominant navy, and when power groups develop which threaten aggression on the Continent, to throw her weight with the weaker side. This has become a sort of law of British nature.

These balances have periodically broken into war, and then, after each costly experience, Britain retreats into a fit of isolation—until driven out again by some new menacing combination.

All this has given to British policy a strong color of opportunism, not perhaps the opportunism of carelessness, but of carefully thought out policy. She knows what is good for her today, but realizes better than most countries the inevitability of shifting balances and change. And this accounts for a striking British characteristic, an invincible reluctance to bind herself as regards unforeseen eventualities.

Continental Powers are given to criticizing British policy for its apparent inconsistencies. But Britain usually shows complete consistency even in her apparent lack of logic or continued affiliations. The oft-expressed continental phrase is, "Perfidious Albion." But Americans can well sympathize with her fits of isolationism, her reluctance to get into continental wars, and yet her necessity to fend off danger by preventing any power from becoming too dominant.

A moment's glance at the history of Europe during the 140-year period shows a series of examples of these shifting balances and crises, although they have been at times obscured by national upheavals and the surge of personal freedom and representative government. There were the combinations of practically the whole of Europe against French aggression under Napoleon. There was a manifestation in the Crimean War of 1853–56, where England, France, and Austria supported Turkey against Russian aggression. After the Franco-Prussian War in 1870, the rising unification of Germany and her drive for colonies and the growth of her navy began to alarm Britain, and in reaction, Bismarck sought strength from an alliance with Russia and Austria. Within a few years Russia withdrew from this triple alliance, but in a very short time Italy, aroused by the French seizure of Tunis, took Russia's place. This German-Austrian-Italian alliance continued until 1914. Britain stayed out of these alliances until 1904, but in 1898, when there was a threat of war between Britain and France over the

Sudan, Britain went so far as to explore the possibilities of an alliance with Germany.

The intensity of French fears, and hatred of Germany for the loss of Alsace-Lorraine in 1870, led her to build industriously a grouping for her own protection. In 1895, France and Russia had made an alliance directed toward the Triple Alliance group, and in 1904, the British loosely joined this group through the Triple Entente.

There is no doubt that alliances in general are not lasting, that they are constantly subject to attempts to dissolve them or to face them with superior force. They always build for competitive armament. All of this leads to unrest and insecurity. Although the balance of power is described as a "just equilibrium," governments are constantly seeking to secure not so much an even balance as preponderance for their own side, and this leads to ultimate conflict. And the effect of these combinations is to make war on a much wider front by drawing in many nations not directly part of the controversy. This was essentially the case in 1914.

But whatever the shortcomings of the system of balance of power, there is no doubt that the ability of the Powers to hold each other in check has gone far at times to avert aggression and violence.

It is a mistake to think of the balance of power as belonging to the past or even to Europe. It dominated Europe after Versailles despite its presumed burial by the League of Nations. And it is as alive today as it ever was.

The Concert of Europe

Out of all these dangers grew a new movement—the Concert of Europe. It marked a feeble growth of general collective action for maintenance of peace—that is, a Council of Nations. It was not an institution but a practice, a practice which automatically grew out of the Holy Alliance and the Quadruple Alliance with the body of decisions remaining from the four great congresses which followed from the latter. These congresses had in emergencies brought the great Powers into consultation to keep the peace as best they could. It was not an agreement, but rather a loose system which simply prevailed.

At the close of the Crimean War—in the 1850s—the Concert of European Powers concluded a number of further agreements with a view to establishing orderly processes of international life. Although the organization of the Concert had never been embodied in treaty agreements, it was clearly recognized, and Turkey was in 1853 specifically admitted to the advantages of "public law and the Concert of Europe."

The same Powers in 1864 signed the Geneva Convention, creating the Red Cross System. In 1874, the laws and customs of war on land were embodied in the Brussels Convention. In 1878, the Concert of Powers at the Congress of Berlin drew up a treaty reconciling the claims of Turkey, Greece, and the Balkan States—at least tiding over the emergency.

The Concert was most active in the period after the Franco-Prussian War, no doubt finding its chief worry in the growing militarism of the German Empire. All the elements of war were present from 1870 to 1914, but war was averted. The Powers remained in constant contact on the thousand and one everyday causes of friction. When a crisis came, the Concert foregathered directly or by communications and arrived at some sort of settlement, as, for instance, in dealing with China during the Boxer crisis of 1900, and with Morocco in 1906 at the Algeciras Conference. The United States took part in both these settlements.

The Concert may not have been greatly concerned with the rights of small countries, but controversies were settled and crises were tided over by this sort of Council of Nations.

It was a precarious way of keeping the peace, and there was always danger that the system would fail. And when it did finally fail in 1914, the failure was due to the accumulation of explosive forces beyond the powers of this form of diplomacy. Or at least statesmanship was so weak as to fail to recognize them.

The Monroe Doctrine

Surprisingly enough, the Monroe Doctrine may be listed with the tried methods of keeping the peace and, more surprisingly, it must be listed among the methods for keeping the peace by force. But it was in itself a participation in the balance of power, for the United States thereby threw its weight to any Western Hemisphere state threatened with European encroachment.

There is no doubt that it depended on force, for it was heeded only because it was known that the armed strength of the United States was behind the President's warning, to make it effective.

When we speak of this force, we must also remember that America did not stand alone behind the Doctrine. There was the interest of Britain in maintaining it as part of the balance of power among European empires, not because Britain supported or even referred to the Monroe Doctrine, but because there happened to be a coincidence of interest which led Canning to declare that Britain could not see with indifference the change in balance by the transfer of any of Spain's possessions to another Power.

The essential part of President Monroe's warning to the Powers of Europe was his statement that "we should consider any attempt on their part to extend their system to any portion of this Hemisphere as dangerous to our peace and safety." Aside from its political implications in defense of the United States, the Doctrine was prompted by the ideological cleavage between the two hemispheres. The interest of the Holy Alliance in support of Spain and its insistence on Divine Right were as repugnant to us as American agitation for personal liberty and representative government must have been horrifying to the statesmen of Europe bent on putting down such shocking ideas.

Two notable incidents arose in connection with this Doctrine. The first was the landing of British, French, and Spanish troops in Mexico in 1861 and the proclamation of Maximilian as Emperor. Engaged in civil war, we were too weak to act at once, but in 1866 we put an end to it. A further action was taken in 1895 in protection of Venezuela from British threats and demands.

At times we went far afield in our interpretations of the Doctrine, especially in the administration of President Theodore Roosevelt. That stretch of interpretation covered the idea that we must keep these Western Hemisphere nations in order to prevent pretexts for European intervention. And with this color of authority, we justified numbers of military and diplomatic interventions on our part to establish internal order and to enforce the commercial contracts of our neighbors. These actions created great fears and resentment against the United States. During the Coolidge Administration, Secretary of State Hughes came out vigorously against this entire conception of the Doctrine, got the Marines out of Santo Domingo, and took the first steps toward getting them out of Nicaragua. To bring this situation definitely to an end, Mr. Hoover, then President-elect, visited the South American governments in 1928 and gave public assurances to them of an entire change in these policies. To emphasize it, he at once directed the withdrawal of American troops from Nicaragua and Haiti. He directed the publication of a memorandum by Under Secretary of State J. Reuben Clark repudiating the whole thesis of intervention which had been built up. This attitude has been maintained and developed by Mr. Roosevelt's Administration under the name of the "Good Neighbor" policy.

In the large sense, the Monroe Doctrine has worked beneficially to maintain separation of Western Hemisphere problems from those of Europe and has contributed to preserve peace in the world.

The Development of Law and International Co-operation

The last half of the nineteenth century marked the great advance in ideas of international law and international co-operation alongside the older forces of balance of power, the Concert of Europe, and the Monroe Doctrine. Indeed, the Concert of Europe played some part in this development, but it was primarily due to the spread of representative government. Inherent in that thesis are government by law and the popular demand for peace. The strength of the movement came from those countries where there was representative government and where the people had a voice. There were faint efforts to champion the same ideas in other countries—but the popular demand for orderly methods in the conduct of international relations was in direct proportion to the popular share in government. At first these attempts to formulate the demand for better-organized peace were only occasional and fragmentary—but as the years went by, the movement grew in volume. We may note some of the more important incidents which mark its progress.

Pan American Union

On May 24, 1888, the United States Congress, as a result of efforts begun by Secretary of State Blaine in 1881, passed an act authorizing the President to summon a conference of the independent nations of the Western Hemisphere. Thus was formulated the great ideal for which Bolivar strove. This conference was to be called for the purpose of considering measures to preserve the peace and promote the prosperity of the several American nations, to establish economic co-operation, and to include a definite plan for arbitration of all disputes between them. These Pan-American conferences met a common need and have long played an important role in the improvement of inter-American relations.

The several succeeding conferences gradually led to the founding of the Pan American Union in 1910. The Union performs valuable statistical and informational services, follows up the decisions of the conferences, and arranges their programs. A long list of treaties bearing upon economic, cultural, and peace promotion has been perfected.

But above all, the Pan American Union has served a useful purpose, in the preservation of peace, through the governing board meeting round a table once a month. It has been able to smooth over many difficulties as they have arisen and thus avoid more serious disputes.

The Hague Conferences

The first fundamental and courageous attack upon the world problems of peace and war was made by the first Hague Peace Conference, called in 1899 by the Emperor of Russia. While it is customary to belittle the work of the first Hague Conference for not going far enough, it must be admitted, in the light of subsequent experience, that its achievements were remarkable in laying a foundation for further progress.

The conference, attended by the representatives of twenty-six countries, resulted in the signature of three important Conventions:

1. A Convention for the Pacific Settlement of International Disputes which set up as an agency a Permanent Court of Arbitration at the Hague, with a permanent organization and a defined procedure for arbitration and inquiry.

2. A Convention Respecting the Laws and Customs of War on Land. This Convention confirmed previous agreements and marked a notable progress in building up a body of international law. The fact that this Convention has been repeatedly and cynically violated does not destroy its value. Its wise provisions still stand and will serve to guide us when we recover our balance.

3. A Convention for the Adaptation to Maritime Warfare of the Principles of the Geneva Convention of August 22, 1864.

In further development of the principle of arbitration of international controversies, a plan was proposed for obligatory arbitration of all questions excepting those "involving vital interests and national honor." It was found impossible to conclude a convention against the strong opposition of Germany, who claimed that these reservations reduced it to nothing.

The second Hague Peace Conference, convened in 1907, was attended by the representatives of forty-four countries and further perfected the procedures in arbitration and the Conventions signed at the first conference. Thirteen Conventions were signed and in large part ratified by important Powers.

In the first thirty-eight years of its existence, there were twenty-one arbitrations before tribunals of the Permanent Court or before special tribunals of such character as to be listed in the reports of the Administrative Council of the Court.

London Conference of 1909

Convention XII of the second Hague Conference initiated discussion upon the constitution of an International Prize Court. In 1909, the British Government called a conference in London upon the law to be applied by such a Court composed of representatives of nine leading maritime nations. This conference drew up a document known as the "Declaration of London."

The Declaration confirmed the terms of the Declaration of Paris of 1856 that a blockade to be binding must be effective. It was the beginning of world demand for clear freedom of the seas during war. It laid down agreed definitions of contraband of war and unneutral service and prescribed rules governing the capture or destruction of neutral prizes and the transfer of ships to a neutral flag, with further rules concerning enemy character, convoy, and resistance to search. The British House of Lords failed to take action on this declaration, which has consequently never become a binding convention, but has nevertheless influenced the development of the law.

Development of Arbitration and Mediation

In 1911, during the Taft Administration, treaties were negotiated with Great Britain and France extending the principle of arbitration to all justiciable questions. These treaties were materially amended by the Senate, and President Taft declined to accept them in amended form, so they did not become effective. They serve chiefly to indicate the direction of progress.

Mr. Bryan, during his term of office as Secretary of State (1913–15), made a definite contribution to the cause of conciliation. He proposed the acceptance of a period of delay, and independent investigation and report before resort to war and concluded a series of treaties incorporating this idea. He prescribed that whenever the methods of diplomacy were found unable to adjust a dispute, it should be submitted for investigation and report to an International Commission, and that the contracting parties should agree not to declare war or begin hostilities during the period of such investigation and report. This in itself insured a cooling-off period which might readily be prolonged by the proceedings of the Commission of Inquiry. This was primarily useful for disputed questions of fact. A number of such treaties were negotiated.

International Unions

During this period can be noted the growth of international unions which have been conspicuously successful in building up international co-operation in fields where it was useful and in the common interest.

First and foremost of these, of course, is the Universal Postal Union, established in 1874 and now comprising every recognized state.

Other unions which follow the same methods for varying numbers of states are the Telegraphic Union; the Metric Union; the Union for the Protection of Submarine Cables; Radio and Communications Union; the Union for the Repression of the White Slave Trade; the Union for the Protection of Industrial Property.

The Transformation of Diplomacy

During this period of 140 years, diplomatic activity was itself transformed from its older dominant occupation with alliances, intrigues, and social contacts into the major purpose of preventing and allaying friction and controversy. Diplomacy is in everyday operation in every capital. It finds its strength in the give and take of ordinary life. By its very elasticity it settles 999 out of 1,000 conflicts or possible conflicts. It was to fill in where diplomacy fails that all the stronger methods were developed. In sequence, there have developed regular diplomatic steps in the use of the "good offices" of other nations; conciliation and mediation with examination and report on the facts by friendly nations; arbitration by independent agencies; or judicial decision of some types of controversy.

The differences between arbitration and judicial decision are perhaps more practical than theoretical. Both are judicial in character, but arbitration leaves broader scope for the elements of compromise and adjustment in the decision. One distinction, however, is that judicial settlement is made by an existing bench of judges, whereas arbitration is by judges chosen for the specific case.

By all these means, hundreds of disputes were disposed of, and by 1914 it seemed that the world was strengthening the methods of peaceful settlement.

We cannot leave this period in development of the methods of peace without reference to the long line of American Secretaries of State who so steadily contributed to the road building of peace. The names of James Monroe, John Hay, and Elihu Root especially stand out in the records of the time.

Summary of Peace Movements

Thus, gradually there developed in this period three pacific concepts: first, the establishment of international rules and law by agreement and precedent; second, the development of methods of settling controversies by arbitration and cooling off; third, the development of co-operation in economic and social fields.

But if we examine all these movements, we again find that the use of military force, or threats of its use to keep the peace, dominantly prevailed at least in practice. The Quadruple Alliance, the Triple Alliance, the Entente Cordiale, the balance of power, the Monroe Doctrine—all belong to that category. But proposals of pacific methods of solution or relief of disputes and tensions through morals and reason made the greatest advances in history up to this time. The Holy Alliance; the Concert of Europe; the development of law and international co-operation, disarmament; arbitration and mediation; and change in purpose of diplomacy—all contributed to these strides.

Despite the great efforts of men devoted to peace, the six underlying dynamic forces of ideologies; economic pressures; nationalism; imperialism; militarism; and the complex of fear, hate, and revenge had culminated in a gigantic crisis by 1914.

Part Two

V THE FIRST WORLD WAR

HERE again we are interested not in military history, but in the forces which make for war and peace. Therefore, we do not describe the military campaigns or battles, or the heroism and sacrifice of millions of men whose deeds are the great rays of sunlight in the gigantic tragedy of the first World War.

In this chapter we shall first review the final pressures of the seven dynamic forces which led to this gigantic explosion, then offer some description of the effect of the war upon the dynamic forces themselves, and finally enumerate the expressed peace aims and purposes of the United Nations in seeking victory.

The Final Explosion

Historians will not be able to measure the relative weight of these seven forces in producing this gigantic upheaval until long hence, when they can be examined in the light of all their consequences. But from this distance of a generation we can make some observations upon them.

The superficial causes of the war started from Sarajevo, in June 1914. But the assassination of an archduke could not alone have provoked a world war had it not been for the antecedent development in the dynamic forces which we have outlined in the last chapters. Six out of the seven had risen to pressures beyond the safety valve of the seventh—the will to peace.

It is a matter of speculation whether with more capable or more clear-minded statesmanship, crises could have been allayed and the debacle deferred. It might be said speculatively that had Serbian statesmen quickly realized the heinousness of the crime of Sarajevo and made immediate amends, even though humiliating, had the Russian statesmen not been looking for war as a diversion from domestic troubles, had

Germany wished to avert conflict, had Britain taken a positive stand earlier in the crisis, the conflict might have been averted for the moment. In other words, the fundamental pressures of the dynamic forces of explosion were present, but inadequate statesmanship did not recognize them, or failed, or did not wish to allay them. Be that as it may, these evil forces were released, and from releasing them were created more evils, and thus came the first *total* war.

Undoubtedly, even had the incident at Sarajevo been tided over, the pressures had become too great for the explosion to be long deferred without constructive allaying of these forces in Europe. That they were tinder for a match is evident from a short review of them.

Ideological Pressures.[1] The pressure of ideological forces—the struggle of men for liberty against subjection—had become potent in the causes of the war. The march of personal liberty and representative government had raised internal explosions in Russia, Germany, and Austria by demands of their people for more liberty. And liberty had inspired the rising forces of nationalism and demands for independence in the races they held in subjection. The men around the emperors welcomed a diversion of their peoples' minds from the internal pressures of nationalism and liberty over into foreign dangers even if at the moment they did not consciously envisage war.

The importance of the ideological forces in the causes of the war were at the outbreak obscured by the military grouping of nations. The alliance of the representative governments of France and England with Czarist Russia would not indicate a military crusade to impose democracy. Indeed, America was not fully convinced of the ideological purity of the Allies until the collapse of Czarist Russia in March 1917, before we entered the war. Nevertheless, the basic conflict was there. The peoples of the western European nations certainly raised these grounds of antagonism to the Central Empires.

There cannot be the remotest doubt that alarm for the ideals of personal liberty and representative government was the major pressure for the entrance of the United States into the war.

It is true that the unlimited submarine warfare, with its attacks upon American shipping, and the Zimmermann note, with its revelation of German designs, had a crystallizing effect.

[1] For outline of these forces, see p. 159; 140 years prior to World War I, p. 178.

No one, however, can read the ideals and aims expressed by President Wilson without accepting the fact that, so far as the United States was concerned, this was dominantly an armed crusade to defeat aggression and to make personal liberty and representative government supreme in the world. These aims were supported by the American people and were quickly coined into popular terms of "war to end war," "to make the world safe for democracy," "to destroy militarism and aggression," "to bring freedom to mankind"—all are ample evidence of the character of the American purpose.

If further proof were needed of our major idealistic purpose, our self-denying ordinances of no annexations of territory and no indemnities amply indicate that there was no imperialism or nationalism behind American purposes. With only a police army, we had no militaristic pressure. We were under no economic pressures of any kind. There was no inherent hate of Germany or Austria. Our declarations that we had no purpose of vengeance or punishment of the enemy peoples further emphasized this. In fact, before 1914 the general feeling throughout the nation was perhaps more friendly to Germany than to Britain. There was no fear of invasion of our continent or loss of our independence. We had no internal pressure of any kind for which politicians needed diversion of public mind to foreign affairs and war. The will to peace ran high among us.

So when we did go to war, it was the most gigantic crusade of all history.

Economic Pressures.[2] The economic pressures of the Industrial Revolution had created great dangers. The push for elbow room and foreign markets, the dependence upon overseas supplies of food and raw materials had created intense rivalries and a consequent growth of huge navies. Everywhere, nations were building barriers around trade and seeking special privilege and advantage. For these reasons the friction between Britain and Germany especially had grown most acute. The push of German capital into the Near East had stirred Russia. Economic pressures had, in fact, risen to the incendiary stage.

Nationalism.[3] The accumulated forces of nationalism were tearing at

[2] For outline of these pressures, see p. 159; 140 years prior to World War I, p. 181.

[3] For outline of this force, see p. 160; 140 years prior to World War I, p. 185.

the vitals of the German, Russian, Austrian, and Turkish empires. A dozen races were striving for independence from the old empires. That became evident enough when these old empires later on split into thirteen independent nations by the rebellions of their subject peoples seeking freedom.

Imperialism.[4] The clash of rival imperialisms was clanging with war. And it came, not alone from economic pressures, but from the impulses of national glory and national arrogance. The two rival centers of imperialism, in Russia and in Germany, were constantly at each other's throats, particularly in the Balkans.

Militarism.[5] Aggressive militarism was rampant in Russia, Germany and Austria. Their military castes had built mammoth armaments and were on the march for glory. The two huge military alliances themselves invited war. The Triple Alliance of Germany, Austria, and Italy had forced France, out of fear, to join in counteralliance with Russia. Britain's policy of balance of power had given friendly support to France. The cost of competitive arms rocketed. The annual expenditure on arms in the Western World had increased from about $1,500,000,000 to more than $5,000,000,000 in the five years prior to 1914. It could not go on increasing the numbers and power of men whose mission was fighting without eventually cultivating a fight. This increase itself was an indication of rising pressures.

Fear, Hate, and Revenge.[6] And impelling to the final debacle were fear, hate, and revenge: French and British fear of Germany; German fear of Britain and Russia; Austrian fear and hate of Russia; Russian fear of Germany; French hate and resolve of revenge against Germany; and all the hates of the subject races.

The Will to Peace.[7] All these pressures were too much to be subdued by the Will to Peace alone. The instruments of the old power diplomacy, the balance of power, the Concert of Europe and even the newer machinery of international law and international co-operation, driven with frantic efforts by the British and French Foreign Ministers, all totally failed to prevent the explosion.

[4] For outline of this force, see p. 163; 140 years prior to World War I, p. 186.
[5] For outline of this force, see p. 161; 140 years prior to World War I, p. 190.
[6] For outline of these forces, see p. 164; before World War I, p. 192.
[7] For outline of this force, see p. 165; 140 years prior to World War I, p. 193.

Changes in the Seven Dynamic Forces Imposed During the War

The seven dynamic forces were certain to be changed by the heat from the furnace of war. Some of these changes developed during the course of the war itself and require examination for the effect they had upon the peace conference—and afterwards.

Total War. The most vital of these changes came from the development for the first time in history of what was well called "total war."

Sometime after the Franco-Prussian War of the 1870s, the whole character of war had changed. Prior to that, the broad art of war had been about the same for over 300 years. It is true, firearms had been perfected in detail, but methods of military organization, tactics, and strategy were broadly of the same character. Sea power changed little in its relationship to the factors in war.

In those earlier times, armies and navies called out only a fraction of the population. Their support required only another fraction. Thus, there was only a fractional disruption of economic and social life during the war. But the Industrial Revolution, with its mechanical inventions, had given birth to total war. It had perfected ability to produce firearms in far greater volume. Improvements in rail, water, highway, and truck transportation had made it possible to maneuver far larger bodies of men. Thus, during the first World War, armies grew to the total man power which could be spared from production of arms and the minimum supply of necessities to the civil population.

The invention of the gas engine had made possible the truck, the airplane, the submarine, and later the tank. Other inventions had made possible the heavier artillery, the improved machine gun and rifle, and poison gas. These weapons had become not only more hideously destructive but more complicated to make and far more expensive. Thus, huge specialized factories and millions more of mechanics were required to support the larger armies.

And the calling of the maximum man power to the fighting front and the need of maximum supply services for them required, for the first time, total mobilization of the civil population under great compulsions and restrictions imposed by governments. Herein was what amounted to a profound revolution.

Starvation of Nations as a Weapon. As we have said, the huge populations resulting from the Industrial Revolution, such as those of Germany, England, and Japan, had become dependent upon overseas imports for food and raw materials. While to besiege and starve a city is as old as Babylon, never until 1914 had the starvation of whole nations been made so effective by blockade. It was proved that sea power could starve whole empires for food, and all their industries for raw material.

Blockade was now aided by another special phenomenon of total war. That was the rapid degeneration of agriculture. Because of the lack of imported fats and animal feed, great inroads were made into the flocks and herds in order to live. Work stock was used up in war. Fertilizers had to be diverted to explosives. Shortage of labor curtailed planting and harvesting of ground crops. In the enemy countries, these shortages undermined the health and the stability of their children. In the Allied countries, the shortage of shipping and man power had the same effects on agricultural production, but the people secured their marginal needs by imports.

The economic consequences of diversion of normal production to war materials—the diversion of occupation, the displacement of populations, the introduction of women into industry—were on a scale never dreamed of in war before.

And the gigantic sums required to finance all these diversions of economic life to war made huge inflation during the war inevitable.

A New Ideology Is Born. In the end, profound consequences were to come to the whole world from the ideological thinking arising out of the organization of whole peoples for total war.

Representative government itself contributed to the beginnings of a malevolent and hostile ideology. In order to mobilize the whole energies of their peoples, all governments at war had to plan and enforce production and to divert men and material to war purposes. They were compelled to restrict production for civilian purposes. Governments had to operate industry and dictate to business, labor, and agriculture. And where men claimed old personal rights, they had to be coerced. All this was as much needed in the countries of liberty as in those accustomed to subjection. Thus, representative government everywhere surrendered economic and personal freedom to the state that they might win the war. Government management of economic life during the war was assisted greatly by the fact that altruism and patriotism replaced self-interest as the basis of economic production and service. But the world at that spot laid the foundations of "managed economy," and thus the economics of a new ideology—Fascism.

The Corruption of Intellectual and Spiritual Freedom. The desperations of total war gave birth to other inroads upon liberty in the democracies themselves.

Truth proved to be the first fatality of war. Total war required government-organized propaganda. And propaganda is, at best, only part truth. The atrocities and wickedness of the enemy must be constantly illustrated. The hates of the people at home, their courage and their aspirations could not be allowed to lag in the face of suffering and reverses. Neutrals must be influenced to keep neutral or to help. The enemy had to be misled. All governments engaged in these processes without any moral restraint. Telling lies was saving the lives of sons. It was further justified among the representative governments on the ground that victory must be had, for defeat in total war meant defeat of liberty itself.

And total war bred total intolerance. National unity was essential in the face of total national danger. But impatience at discussion rose to rabid intolerance, even at discussion of constructive character. There was no need for government in the democracies to suppress free speech. The crowd howled it down. And government-inspired propaganda could and did injure many of its own citizens, no matter how pure their patriotism.

Total war created more hideous brutalities than had any war since the Middle Ages. Total war was a war of civilian effort against civilian effort as well as of armies against armies. Therefore, to dislocate civilian activities on the enemy side became a part of military action. Thus, it became also a war of armies against civilians. No longer was there chivalry of armed men for women and children. Starvation of nations brought not only agony to civilians, but stunting of their children and decimation of millions from inevitable pestilence. Terrorization of civilians was organized as an act of war. Towns were burned by the Germans as warnings, and innocent hostages were mowed down by machine guns. Airplanes and zeppelins were used to drop iron and fire upon helpless civilians, to burn their homes and their cities. Civilian sailors were sunk by submarines without a chance of survival.

One bright spot in all this welter of brutality was the efforts of people of good will to alleviate suffering. The Commission for Relief in Belgium, through consent of both sides, preserved the lives of 10,000,000 invaded and blockaded people over the period of four years. During and after the war, the American Red Cross, the Friends' Service Committee, and other organizations played a splendid role in alleviating the sufferings of war.

The Growth of Hate. And total war, from the brutalities to civilians, produced total hate and total demand for revenge. Hate enveloped the mind of every man, woman, and child. It was not directed solely to the enemy leaders, but to every individual in enemy countries. Soldiers fighting at the front had far less hate than civilians.

During 1916 there came a moment when reason said there should be a negotiated peace. The Central Powers might thus have avoided collapse into chaos. The Allies stood to gain more substantial and lasting advantages. President Wilson tried to initiate such a peace. There is little doubt that most of the European statesmen on both sides recognized the desirability of such a peace and would have been glad to consider it. But the peoples on both sides had been aroused to such a pitch of anger and hate that they would have overthrown any statesman who manifested a readiness to consider a negotiated peace. Total war, flogged on by the propaganda of hate, had no terminal short of the surrender of one side or the other through defeat or exhaustion. And in that respect the victor was but one lap ahead of the vanquished.

War Aims. As the war moved on, there were profound changes at least in its aims. These changes were in considerable part due to the entrance of America and the emphasis given to ideological purpose.

Before the war was ended by the Armistice, President Wilson had repeatedly expressed America's aspirations in the aims and principles of the peace to come. Because of their profound effect upon ending the war and upon the peacemaking, we must examine them closely.

At the end of this chapter we have grouped his aims and proposals on the basis of their relation to the seven forces: ideological; economic; nationalistic; imperialistic; militaristic; the complexes of fear, hate, and revenge; and the yearning for lasting peace.

The Armistice. During the year before the Armistice, Mr. Wilson had enumerated these aims in his Fourteen Points, and later extended them to twenty-five points in the subsequent addresses covering the basis of peace, which we give at the end of the chapter. The moral, economic, and military strength of the United States had swung the balance over to victory. The Allies, bled white by their efforts, had arrived at a stalemate. But for the United States, the Allies could not have attained victory. The American people never organized, co-operated, or sacrificed more efficiently in their national history, nor did their sons ever rise to greater heights of discipline and valor. Nor did American military leadership ever rise to greater heights than under General Pershing and Admirals Benson, Pratt, and Sims.

During the month of October 1918, at Germany's request, Mr. Wilson negotiated the basis of the Armistice on behalf of all the Allies. That basis was Germany's specific acceptance of the Fourteen Points and the "subsequent addresses." But before closing the agreement with Germany, the President submitted the entire proposals to the Allied Powers and received their formal acceptance except for one point—the freedom of the seas.

With these ideas and ideals established, the war was won and the Armistice signed. It provided for the complete surrender of the arms of Germany, and her retreat into her own borders. A peace was to be negotiated later, and the Armistice promised that food would be provided in the meantime.

The destruction of life and property were unparalleled in their proportions to any previous war in history, except perhaps the Thirty Years' War. Government debts of somewhere near $250,000,000,000 were piled up. Huge numbers of ships, factories, homes were destroyed. Some 10,000,000 men were killed or maimed, probably 10,000,000 civilians died of starvation or disease resulting from the war. And 350,000,000 people were left disastrously short of food, heat and clothing. The third and fourth Horsemen of the Apocalypse—Famine and Pestilence—were the rulers of men. And a fifth Horseman was to appear—Revolution.

Declared War Aims

For later reference, we have here paralleled President Wilson's declarations with those on the present war made thus far by President Roosevelt.

IDEOLOGICAL AIMS

WILSON

The soldiers at the front . . . They are crusaders . . . are giving their lives, that homes everywhere . . . may be kept sacred and safe and men everywhere be free as they insist upon being free.

Sept. 1, 1918

Longing of the oppressed . . . to hear something like the "Battle Hymn of the Republic"; to hear the feet of the great hosts of liberty going to set them free, to set their minds free, set their lives free, set their children free. . . .

May 18, 1918

It is our inestimable privilege . . . to make not only the liberties of America secure but the liberties of every other people as well. . . . We have heard and watched the struggle for self-government spread and triumph among many peoples. We have come to regard the right to political liberty as the common right of humankind. Year after year . . . we have continued to rejoice in the peaceful increase of freedom and democracy throughout the world. . . . We are confronted with a menace which endangers everything that we have won and the world has won. . . . In all its old insolence, with all its ancient cruelty and injustice, military autocracy has again armed itself against the pacific hopes of men. . . . We are face to face with the necessity of asserting anew the fundamental right of free men to make their own laws, choose their own allegiance, or else permit human-

ROOSEVELT

In the future days which we seek to make secure, we look forward to a world founded upon four essential freedoms.

The first is freedom of speech and expression—everywhere in the world.

The second is freedom of every person to worship God in his own way—everywhere in the world.

The third is freedom from want, which translated into world terms means economic understandings which will secure to every nation a healthy peacetime life for its inhabitants—everywhere in the world.

The fourth is freedom from fear, which translated into world terms means reduction of armaments to such a point and in such thorough fashion that no nation will be in position to commit an act of physical aggression against any neighbor—anywhere in the world.

Jan. 7, 1941

We will accept only a world consecrated to freedom of speech and expression—freedom of every person to worship God in his own way —freedom from want and freedom from terror.

May 28, 1941

The essence of our struggle is that men shall be free.

Nov. 6, 1941

There must be no place in the postwar world for special privilege, either for individuals or nations.

Nov. 6, 1941

This duty we owe . . . is to make the world a place where free-

WILSON

ity to become the victim of a ruthless ambition that is determined to destroy what it cannot master. . . . The past and present are in deadly struggle. . . .

What we seek is the reign of law based upon the consent of the governed and sustained by the organized opinion of mankind. I ask you, fellow citizens, to unite with them in making this our Independence Day the first that shall be consecrated to a declaration of independence for all the peoples of the world.

July 4, 1918

What is the war for? . . . It is a war of emancipation. Not until it is won can men anywhere live free from constant fear or breathe freely while they go about their daily tasks and know that governments are their servants not their masters. . . .

Sept. 1, 1918

What we are striving for is a new international order based upon broad and universal principles of right and justice, no mere peace of shreds and patches.

Feb. 11, 1918

Our desire for a new international order under which reason and justice and common interest of mankind . . . shall prevail . . . without that new order the world will be without peace.

Feb. 11, 1918

Our passion for justice and self-government is no mere passion which once set in motion must be satisfied.

Feb. 11, 1918

ROOSEVELT

dom can live and grow into the ages.

Nov. 6, 1941

We are fighting today for security, for progress, and for peace, not only for ourselves but for all men, not only for one generation but for all generations. We are fighting to cleanse the world of ancient evils, ancient ills . . .

Jan. 6, 1942

We are fighting, as our fathers have fought, to uphold the doctrine that all men are equal in the sight of God. Those on the other side are striving to destroy this deep belief and to create a world in their own image—a world of tyranny and cruelty and serfdom.

Jan. 6, 1942

The present great struggle has taught us increasingly that freedom of person and security of property anywhere in the world depend upon the security of the rights and obligations of liberty and justice everywhere in the world.

Feb. 24, 1942

ECONOMIC AIMS

WILSON	ROOSEVELT

The removal as far as possible of all economic barriers and the establishment of equality of trade condition among all nations consenting to the peace and associating themselves for its maintenance.

Jan. 31, 1918

There can be no special selfish economic combinations within the League . . . no economic boycott or exclusion . . . except by the League.

Sept. 27, 1918

[Mr. Wilson's specific labor aims were expressed in the creation of the International Labor Office.]

Absolute freedom of navigation upon the seas outside territorial waters (except where closed by international agreement).

Jan. 8, 1918

The desire to bring about the fullest collaboration between all nations in the economic field with the object of improved labor standards, economic advancement, and social security.

Churchill-Roosevelt,
Aug. 13, 1941

They will endeavor with due respect for existing obligations to further the enjoyment by all states, great and small, victor and vanquished, of access on equal terms to the trade and to the raw material of the world which are needed for their economic prosperity.

Churchill-Roosevelt,
Aug. 13, 1941

Such a peace should enable men to traverse the high seas and oceans without hindrance.

Churchill-Roosevelt,
Aug. 13, 1941

. . . No nation has the right to make the broad oceans of the world at great distances from the actual theater of land war unsafe for the commerce of others.

Sept. 11, 1941

SELF-DETERMINATION AND NATIONALISM

WILSON	ROOSEVELT

. . . National aspirations must be respected; peoples may now be dominated and governed only by their consent. "Self-determination" is not mere phrase. It is an imperative principle of action. . . .

Feb. 11, 1918

The respect the right of all peoples to choose the form of government under which they will live.

Churchill-Roosevelt,
Aug. 13, 1941

They desire to see no territorial changes that do not accord with

WILSON

Satisfaction of those deep-seated longings of oppressed . . . and enslaved peoples.

Sept. 27, 1918

Peoples are not to be handed about from one sovereignty to another by an international conference.

. . . Peoples and provinces are not to be bartered about from sovereignty to sovereignty as if they were mere chattels and pawns in a game. . . . Every territorial settlement involved in this war must be made in the interest of the populations concerned and not . . . adjustment or compromise of claims among rival states. . . .

Feb. 11, 1918

[President Wilson, in the Fourteen Points, proposed specifically the restoration of Belgium, Alsace-Lorraine, Rumania, Montenegro, Poland; the creation of Czechoslovakia, Yugoslavia; the union of the Italian-speaking peoples; the autonomy or freedom of non-Turkish races (Armenians, Arabs, Syrians, Palestine); and the freedom of the Dardanelles.]

Jan. 8, 1918 and Oct. 26, 1918

[Russia] an unhampered and unembarrassed opportunity for the independent determination of her own political development . . . a sincere welcome into the society of free nations under institutions of her own choosing. . . .

Jan. 8, 1918

ROOSEVELT

the freely expressed wishes of the people concerned.

Churchill-Roosevelt, Aug. 13, 1941

They wish to see sovereign rights and self-government restored to those who have been forcibly deprived of them.

Churchill-Roosevelt, Aug. 13, 1941

We of the United Nations are agreed on certain broad principles in the kind of peace we seek . . . disarmament of aggressors, self-determination of nations and peoples. . . .

Feb. 24, 1942

NO IMPERIALISM

WILSON	ROOSEVELT
There shall be no annexations. . . .	Their countries seek no aggrandizement, territorial or other.
Feb. 11, 1918	*Churchill-Roosevelt,*
	Aug. 13, 1941

Free, open-minded, and absolutely impartial adjustment of all colonial claims . . . based upon the interests of the population concerned. . . .

Jan. 8, 1918

"German colonies should be declared the common property of the League and administered by small nations."

Dec. 12, 1918 [8]

DESTRUCTION OF MILITARISM

WILSON	ROOSEVELT
The day of conquest and aggrandizement has gone by.	After the final destruction of the Nazi tyranny. . . .
Jan. 8, 1918	*Churchill-Roosevelt,*
	Aug. 13, 1941

But it is necessary we must frankly say, and necessary as a preliminary to any intelligent dealings with her [Germany] on our part that we should know whom her spokesmen speak for when they speak to us, whether for the Reichstag majority or for the Military Party and those men whose creed is imperial domination.

Jan. 8, 1918

. . . She [the United States] entered this war because she was made a partner . . . in the sufferings and indignities inflicted by the military masters of Germany

Since no future peace can be maintained if land, sea, or air armaments continue to be employed by nations which threaten aggression outside their frontiers, they believe pending the establishment of a wider and permanent system of general security that the disarmament of such nations is essential. They will likewise aid and encourage all other practicable measures which will lighten for peace-loving peoples the crushing burdens of armaments.

Churchill-Roosevelt,
Aug. 13, 1941

[8] Ray Stannard Baker, *Woodrow Wilson and World Settlement*, Doubleday, Page, Vol. I p. 19.

against the peace and security of mankind.

Feb. 11, 1918

Not . . . even the great game now forever discredited of the balance of power.

Feb. 11, 1918

. . . These great ends cannot be achieved by debating and seeking to reconcile . . . their projects of balances of power and of national opportunity.

July 4, 1918

We know that there cannot be another balance of power. That has been tried and found wanting.

Dec. 2, 1918

Special alliances and economic rivalries and hostilities have been the prolific source in the modern world of the plans and passions that produce war. It would be an . . . insecure peace that did not exclude them in definite and binding terms. . . .

There can be no league or alliance or special covenants and understandings with the general and common family of the League of Nations.

Sept. 27, 1918

Adequate guarantees given and taken that national armaments will be reduced to the lowest point consistent with domestic safety.

Jan. 8, 1918

We of the United Nations are agreed on certain broad principles in the kind of peace we seek . . . disarmament of aggressors. . . .

Feb. 24, 1942

TO ALLAY HATE, FEAR, AND REVENGE

WILSON

The war shall not end in vindictive action of any kind; that no nation or people shall be robbed

ROOSEVELT

After the final destruction of the Nazi tyranny they hope to see established a peace which will afford

WILSON

or punished because irresponsible rulers of a single country have themselves done a deep and abominable wrong.

Dec. 4, 1917

We wish her [Germany] only to accept a place of equality among the peoples of the world . . . instead of a place of mastery.

Jan. 8, 1918

I call you to witness, my fellow countrymen, that at no stage of this terrible business have I judged the purposes of Germany intemperately. I should be ashamed, in the presence of affairs so grave, so fraught with the destinies of mankind throughout the world, to speak with truculence, to use the weak language of hatred or vindictive purpose.

April 6, 1918

There shall be no . . . contributions, no punitive damages.

Feb. 11, 1918

The settlement of every question whether of territory, of sovereignty or economic arrangement, or of political relationship upon the basis of free acceptance of that settlement by the people immediately concerned and not on the basis of the material advantage of any other nation. . . .

July 4, 1918

The impartial justice meted out must involve no discrimination between those to whom we wish to be just and those to whom we do not wish to be just.

Sept. 27, 1918

ROOSEVELT

all nations the means of dwelling in safety within their own boundaries and which will afford assurance that all men may live out their lives in freedom from fear and want.

Churchill-Roosevelt,
Aug. 13, 1941

We are now in the midst of a war, not for conquest, not for vengeance, but for a world in which this nation and all this nation represents will be safe for our children.

Dec. 9, 1941

WILSON

It is the principle of justice to all peoples and nationalities and their right to live on equal terms of liberty and safety with one another whether they be weak or strong.

Jan. 8, 1918

THE WILL TO PEACE

WILSON

A general association of nations must be formed under specific covenants for the purpose of affording mutual guarantees of political independence and territorial integrity to great and small states alike.

Jan. 8, 1918

The indispensable instrumentality is a League of Nations . . . without such an instrumentality by which the peace of the world can be guaranteed peace will rest in part upon the word of outlaws . . . the constitution of the League of Nations . . . must be . . . the most essential part of the peace settlement itself.

Sept. 27, 1918

Open covenants of peace openly arrived at—diplomacy always frankly in public view.

Jan. 8, 1918

VI THE SEVEN DYNAMIC FORCES
DURING THE ARMISTICE AND
PEACEMAKING 1918–19

JUST as neither sin nor goodness can be abolished from the world, the seven dynamic forces that make for peace and war cannot be eliminated. The real problem before the peace conference was to allay those forces that made for war and to strengthen those which made for peace.

Some were altered during the progress of the war. Some were altered as a consequence of the war. But they were all in action the day after the Armistice, and, for that matter, always will be this side of the millennium. And statesmen are too often dominated by the less peaceful ones.

It is not our purpose to describe the drama of peace negotiations, the gilded halls, the pomp and circumstance surrounding these scores of nations with their celebrated representatives and their protocols of politeness. We are interested in the grim unseen forces which haunted the halls of peace and shaped the coming world.

After the Armistice, the American peace argosy, with President Wilson on board, sailed from America, confident that victory had now brought the opportunity to build a new order of "freedom to mankind," "based upon the broad and universal principles of justice" in which "reason and justice and the common interest of mankind shall prevail," a "lasting peace"—not "a mere peace of shreds and patches," in which economic wrong, selfish nationality, imperialism, militarism, hate, revenge, and fear should be forever buried in the new order.

Americans generally failed to realize how far, in our 300 years of separation, our outlook, our political and social ideas and ideals had grown apart from the practical methods and problems of Europe. This is not said in contention that our ideals were superior. It is merely an indication of a development which was to have a profound influence upon events.

Our freedom from age-old hate of our neighbors, our freedom from fears of invasion, our centuries of national safety, our abundant resources, our ease of living, and the blessings of liberty allowed us to indulge in the luxury of concepts wholly different from those of Europe. Having made a fresh and independent start in the New World, our concepts of democracy had grown apart from the class stratifications and class barriers and class governments of democratic Europe. We had grown far apart in our thinking.

Our warm hopes met at once the freezing blasts of centuries of European mores. To them we were bearers of impractical and strange notions for dealing with their problems. Our ideas clashed against the backgrounds of their realistic necessities. Our representatives had little appreciation of the subtle forces moving in these scores of nations and of the genuine obstacles to the acceptance of some of our ideas.

Our European Allies lived in a grimly practical world in which they believed the tried principles of old power diplomacy afforded the only way to deal adequately with the forces of economic nationalism, economic necessity, imperialism, age-old hates, punishment, revenge, and general disorder. Their nations had lived amid a struggle for existence where every proposal was examined in the cold light of national advantage.

To handle this new phenomenon from the Western World, they summoned the skilled hands of the old diplomacy. It was the process with which over the centuries they had dealt with a hundred European crises. Their representatives belonged to classes and schools which had been born to this profession. They practiced the art with skill that comes from centuries of inheritance and training. Their formulae were seasoned in the history of Europe. The shades of Machiavelli, Marlborough, Pitt, Castlereagh, Talleyrand were all about in their spiritual descendants. To them, this was simply another crisis and no crusade of idealists. They were not impressed—below the skin at least.

The proofs of this lie not only in the incidents and outcome of the peacemaking, but in the official actions and the subsequent ample writings of the European statesmen on the Allied side. They are now the open book of history and need no specific reference.

Here was the greatest chance of all history for statesmen to dominate the evil dynamic forces, but statesmanship ignored them or proved unequal to the task. However, in all this we must recognize the desperation of the situation, the wholly different points of view and ideals of nations separated by centuries of different development and environment.

The misfortune of the world is that, instead of the destructive dynamic forces being allayed, they were given new impulses which plunged the world into World War II.

But American ideals, so well formulated by President Wilson, were not without some victories. Their very vitality carried some of them at least into temporary acceptance.

Here we have the advantage of hindsight and here we may again examine the problem, not in a spirit of captious criticism, but in a desire to extract what lessons we can. Man is not blessed with as much foresight as he is with the ability of availing himself of his hard experience.

The Ideologies [1]

The outstanding immediate result of the war was the advance of representative government. Indeed, this victory came before the peacemakers could meet. It had only to confirm accomplished facts.

The ideals of representative government and of personal and national liberty, so much emphasized by America, had stimulated democratic revolutions which, at the Armistice, swept over the enemy states up to the Russian border. President Wilson's insistence upon "self-determination" and the right of races to their own self-government had started a potent ferment long before the Armistice. A dozen races had completed their independence before the peace conference assembled.

Revolutions in old enemy states installed representative government in full. Long before the war, the great mass of common people in the enemy areas were already fertilized by its preachments. Now their own struggles to attain personal liberty installed at least the forms of representative government. Germany, Hungary, Austria, dismissed the last shreds of despotism. Unfortunately, they went too far and nullified much of the good that might have been achieved by more moderate measures. The revolution was no doubt made easier by the acquiescence of the

[1] For outline of these pressures, see p. 159; before World War I, p. 178; in World War I, p. 207.

warrior classes, hoping for softer terms in defeat. But, nevertheless, the men who came to the top in this revolution were for the most part genuinely liberal and wanted fervently to make democracy work. They especially wanted to turn Germany's face from militarism; they hoped to direct her toward social and economic advancement. They wanted her to co-operate with the other representative governments.

The liberated peoples of Finland, Latvia, Estonia, Lithuania, Poland, Czechoslovakia, Rumania, Croatia, Serbia, Slovenia all adopted personal liberty and representative government as the foundation of national life. Britain, France, Italy, Belgium, Sweden, Norway, Holland, Denmark, Switzerland, and Greece had long since adopted various liberal governmental forms.

Thus, representative government had spread over the whole of Europe up to the Russian frontier. It seemed that the freedom of men had triumphed over almost all the civilized world. It seemed that the World War was but a triumphant incident in the glorious march of mankind toward freedom.

To the Americans, this was not only a crowning success in their purpose, but it was their policy in peacemaking to sustain these representative governments. And here came the most severe clash of American concepts with the Allies and old diplomacy. In the roots of what was done about this problem lay much of the woe to come to the world.

To thoughtful Americans the cornerstone of the edifice of lasting peace after Versailles was not the League of Nations. The real hope lay in representative government. That in itself signified the overthrow of the spirits of aggression, autocracy, militarism, the Junker landlord castes, the remnants of feudalism, the re-establishment of the rights of men as against slavery to state and class. It was the American belief that these newly freed peoples, if able to act, would refuse to stand for militarism and the burdens of aggressive arms or to vote themselves into war—except against attack. But their ability to assert themselves in this peaceful sense depended upon growth of the tender plants of representative government and personal liberty which had sprung up with the Armistice in the old militaristic areas. A chief purpose of the League, as we saw it then, was to safeguard the growth of these forces of freedom.

Yet subsequent revolt from these forces was in part born in the peace treaty itself. We discuss elsewhere the question of punishment of the enemy states. The treaty certainly leaned to the side of hate, fear, and revenge rather than toward statesmanship. The real problem was not one of abstract justice. Justice could never liquidate the wrongs which the ruling caste of Prussia had done the world. The practical fact was that the evil should have been charged to their leaders, as had been promised, and the people should have been given a chance.

Many actions by the Allied governments during the Armistice and in the peace treaty weakened the liberal movement in the enemy states. The German people unquestionably believed they had surrendered upon the basis of the Wilson points. That these points were not applied to Germany very exhaustively is manifest. Whether Germany would have surrendered anyway, or whether she kept her own promises, is not to the point. The point is in the beliefs and emotions of a whole nation.

The leaders of Germany bore a heavy weight of responsibility for the origin and conduct of the war. Their armies had spread grief and suffering and devastation far and wide. No amount of punishment could have been devised to do full justice for the crimes and brutality of those four years. Nothing we may say in criticism of the course followed by the victors in dealing with Germany can soften the judgment of the behavior of her war leaders. But entirely aside from the question of their responsibility, we have an unfortunate record of actions which undermined the edifice of peace while it was being built.

One of the most humiliating of all actions to the Germans was the requirement that the democratic regime sign a war-guilt clause—a confession that the whole nation was guilty of causing the war. This did not bother the militarists—they all escaped—but the millions who had no voice on the war did object, and the foundation was laid for their later support of the militarists in wiping out this stain. The avowal of guilt, signed under duress, brought us no advantage, but, on the other hand, gave successive German agitators a ready-made grievance to exploit.

Another futile and even wicked thrust of Allied militarism and punishment was continuing the food blockade against Germany after the Armistice on November 11, 1918. The provisions of the Armistice promised food, but no food was allowed in until nearly five months later, in the latter part of March 1919. And expanding the blockade after the

Armistice, by the British and French fleets to the Baltic fisheries, made it worse. All this is a black chapter in human history for which no blame attaches to the American people. Our representatives fought against this action daily and hourly during the entire period, and that its ultimate relaxation before peace was signed was due to American insistence. We did have the strong support of certain liberal-minded Englishmen, such as Lord Robert Cecil and Lord Eustace Percy. The suffering of the people in the enemy states after November 11 under the continued blockade was far more acute than that prior to the Armistice. With revolution and weakened government the old distribution and rationing machinery greatly deteriorated. Between farmers hoarding and the richer people bootlegging, a blow came to the children of Germany which subsequent large-scale American charity was not able to remedy.

A further action which was to carry seeds of destruction into the new regime in Germany was the absurd levying of indemnities or "reparations" of $40,000,000,000 upon a people that even under no concept of economic slavery could deliver half the interest on that sum in foreign exchange. Under the terms of the treaty, the Germans were stripped of ships, of much of their private property in foreign lands and even at home. The reparations in kind, chiefly coal from the New Reich and the separation of coal districts, undermined her industrial strength. Just or unjust, wise or unwise, the consequence of these things was to destroy hope and incentive, constantly upset stability, and deter economic recuperation of the world. The whole was punishment for original sin rather than reparation.

The separation of fragments of the German race by Danzig and the Polish Corridor, by territorial changes, and by the prohibition of union with Austria were more punishment than weakening of Germany. Altogether, it decreased Germany's possible population by about 10 per cent. Likewise, the same sort of action toward Hungary, Austria, and Bulgaria sowed dragon's teeth for the future.

It can be said here, and with emphasis, that it was not the fault of Americans that brought these things about. Nor should the statesmen of the Allies be judged too summarily, for there were many desperate forces in operation which often dominated their actions. Our purpose is not to accuse or blame. It is to diagnose.

The freedom of men is again the American purpose in war. If we still hold that it is the cornerstone of a future and lasting peace, we shall need to study all these lessons again.

Economic Pressures [2]

We are not at this point concerned with the economic consequences of the war itself so much as with the pressures which surrounded the peace conference and which were created by the making of peace. Howling storms of economic demoralization surrounded the peace conference with shrill winds crying, "Hurry, hurry, or we perish."

The whole area of the four old empires—Russia, Germany, Austria, and Turkey—was economically exhausted. Italy and France were only one lap behind. Even England was dependent upon the United States for food credits on which to live. The European degeneration in agriculture, with its inevitable famine, demanded relief. The whole of 350,000,000 people were either dangerously short of food or starving. And they had to have food at once or the remnants of civilization would collapse in anarchy or would yield to the seductive call of Communism, now organized and spreading from Russia, subsidized by captured Russian gold. The 200,000,000 people between Russia and the Hindenburg Line had scarcely seen new clothing for four years. They were ragged, tattered, and cold. Then the fourth of the Four Horsemen appeared—Pestilence.

With the Armistice, two new factors made the situation of all these peoples worse than during the war itself. With defeat, the sweep of revolution and the emergence of the thirteen independent nations from disintegration of the four old empires, the wartime controls and restraints collapsed. As mentioned before, the rationing systems of food, clothing, and coal broke down with the removal of the iron hand of military government. Farmers and villagers hoarded what food there was away from the cities.

The economic recasting done by self-determination added another confusion. Each of the thirteen new governments which evolved from the four old empires at once seized all the railway rolling stock and canal boats they could lay hands on. Out of their fears, their hates, their jealousies, and their bad-neighbor policies, they would not allow trains

[2] For outline of these forces, see p. 159; before World War I, p. 181; in World War I, p. 208.

to pass their borders. The railway systems which before the Armistice had fitted the economic life of the old empires were thus broken into fragments. The currencies of the old empires disintegrated and the new states had little security upon which to re-establish them or credits for purchases outside their borders. Thus, the transportation and exchange of goods between surplus areas within Europe were stopped. Coal supplies were inadequate for the minimum of municipal necessities. Hundreds of millions of people in the midst of winter were without heat and light as well as food. Industry was paralyzed; from fifteen to twenty million workmen were unemployed and on public doles.

And add to this the fact that the officials of every one of these new states were for the most part without experience in government. They were nearly all revolutionaries, burning with zeal for the New Order and world politics and so engrossed in that zeal that they had little time or thought for keeping the machinery of everyday life in motion.

The Americans, having the only substantial resources left, and being trusted everywhere as politically disinterested, assumed the burden of finding food; co-ordinating railway, canal, transportation and communication facilities; rehabilitating coal production; improvising credits and currency; organizing new exchange and new systems of rationing supplies; and fighting pestilence. It was not alone a job of saving hundreds of millions from starvation, cold, and disease. It was the job of building stability in government, defeating anarchy and Communism, in order that foundations for any sort of peace could be built. And it was a job of restoring spirit and faith in peoples.

And America did it by the sacrifice of billions of dollars in charity and bad credits, by the distribution of thirty million tons of food, scraped from all parts of the world, by furnishing a dozen governments with expert technical guidance in mobilizing their internal energies to salvation.

Our second intervention in Europe in the name of humanity immediately after the Armistice saved Europe from another collapse such as that after the Thirty Years' War, when it was said a third of the people in Europe had died.

All these economic pressures called for haste in peacemaking. Haste that industry, credit, foreign exchange, and stability might be restored, and haste from fear of impending collapse.

The economic consequences of the peace were not gentle rain on either the just or the unjust. President Wilson had originally denounced all "indemnities or punitive damages," but under the term "reparations" they came into full blossom. There can be no doubt of the ghastly injury the Allies had suffered and the propriety of the old enemies' paying everything within their capacity. The practical question that arose was to assess reparations in such amounts as would not create despair and repudiation or undermine the economy of the enemy states so as to decrease the payments themselves. "You cannot have reparations and revenge at the same time" was the attitude of the Americans. Our delegation wanted to assess a definite annual sum over a limited period of years which would be within the capacity to pay, and by limiting the term, would give hope of eventual release. They also protested at the seizure of private property of enemy citizens all over the world without compensation. But the Allied purpose, particularly that of the French Government, was to devitalize Germany with economic anemia. The preposterous sums levied in the treaty at once started forces that ended by bringing economic degeneration to the world. And from this collapse came a large part of the forces which created Hitler.

The economic systems of the old empires had been integrated over long periods, and their dissolution into a multitude of new states all afire with nationalism played havoc with production and the channels of distribution. Much of this should have been remedied by the peace treaties, but it was not done.

Any American hopes for the reduction of trade barriers were thwarted by the independent action of every new government in Europe at once raising tariffs and setting up special trade agreements partly for political purposes and without even consulting the peacemakers.

In no single case were the prewar economic strains or the strains from the war itself eased by the treaty. They were violently increased.

Nationalism [3]

A new and vigorous nationalism blew full blast through every anteroom, every committee room, every conference, every action. The racial

[3] For outline of this force, see p. 160; before World War I, p. 181; during World War I, p. 208.

fevers of the Allies had been stirred to white heat by the war. And it was even more violent in the liberated nations.

In the Armistice period and under their proclaimed right of self-determination, the oppressed races—the Finns, the Estonians, the Latvians, the Lithuanians, the Poles, the Czechs, the Slovaks, the Croats, the Serbs, the Slovenes, the Armenians, the Georgians, the Azerbaijanese, and the Arabs—all declared their independence. The exiled governments of Belgium, Serbia, Rumania, and Greece returned to their plundered hearths.

There is no hard and fast line where advantageous development of national spirit ends and selfish destructive nationalism begins. Certain it is that at once every one of these new governments organized an army. They occupied the utmost boundaries that they could secure. They fell into a multitude of conflicts among themselves over how far their racial or historic or economic boundaries should extend. Thus the nations and boundaries of Europe were mainly determined before the peace conference could even convene. Many territorial and other enormities, for which the peace conference has been blamed, were committed before it began—and in some cases against its wishes.

Each country, except the enemy states, sent delegates to Paris at once, not only to secure recognition of their newborn independence, but to oppose the claims of their rivals and to take part in the peacemaking. At once they formed combinations among themselves or adhered as satellites to some major power to influence the decisions of the conference. And they absorbed much of the time and vitality of the conference in their problems.

Just as sure as fate, that will happen again at the next peace. For again, we have quite properly proclaimed the right of peoples to freedom, to self-determination, and self-government. But these concepts are the very fires of nationalism, and these nationalistic forces, with their interests and influences, will again bring their problems for settlement to the confusion of the peacemakers if they are not well prepared and united in advance.

Some of these countries are active through their "free governments" in exile, contributing troops, merchant shipping, and colonial resources to the Allied cause. They will demand repayment in the form of restoration of their national existence and the reconstitution of their boundaries.

Imperialism [4]

Imperialism, which was laid out in death by the American peace aims, had even a rebirth. It not alone had the usual appetites, inherited from the Babylonians, Assyrians, Egyptians, Persians, or some other ancient breed, for territory, exploitation, expression of national growth and glory to returning statesmen, but it also had another impulse. The losses of the war were so high that real economic reparations could come to the Allies only by taking Germany's and Turkey's territorial possessions.

It may be said at once that hopes of indemnities and reparations from impoverished, defeated nations have always proved a delusion. Consequential economic compensation for war is to be found only in the form of territories and peoples to exploit. Whatever its form may be, with the impoverishment of the victors and with their blood shed to protect life and living for other nations, and with many backward races incapable of maintaining self-government, the pressures are to get compensations in exploitation in some fashion.

Under the mandate system, set up in the peace treaty, the British Empire grew by 1,607,053 square miles with 35,000,000 inhabitants; the French Empire gained 402,392 square miles with 4,000,000 inhabitants; the Belgian Empire got 53,000 square miles with 3,387,000 inhabitants; the Japanese Empire was awarded 833 square miles of islands with 113,154 inhabitants. Italy got no mandates. America got nothing—and wanted nothing.

These areas contained valuable raw materials and markets. They gave valuable outposts for land, air, and naval forces. They certainly stripped Germany from a world empire down to a local state, but they sowed more dragon's teeth. For one thing, they practically gave to Japan the strategic Pacific islands north of the equator that had belonged to Germany. The use made of these islands since was hardly that envisaged by the mandate. For instead of keeping them unarmed, as the mandates required, they were equipped to serve as the naval and air bases from which America is now being attacked.

[4] For outline of this force, see p. 163; 140 years prior to World War I, p. 186; in World War I, p. 209.

Militarism [5]

The Armistice terms were designed to expunge the force of militarism from the world. German, Austrian, Hungarian, and Bulgarian weapons were taken and destroyed. Germany was disarmed to 100,000 men with no planes, no heavy guns, no tanks, and but few warships. The other enemy nations were allowed but scraps of armies. Herein the peace treaty made a start toward achievement.

But one fatal mistake was made. The old warrior caste was allowed to organize and command the 100,000. Thus they were able to provide for the survival of their class. Under this cover they carried on the tradition of militarism in all its worst forms. They carried on a continuous conspiracy against the peace of the world. It is to them that punishment should have been applied, rather than to the mass of the people.

The treaty provided also for disarmament of all Allied nations by conference later on. This deferment was one of the greatest of all treaty mistakes. It should have been done on the spot. General Bliss, the military member of the American delegation, recommended drastic measures of general reduction of armaments to levels essential for internal security. In a letter to the Secretary of War, written from the peace conference, he made this comment:

Judging from the spirit which seems more and more to dominate our European Allies, I am beginning to despair that the war will accomplish much more than the abolition of *German* militarism while leaving *European* militarism as rampant as ever.

We shall deal with this more fully later on.

Fear, Hate, and Revenge [6]

The evil spirits of fear, hate, and revenge never did more destruction to civilization than at the Paris Conference. They will certainly rise again. As we have said, total war is war on civilians. It is war on women and children. Among our allies, not only had the best of their races been killed upon the field of battle, but their homes had been destroyed, their women and children had been ruthlessly killed from the sky, they had

[5] For outline of this force, see p. 161; 140 years prior to World War I, p. 190; in World War I, p. 209.

[6] For outline of these forces, see p. 164; 140 years prior to World War I, p. 192; in World War I, p. 209.

been deprived of food, their sailors had been drowned without mercy, and their peoples had been impoverished for years to come. Total war sank deep its sufferings and hates into every cottage and fireside, arousing a resentment unknown under the older forms of war.

Moreover, the French had suffered two invasions from Germany in the memory of people then living. The liberated peoples had lived under the heel of the oppressor for generations. And fear is even less tolerant than hate.

Statesmen were not free agents at Paris. It was their people who demanded violent punishment and revenge. To secure re-election, Lloyd George had made a campaign on "Hang the Kaiser" and "Pay to the last farthing." Clemenceau had carried a vote of confidence in the French Assembly only upon the fervid assurance that the German race would be dealt with once and for all. Neither of these statesmen could have continued in office on any assurance of moderation. Even in the American people, where suffering had been infinitely less, there was full flow of hate and a determination for violence in punishment.

Herein was the most difficult of all problems which faced that conference and will face the world again. Statesmen at Paris, looking to the future, realized that here were 100,000,000 people in the enemy countries who could not be exterminated and who had to be lived with. If there was to be lasting peace, the people had to be influenced into the paths of peace; they had to be given an alternative more advantageous than war, and, at the same time, they had to have a definite reminder not to do it again. It required a delicate balance of tolerance and grim justice. The liberal-minded wished to discriminate between the "people" in the enemy countries and their leaders, and upon this theory moved toward tolerance.

But fear, hate, and revenge overweighed the scale. By device after device, they appear in the Treaty of Versailles. We shall later recount the consequences.

The Will to Peace [7]

Principally under American and British guidance, the peace conference created the League of Nations. The League was a convenient re-

[7] For outline of this force, see p. 165; 140 years prior to World War I, p. 193; in World War I, p. 209.

pository for continuing problems. Of vastly more importance, however, it constituted the greatest experiment and the greatest effort that mankind has ever made to assure the peace of the world. It did not come into operation during the period we are discussing.

Effects of the Peacemaking. We may at this point summarize the effects of the peacemaking upon the seven dynamic forces which make for peace and war.

In the field of ideologies, the hopes for freedom of mankind reached the highest point of ascendancy in all history. Subjection of men and class government seemed on the way out of the world. And as a consequence the foundations of peace seemed far more secure than in all past history.

Destructive economic pressures were vastly increased by the war itself and still further increased by the treaty.

Nationalism in its proper forms of freedom and self-government of peoples made the greatest stride of a century. But within it were seeds of selfishness that were destructive.

Imperialism had not died. There was only a shift of possessions of empire. These shifts left destructive hates and destructive aspirations.

Militarism and aggression were stunned but still alive.

Fear, hate, and revenge were swept on to new intensities by both the war and the peace.

The will to peace had brought forth the greatest experiment in international maintenance of peace of all history. Mankind was inspired with a new hope.

But underneath it all the old power diplomacy had given scant regard to American ideas about balance of power, military alliances, disarmament, self-determination in border provinces, annexations, imperialism, freedom of the seas, indemnities, economic aims, negotiated peace, the new order, impartial justice, and many others. Altogether, out of President Wilson's twenty-five points, he had fully succeeded in but four or five.

But he had represented the best ideals of America. He made a magnificent fight for them.

VII THE SEVEN DYNAMIC FORCES IN THE TWENTY YEARS AFTER VERSAILLES

WE have, in this chapter, to examine the swiftest and most explosive revolution in the whole history of Western civilization. During this period of twenty years between 1919 and 1939, the seven dynamic forces moved in confusion and in violence. They, with the help of inadequate statesmanship, ultimately thrust the world into a second World War.

They moved with such rapidity and such interaction upon one another that their separate discussion becomes most difficult. However difficult this separation may be, it requires the most critical examination for such lessons as we can perceive. Hindsight is always more assured than foresight. But the hindsight gained from being singed by fire is good training for acquiring foresight. We can perhaps learn something from experience as to how the forces of good are to be made to dominate the forces of evil.

Ideological Forces[1]

The spread of representative government over the whole of Europe up to the Russian border at the time of the Armistice had inspired high hopes of a new era of freedom, peace, and progress for mankind. But soon it was to weaken in a thousand frustrations. The renewed hope of a golden age was transformed into an era of fear plagued by a thousand miseries.

Then came the gigantic revolt from personal liberty and representative government. Man seemed to be fighting blindly for some new way

[1] For outline of these forces, see p. 159; before World War I, p. 178; in World War I, p. 207; the Armistice and peacemaking, p. 225.

out. He seized upon the word "new" as if it contained salvation in itself, without realizing that the tasks of today were created yesterday.

The age-old idea of enslavement of men to the state returned in two new forms. We have mentioned that Socialism and its brother, Communism, were born even before the first World War. We have mentioned that Fascism had its birth during the war. And it was to find a still more ruthless partner in Nazism. Communism and Fascism were to be rivals, and both were hostile to all liberty.

Indeed, the greatest ideological explosion in all modern civilization was the revolt from the spirit of Liberalism over the world. Beginning with the defeat of the Kerensky regime in Russia in 1917 and the rise of Communism, it broke out again with the rise of Fascism under Mussolini in Italy in 1922, the ascendancy of the military party of Japan in 1931, the rise of Hitler in 1933, and a score of lesser dictators in various parts of the world. And the infection of their ideologies was to reach into and modify concepts of liberty everywhere.

The ideologies of Communism and Fascism have much in common. They have in common their political forms of dictatorship, domination by a single political party, brutality, ruthlessness, and rule by terror. They are both determined enemies of free economy and private rights. They are both founded upon sheer materialism. They are both intensely militaristic and imperialistic. They both ruthlessly oppose intellectual and spiritual freedom.

There is one broad distinction between them. Communist revolution is a complete overturn of society in the name of "the proletariat." It is a cult of supposed complete economic equality. Fascism is an overthrow in the name of the elite. It is a cult of national efficiency. There is less murder and "liquidation" under Fascism, but the moral base is no higher. Communism is brutally opposed to all religious freedom. "Religion is the opiate of the people." Fascism seeks to use religion for purposes of the state. There is another distinction in that Communism is a total expropriation of private property to the state, whereas Fascism continues the private ownership of property but compels its operation for the state. Either is slavery. And Fascism came to power largely as the result of middle-class despair over the failures of representative government to repel the inroads of Communism.

These ideologies are of the most militant type. The Communists, in

1917, organized an attack upon personal liberty and representative government over the entire world, with Moscow as their holy of holies and with the gold of Russia to finance it. The Fascists have been somewhat less energetic in foreign penetration, but with no less intent, as witness their Fifth Columns and their Quislings.

Representative government, which seemed to have established itself as a triumphant concept in the world, was left fighting for its life in World War II. Few Americans even today realize the almost total revolt from Liberalism on the Continent, not only in form, but in the beliefs of men. But Americans should observe the march of these revolutions. This gigantic revolt involved 500,000,000 people in Russia, Germany, Italy, Austria, Poland, Estonia, Latvia, Lithuania, Yugoslavia, Turkey, Hungary, Rumania, Bulgaria, Greece, Japan, Spain, and Portugal. And yet the initial overturn from representative government in all but Russia and Spain was accomplished with the loss of but little blood. It is useless to deny that the peoples of many of these countries welcomed this overthrow of freedom. In many of them, the people voted the new ideologies into being.

The soil upon which all these revolutions throve was prepared by the destruction, the miseries, the disillusions and the moral degradation of the war. The peace treaty had responsibilities in its legacies of selfish nationalism and imperialism and in hate, fear, and revenge. The conduct of the dominant powers in the years following the treaty had a responsibility in driving peoples to further desperation.

There were other contributing causes. These were the trumpetings of new Utopias to despairing peoples. And to their propaganda and borings from within, the very freedoms of free government gave full license. Thus freedom was destroyed by the waters from her own well —free speech, free press, and right of assembly.

Racial mores which were yet unacclimated to the freedoms of personal liberty and its self-disciplines led to license. The faulty structure of these new representative governments created a multitude of factions or parties in legislative halls, whereas democracy can really function with stability only in more disciplined party systems.

In the Fascist revolutions, as we have said, the fear of Communism played a considerable part. The Communists bored from within especially by corrupting the labor groups and using them to create disorder.

The fear of Communism was the immediate turning point in the movements to Fascism.

Finally, two thirds of the people of Europe, starving and idle, despaired of finding their way out through personal liberty and representative government. Allured by the Fascist promise of food, protection of property, and restored order, they welcomed "men on horseback." They voted most of them into power. Truly, they voted their own doom. And doom of all their freedom it has been.

Initially, these were to be revolutions in the economic systems and political organizations only. But quickly the dictators found that they could not secure economic recovery and political ascendancy without more and more coercion and without suppression of every form of actual or possible opposition. Having lost the whole mainspring of economic production through the loss of confidence and the fears of men, they substituted fear of the concentration camp. Quickly they shifted the ideological pattern into the shapes of despotism, terrorism, and slavery.

Economic Pressures [2]

As we have said above, the economic pressures were a large contribution to the revolt from Liberty. The first World War left the world a hideous economic inheritance. It depleted the best manhood; it destroyed skills; it brought moral degeneration and lifted brutality to a profession. It left damaged or wrecked factories, mines, railways, ships; depleted herds and soil; and ruined orchards. It disrupted the machinery of economic life. It destroyed savings and capital, left gigantic internal and international debts and inflation. The very delicacy of adjustment and international interdependence of the economic life before the war contributed to ruin by the disruption of the machinery of trade and credit. Its net result was to be seen in tens of millions of unemployed, starved, and pestilence-ridden peoples.

To analyze the contribution these disasters made to the revolt from representative government and toward war presents one immediate difficulty. The forces of destruction on the march did not march in step between different countries. They were modified by racial characteristics and leadership. The reactions of political and other pressures affected

[2] For outline of these pressures, see p. 159; before World War I, p. 181; in World War I, p. 208; the Armistice and peacemaking, p. 229.

each country differently. But certain generalizations can be discovered which are of importance to our later conclusions.

After Versailles, all the world except Russia went to work to resuscitate free economic systems. The first task was to reorient economy from purposes of war to civilian production. But they were soon to realize that after total war, it was not a simple process to turn swords into plowshares. Under the absorptions of their economic systems during the war, nations did not feel their real economic wounds until the war was over. All nations were soon to realize that there were wounds in the complicated economic system of industrial age that were deep and festering. These were most severe in the former enemy states and most of the newly liberated nations—with Italy and France but a short distance behind. The United States, Britain, and the neutrals suffered less, but even there the shock upon the delicately adjusted economy of the Machine Age was disastrous. And these shocks continued to reverberate over the whole world from the center of worse confusion of the Continent. Britain and America were still strong enough to have pulled out quickly to recovery but for economic shocks and ideological infections from the Continent.

With the Armistice, most nations tried to drop their government-managed or -dictated economics. Most of them first tried to heal the wounds of war the hard way—by freeing enterprise, honoring debts, and stabilizing currencies; stimulating thrift and savings as the basis of recuperation of capital; driving to balance budgets; and generally hoping for the growth of individual initiative, self-discipline, and self-reliance. Practically all governments, in the meantime, directly or indirectly gave support to the unemployed against hunger, cold, and disease. It was the method of healing wounds by the natural growth of cell upon cell, with governmental protection from suffering. The more-exhausted countries and those of less vitality on the Continent responded slowly. Other countries, such as Britain, the United States, and the neutrals, progressed on these lines until the more exhausted countries collapsed. In the more exhausted countries, men lost patience with the hard way. And in different countries at different times men's minds began to revert consciously or unconsciously to resurrection of wartime economic regimes as the way out.

As we have said, war organization, even in the democracies, had of necessity to take regimented forms. With the pains of after-war dis-organization and the aches of the hard way, men quickly became candidates for public favor who proposed to speed up convalescence by restoring some degree of the coercion economics of war. These ideas were arrayed in new garments of fine colors and heralded as the salvation of mankind. They gave the people hope of a new road out of misery. Everywhere these men promised punishment to economic evildoers, a division of supposed stores of wealth, with assured security and comfort for everybody.

There thus emerged what can perhaps be defined as another ideology—that is what is called "managed economy." Its essential characteristic is an attempt to maintain personal liberty and representative government with some considerable degree of totalitarian methods in the field of economic freedom.

The subject has a relation to the problems of peace and war in many aspects, which we discuss later. It bears upon the revolt from liberty and representative government. From its failure to restore employment came pressure to rearmament as a relief measure. In many countries it was a transition stage in the rise of dictatorships. And it enters into foreign relations through governmental action in foreign trade. It therefore merits some amplification.

Before we discuss the subject further, it is desirable that we define what we mean by economic freedom. To be free, men must choose their callings, bargain for their own services, save and provide for their families and old age. And they must be free to engage in enterprise so long as each does not injure his fellow man. And that requires laws to prevent abuse. And when we use the term "economic freedom," "free enterprise" or "Fifth Freedom," we use it in this sense only, not in the sense of *laissez faire* or capitalistic exploitation. Such freedom does not mean going back to abuses. It in no way inhibits social reforms and social advancement. Economic freedom furnishes the resources for such advancement and flourishes only with such advances.

Laws to prevent men doing economic injury to their fellows were necessary and universal in civilized countries long before the first World War. Government regulation of monopolies, banks, utilities, coinage; prevention of combinations in restraint of trade; government support to credit in times of stress; public works; tariffs; limitations on hours of labor; relief of suffering; etc. might be called "managed economy." The essence is one of degree—that is, the extent of government action and centralization of power. At some point of this expansion of government into the economic field, it begins to stifle initiative and enterprise, with consequences in unemployment and lowered standards of living. At some point it weakens the constitutional safeguard of personal liberty and representative government and begins to trespass upon liberty itself. At these points it could be more appropriately called statism.

The development of managed economy on the continent of Europe covered a varied range of activities and in different degrees of intensity. It included manipulation of currency, credit, and markets. It included huge government expenditures for public works and in other efforts to prime the economic pump, with consequent unbalanced budgets, increasing public debt, and inflation.

Governments sought to lift prices and wages by restriction of production. They undertook the operation of some types of business, and thus included strong draughts of Socialism. They undertook dictation to business, labor, and agriculture, and thus included the strong doses of economic coercion of Fascism. The spirit was hostile to free enterprise. Much-needed reforms of economic abuse were undertaken not through thoughtful development of definite rules of law but by short cuts through wide authorities to bureaucracies. Every advance in economic power of governments brought needs and demands for more and more power.

As these regimes progressed, they overwhelmed legislative bodies with tasks impossible of deliberative digestion. They secured acquiescence of legislators through pressure groups, coercions, and the bait of political privilege. They undermined the independence of legislative bodies. They weakened them by their undermining of constitutional safeguards of liberty. They brought the degradation of privilege. They brought back the very system of ruinous bureaucracies from which the French Revolution had originally started.

Managed economy was thus a mixture of free enterprise, together with Socialism and Fascism. The proportions varied in different countries. We have constantly to remember that free economy is governed by the most delicate of hairsprings—confidence of individual men who operate it; confidence in money, in open markets, in credits, in stability of government finance; and, above all, confidence in the future. And as free enterprise is based upon voluntary co-operative action and security from fear, it was easily stifled by the interferences, uncertainties, confusions, and fear of political action. The way was paved for the full Fascist stage, where production is secured not by confidence of free men but by coercion and fear.

No one country engaged in all of these practices at one time. But Italy, Germany, Spain, and some lesser nations embraced them in part. In France, the attempt by Blum to mix larger doses of totalitarian economics into free economy contributed to the demoralization of the country which had so tended the cradle of economic liberty. It can be observed that every European nation of a totalitarian or managed-economy system turned to the manufacture of arms before they secured employment and war markets.

From the other economic and political repercussions of war aftermaths which we have enumerated, together with the failure of managed economy, the economic collapse on the Continent could not longer be staved off. The crash and panic beginning in Austria in 1930 swept Germany and all Europe, finally dragging the whole world down into the "Great Depression." From the miseries of the depression came renewed impulses which contributed to the revolt from all personal liberty and representative government. One after another, nations comprising hundreds of millions of people went over to dictatorship and Fascism.

Britain and the United States and most neutrals had made real recovery from the war. There were weaknesses. One of the worst in both Britain and the United States, the least-hurt of all nations, was a wild speculative boom. It arose initially from the moderate war inflations, the postwar food and raw material shortage abroad, and the war suppression of housing and other construction at home. The speculative temper was made worse when the Federal Reserve Board and the Bank of England in 1927 yielded to the urgings of Europe to inflate credit further. That action may have staved off the European collapse for a year or so, but inevitable disaster could not be long deferred. The real effect was further to stimulate our own speculative orgy, which finally, in 1929, collapsed, partly of its own weight and partly from foreign causes.

But the real detonator of the crash was central Europe when, in 1931, their panics, their defaults of private and public credits dragged down the entire world. America could have recovered from its own misdoings in a year, but with the European collapse, we were dragged into the depths of depression as great as that which followed ten years after our Civil War. There were many other contributing factors to this depression, but the subject is not part of this discussion.

Managed economy infected Great Britain for a short period only under the Labor Government. That stanch people had shaken it off, and, continuing the hard way, they made real recovery both from the war and the depression. The United States, impatient with recovery from the world depression by the hard way, became infected with managed economy in 1933.

Whether managed economy in the United States had extended over the line where recovery by voluntary and co-operative action of free enterprise was stifled and liberty infringed is not part of this discussion.

There is, however, an illusion and a warning to Americans in all this world experience with managed economy, including our own. The illusion of its advocates is that there can be totalitarian (or coercive) economics and at the same time a survival of the personal liberties of free speech, free press, free assembly, freedom of worship, and free representative government. The moment that managed economy steps over the line where voluntary action, co-operative movement, and individual initiative reign, protest begins. Soon the bureaucracy loses patience with opposition and starts limiting personal expression by direct or indirect coercion. Moreover, when the voters in large numbers become dependent upon the state, the rule of the majority may become tyranny.

This whole period of twenty years was everywhere marked by frantic nationalistic economics. The pressures for individual recovery within nations led to a deluge of increased tariffs, which America followed after some two-score nations had increased their tariffs against us. The many new small nations freed by the war developed such economic and political excesses as to impoverish themselves. Then came special trade agreements; reciprocal agreements; quotas; manipulation of currencies to influence international trade and other barriers to commerce. The whole of these excessive nationalistic economics contributed to world economic disorganization.

The tendency of politicians in each country has been to blame immediate local causes for the world economic collapse, but no capable student of peace and war ignores the fact that the dominant cause was in the inheritances of the war itself. Had there been no war, such a collapse would not have occurred.

Nationalism [3]

Nationalism rose steadily during the whole fateful twenty years. The newborn states expressed it culturally, economically, diplomatically, and in armament, with great vigor. Especially in the economic and military fields did excesses contribute to the general degeneration. Germany moved under Hitler into the grotesque concepts of racialism and the "Master Race." These concepts were part contribution to their persecution of the Jews and other racial minorities.

In addition to the small countries which set up national existence at the end of the first World War, there were various lands throughout the world which had not progressed so far, but where the ferment of nationalistic agitation was preparing the way to more independence among nations. Such movements were pronounced in China and its resentment of foreign occupation of parts of its territory; in India and Burma for dominion status in the British Empire; and to some extent among the Malayan and other races.

A side issue of explosive character in nationalism of this period lay in the handling of the irredentas of Europe by the Versailles Treaty. There are many of these areas of mixed populations where a reasonable boundary is difficult if not impossible to draw. For any boundaries through the areas of mixed population leave great masses of people separated from their homelands. Nationalistic agitations and repressions began on both sides. With the Treaty of Versailles these boundaries were stretched everywhere to the advantage of the victors. Many festering irredentas still remained, and some new ones were created. The treaty placed many Russians, Lithuanians, and Germans under Poland;

[3] For outline of this force, see p. 160; 140 years prior to World War I, p. 185; in World War I, p. 208; the Armistice and peacemaking, p. 231.

it placed many Hungarians, Bulgarians, and Russians under Czecho-slovakia, Yugoslavia, and Rumania; it placed many Germans under Czechoslovakia and France, Arabs under Britain, etc. It all added to clamor and chaos.

Imperialism [4]

Imperialism again put its ugly hands into the chaos of these twenty years. Imperialism, punishment, and reparations had shorn Germany of her possessions. When Hitler came to power in 1933, he at once raised the banner of unification of his race and the cry for territory to exploit. His invasions of Austria, Sudetenland, Memel, even before the present war, are evidence enough of the rising imperialism of Germany. Japan took Manchukuo by conquest from China. Italy was aggrieved at her failure to secure imperial possessions at Versailles and undertook the conquest of Ethiopia. The appetite for possessions was not quieted in the world.

Another form of imperialism emerged in this period: that is, the political subjection of nations by penetration of ideologies. By this means the Communists sought to extend the domain of Moscow influence, and the Germans the domain of Berlin influence. By this method Russia at one time gained temporary dominion over Finland, Estonia, Latvia, and Lithuania, and reached into Hungary. She succeeded in Georgia, Azerbaijan, and Outer Mongolia.

Fascism and Nazism have directed their policies to the creation of ideological blocs by such penetration combining them by military and economic alliances. Therefrom we have the "Axis" and its adherents. Nor are these ideological penetrations limited to acquiring territory. They are used to disturb the policies of other countries. Both Communist and Fascist Fifth Columns worked increasingly to these ends throughout the world in this period.

Militarism [5]

Militarism quickly demonstrated that it was not killed by the treaty. As a matter of fact, its greatest triumph was the defeat of disarmament in the Allied countries.

[4] For outline of this force, see p. 163; 140 years prior to World War I, p. 186; in World War I, p. 209; the Armistice and peacemaking, p. 233.
[5] For outline of this force, see p. 161; 140 years prior to World War I, p. 190; during World War I, p. 209; the Armistice and peacemaking, p. 234.

Communist Russia led rearmament in a stupendous fashion at once after the war. Mussolini immediately built a militarist state as part of Fascism. When Hitler came to power he repudiated the disarmament of Germany and began the building of huge armaments. The military alliances of the Axis which followed provoked vast counter rearmament in the liberal nations.

From 1932 to 1938, the annual arms expenditure of the world increased from about $4,000,000,000 to about $18,000,000,000. Such a sum would have probably relieved most of the acute poverty in the Western World had it been applied to productive purposes. And this sum of $18,000,000,000 compares with $1,500,000,000 five years before the first World War. And it meant a vast military machine in the world whose inclinations turned in 1933 toward war, not peace.

Fear, Hate, and Revenge [6]

We need add little to what we have already said to indicate that the evil forces of fear and its allies, hate and revenge, continued and grew steadily more bitter in many parts of Europe from the treaty in 1919 down to 1939.

Wars seldom bring about the brotherhood of man. Hate lives on, and it becomes entrenched in the mores of a people. The defeated are always humiliated, no matter how just the peace. No nation ever recognizes or admits that it was wrong. No leader in that nation would dare to suggest such a thing. We saw Germany, Austria, and Hungary refuse to accept the terms of peace except technically. The forces of new wars began to gather emotional strength the day the treaties of peace were signed.

It is an interesting observation that neither the reactionary Treaty of Westphalia nor the Treaty of Vienna attempted to punish the defeated. Those treaties proved more lasting than Versailles, which, except for its punishments, was far more liberal in character.

And worse still, the process of modern total war, with its hideous brutalities to women, children, and noncombatants, breeds a deeper hate, a greater demand for punishment; and the total humiliations of defeat in modern war create an undying demand for revenge. Certainly

[6] For outline of these forces, see p. 164; before World War I, p. 192; during World War I, p. 209; the Armistice and peacemaking, p. 234.

this twenty-year period was one of ascending hates. During this time the burden of reparations and international debts left over from the war were unceasing causes of hard feeling. But outstanding in threat to the peace of Europe was the fear and hate between France and Germany. The Hungarians never ceased their hymns of hate against their neighbors for the dismemberment of their territory. The French and Italians, once comrades in arms, steadily developed ill feeling. Hate between the Japanese and Chinese rose steadily from the aggressions of Japan. The Czechs, the Poles, the Baltic states, and the Balkans could not easily forget their centuries of oppression.

However, the British and Americans did allay their hates toward former enemies and gave to them great aid until the rise and threats of the Fascist groups.

Toward America for her generosity and service in saving millions of lives in a score of friendly and enemy nations of Europe, and for her part in the liberation of many of them, came an affection that has never before been witnessed in this world. But aside from this, only in the Western Hemisphere can it be said that universal good will among all the nations made gains in this period.

The Will to Peace [7]

This twenty-year period represents in the whole history of civilization the greatest definite effort of mankind to organize peace and international co-operation. The League, the World Court, Locarno, Lausanne, the conferences for the reduction and limitation of armaments, the Kellogg-Briand Pact are monuments to that effort.

As the world, twenty years after one dreadful war, blew up in a second and more fearful conflict, all the work of buttressing peace has been condemned as futile. We do not believe that such condemnation is justified. The world will attain peace only by sore trial and error. The League of Nations, above all other efforts, has given us a vast fund of experience. We will elsewhere critically examine the directions of its success and the causes of its failures.

We may emphasize here, however, that it was not the League that brought the collapse of the world into a second total war. The League

[7] For outline of this force, see p. 165; 140 years prior to World War I, p. 193; in World War I, p. 209; the Armistice and peacemaking, p. 235.

was the creation of representative government, and when representative government and personal liberty died, the League died also. The present war came from the revolt from Liberalism, the rise of totalitarianism, of selfish nationalism, of imperialism, of militarism, of fear, hate, and revenge. These evil forces were not allayed by the Treaty of Versailles. They found roots of growth in it. And the efforts to organize peace failed because of these foul growths.

We cannot avoid the haunting fear that the decline and fall of the League and other liberal efforts were a part of a decline and fall of civilization on the continent of Europe—a vast compound of impersonal forces driving inexorably to some dreadful fate.

The Attitudes of the Principal Nations during the Twenty Years

It is of the first importance that the world examine and understand the experience and lessons from the gigantic peace efforts of the period. But to do so more effectively we will first examine the effect of the six dynamic forces of degeneration upon the attitudes and actions of the principal nations during this time. Especially we must examine the relation of that conduct to the great revolt which precipitated the present war.

This twenty years was a period of heartbreaking divergences of attitudes and degenerations in relations between nations. After the peace treaty Britain, France, Italy, and Japan remained the only substantially armed nations, with Russia rapidly rearming. The British and French, acting together or separately, were able to impose their will upon all Europe up to the borders of Russia. With the Italians, they dominated the League and could determine its European policies. But at once there grew up differences between them, and an entire lack of cohesion in action in their relations with Germany, Russia and the Liberated Nations.

France and Germany. The dominating factor in French foreign policies was fear of Germany. These fears had dominated French policies for two generations. It is easy to understand French apprehension. As we have said, within the recollection of living Frenchmen, France had been twice invaded by the Germans, her lands and homes destroyed with fire and sword, the best of her manhood killed or maimed. Her population was less than two thirds that of the Germans, and it was not unnatural that she should believe her security could be obtained only by keeping Germany prostrate or by international alliances against her.

In any event, at the end of those four years of the World War, again exhausted and bled white, France was determined to keep Germany in military and economic bondage when she had a chance. Her fears were such that she would not participate in limitations of naval arms except in words, although her naval superiority to Germany was always conceded; she would participate in no reduction of land arms, though armies overwhelmingly greater than those of Germany were always proposed for her defense. She yielded unwillingly to every effort at amelioration of the impossible and unworkable reparations. Meantime, to buttress herself with international support, she was frantically building rings of military alliances around Germany. She drained her resources to arm the Poles, the Czechs, the Yugoslavs, and the Rumanians. She entered into a military alliance with Communist Russia. The reaction of French policies upon the Germans was to heighten every German hatred and to confirm every fear of encirclement and destruction.

France had one of two courses to follow. The one was to hold Germany down by grim force of arms. The other was to join in sustaining a democratic regime in Germany, giving her an economic chance; holding to German disarmament, but joining with other nations to lower all armament and thus relieve economic burdens everywhere. France followed neither course consistently, and the latter least of all. During the whole period from 1918 to 1939, she was the stumbling block to every proposal for world advancement, constantly demanding guarantees for her own security as the price of co-operation with other nations in any direction. At the same time, she alienated her major and natural allies, Italy and Britain.

France and Italy. The French attitude toward Italy drove Italy into the arms of Germany, and thereby greatly increased the menace to French safety. It began when the Italians were denied the promised lands enumerated in the secret treaty upon which they had entered the war. Then followed French affronts and pinpricks. Her repeated rebuffs of Italian advances wasted the period when Italy would have accepted almost any reasonable solution of colonial and naval questions.

Nor was France constant to her major protector, Britain, or to the League of Nations, as witness the abandonment of the British in the economic sanctions against Italy at the time of the aggression against Ethiopia. French conduct generally helped to alienate the United States from all European problems. At this distance, the whole course of French diplomacy, except in certain intervals of Briand's ascendancy, is incredible. We have here the age-old forces of fear and hate doing their suicidal worst.

In the course of this discussion we have frequent occasion to criticize the policy and action of the French Government. We wish to stress the fact that our criticisms are directed at political leaders, not at the nation. It is a tragedy for our civilization that a people of such magnificent virtues and intelligence should have entrusted their destinies, with honorable exceptions such as Briand, to a class of politicians unable to rise to the need of the times. The French people should have every sympathy and support in their blood and tears. We should not lose sight of the fact that it is essential to any real rehabilitation of Europe that France should be restored to a position of weight and influence worthy of her great national qualities.

The United States and Germany. The attitude of the United States of giving aid and support to the building of a representative government in Germany was not confined to the treaty negotiations, but continued in every crisis during the whole life of the Weimar Republic. The friendly offices of Americans brought above the Dawes Commission in 1924, the Young Commission in 1929, the Hoover Moratorium and the Standstill Agreement in 1931, all in endeavors to save the republic from economic collapse under reparations pressure. Our arrangement of the meeting of Premiers at Geneva in 1932 in an endeavor to relax the unnecessary burdens of the treaty, and our calling of a World Economic Conference of 1932 are but part of our interest and effort. In all these efforts we had the full co-operation of Britain and usually of Italy, but always the opposition of the French Ministers.

Britain and Germany. The intermittent and intransigent courses of French policy were a constant anxiety to Britain. Britain did endeavor to support the growth of liberal forces in Germany, but in every crisis had to yield something to France. Outstanding instances of this desire of the British to give the democratic regime in Germany a chance were their opposition to the French occupation of the Ruhr in 1923 and their refusal to join in the French schemes against democratic Germany or the alliance with Russia. British leadership of reconciliation at Locarno gave great hope. Her initiative in the move to admit Germany to the League of Nations, her urging the French to accept the Hoover Moratorium in 1931, her support to the American proposals to strengthen Bruening and German economic stability in 1932 were all instances of British anxiety to strengthen the forces of freedom and economic recovery.

Americans can perhaps better understand British policies in Europe if they will constantly realize that she has always had intermittent spells of isolationism and disgust with continental power politics and continental wars. But finally driven by ascending crises, and without any effective machinery for common action, she falls back upon the familiar methods of balance of power.

Nevertheless, all through the period of German democracy, the British were constantly seeking opportunities to strengthen the liberal forces within Germany. When Germany did revolt from representative government to dictatorship and did become a menace, then Britain supported France and the balance of power against Germany and Italy.

Italy and Germany. Italian policy has been described as the antithesis of British policy. Whereas Britain seeks to prevent any Power acquiring domination, Italy is on the lookout for rising stars and seeks to throw in her lot with the winning side. She had real grievances from the Treaty of Versailles and from the domineering attitude of France. And indeed, these grievances contributed to the rise and popular support of Mussolini, with his trappings of Fascism and dictatorship. With this ideology, the new Italian Government had initially no sympathy with republican Germany.

Germany. Germany came out of the Treaty of Versailles with real and fancied grievances. She deserved punishment. But as we have stated before, that punishment took forms which brought no benefit to the Allies and which made it doubly difficult for the men to succeed who were struggling to liberalize Germany. Certainly, if establishment of representative government is the cornerstone of lasting peace, then many of the Allied acts were most utter folly.

The aggressive and bitterly nationalistic character of the German ruling class has been one of the fundamental causes of European wars for centuries. The almost constant formula of other European nations in repression of Germany has been to divide the race into separate states. But the resultant agitation of this virile people for union has been one of the prime causes of European wars. Even customs union with German Austria was prohibited, and in the subjection of large groups of Germans to Poland and Czechoslovakia was laid a powder train to the new explosion. Added together were the weakening of representative government, economic demoralization, the penetration of Communism, and the growth of real or fancied grievances, which brought Hitler to power.

How just was the German complaint about its treatment is not the whole question. When a nation is humiliated by defeat and becomes indurated with such beliefs and resentments, she becomes hopeless of reasoned action—and this, regardless of real rights and wrongs.

With all these different attitudes, it is not surprising that European developments have been complex and confusing. It would have been surprising if, during this troubled period, the divergent policies in the leading nations had led to solution and peace.

VIII THE WILL TO PEACE DURING THE TWENTY YEARS AFTER VERSAILLES

THE efforts at international organization to preserve peace rose to greater heights in the period of twenty years from 1919 to 1939 than ever before in all the history of man. Great experiments were tried and failed. But from this very experience the world may have found real guidance to the Promised Land. It is our purpose to explore these efforts in this chapter.

The League of Nations

The nursery of the League of Nations was not only set in the middle of conflict among leading nations which we have outlined in the last chapter. It was also surrounded by the grim misery, the strife, the revolution and the ascending nihilism of reaction from the greatest shock that has come to man—total war. An analysis of the League and its results becomes at the same time a recitation of the effect of the seven dynamic pressures and the treatment of the League by the various governments after the war.

The immediate spread of representative government over the world gave a foundation upon which such a liberal institution as the League had a chance to take hold. But, as said above, the League, born of Liberalism, could not survive after representative government had perished.

It is not necessary here to recount the origins of the League of Nations idea. In various forms it had appeared in the discussion of thinking men long before the outbreak of war in 1914. The ideas of military and economic sanctions to be applied collectively by all nations against an aggressor were a part of this thinking. Organizations had been

established in various countries to promote the League idea early in
the last war—and various drafts had been proposed before the peace
conference. But the drafting of the actual League Covenant was done
under great pressures for haste and many conflicts of interest. Of
necessity, there was much compromise which led to subsequent confusion.

The League Machinery

The League machinery consisted of an Assembly, a Council, a Secretariat, and co-ordinate international organizations. The Assembly comprised representatives of all member nations, meeting once a year and
on call for emergencies. In the Assembly, each member state had one
vote. The Council, which met periodically or on call in emergencies,
envisaged a permanent membership of Britain, France, the United
States, Italy, Japan, and certain others elected by the Assembly to
temporary membership. The number of these temporary members rose
from four at the start to ten, which gave the Council a total membership
of fourteen. Action by the Council and Assembly was required to be
by unanimous vote with certain exceptions. These exceptions related
mostly to procedure, election of members, and exclusion of those members engaged in dispute from the right to vote. In effect, no action of
the Assembly could become binding except with the approval of the
Council.

With the requirement of unanimous vote of the Council, each of
the principal Allied governments of the first World War had in effect
a complete veto on any action by the League.

The League membership at one time or another embraced sixty-two
nations, constituting about nine tenths of the world's population. The
"enemy" countries were to be admitted and were in fact admitted after
some years. The United States and a few minor states did not join,
while Brazil, Italy, Germany, Japan, and a few others ultimately withdrew, and Russia was expelled.

The permanent Secretariat at Geneva functioned admirably under
a secretary-general and an efficient international civil service at Geneva.
The International Labor Office was affiliated with the League. The
League was entrusted with the duty of establishing and supporting
the Court of International Justice at the Hague. And the League en-

couraged and co-ordinated many other agencies of international co-operation.

The League Purposes

The declared purposes of the League were to establish "international co-operation," achieve "peace and security," "an obligation not to resort to war," "the firm establishment of international law," "maintenance of justice," and "respect for treaty obligations."

The separate fronts of the League's attack upon war were:

1. A commitment of members to respect and "preserve as against external aggression the territorial integrity and existing political independence of all members."
2. A commitment of members to seek settlement of controversies by negotiation, conciliation, arbitration, judicial settlement, and reports upon fact, with a pledge not to resort to war until three months after these processes were exhausted. All these may be called the pacific methods.
3. Agreement that if a member were unwilling to proceed through these alternative processes and went to war, "it shall be deemed to have committed an act of war against all other members of the League." Then all members were committed to consider severance of trade and financial relations and all intercourse with nationals of the offending state. And finally the Council was authorized to recommend economic and military sanctions (Art. 16). All these may be called the force methods.
4. General disarmament was to be vigorously undertaken.
5. There was to be reconsideration of treaties which had become "inapplicable"—peaceful revision.
6. The League was to promote international co-operation in suppression of crime, and advancement of public health, of trade, labor standards, intellectual exchanges, etc., etc.
7. In addition, the League had certain duties and responsibilities in the administration of former German colonies and the former Arab possessions of Turkey.
8. The League was further charged with important duties for the protection of national minorities.

Thus there were five major principles of peace preservation running through the League Covenant. The first one was a joint guarantee against infringement of the *status quo*. The second principle was the commitment to submit all controversies to arbitral procedure or conciliation. The third was to enforce peace by economic and military alliance of members. The fourth was to relieve strain by peaceful revision of onerous treaties. The fifth was to build international solidarity by co-operation in welfare, economic, and intellectual fields.

Thus, the League was to combine in one organization both force and pacific methods of preserving peace. Generally, the principle was called "collective security."

Areas of Success in League Operation

There were two areas of real success by the League:

The first was the settlement of a good many disputes by pacific methods. Several important disputes were brought before the League or its agencies and disposed of in some fashion by pacific methods which prevented bloodshed. Sometimes no tangible final agreement was secured, but conflict was staved off. There were successful solutions in some minor disputes. But even these minor settlements prevented the growth of antagonisms which might have developed into more serious problems. The success in this direction brought prestige to the League. We give a résumé of these actions in the Appendix.

The second area of success was the non-political co-operation between nations and welfare activities. Co-operative action was effective in labor questions; child welfare and refugees; white and black slavery; public health; drug regulation; economic and tariff standards; double taxation; treatment of nationals; whaling regulations; intellectual co-operation; communications; and various transportation, transit, and power transmission questions. This multitude of services was accomplished partly by way of distributing information, partly by way of international agreements, and is beyond praise. This picture fulfilled every hope of the well-wishers of the League. More, in fact, was accomplished by the League in twenty years in advancement along these lines than in the whole of the previous century.

Areas of Failure in League Operation

The areas of failure are no less instructive. The causes of failure lay in:

1. The survival of power diplomacy.
2. The inability to formulate a European policy of peaceful reconstruction.
3. The total collapse of the force methods in practical application.
4. The failure to secure disarmament.
5. The failure of effort or real intent to revise the onerous treaties and thus make the readjustments between nations which the injustices of the Versailles Treaty, and other treaties marking the end of the war, and normal change constantly required. That failure permitted the growth of an accumulation of conflicts and grievances, with war as the only available solvent.
6. Internal weaknesses in the League structure.

1. Survival of the Old Power Diplomacy. It is important to consider the political climate in which the League functioned.

The League was to be the instrument of co-operation and collective security. It was *ipso facto* to replace and liquidate the old diplomacy, military alliances, balances of power, the Concert of Europe, etc. It was to be the clearinghouse of disputes that might lead to war. But it did not work out this way in practice. The great Powers—Britain, France, Italy, Japan, and subsequently Germany and Russia—and even the smaller Powers, when they became members, preferred to rely upon their own right arms rather than any "common opinion of mankind" or "collective security." The British asserted publicly time and again their resolution to maintain the naval domination of Europe, and the French with equal vigor asserted their determination to maintain the dominant continental land forces. And they jointly resolved to maintain complete military domination of Europe. Various military alliances, such as the Anglo-French Alliance and the Little Entente, were doing business from the start of the League or even before the start. Others grew like weeds all over Europe.

From the League's first day it found itself paralleled by and in competition with the functioning of the old power politics. Before the

Covenant was sealed, before the United States had declined to join, power diplomacy was operating with the old vigor. The old order was not dead. The Council of Ambassadors continued to handle matters of common concern after the League began to operate. Not only was the League ignored on many major issues, but many policies for the League were planned outside its halls.

Power diplomacy penetrated the League itself. The hard fact is that nations have friends, and these friendships could be called upon to prevent any action by the League. And thus the League was pulled and hauled behind the scenes, as in the cases of Hungary, Japan, and Italy. Moreover, nations have friends among officials, institutions, societies, and individuals in foreign countries, and these too were brought into action in creating influence and public opinion in foreign countries to influence League action.

Quickly, also, the important nations established permanent organizations to deal with League affairs, which grew into a sort of periphery of diplomacy around the League. One of their concerns was the possible encroachment of the League upon national sovereignty or upon independence of action by the individual members of the League. A part of the duties of these representatives was to see that no action was taken by the League that would be inimical to their national policies at home. And for this purpose, groups quickly grew up for mutual aid, especially in satellite smaller Powers attached to the major Powers.

Another of the crosscurrents was the urge of the very human egoism in individual representatives for leadership in activities of the League and for prized positions as members of the Council. In these maneuvers, the old power diplomacy clearly showed its hand. One reflex of it was the increase of the number of members of the Council from eight to fourteen.

Out of these same very human qualities the meetings of the League became forums for a vast amount of camp meeting oratory on peace which the world did not take seriously.

The result of it all was materially to lower the prestige of the League.

On the other hand, the Secretariat embraced a group of men and women of great capacity and intelligence. They believed in the League and served it with most efficient zeal.

2. The Inability of the League to Formulate a European Policy of Peaceful Reconstruction. But more important was the inability of the League to formulate a broad policy for dealing with European problems.

The major scene of danger of war in the world has always been the continent of Europe. Although it was the transcendent need of the times, the League never had a European policy, even at the moment when every European nation was in its membership. The League Covenant, in Article 19, provided not only for revision of treaties which we refer to later on, but there is the implication of consideration to be given to "international conditions whose continuance might endanger the peace of the world." There seems to have been no serious discussion or consideration of the crisis generated by the rise of the Axis. That is, the major danger to the world was ignored by the League.

The League considered that its prime function was to settle controversies. One purpose of the victors in the last war and the real foundation of peace was to implant and hold representative government in Europe. That concept the League never seemed to have grasped and certainly did not vigorously assert or guard.

Fundamentally, the policies of Europe remained in the hands of the larger Powers—with final determination by the old Allies until the general European revolt from Liberalism and the creation of the Axis.

As an indication of the unwillingness of the principal powers to make use of the League to formulate European peace policies, we give in the Appendix a list of nineteen international diplomatic conferences upon important measures in which the League played no part. We give a list of thirty-six military alliances and non-aggression pacts between European states which ignored the League and its potency to keep peace. And we give a further list of twenty violent actions between nations where the League was too weak to intervene or was not allowed to take action.

We do not contend that the League should have been the center of all these conferences or that it should have intervened in all these actions which affected peace and war. But they at least indicate that the League never was able to replace power diplomacy, military alliances, the balance of power, with collective security on its home ground—Europe.

The whole experience would seem to indicate that one of the first functions in the prevention of war is the development of regional policies in the different major areas of Europe, Asia, and the Western Hemisphere.

Most of the broad policies of long-view peace are regional either to Europe, Asia, or the Western Hemisphere. In the Western Hemisphere, the Pan-American conferences had long and successfully performed that function. Certainly the League failed or was unable to formulate a similar broad policy of European co-operation and of constructive peace.

3. *The Total Collapse of Force Methods in Practical Application.* The attempt to use or the failure to use the gigantic powers of force at the disposal of the League against the two first great imperialistic aggressions after Versailles broke the back of the League's authority. The Japanese aggressions in Manchuria in September 1931, and during the next year at Shanghai, violated every implication of the Covenant in spirit and letter. The authority of the League was here brought to test in dealing with major Powers. The League failed utterly in its dealings with this gross breach of the Covenant, and the real reasons are important to note.

The Council attempted to apply the pacific methods with painstaking persistence. But when these failed, it did not exercise the measures of force. The commercial and political relations of the major Powers in the Council were such, together with the military consequences involved, that they withheld from the League the powers necessary to effective force action.

Following the Council's failure, the controversy was transferred to the Assembly, where the smaller Powers were more largely represented. But despite brave talk about applying the economic sanctions through a worldwide boycott of Japan, they also soon discovered that the major European Powers would not follow. The small Powers were, it is true, insistent on drastic action. But it soon became obvious that they were less intent on remedying the situation in Manchuria than in establishing a precedent of force action which they could later invoke for their own protection in case of aggression by Germany or Russia. Nor could this failure of the League be blamed upon lack of American co-operation, for upon Mr. Hoover's instructions and under the able guidance of Mr.

Stimson, the United States consistently supported the League through-out. Finally, the United States injected a new moral sanction—that is, an agreement of non-recognition of territory gained by aggression.

The second defiance of the League came in October 1935, with the flagrant Italian aggression against Ethiopia. In this case, the Council and Assembly voted partial economic sanctions, but Britain would not go the whole distance and France defaulted in even the partial action upon which she had agreed.

Both attempts to apply force were abortive and were terribly de-structive to the prestige and effectiveness of the League. It greatly weakened the League's influence even in the field of pacific settlements.

Brought face to face with the application of economic sanctions, it quickly developed that they had deeper implications than appeared upon the surface. The theory was assumed that by use of the economic sanctions or a universal boycott, any nation could be brought to its knees, and that such sanctions were a measure "short of war." That may be true against a weak nation. But it was soon proved that no strong nation would endure such action. Economic sanctions, if effec-tive, involve the internal economic disorganization of the penalized nation, with vast unemployment and the danger of starvation. These are penalties as great as war itself. It soon became evident that strong nations at least will risk war rather than submit to such action.

The advocates of collective military or economic force against evil-doers, aggressors, outlaws, or whatever they may be called are also misled by an analogy. That analogy is that every court has a policeman to enforce its decrees. The analogy proved false, in actual experience, for in international cases the policeman is not under the authority of the tribunal and is free to do as he pleases. Stated in another way, there are a score of policemen, each under different command. And it is assumed by theorists that not only the international tribunal but the international community will be unanimous and that there will be no clash of interest among the states not involved in the controversy and who must furnish the policemen.

Moreover, when the question came to practical test, where aggres-sion was so patent as in the invasion of Ethiopia by Italy, or of China by Japan it was soon proved that those nations can count upon friendly or allied nations, whose interest or whose situations were such that while they might disapprove morally, they could not or would not join in military or economic force. Certainly, the powers of military and economic force, such as the League possessed, proved beyond its strength to exert. When it failed to exert these powers, its prestige was gone. If it exerted them ineffectually, then again its prestige suffered. That is what happened. And in happening, it destroyed the strength of the League in its other field, that of pacific methods.

Later in this book we discuss this dual function of promoting peace by pacific methods and at the same time using force to preserve peace.

4. Failure to Secure Disarmament. Article 8 of the Covenant clearly recognized the need for the reduction and limitation of armaments:

1. The members of the League recognize that the maintenance of peace requires the reduction of national armaments to the lowest point consistent with national safety and the enforcement by common action of international obligations.

The United States participated in all League efforts at reduction and limitation of armaments. And the only consequential disarmament was brought about wholly outside the League by the initiative of the United States. The Naval Treaties of 1922 and 1930 brought real reduction and stopped unrestricted naval competition in the world for fifteen years. But throughout, the League, hamstrung by France and the Little Entente, made no contribution.

While lip service was paid to the need for reduction, the subject was shunted from committee to committee for some years, during which, it is true, much valuable technical work was accomplished. Finally, when public opinion on the matter could no longer be ignored, the subject was referred for more exhaustive examination to a "Preparatory Commission for the Disarmament Conference." This body sat intermittently from 1926 to 1931 and produced a fund of valuable material and a most unedifying spectacle in the determination of many governments to avoid coming to grips with the problem. The French were resolved to maintain a vast military dominance of the Continent as a vital major policy. Britain had already reduced her land forces, and while determined to maintain naval dominance over Europe, was always prepared to co-operate with the other naval powers in reduction. The enemy states were disarmed, so far as treaty provisions went, for all time.

Finally, the Disarmament Conference of 1932 was convened, in which, as in previous limitation of armament conferences, the United States took full part. As after some months no serious intent was apparent, the United States delegation, upon the instructions of Mr. Hoover, made a direct and blunt proposal covering the abolition of aggressive weapons and a systematic base for reduction of land armament. These proposals, advanced by Hugh Gibson, chairman of the American delegation, were supported by the technical committees and most of the governments represented. But the French and Japanese opposed the plan. Great Britain submitted an alternative plan which was also buried. It was the last call, not only for disarmament, but for the peace of Europe. President Roosevelt revived and strongly advocated this proposal for reduction of aggressive arms in 1933, but no reply was given him.

The idea was to abolish bombing planes, tanks, mobile guns, poison gas, and submarines; reduce battleships; and reduce armies by a coefficient above the necessary police component. The consequence would be to increase the defensive power of every nation.

Throughout the five years of the Preparatory Commission and the life of the Disarmament Conference, France and her followers effectively blocked all efforts to come to grips with real measures of reduction and limitation of armaments. Only so long as a vast dominant military position could be maintained did the French feel secure. We have referred to this in the previous chapter.

However shortsighted their course, it is far easier to be objective about this sort of thing from our position across the Atlantic. The fact remains, however, that great opportunities were lost.

One of the consequences of this failure was Germany's denunciation of the arms provisions of the treaty. She based her right on the preamble to Part V (Military Clauses) of the Treaty of Versailles:

In order to render possible the initiation of a general limitation of the armaments of all nations, Germany undertakes strictly to observe the military, naval, and air clauses which follow.

The Germans contended that this was a contract between the victors and vanquished by which the former were to reduce armament. They demanded that this contract be performed. Alternatively, they demanded that they be released from the military clauses. The fact remains that, unless the text was pure humbug, it meant something substantially like the German thesis. It may have been unwise to embody such a phrase in the treaty, but once there, it gave German agitators what they needed most—an appearance of injustice and grievance.

As late as 1932 it would still have been possible to reach an agreement by which Germany accepted the perpetuation of her inferior military status in return for some minor adjustments and face-saving clauses. This would have justified some first measures of reduction on the part of the victor nations—but above all, it would have done away with the dangerous sense of grievance felt by the Germans over the military clauses of the treaty and would have helped Chancellor Bruening to keep alive the German Republic.

It is here perhaps that we find the most tragic failure of the League, or, to put it more accurately, the failure of the member states. For if agreement had been reached on reduction of arms at this time, the effect would have far transcended its importance in terms of figures. It would have removed for a time at least one sense of grievance which led to Germany's revolt from Liberalism, on which Hitler came to power.

5. *Failure in Peaceful Revision of Treaties.* From the League's failure to function in its authority to revise inapplicable treaties came some part of the causes of the present war. Article 19 of the Covenant provided:

The Assembly may from time to time advise the reconsideration by members of the League of treaties which have become inapplicable and the consideration of international conditions whose continuance might endanger the peace of the world.

It is an exaggeration to say that this article provides for change. All it does is to authorize the Assembly of the League to advise members to reconsider treaty provisions which have become inapplicable and which might constitute a threat to peace. As a matter of fact, even this attenuated reference was based less on recognition of normal evolution in interntaional affairs than on Mr. Wilson's belief that it would afford a method for correcting unwise territorial provisions in the Treaty of Versailles.

This Article 19 was not enough to save the League of Nations. It was disastrous in that it offered no effective means of discussing peaceful change, however necessary it might become. The only alternative that remained at the disposal of governments was the use of force. Here Article 10 stepped in with the provision:

The members of the League undertake to respect and preserve as against external aggression the territorial integrity and existing political independence of all members of the League. In case of any such aggression or in case of any threat or danger of such aggression, the Council shall advise upon the means by which this obligation shall be fulfilled.

What this boils down to is that, in the absence of any opportunity for change by agreement, any attempt to change the *status quo* must lead inevitably to one of two things—either to war or, on the other hand, to universal tacit acquiescence in aggression and breach of the Covenant. It would be difficult to devise a more effective way of bringing the orderly processes of law into disrepute.

As a matter of fact, Article 19 was no more than the expression of a pious hope that the members of the League would be reasonable. Unless all the members of the Council agreed, there could be no readjustment of provisions that had become irksome or intolerable. That this was inadequate is shown by the fact that although there was frequent appeal for revision under Article 19, it was never put into operation, and for a simple reason. The members of the League who opposed any revision had the power of veto. The Powers who have the better of a bargain will always oppose any attempt at revision.

There can be no doubt that the preponderant judgment of the world was that provisions in the Treaty of Versailles, formulated in the hot emotions of the war, with its violations of President Wilson's Fourteen Points and his "subsequent addresses," were destructive of peace and recuperation in Europe. Mr. Wilson's hope and contention was that, with the cooling of war emotions and a wider vision of reconstruction, these matters would be corrected by the League.

However, the veto power of the Allies over every League action made it merely a tool to preserve "the territorial integrity and political independence" of those Powers and their allies and perhaps worst of all the rickety structure of the jerry-built Balkans—in short, the *status quo*.

Boundary and peace treaties are not inspired documents. Sometimes shifting and unforeseeable conditions render change imperative. Sometimes such conditions are highhandedly and unjustly imposed by treaty on no other ground than that one party is strong enough to compel the other to accept. But relative positions have a way of changing. When the underdog becomes top dog, he is hardly likely to go on considering himself bound by a bad bargain he entered into unwillingly. As a rule, he would be willing to readjust matters without going to war. But if all change is opposed, war is the only alternative to continuing under constraint.

It may be as well to examine specific instances in which peaceful change would have averted violence. One of the clearest recent examples of this is to be found in the handling of the Sudeten problem. Under the terms of the Treaty of Versailles, 3,500,000 German-speaking people were incorporated in the Czech state, which thus did violence to the principle of self-determination on which Czechoslovakia was founded. The protests of these people were ignored, and they were denied a plebiscite. Their annexation to Czechoslovakia was justified at Versailles on strategic and geographical grounds. Perhaps this decision was really imposed by circumstances, but it created a dangerous situation, and having created it, there was obvious need to keep an eye on it and keep injustice to a minimum.

During many years, this German-speaking minority sought to obtain consideration of their lot, which was made intolerable chiefly by the behavior of petty Czech officials. No doubt their own antagonisms to the Czechs played a part also. They sought to appeal for consideration under the Treaty for the Protection of National Minorities but they got short shrift. Nevertheless, they were convinced that under any reasonable regime they could best work out a solution of their troubles within the framework of the Czech state. Representatives of this minority got no consideration and scant courtesy at Geneva. On appealing to the principal Powers, they were denied a hearing and, in some instances, were given to understand that they were no better than traitors in that they appealed to foreign Powers against their own government. This was a clear case where even a brief inquiry would

have sufficed to show the existence of definite grievances and the necessity for some sort of revision if violence was to be averted. And failure
to deal with the problem made for the disintegration of all treaties. We
discuss this incident further, but in fairness to the Czechoslovak Government it must be said at once that the incorporation of the Sudeten
area into Czechoslovakia was the result of French pressure at Versailles
and in spite of the expressed misgivings of President Masaryk and
Dr. Beneš. They found themselves with a responsibility that should be
charged to the great Powers rather than the Czech state.

Another case of insistence on treaty terms regardless of possible consequences is to be found in connection with the military clauses in Part
V of the Treaty of Versailles, to which we have already referred in
discussing disarmament. It has, however, a wider implication. When
the Disarmament Conference met in Geneva in 1932, it was obvious
that the German attitude would determine the possibilities of success.
Chancellor Bruening took the ground, at once enlightened and practical, that Germany wanted to contribute toward creating a situation
where there could be a general reduction of armaments. He did not ask
to be relieved of Part V of the Treaty of Versailles, under which Germany was completely disarmed, but suggested some unimportant
changes which would have lessened the sense of humiliation and in-
feriority and would have enabled him to turn the thoughts of Germany
away from their sense of grievance to more constructive tasks. The
American, British, and Italian governments saw his proposals as opening the way to possible success, but the French Government, clinging
to the letter of the bond, declined even to discuss any suggested changes
in the treaty, maintaining that the Germans had made a bargain—that
they must stick to it.

Chancellor Bruening stated at the time that he felt the greatest contribution that Germany could make to the general cause of disarmament would be to shake off the sense of grievance which might lead to
an attempt at forcible revision of the Treaty of Versailles. He was
convinced that this was just as much in the interest of Germany as of
the other Powers, but saw clearly that if there was to be no relaxation
even in the appearance of the military clauses, there was the danger
that demagogues could stir up a sense of grievance which would lead
to dangerous results. His forebodings were only too well founded. Only

a few months after his proposals had been scornfully rejected, Hitler came to power, largely upon the indignation he had been able to arouse in Germany over real and fancied grievances. And liberal government in Germany was destroyed.

Here we have another example of the inadequacy of concessions made too late. As soon as Hitler came to power, the French Government manifested a quite different attitude and made a series of proposals which would have been more than adequate while Bruening was in power. Greater and greater concessions were offered by France and rejected by Hitler. And even in France there was a considerable feeling that if Chancellor Bruening had been met in a reasonable way, and helped to dispel the sense of wrong and humiliation, it is highly improbable that Hitler would have succeeded in gaining mastery of the government. The failure to act reasonably on this matter contributed to the success of the Nazi party, with all its disastrous consequences.

Bearing upon this question of revision of treaties, the League had certain duties in protection of national minorities. But the intervention of the League was greatly limited and the task delicate. The very existence of this authority no doubt had a beneficent influence. A number of solutions were found and actions taken in such cases. But the real cancers of Europe—the irredentas—were untouched. That would have involved revision of treaties and boundaries. This malady of irredentas became one of the contributing causes of the second World War.

We believe it is desirable further to emphasize this whole question. One of the greatest and most disastrous of all defects in methods to promote peace, which was proved by League experience, was on the question of revision of treaties.

The pacific methods of preserving peace by conciliation, arbitration, or judicial settlements are based upon existing treaties, and they become instruments to maintain those treaties, no matter how unjust. Experience now demonstrates that there are whole areas of most dangerous controversies which rise from the pressures of change in the relations of nations. Such are the cases we have mentioned of treaty provisions imposed after the heat of war, shifts in economic pressures, and population pressures. There are also the backward nations which become conscious and capable of self-government, governments which fail in their obligations to minorities, boundaries which become inappropriate, and a score of other questions. In the main, arbitral questions are those of damages, boundary disputes, and the rights of citizens based on existing documents. Unless the possibility of revision of treaties can be brought into active reality, then neither can real aggression be defined nor can pacific processes function.

It will be objected that a defeated Power must observe a treaty concluded at the end of a war. We may as well recognize that the length of time during which the defeated Power will continue to observe the treaty will be largely dependent on (a) how harsh the treaty may be upon the defeated people as a whole, and (b) the time it takes the defeated Power to regain strength. If the treaty is unduly harsh, it will be observed just so long as the defeated Power remains too weak to disregard it with impunity. But it is not realistic to expect a defeated Power to go on accepting an intolerable position when able to throw off the bonds of the treaty. We would do well to base our thinking on the recognition that treaties are on no superhuman plane; that they are sacred only as commercial contracts are sacred. Treaties forced upon nations are not upon the same plane as those that are entered into freely and willingly.

All these analogies were indulged in after the last war whenever there was an appeal for revision. The opposition was on high moral grounds. The world was flooded with speeches on the "sanctity of treaties," and it was represented that any attempt to reconsider a single article of the Versailles Treaty was nothing less than a sinister attempt to undermine its entire fabric and must be resisted as such by all law-loving people. This propaganda was so successful that many people were led to believe implicitly that all change was to be resisted on high moral grounds. We can agree as to the sanctity of the pledged word—but most of this talk meant something quite different. What was really meant was not the "sanctity" of treaties but the "immutability" of treaties or the "sanctity of the *status quo*."

Each and every plan for preserving peace, whether it be the Pax Romana, the balance of power, the legitimist theory at the Congress of Vienna, or collective security at Versailles, however divergent they may appear outwardly, have one thing in common. They set up a new order, and knowing it to be good, they provide that it shall be kept unchanged. On the surface this may appear logical and prudent—but it is a vital defect. For change, instead of being the enemy of peace, is essential to its preservation.

If we are going to accomplish anything in our time, we must approach our problem in the knowledge that there is nothing rigid or immutable in human affairs. History is a story of growth, decay, and change. If no provision, no allowance is made for change by peaceful means, it will come anyway—and with violence.

6. Internal Weaknesses in the League Structure. One of the weaknesses of this great experiment was inherent in the Covenant itself. Its articles left several gaps and conflicting interpretations. This led to endless legalistic discussions of constitutional construction. Where controversies were brought before the League, the parties resorted to every artifice to avoid League jurisdiction. Whole volumes have been written upon these questions, with interminable discussions of the interpretation of words and phrases of the Covenant and the use of hairsplitting distinctions and disputes to contest its authority or to avoid action. The Covenant's gaps were never cleared up, although various attempts were made to do so.

An indication of such confusion is to be found in the provisions governing the commitments of members. It starts with the positive agreement in Article 12 that "the members of the League agree that should there arise among them any dispute likely to lead to rupture they *will* submit the matter either to *arbitration* or *judicial settlement* or to *inquiry by the Council* and they agree in *no case* to resort to war until three months after the award. . . ."

These commitments became less positive in Article 13: "The members of the League agree that whenever any dispute shall arise between them *which they recognize to be suitable* for submission to arbitration or judicial settlement and which cannot be satisfactorily settled by diplomacy they will submit the whole subject matter to arbitration or judicial settlement."

The commitment becomes still less positive in Article 15: "If there should arise between Members of the League any dispute likely to lead to a rupture which is *not* submitted to arbitration or judicial settlement in accordance with Article 13, the Members of the League agree that they will submit such matter to the Council. . . . The

Council shall endeavor to effect a settlement of the dispute . . . and [under varying circumstances] "the Council may make public a statement of the facts and of its conclusions regarding the same."

Whether members were completely committed *to submit* questions went to the very heart of the League. Despite interpretations which might be put on the Covenant it developed that nations would not pledge themselves in advance and in unknown contingencies and unknown claims to arbitral or judicial verdict by some tribunal, the personnel and constitution of which could not be foreseen. Perhaps the original intent of the framers of the League was complete commitment to this, but they were not able to get it wholly accepted in the Covenant. The subsequent British attitude that they could not be found to submit any dispute to be decided by an international body of uncertain character and composition was probably the general attitude of members who expressed it less frankly. That attitude would seem to have torn the heart out of the pacific sanctions of the League.

In any event, the constant conflict of views over jurisdictional and interpretative questions weakened the League and some nations even withdrew over such disagreements. The experience of the League seems to prove that the Covenant, as framed, attempted too detailed and too binding and at the same time too indefinite an agreement for practical working in respect to pacific methods. Had the whole of the articles on methods of pacific settlement of controversies been condensed into a simple declaration of purpose and a general direction to the League to promote peace, it would have probably proved more binding and in practice less disintegrating to the League setup.

Another primary difficulty was that the League was founded upon two entirely different concepts, one organizing the preservation of peace by military or economic force, and the other the prevention of war by settlement of controversy through pacific methods. The League undertook to carry out its mission by combining both methods. The two concepts proved to be in both philosophic and practical conflict. The idea of promoting co-operation by threatening war weakened the influence of the League in persuasion to pacific methods. Nations were not willing to accept jurisdiction of the League when the end might be such penalties.

The question of the borderline where pacific methods were to be abandoned and force introduced raised another weakness. The original assumption was that this borderline could be so clearly defined that anyone was an aggressor who refused to settle controversies by pacific methods, or further that aggression was always proved by military invasion. The economic and military force was to be then applied. Sometimes, in flagrant cases, aggression could be so defined.

But aggression does not necessarily begin with actual or threatened military invasion. Nations may be in subjection as the result of aggression long previous. Such nations have a right to be free from oppression even if it takes war. It may not be aggression to aid them to freedom by military means. And aggressions may comprise economic domination or pressure such as boycotts from other nations until they become intolerable and military action is justified in defense. It may be in provocative action or even in provocative words, which humiliate nations or reflect upon their honor.

Another difficulty of defining aggression is that treaties represent the *status quo* of nations at a given moment. Many controversies and current incidents which need to be quieted are based upon insistence on maintaining such an established relationship. Pacific methods are indeed applicable to a large number of run-of-the-mine international difficulties. But those which arise from treaties which were onerous to start with or have been made inapplicable by a thousand circumstances raise problems which are beyond arbitration and judicial decisions.

For arbitration or judicial settlement is necessarily based upon existing treaties. Such action is inherently an assumption of maintaining the *status quo* of such treaties. Thus, these processes are not usually applicable to fundamental changes in treaties. In any event, after long debate by the League in trying to define aggression as refusal to accept pacific methods for the settlement of controversies or to entrust to the Council full authority to make such a determination, the idea failed of acceptance by a large majority of its members. The net of all this seems at least to affirm that the Covenant attempted too detailed a program.

The Effect of American Non-Participation

The American opposition to joining the League was in some part due to sheer vindictive hate against President Wilson. At one period in the Senate debate, however, a less rigid attitude on Mr. Wilson's part would have secured ratification with reservations which were, in fact, immaterial to the larger purposes of some form of organized international co-operation. This opposition could not have prevailed, however, if there had not existed a debatable ground which troubled many Americans. It came largely from the feeling that other features of the Treaty of Versailles were far from the ideals for which America had joined the war. The specific argument in the United States against joining the League, however, revolved around the supposed commitments to a military alliance and abrogation of sovereignty. Such questions presented no difficulties to the European Powers, as they understood perfectly that their veto power as members of the Council and the pressures they could bring to bear would prevent any such interpretations. The obvious ganging up on the United States during the treaty negotiations was the ready answer to American argument for this sort of protection to the United States.

The question of what the destiny of the League would have been had the United States joined is purely speculative. Certainly, Europe and many Americans blamed its failure upon our absence. This constant condemnation of the United States was itself a confession of inability of Europe to keep the peace. At one moment the League embraced every country in Europe and seemingly could have settled upon a European policy of peace.

At the first real threat to world peace from outside Europe (the Japanese-Chinese conflict), the United States co-operated fully with the League, yet that worst of League failures was made because of lack of cohesion among the great Powers of Europe. Likewise, the United States participated in the disarmament and many other international conferences with a full will to succeed.

In considering the possible effect of American participation in the League it must be remembered that the old power diplomacy would in any event have dominated Europe because of the fundamental determination of Britain and France to maintain military domination and to settle the important European policies outside the League.

Thus, the assumption that the United States could by membership in the League have prevented a second World War is a very large assumption that the United States would have been willing to resist the military power of France and England in order to carry out her original ideals of peace. Moreover, it is an assumption that all the other destructive forces set in motion by the treaty and nations acting outside the League could be controlled by the United States.

In any event, time proved that there was no moment after the defeat of adherence to the League Covenant in the Senate when any political party could carry the League with the American people. And no political party did thereafter propose it. The constant refrain in the news columns of conflict, military alliances, intrigue and power politics from Europe was a requiem on American participation. The fact that every President since the war—Harding, Coolidge, Hoover, and Roosevelt—failed by every influence to secure approval of the Senate even to membership in the World Court is evidence of the hardening of American reaction. And this is written regretfully by the authors of this book, who ardently supported adherence to the League and the Court as at least an experiment in preserving peace.

IX PEACE ORGANIZATION OUTSIDE
THE LEAGUE FROM 1919 TO 1939

DURING the twenty-year period between the first and second World Wars, the will to peace was manifested in many activities conceived and carried on outside the League. In the Appendix we list nineteen such cases, and the list is by no means exclusive. We here discuss those of greatest importance.

International Labor Office (*1919*)

The International Labor Office was created by Part 13 of the Versailles Treaty. In the preamble to this part of the treaty, it is stated that "a peace can be established only if it is based upon social justice . . . conditions of labor exist involving such injustice, hardship, and privation to large numbers of people as to produce unrest so great that the peace and harmony of the world are imperiled."

The International Labor Office has proved a most beneficent institution. Although it has little relation to the direct problem of peacemaking, it has an indirect value as a constant stimulant to international co-operation.

Washington Conference of *1921–22*

The Washington Conference in 1921–22, called by the United States, was not wholly devoted to naval reduction and limitation. It sought, by treaties, to improve the whole climate of peace in the Pacific area.

In November 1921, the delegates of France, Great Britain, Italy, Japan, and the United States, under the outstanding leadership of Secretary Hughes, reached an agreement on the limitation of ships over 10,000 tons. No agreement could be reached upon cruisers, destroyers, submarines, and auxiliary ships. In capital ships, building programs were abandoned, and some partially completed ships were scrapped.

The principle established was a ratio of naval strength responsive to naval needs and strategic equality. As between the three strongest naval Powers, the United States, Great Britain, and Japan, the ratio was established at 5-5-3, and 1.75 each to France and Italy in ships over 10,000 tons and with guns above 8-inch caliber. The treaty fixed the maximum tonnage of all the larger types, capital ships, aircraft carriers, and cruisers. In order to induce Japan to accept the ratio, the United States undertook not to fortify the Philippines and Guam. Great Britain gave a similar undertaking as regards Hong Kong and various other Pacific possessions.

Japan was already committed by the mandates agreement of the Versailles Treaty not to fortify a number of islands specified by name "and any insular territories or possessions in the Pacific Ocean which Japan may hereafter acquire." But she promptly did fortify them without awaiting the approval of the League.

One of the greatest of all accomplishments of Secretary Hughes was the comprehensive way in which he led the conference in dealing with Pacific and Far Eastern questions, in which the representatives of China, Belgium, Holland, and Portugal participated. Two major treaties outside the Limitation of Arms Agreement were agreed upon.

By the Four Power Treaty the United States, Great Britain, France, and Japan guaranteed each other's insular possessions in the Pacific and provided for peaceful solution of controversies about them. The chief significance of this treaty was the provision that on its ratification the Anglo-Japanese Alliance should terminate.

The Nine Power Treaty guaranteed respect for the territorial integrity of China and the "Open Door." It provided "that, whenever a situation arises which in the opinion of any one of them involves the application of the stipulations of the present treaty, and renders desirable discussion of such application, there shall be full and frank communication between the contracting Powers concerned."

The great purpose of these treaties was to give China an unmolested chance to recover from the anarchy of revolution in which she was then plunged. She was unable, however, in the following ten years to build up the national solidarity necessary to defend herself adequately.

London Naval Conference of 1930

We may here digress from chronology to show the continued American effort in naval reduction. In 1927, President Coolidge issued invitations to a naval conference at Geneva to deal with cruiser, destroyer, submarine and other craft upon which the Washington Conference had failed to find agreement. This conference failed also.

As these craft constituted two thirds of naval strength, and great competitive building was going on, Mr. Hoover, in March 1929, through Mr. Gibson, who was then at the preparatory Arms Conference at Geneva as the American representative, proposed another conference to deal with the subject. It was finally settled that the conference should be called in London. The President, through the able and patient negotiation of Secretary Stimson, Ambassador Dawes, and others, took the precaution of settling the main lines of agreement in advance by direct negotiations with the various Powers.

The conference came to agreement and placed further effective reductions upon all craft, including battleships. This agreement held until it expired in 1936, when the Japanese refused to renew it.

This treaty fully established the parity of the American Navy with that of the greatest other Power, and by this American leadership, billions of dollars of waste in competitive building were saved and much international ill will was avoided.

The Permanent Court of International Justice (1922)

The idea of establishment of a world court which could decide questions between nations suitable for justiciable determination, as distinguished from subjects for conciliation and arbitration, had long been advocated as having a part in the creation of lasting peace. The idea was developed particularly at the Hague Conference of 1907. The Covenant of the League of Nations provided for the adoption of a plan for the establishment of such a Permanent Court of International Justice. "The Court shall be competent to hear and determine any dispute of an international character which the parties thereto submit to it. The Court may also give an advisory opinion upon any dispute or question referred to it by the Council or by the Assembly."

The Statute of the Court was worked out by the League with the aid of the ablest jurists in the world in consultation with the foreign departments of the principal governments; in this, Secretary Bainbridge Colby ably participated.

The Protocol covering agreement to the Statute was completed late in 1920 and submitted to the various nations for adherence. The members of the League signified their adherence, and the Court opened February 15, 1922.

President Harding and Secretary Hughes recommended the Protocol to the Senate in 1923, despite the fact that the United States was not a member of the League, with recommendations as to special agreement by which the United States would participate in all questions respecting the Court. The Senate approved it three years later, but with reservations concerning Advisory Opinions that would require serious alteration in the Statute of the Court. No modification of the attitude of the Senate could be obtained, despite the urgings of President Coolidge and Secretary Kellogg. In 1929, Mr. Hoover asked Mr. Elihu Root to go to Europe and endeavor to find a formula meeting the Senate reservations. This Mr. Root was able to do, and Mr. Hoover and Secretary Stimson repeatedly urged it upon the Senate, but without avail. President Roosevelt and Secretary Hull have likewise urged it, but unsuccessfully.

The Court has functioned under eminent judges and has successfully resolved some seventy international controversies. The Court, however, received a blow, especially in American opinion, when in 1931 it gave a decision on a case affecting a customs union between Germany and Austria in which the judges voted 7 to 8, largely, it is alleged, on purely nationalistic grounds.

The Court can serve a most useful purpose in preserving peace in a sane world, and such incidents as this could be solved by disqualifying any judge of the nationality of one of the parties to the case from sitting in judgment.

Locarno Treaties (1925)

The Locarno Agreements of October 16, 1925, marked a real attempt to heal the wounds of war and to allay the ancient Franco-German feud. Various attempts to bring about better relations during the previous three years finally found a propitious moment when Austen

Chamberlain, Briand, and Stresemann, all men of good will, were at the same time Foreign Ministers of Britain, France, and Germany respectively. A series of treaties resulted in mutual guarantees of the frontiers of France, Belgium, and Germany, with a supplementary guarantee by Great Britain and Italy; arbitration treaties between Germany, on the one side, Belgium and France, on the other; treaties of mutual assistance between France, Poland, and Czechoslovakia in case of aggression. The agreements also provided for the admission of Germany to the League of Nations.

This Locarno settlement represented a brave attempt at regional agreements to solve particular problems. The spirit of these settlements was more important than the actual achievement. At the ceremony of signature in London the oratory became lyrical. Chamberlain described the pact as "the real dividing line between the years of war and the years of peace." Briand said that "in the light of these treaties we are Europeans only." And finally Stresemann, not to be outdone, appealed: "Let each one of us first be a citizen of Europe linked together by the great conception of civilization which imbues our continent."

Some things may, however, be observed about this settlement. Except for lip service, it totally ignored the League, whose real function it was to provide a policy of reconciliation in Europe. Beneficent as it was, it did represent the human quality of Ministers of Foreign Affairs to want the stage. Its spiritual forebear was essentially the Concert of Europe, not the League. And behind it was still the destructive drive of six of the seven dynamic forces which it had done little to remedy or to allay.

The end of the Locarno Agreement was indeed sad. Hitler, alleging that the Franco-Russian Military Alliance had violated the Locarno Agreement, sent his troops into the Rhineland (March 7, 1936) on the ground that Germany was released from her Locarno obligations.

There is no doubt that, under any reasonable construction, this step called for action under the Locarno Agreement. But in the meantime, great fissures had grown up between Britain, France, and Italy. France appealed to Britain and Italy for military assistance. France and Belgium would not act alone—partly because they felt need of support —possibly through fear of alienating Great Britain. Italy was fully engaged in her Ethiopian campaign and, smarting under economic sanctions from Britain and France, was hardly disposed to take military action against Germany on behalf of France. The British Foreign Office found difficulty in seeing any "flagrant violation" or any "unprovoked act of aggression." It was considered that Germany was merely sending her troops into German territory and that this hardly called for steps that might end in war. In these few short years a situation had developed where not one of the guarantors would act to save the Locarno system from ignominious collapse. Neither did the League intervene.

The Kellogg-Briand Pact (1928)

On June 20, 1927, Mr. Briand, then French Minister for Foreign Affairs, proposed to the American Government a bilateral treaty renouncing war between the United States and France. Secretary Kellogg replied to this proposal on December 28 with the suggestion that, instead of a bilateral declaration, an effort be made to secure general acceptance of the project.

As a result, the Kellogg-Briand Pact was signed in Paris on August 27, 1928, with reservations by some Powers to make war in self-defense, although, of course, Mr. Kellogg maintained that the right of self-defense was inherent in the pact itself.

This pact which was originally signed by fifteen governments, including all the principal nations, has considerable significance in the moral definition of war and the implementing of public opinion for the preservation of peace.

The idea had been advanced over a generation and is fundamentally to outlaw war morally, just as society outlaws crime. The advocates of the "Outlawry of War" insisted that the attempt to control and humanize methods of warfare merely tends to recognize war itself as inevitable and almost respectable; that the evil itself will not be extirpated so long as war has a recognized place in the field of international relations.

They held that international agreement on this principle would at least establish standards of conduct. The question, of course, at once arose as to enforcement, any form of which would trespass upon the functions of the League and possibly other existing peace machinery. The common view was, however, that at least at the start it must depend for enforcement upon moral force, enlightened public opinion, and the fidelity of nations to agreement. The essential part of this treaty was embodied in two articles, as follows:

ARTICLE I

The High Contracting Parties solemnly declare in the names of their respective peoples that they condemn recourse to war for the solution of international controversies, and renounce it as an instrument of national policy in their relations with one another.

ARTICLE II

The High Contracting Parties agree that the settlement or solution of all disputes or conflicts of whatever nature or of whatever origin they may be, which may arise among them, shall never be sought except by pacific means.

The moral vitality of the pact was somewhat reduced by its reservations, but it was strengthened by the action of the United States under the leadership of Mr. Hoover and Secretary Stimson during the Japanese-Chinese conflict of 1932. It was then proposed that territorial or other gains made in violation of the pact should not be recognized by other governments. Such a non-recognition declaration was signed by nearly all nations of the world in respect to that act of aggression.

It is a significant fact that no important representative government has ever violated the pact. Totalitarian Germany, Russia, Japan, and Italy have all done so.

Briand's United States of Europe

M. Briand's proposals, undertaken under authority of the League, for a "United States of Europe" have caused a great deal of confusion in discussions as to the possibilities of international federation and the building of supergovernments. Most people have not gone beyond the title, and this title is entirely misleading. It is generally assumed that what M. Briand had in mind was to amalgamate the many nations of Europe under a single central government. This illusion has served to convince many people that a drastic plan of welding together all the nations of Europe must be practical because it was advocated by a practical statesman and was seriously discussed by the governments of Europe.

Briand proposed no more than an organization to serve as an adjunct to the League of Nations to facilitate the solution of problems regional to Europe. Its intellectual progenitor was the Concert of Europe rather than the United States of America. In fact Briand was preparing a definitely organized Concert of Europe. He said, in putting it forward to the Assembly of the League:

It cannot be a question of a real United States, because each nation of Europe must retain its sovereignty. But since Europe is geographically a unit, there are problems which exist for all. The economic question should be the first one to be considered, but even in political and social problems, it would often be to the advantage of the various countries to meet and solve questions in common. . . .

Briand was most specific in his statements that the proposed organization was not in any way to affect the absolute sovereignty of its members and their complete political independence. In spite of this, much of the current discussion is based on the assumption that he proposed a "federation" of Europe—that is to say, a central federal government. Study of the correspondence fails to reveal any ground whatever for this assumption. On the contrary, Briand is at pains throughout to make it clear that what he has in mind is to promote "study, discussion, and adjustment of problems which might be of common interest." He proposes "determination of the field of European co-operation—general economy, economic machinery, communications and traffic, finance, labor, hygiene, intellectual co-operation, interparliamentary reports, etc."

All this was clearly a plan for co-operation limited to the European field rather than for federal government—a sort of subsidiary League of European Nations. The plan was viewed with a good deal of skepticism by the League, but Briand was authorized to sound out the various twenty-seven governments, twenty-six of which replied. All of them made reservations of one sort or another. Some felt disarmament must come first; some feared it would weaken the League. Some raised questions of the equality of nations; there was question as to the possible admission of Russia in dealing with questions of free economic systems. The project got nowhere. A Commission of Inquiry for European Union was set up to study the problem. It met three or four times without making any progress, and soon lapsed into a comatose condition. The men who might have given it an impulse were gone. Stresemann had died. Chamberlain was no longer in office, and Briand no longer enjoyed the same free hand under the governments of Tardieu and Laval. The fact that Briand did not envisage or advocate setting up the United States of Europe in the sense that it has been generally understood does not mean that there was no importance in his proposal. As a matter of fact, the regional proposal is probably of greater value because time may prove that this was the first important step towards systematic regional treatment of world problems—a method which would seem to be dictated by common sense and to offer real hopes of progress and achievement.

During this period, the United States made other efforts to combat the vicious forces which were undermining peace and stability in the world. The Economic Conference instigated by Mr. Hoover's administration in 1932 for removal of trade barriers and the stabilization of currency met at London in 1933, but did not meet the approval of Mr. Roosevelt. As we have said elsewhere, at the first Japanese aggression on China in 1931, the United States co-operated with the League in attempts to protect China. When the second Japanese aggression on China occurred in 1937, President Roosevelt secured the calling of a conference of the signatories of the Nine Power Treaty, but it was unable to accomplish anything. When the Munich crisis arose in 1938, Mr. Roosevelt and Secretary Hull exerted the "good offices" of the United States in urging settlement. And President Roosevelt repeatedly proposed undertakings toward peace to the Axis governments. Of more successful issue, however, was the strengthening of Pan-American co-operation under the unflagging leadership of Secretary Hull and Under Secretary Welles.

Other Peace Efforts in Europe—1919–39

We have given in the Appendix a list of many other peace efforts outside the League. It is certain that hundreds of statesmen and millions of citizens worked to this end. The numerous conferences and the sweat of good men are proof that the will to peace was struggling for a chance.

Perhaps even military alliances can be interpreted as efforts to keep the peace—or balance of power. Non-aggression pacts certainly have more of a peace flavor.

But the whole failure of them presents a disheartening picture—attempts of old diplomacy to put temporary lids upon growing explosive forces underneath and, above all, a failure to realize prior to Hitler that the one hope lay in sustaining representative government in the former enemy areas.

And never to be forgotten was the undermining of the whole will to peace by the flagrant repudiation of non-aggression and other treaties which had been entered into in full free will by Hitler, Mussolini, and Japan. No one can say that Locarno, the Kellogg Pact, the Four Power and the Nine Power treaties were dictated or forced upon them.

Summary of the Forces Leading to the World Explosion of 1939

In the last two chapters we have outlined the movement of the seven dynamic forces in the twenty years after Versailles. It requires but a few words to indicate their cumulative effect in the explosion of the World War of 1939.

Again, as in 1914, the immediate causes of the gigantic explosion into the present war were only superficially to be found in the immediate incidents. Again the real causes lay in the dynamic forces of ideologies, economic pressures, nationalism, imperialism, militarism, and the complexes of fear, hate, and revenge.

It is not clear at what point in matter of time the face of the world began to turn from peace toward war. Certainly, at the end of 1933 confidence of economic recovery from the last war and continued peace were general in men's minds, and nowhere was such an immense catastrophe as another World War thought possible. It is equally certain that four years later, during 1937, men everywhere had become fearful, and all the world had joined in arming against renewed war.

It might be remarked that prior to the outbreak in 1914 this change in men's minds took place scarcely thirty days before that outbreak. The change at the present crisis was at least two years before the explosion, the delay of which might be attributed to greater reluctance at starting war or to more capable effort to maintain peace. The observation is a slender tribute to world progress.

The political turning point was probably the refusal of France in

1932 to co-operate in support of representative government in Germany, with the consequent overthrow of the republic by Hitler, with its sequence of Fascist revolutions in some fifteen nations.

Beginning in 1934, ideologic forces rose steadily to a full and fierce world-wide conflict. Fascism and Communism were at war with each other in every respect except actual gunfire. Russia on one side, Germany and Italy on the other, were planting Fifth Columns and propaganda, endeavoring to create internal revolutions in each other's territory, and both executing each other's sympathizers and agents. The Anti-Comintern Pact by Germany, Japan, and Italy was signed late in 1936. Russia, Germany, and Italy had a hand in creating the Spanish Revolution beginning in 1936. The mortal conflict between these ideologies was the more evident when the Fascist Powers gave military aid to Franco in Spain while Communist Russia and the French Government gave like aid to the Republican Government.

Both the Communists and Fascists also carried on war against the democratic governments everywhere with Fifth Columns and propaganda. In the American recognition agreement with Russia in 1933, that country agreed not to stimulate such propaganda but promptly violated the agreement by subsidizing subversive action in the United States. Thus ideologic forces were explosive enough.

Economic pressures induced by the depression had begun to relax with the turn to recovery in the spring of 1932. But many forces, economic and political, intervened to retard recovery, and the world as a whole by 1939 had found little relief from unemployment and a distracted agriculture. The World Economic Conference in 1933 had failed to give relief from unstable currencies and mounting trade barriers. How far these pressures turned nations to making arms and armies as a method of relief cannot be surmised.

Nationalism ran riot in economics by increased trade barriers, through new devices of special and exclusive agreements, quotas, manipulated currencies, and restrictions on production. And in the Fascist countries, nationalism took on forms of extreme racialism, with persecution of minorities and the Jews.

The old monster of imperialism revived in Japan's conquest of Manchuria in 1931, Italy's conquest of Ethiopia in 1935–36, Japan's revived conquest of China in 1937, and the whole purpose of the Axis in the same year.

Militarism did not die even in the victorious countries, and was fed by the French alliances before the Fascist rise. It was obviously an integral part of the whole totalitarian philosophy and organization. After the failure of the Disarmament Conference of 1932, the military expenditures of the world rose from about $4,000,000,000 per annum to about $18,000,000,000 in 1938.

Hate, fear, and revenge were rampant, not alone from nationalist inheritances of the last war, but from the added fuel of ideological conflict.

In these last years before the war, the will to peace still strove to find a way out. It was sustained, partly by the memory of the horrors of the last war, partly by the efforts of statesmen of good will, particularly in Britain and in the Western Hemisphere; but the destructive forces in Europe and Asia, cultivated by malign leadership, had reached the explosion point. Yet the peoples themselves in no country wanted war. When it came to Europe in 1939, and America in 1941, it came with no popular enthusiasm in any nation. Unlike 1914, there were no bands, no flowers, no flag waving, no cheers.

Part Three

X THE FOUNDATIONS OF LASTING
PEACE

Some Deductions from Experience

EVEN with victory, after the dreadful degenerations of these thirty years of war, revolution, and disorder, if Western civilization is to be saved from another relapse into the Dark Ages, it must be saved at the peace table. Never will humanity need more objectivity, more tolerance and more vision, more open and more prayerful minds.

Again we may repeat, we are not here proposing a plan for peace. We are discussing, from an analysis of experience, the principles which will need to be considered if peace is to be built upon solid foundations. Discussion, debate, and understanding by our people prior to ending of the war are necessary if adequate plans are to be drawn. And the American delegates to the peace table should not only be armed with the principles of peace which America believes workable, but they should have an understanding people behind them.

We may again observe that, if we scan the history of modern Western civilization, we can see that following long periods of world wars and world disorder, new shapes and new forms of nations have emerged. Civilization has taken on new impulses and new directions. We must expect new forms and new directions from the gigantic explosion beginning in 1914. No one can pretend to see these coming shapes and forms clearly. All that can be known only in the minds and hearts of men and women who live to see those days.

Yet we do know we must make peace when the cheering bugle blows "Cease Firing" at the end of this war. And we know beyond all doubt that the seven dynamic forces will sit at the peace table, as they did in 1919, even though six of them come as unbidden and unwelcome guests.

Ideologic, economic, nationalistic, imperialistic, and militaristic pressures, and the witches of fear, hate, and revenge will participate in every discussion.[1] But on the other hand, the prayers of a stricken world for a lasting peace will echo through those halls. The seven dynamic forces have survived every crisis. They will be with us again. We know all this from the nature of the human animal, from his long, toilsome experience.

We propose to discuss the problems which these forces will lay upon the next peace table—and to search for some specific deductions, some experience, and some lessons that emerge from the long struggle of humanity to deal with them. We shall suggest some fifty such specific conclusions.

The first of these conclusions is:

1. We have had experience with misunderstanding and divided views on peace aims, such as developed immediately after the Armistice in 1918 despite the Fourteen Points of President Wilson; therefore, before this war ends, the war aims and the principles of peace should be reduced to more specific and more practical terms than those expressed in the Atlantic Declaration of President Roosevelt and Prime Minister Churchill. And there should be agreement now on the methods by which the machinery of peacemaking is to be handled by the United Nations.

The next of these conclusions from experience is:

2. Any structure of lasting peace must consist of two parts. The first is its foundation of political, territorial, military, economic, and ideological settlements which restore order and recovery in the world. The

---

[1] In describing the seven dynamic forces early in this book, we said:
"These forces are not arranged in order of their importance. That varies in different periods. They overlap and are interwoven in the whole fabric of civilization. Other students may prefer different divisions and different designations for these parts of world anatomy. We have reached the conclusion, however, that these divisions and separations most nearly represent not only these dominant world movements but are historically the more conclusive basis and they furnish a new approach in discussion of these problems.

"The history of peace and war is largely a recitation of the operation of these forces and the failures of men to comprehend and control them. Much of it is mistakenly written into terms of personalities both good and bad. Now is the time when the problems of this peace must be studied in far larger patterns than ever before" (p. 158).

second is the erection thereon of some instrumentality to preserve peace.

The temple where the flame of peace is to be kept will not endure unless the foundations are more deeply and more securely laid than those of Westphalia, Vienna and Versailles.

On those occasions, strains and pressures of the seven dynamic forces were ignored or only partially allayed, or even increased. The world must now lay those foundations rightly, or any superstructure to preserve peace will fail.

Before we discuss the architecture of the temple itself, we must sift from reason and experience the definite methods which will allay the destructive dynamic strains and will give stability to the world. Here history is positive and experience extended.

We may perhaps be a mite critical that most thought is being devoted to alternative architectural forms of the temple rather than to the foundations. And many who contemplate the nature of the foundations assume that, because the pressure and strains are great and strong, they must be inexorable and little can be done about them. If we enter into the drafting room in this despair, we may as well accept the utter futility of all human efforts to keep the peace.

The authors believe, on the contrary, that a recognition of these forces themselves, together with the lessons to be drawn from experience, does point to avenues of hope for the future.

Ideological Forces

We will first deal with the ideological forces. And we refresh the reader's mind with our early description of this force.

The importance of religious faith, of social, economic, political, artistic, and scientific ideas in shaping the form of the world and the making of its wars and peace is not to be estimated as less than that of other basic forces. Over the long range of history, they are the determining factors in civilization.

One thing is certain: that is, that the ideas which involve human belief and faith contain a militant crusading spirit. Within them is inherent aggressiveness. Great and revolutionary ideas have within them at least a period when they are borne aloft by military action. Christianity, the Divine Right of Kings—with all its descendants in the armor of feudalism—Mohammedanism, the Protestant Reformation, and Liberalism have all in their time marched with the sword. Now, new ideologies—Communism, Fascism, and Nazism—are on the warpath.

And ideological wars, whether religious or temporal, are more cruel and more bitter than were the wars of mere conquest or exploitation. While the ideology of personal liberty is today less aggressive than the ideologies of collectivism, it can rise to crusading heights.

Ideologies can also make for peace. For these nineteen centuries, Christianity has been unique among religious faiths in its preaching of peace and compassion. Personal liberty and representative government as a political concept have also preached the gospel of peace. Both, at times, have sought to impose their beliefs with the sword. But their final purpose is peace. And as long as men have beliefs, they will strive to protect and expand them (p. 159).

We have before us today certain declared pledges and peace aims in the Atlantic Declaration and other statements of the President. They are in part ideological.

3. Indeed, so far as America is concerned, this war is a crusade for personal liberty against totalitarianism and dictatorship. The direction to destroy these and to substitute personal freedom and representative government "everywhere" has already been assignd to the peacemakers by our expressed purpose in entering the war.

It will be seen from our statement on page 214 that Mr. Roosevelt's announced ideological aims parallel those of Mr. Wilson. President Roosevelt has given added emphasis by his statement of the four "essential freedoms"—"freedom of speech" and "expression," "freedom of worship," "freedom from want," "freedom from fear," "everywhere in the world." Thus, Mr. Roosevelt again states the same major purposes in America's participation in this war—a second crusade to establish American ideals.

Again America asks for no territory; it asks for no indemnities; but this time we want the foundations of peace built on rock and not on sand. The fact that we built on sand last time was partly due to the fact that, during the war, Mr. Wilson contented himself with inspiring generalizations, the meanings of which were differently construed by different nations and differently construed before and after the Armistice. Further than that, no one can review[2] the malign forces which surrounded that peace conference without the conclusion that no such assembly should again be convened. We discuss this at length in Chapter XIV, but at this point we may present our first deduction.

[2] See Chapter VI.

Representative Government as the Foundation of Peace. We believe that the whole experience of the last 100 years as reviewed by this book supports the conviction that the will to peace can genuinely flourish only in the soil of representative government. We do not suggest that it is a perfect guarantee of peace. Nations with representative government are not free from wars. They are capable of military crusades to establish their gospel, and even of imperialistic conquest.

As distinguished, however, from dictatorships and totalitarianism, the aims of representative governments are more generally peaceable. Dictatorships and totalitarianism are in their very nature aggressive, militaristic, and imperialistic in character. In contrast, personal liberty and representative government can flourish only in peace. The price of war to democracy is the immediate sacrifice of personal freedom and the uncertainty of its recovery. Its price is prolonged impoverishment after the war and infinite grief from loss of its sons. Thus, in representative government, there is always the live voice of opposition and warning against incurring these consequences.

A further proof of the pacific character of representative government is that during the last fifty years the major development of pacific settlement of controversies by international law, international co-operation, mediation, and arbitration, have mostly been at the hands of such nations. In such self-denying agreements as the Kellogg-Briand Pact, based entirely on morals and reason, there has not been a single violation by important representative governments. Moreover, there was no spirit of war or imperialism during the democratic regimes of Germany, Austria, or Hungary.

4. Our next deduction, therefore, is that the American thesis of 1919, that peace should be built on fostering representative government, was correct, and the best foundation of hope for lasting peace.

There are some profound lessons to consider, however, in any attempt to force personal liberty and representative government upon other nations.

5. Ideologies of personal liberty and free will cannot be imposed by machine guns. Wrong ideas cannot be cured by war or by treaty. They are matters of mind and spirit. The lasting acceptance of any governing idea lies deep in the mores of races and in their intellectual processes.

Liberty does not come like manna from heaven; it must be cultivated from rocky soil with infinite patience and great human toil.

Totalitarianism, on the other hand, can be imposed by terror, execution, and the suppression of any thought except that permitted by the masters. Yet there is an instinctive craving of man for personal freedom. He tasted of its invigorating waters in every civilized nation during the last century.

If we were wise enough in the peacemaking, we might start the rebuilding of freedom in some form. Probably not in our exact forms, for every race moves in the orbit of its own mores. But here is the hope of the world. If it can have a reasonable opportunity, freedom will rise again. While personal liberty and representative government, with all their social and economic forms, cannot be imposed, it is a certainty that they cannot even start to grow unless one minimum foundation is laid.

6. Our deduction from all experience is that at least the forms of representative government must be accepted by the enemy states if we are to have lasting peace. Moreover, unless the representatives of a people accept the terms, there can be no lasting peace.

But that alone is not enough. Personal liberty and representative government are a delicate growth. At the end of the last war, the victors set up, or encouraged the setting up, of such governments. But instead of nursing them through their infancy, we allowed them to disintegrate. In some cases, indeed, the older representative governments by their attitudes destroyed them.

7. Therefore, if we want the principle of representative government to prevail, we must make up our minds now to make such a peace as will not only initiate it but nurture it in the enemy states for long years to come.

Economic Forces

We defined the economic forces in Chapter I:

While we have no faith in theories of complete economic determinism in history, yet they occupy a large place among these seven forces. Since men must have food and living, the striving for them creates eternal economic forces and pressures.

Certainly, through the history of modern civilization, economic forces have played a large part. It was the wealth of the Indies which stimulated the great explorations and conquests of the fifteenth and sixteenth centuries. Pressures of overpopulation to find outlets for men and goods play a striking part on the world stage today. The cravings for security of supply of raw materials and places to sell surplus products have led to incessant friction, hate, fear, and war. Insistence that "trade follows the flag" has cost rivers of blood and untold sorrow. All these are part of the incentives to imperialism.

Whatever may have been the weight of economic pressures in creating the World War of 1914, the economic aftermaths of that war were among the primary causes of the collapse of the world into this second World War. War's disruption of economic life has been burned into the consciousness of nations, yet not so deeply as was hoped by some observers. But economic forces have also in other times and other circumstances acted as a restraint on war (p. 159).

The relief from economic pressures which make for war is one of the greatest of all problems that must be solved by the peace.

Experience of the last war and its aftermath proves that these problems fall into two categories. One is the instant problem which arises from the disruption of war. The other is the long-range problem of rebuilding prosperity in the world.

Instant Economic Problems. Famine and pestilence will be rampant over most of Europe and Asia. Agriculture has already degenerated under war pressures in all parts of Europe. And added to that is the suffering from the blockade and the German seizures. Millions of women and children in the occupied democracies are already sickening and dying. With the disorder and collapse of discipline that will follow upon defeat, there will come the weakening of the rationing systems and distribution of what food there is in the enemy countries. The farmers and villagers and those who can pay black-market prices will get the food, and the poor of the cities will be worse off than they were before the Armistice. To create any sort of order and maintain it pending reconstruction, at least as much food will be needed immediately as after the last war. The volume of relief pending the establishment of normal production and trade will probably exceed 30,000,000 tons of overseas imports of concentrated food.

We have already described (p. 226) how, despite American protests, the blockade of enemy states was continued for months after the last armistice. And it was continued until anarchy and bolshevism had broken out in a dozen centers.

8. Our certain deduction from the last experience is that unless food blockade is instantly removed when firing ceases and the enemy surrenders his military strength, and unless extensive and instant relief is undertaken to enemy and friend alike, there will be no hope of stability in governments upon which peace can be built, and no allaying of war hates.

The immediate economic demoralizations from this present war are likely to be even greater than those of the last war. The world financial exchanges and currencies will be greatly dislocated. Industry will need to be furnished with raw materials to get employment started again. Nations will be without resources with which to buy either food or raw material. Thus, there will be a period where private enterprise and private charity will be totally unable to meet the situation.

9. We conclude, therefore, that the governments of the world must bear the burdens of shipping, credit, and distribution of supplies. And they will have to bear these burdens for the enemy as well as for liberated countries if there is to be peace and recovery.

Long-view Economic Problems. International economic relations are obviously the exchange of goods and services. That was the basis of prewar international economy and will be the basis of postwar economy. Any action by governments is merely the stimulation or retarding of exchanges. The longer-view economic problems of peacemaking will be, first, to start the forces in motion by which economic recovery can be attained, and, second, to turn future economic pressures away from war and toward lasting peace.

The problems of reconstruction will in themselves be gigantic. War destruction, the imperative need to return armies and war industries to civilian employment, will present huge problems in every country, whether victor or vanquished. Every nation will be impoverished. Inflation will be in action, for the national debts will be far more enormous than after the first World War. Every country will be in domestic financial disorder.

Moreover, the stock of goods will have been more exhausted than in the last war. Even the scrap and waste will have been mopped up and used. The standards of living will have been reduced greatly in every country before the war ends—even where there still is food and clothing—and the people will be clamoring for resumption of work and living. And they will be demanding haste.

The major problems of economic recovery will arise inside the boundaries of each country. Lasting peace will greatly depend upon such recovery, but those problems go too far afield for this essay. Domestic recovery will, however, be effected by international action— somewhat proportionate to each country's dependence upon foreign trade. In that particular, the United States, with its dependence of only 7 per cent of its national economy on foreign trade, is the most fortunate of all the large countries. Nevertheless, there are most important phases of long-view peace involved which affect recovery of all nations.

The long-range economic tasks of the peace table will be concerned chiefly with the international phases of trade, credit, and currency. Their successful solution affects not only domestic recoveries in the world, but will reduce the economic pressures which militate against lasting peace.

Before we can make deductions from experience as to these problems, we must determine the ideological approach to them. As we have said, for an emergency period these international functions of commodity supplies, shipping, credit, and monetary exchanges will need to be in the hands of governments. That is, of course, a continuation of the totalitarian war economy, partly Fascist, partly Socialist, which is being established in every country as a necessity of war organization.

The ideological question is, will the peacemakers set up a system which will continue this regime beyond the emergency? Or will they set the stage for the return of international economy to private enterprise as fast as it can be taken over? Or will they set the stage to preserve a mixed economy, partly free enterprise, partly totalitarian?

This query rises more insistently because the peace aims so far declared do not include the "Fifth Freedom"—that is, economic freedom.

FREE ENTERPRISE IN INTERNATIONAL TRADE. A number of books and addresses otherwise intelligent upon the problems of lasting peace are yet founded upon the advocacy of some sort of collectivist world economy. It would be ironic that a war for freedom should end in such a defeat of personal liberty.

We must explore these questions further, for they relate, first, to freedom of men (the declared purpose of this war), and, second, to lasting peace. If the purpose of world reconstruction is to give freedom to men, then the return of direction toward economic freedom is essential. We may repeat again:

To be free, men must choose their callings, bargain for their own services, save and provide for their families and old age. And they must be free to engage in enterprise so long as each does not injure his fellow man. And that requires laws to prevent abuse. And when we use the terms "Fifth Freedom," "economic freedom," or "free enterprise," we use them in this sense only, not in the sense of *laissez faire* or capitalistic exploitation.

Such freedom does not mean going back to abuses. It in no way inhibits social reforms and social advancement. Economic freedom furnishes the resources for such advancement and flourishes only with such advances.

We have elsewhere touched upon the economic consequences involved in the mixture of totalitarian economic systems into free enterprise under the term "managed economy." We pointed out that the danger to free men arises if the expansion of government over economic life reaches the point where it slows down initiative and enterprise and where centralization and bureaucratization of power encroach upon the safeguards of liberty. The further danger is the inherent spirit of bureaucracy, which makes it seek for more and more power. The problem is somewhat a matter of degree, for at some point along this road economic freedom collapses. Intellectual and spiritual freedom will not long survive the passing of economic freedom. The question becomes insistent because we must move more and more into these dangerous fields in order to win the war.

It would be ironical if, having fought a war to establish freedom, we should have fastened any form of collectivism on our own country.

The transcendent thing in ideological forces is the direction in which they are moving, and that depends upon our ultimate aims.

10. *In our view, the ideals of freedom, national unity during the war, economic recovery after the war, and lasting peace all require a strong reassurance now that the ideals and objectives of the war include eco-*

nomic freedom regulated to prevent abuse. Such a determination is vital if the hopes, confidence and initiative of men are to survive.

As we said above, these questions of economic freedom bear not only upon the restoration of freedom itself. The direction that we take determines the method of handling economic problems at the peace table, and it affects the whole question of lasting peace.

For instance, under any form of economy, when governments engage in exchange of commodities, or credit or financial controls, or in the conduct of shipping, they become higglers in the market with other governments. Thus, all the natural conflicts and frictions of the market as to price, quantity, credit, and a thousand other things become conflicts and frictions between governments. When governments engage in these activities, they become competitors with other governments in world markets, both to buy scarce materials and to sell surpluses. Under private traders, such activities do not involve governments, and thereby avoid centralizing their cumulative effects into national emotions. Moreover, government trading also involves the creation of domestic conflicts within their own borders. Agriculture, labor, and industry bring pressures to bear on government, on legislatures and administration to advance their special interests—and all these pressures become political in character.

11. We believe the whole experience of the last twenty years of government trading in commodities, credit, and shipping has demonstrated that it is alive with international friction and threats to peace. And therefore, from the standpoint of lasting peace, the long view should be to restore international trade to free enterprise.

12. There also enters the fact that international economy must be a reflection of domestic economy. International economic freedom cannot function if there is to be a degree of domestic managed economy which stifles free enterprise, for then there would be no substantial force behind private trading, and governments must take over.

Nor can there be domestic economic freedom parallel with government international trading, for free enterprise could not survive against the power of governments in international trade.

XI THE FOUNDATIONS OF LASTING
PEACE (*Continued*)

Economic Forces (*Continued*)

BULKING large in public discussions today are the reduction of trade barriers after the war, freedom of supply in raw materials, and freedom of the seas. These are indeed essential for economic recovery.

Trade Barriers. In order of importance, there are six varieties of the barriers to trade:

1. Governmental buying and selling.
2. Unstable currencies.
3. Special agreements, such as reciprocal treaties and preferential agreements.
4. Quotas.
5. Monopolies and cartels.
6. Tariffs.

Most of these practices, except tariffs, were the product of the demoralization from the first World War. Each frantic to secure its own recovery, all nations drove toward self-containment under the pressures of unemployment or demoralization of credit and currency and markets or the recollection of the privations imposed during the war by shortage in shipping and the blockade.

Government Buying and Selling. As to governmental buying and selling, solely in their economic aspects, it may be said at once that the whole process is restrictive to volume in the movement of trade. It is, therefore, a barrier to trade. It is only the efforts of a multitude of individuals and of enterprises, seeking every opening for production and sale, that can move the maximum of goods. Bureaucrats, hampered by the red tape of governments, cannot find or create the maximum, either of supplies or markets.

13. In any event, if there is to be a restoration of a real volume of international trade, there must be assurance of ultimate removal of all government buying and selling in foreign markets except for possible storage of raw materials for international stabilization, to which we refer later.

Moreover, if governments are to conduct trading, there is no need to worry over trade barriers. The very assumption of removal of barriers implies free enterprise because barriers are questions of private trading, not trading by governments. In government trading, barriers are replaced by barter.

Unstable Currencies. Next to government trading, probably the worst of all barriers to the growth of trade is to be found in unstable currencies. The failure to secure monetary stability after the last war was a major contribution to the economic disaster of the world and added impulse to the revolt from liberalism.

The whole question of stability of currency is greatly involved with credits, but credits are not the whole problem. When a nation devalues its currency, it, in effect, increases its tariffs. After the American devaluation of the dollar in 1933, the American people had to pay more dollars for British or other foreign goods. Theoretically, it was an increase equivalent to a raise of more than 100 per cent in the tariff. Its effect was at once to stifle imports. Similarly, the repeated devaluations in foreign countries had the same effect of stifling exports to them. Of equally great importance is that any fluctuation or uncertainty of currencies creates a wide hazard for merchants, which they must cover with higher prices.

The universal introduction of governmentally managed currencies since the last war presents a huge problem. Dependent as they are upon bureaucratic action for their value, the hazard of uncertainty at once enters into trade. Moreover, experience proves that such currencies inevitably become a nationalistic device to influence the movement of goods. In so doing, they create a mass of barriers to trade in themselves.

It may be that the world's solution over 6,000 years by the use of gold convertibility to give stability to currency and to enable the settlement of international balances is, after all, the only device humanity has found which will serve these purposes.

It is impossible to create currency and credit stability by loaning America's hoard of gold to other governments. They would at once send the gold back to us in exchange for our commodities. There is no reason in all experience to believe that they would repay the loans. We would simply be giving presents of our commodities and labor and we should have the unjust impoverishment of more Americans. The real solution is to distribute this gold hoard by the purchase of foreign goods of the types which we do not produce in sufficiency—and thereby enrich both buyer and seller.

14. Experience shows that this problem of monetary stability must be taken up at the peace table. We should begin again the work of the economic conference instigated by Mr. Hoover in 1933, where the combined resources and co-operative policies of all nations were to be brought to bear. It must be solved by calling upon the resources of all nations, not of America alone.

Solution of the co-related credit problem will probably have to be found through some sort of credit pool in which all nations pledge their resources. In this problem it will be necessary to examine the possibility of using a reserve of raw materials to be created in times of lower prices and depressions as an adjunct to international credit and currency stabilization.

Special Trade Agreements. The whole essence of reciprocal trade agreements—whether by tariffs or other devices—results in the creation of special favor or trade between a few nations.

The effect of reciprocal tariff agreements is somewhat modified by the "most favored nation clause." But all nations do not have the benefit of that arrangement. It must be said, in support of Mr. Hull's efforts in this regard, that reciprocal agreements by America were mostly for the purpose of lowering the American tariff. But from the point of view of world trade as a whole, most of the governments at the other end of these agreements were moved by special advantage to themselves.

There is another type of special trade agreements among certain nations which seek sheer discrimination and privilege against others. These are at once a barrier to free movement of world trade. After the last war, the whole world set to work spinning this particular web of barriers to trade. It was one reason for retarded recovery everywhere.

15. All special trade agreements which establish privilege between either two nations or groups should be abolished.

Quotas. One of the worst of all human inventions in trade barriers is the quota. That invention, discovered since the last war, is a complete wall against trade, which doors open only to favored nations and in favored amounts. It sums up to a 10,000 per cent tariff with a special privilege attachment. Quotas, plus special agreements, have been developed by the totalitarian nations into a practical control of the foreign trade of some other nations.

16. All quotas everywhere in the world should be abolished.

Monopolies and Cartels. Monopolies and cartels created within a nation or between nations at once reach into control of prices and distribution of goods to other nations. They are again a vicious barrier to trade and they enter into the problem of access to raw materials which we discuss later.

17. All monopolies and cartels which limit foreign trade should be prohibited by the peace.

Tariffs. The old-fashioned tariffs—which have existed for 2,000 years—can be serious barriers to trade. They, however, occupy an exaggerated importance in public discussion as compared to these other barriers. And unlike the other barriers developed mostly since the last war, they are, through centuries of universal use in all countries, deeply imbedded in the economy of nations. They are not easy to deal with. In the first instance, we can be sure they will be continued upon luxury goods as a necessary source of government revenues. And the definition of luxury goods varies somewhat with every country.

The roots of the protective principle as distinguished from revenue lie in its use by every democracy to safeguard their workmen and farmers from goods produced under lower standards of living and longer hours of work. This protection will be hard to move, because industries, cities, schools, churches, and skills have been built under these walls.

Total war has also added new impulses for the use of tariffs as a protective device as well as all the other barriers. During the last war and in this war, many neutral nations were, and are, deprived of essential goods by inability to secure supplies from belligerents either because of shortage of shipping or diversion of production by belligerents to their own use. In consequence, when Argentine children were unable, during the last war, to attend school because shoes could not be had, it is not surprising that Argentina proceeded to nurture a domestic shoe industry by protective devices. The nations which, before the first World War, were dependent upon imports of food, clothing, and other necessities, found themselves reduced to great suffering by blockade and shipping shortages; in consequence, they resolutely stimulated their own agriculture through tariffs as a primary defense measure. Another impulse to protective tariffs of the same sort arises from the synthetic raw-material industries upon which nations have desperately expended billions for defense supplies, such as rubber, chemicals, and minerals. They will want to retain these defenses. Another impulse arises from the breakdown of credit for foreign purchases in the after-war economic demoralization. It again drives towards self-containment through trade barriers.

The probability is that if protective tariffs had not been invented prior to the World War of 1914, they would have been invented afterwards. In any event, after the last war, a large number of nations established tariffs or increased them prior to the general American increase of 1931. It will take a long period of peace and order to allay these fears and restore confidence that foreign supplies can always be obtained. The tariffs will be a harder nut to crack than the other barriers. The most practical thing to do is probably to place tariffs on a basis of reasonable competition between imports and domestic production and, above all, have them equal to all nations. That was first attempted in the United States through the flexible tariff provisions based upon relative cost of production at home and abroad and determined by a non-political body. If every country adopted such principles, the worst of the tariff question would disappear.

TARIFFS. The United States has always been the world's whipping boy on tariffs. Yet all the major nations in the world have maintained tariffs against us from the day we became an independent people. And after Versailles, fifty-seven of them increased their tariffs before the upward revision by the American Congress in 1931. World trade would undoubtedly be benefited by reduction of this barrier, but we need some clear thinking as to how it can be accomplished. There is a widespread and mistaken notion that unilateral self-denying action by the United States would suffice to solve the problem. As a matter of fact such action would merely place us in a disadvantageous position, deprived of bargaining power. If tariff barriers are to be effectively reduced, all nations must act simultaneously.

18. For world recovery and world good will, tariffs certainly require two restraints: first, that they be equal to all nations; second, that they be no higher than will preserve fair competition of imports with domestic production.

Furthermore, both experience and common sense declare that all forms of trade barriers—whether governmental buying and selling, unstable currencies, reciprocal agreements, preferences, quotas, monopolies, cartels, or excessive tariffs—must have vigorous overhauling in the next peace. Certainly, if there is to be relief from trade barriers, there must be equal rights and no discrimination between nations and no agreements should be permitted that are not open equally to all nations.

Access to Raw Materials. Access to raw materials has also loomed large in public discussion and is often prescribed as a panacea for both political and economic peace. Few of those who prescribe it realize its origin. This cry was originally raised by Germany and became one of the cornerstones of her propaganda for return of her colonies. And in this propaganda, the Germans originated the cry of the "have" and "have not" nations. The "have not" nations we heard about were always Germany, Italy, and Japan. Yet no nation produces all of its own raw materials—not even the United States or Great Britain. They are also "have nots" in the sense of this argument. But they have somehow contrived during peace to trade with other nations for ample supplies of their deficient raw materials.

All this agitation has tended to create an illusion in the world that raw materials have a direct relation to lasting peace and an acceptance of the idea that a great problem exists somewhere in this connection. We believe the importance of the problem is entirely overestimated from an international point of view.

19. The economic fact is that there have always been and are ample raw material supplies available to any nation during peace if they will produce the goods to exchange for them. Too often, nations have consumed materials and labor in making arms and munitions that otherwise could be converted into goods that could be exchanged for raw materials.

That there are ample supplies is indicated by the fact that the energies of many governments have been devoted to restricting production of rubber, wheat, sugar, coffee, cotton, nitrate, potash, tin, oil, coal, and fats and fibers in order to hold a living price for the producers of these commodities. There are large reserves of raw material in the world which are undeveloped because they will not provide wages of a decent standard of living or a return upon the capital needed. If, at any time, the world is prepared to pay a little larger price, further supplies are available.

And chemistry is also rapidly solving the question of imported raw materials. Nitrates and light metals can now be produced in every country. Oil, rubber, and textiles are on their way.

As to price, many raw materials have been sold over long terms of years—all but boom years—at less than the real cost of production to the exporting nation. That is particularly the case in more speculative products, such as oil, copper, lead, zinc, tin, and other nonferrous metals. In these speculative industries, some ventures are profitable, but in many there is total loss, and these losing ventures are not included in the costs and prices of the successful ones.

Agricultural raw materials are obviously in ample supply and at reasonable prices, and, except in wartime, their prices do not, over long periods, produce for the farmer as high a standard of living as that of the mechanic.

There have been cases of onerous restrictions on price or supply of raw materials beyond a mere desire for decent living standards through monopoly controls, such as the British rubber and tin controls, the German potash, the Dutch quinine cartels, and the international steel control. These obstructions have to be abolished.

In war, of course, the control of raw-material supply becomes a military weapon. The cry for "equality in raw materials" is partly a cry that comes from a desire for assured war supplies. The inequality of the "haves" and the "have nots" is vivid enough then.

If anything is meant by the discussion of this subject other than equal rights for all citizens of all nations to purchase raw materials of the world, then it reaches into questions of sovereignty over such materials. This sort of "access" question is, in reality, a nationalist and military question, not an economic one, and is a matter of satisfying the national spirit. Nations do like to have sovereignty over areas of raw materials so that they may have an outlet for population, for skills, and satisfactions of national pride—a place in the sun. It also gives still more assurance of supplies in war. In these practical phases, this becomes a question of colonies. But even a redistribution of colonies would not provide everybody with raw materials. Anyone familiar with their distribution in the world would realize that to give parts of all the different raw-material areas to everybody is wholly impossible. That would not be limited to colonies but would disintegrate nations. Would we consider giving copper and oil to Britain or Germany by ceding a part of Montana or of Texas? Are we going to claim parts of Russia or Brazil which contain manganese?

20. The whole experience of the past hundred years shows that the assurance of supplies of raw materials requires only a dissolution of monopoly controls, an assurance of equal prices, open markets—and peace.

Immigration. Another difficult phase of economic pressures to be allayed if we are to have lasting peace is the problem of elbow room for expanding and virile peoples. There is also a problem in refuge for minorities.

The problem is, however, one which involves questions of racial identity, of cultural prejudices, spiritual unity, competitive economic standards of life, and many other difficulties. It must be approached realistically. There is no such thing possible as free immigration. Every self-governing nation is going to determine what sort of people it will admit through its boundaries. It will certainly continue to prevent the ingress of people mentally deficient, diseased, criminal, illiterate, or likely to become a public charge. It can hardly be expected that the Western governments will permit indiscriminate and unlimited immigration. This is not a matter of racial prejudice. The objection is on quite other grounds. Some of these races, notably those of Asia, are trained by a hundred generations to eat less, wear less, seek less shelter, and work longer hours than any Western race can endure. No Western standards can compete with them in their midst. Nor should nations with great unemployment be asked to support floods of unemployed from other quarters.

21. The constructive thing is to direct the streams of immigration toward undeveloped countries. The whole requires a definite plan of preparation which should be taken up at the peace table. There are large suitable areas in South America and Africa.

We shall make a suggestion upon this subject later.

Freedom of the Seas. The freedom of the seas as a problem of peace is a much overestimated issue. During peace, except for the rare revival of old-fashioned piracy, there has been no consequential interference with free movement of merchant ships for a century or more.

The question is wholly one of freedom of the seas during war. And that revolves around the blockade measures of belligerents. With the modern development of blockade in total war, there is no freedom of the seas in war. Even trade between neutrals is controlled by the belligerents through pressures upon their coal and other supplies and blacklists upon merchants.

However, this question has agitated the world for centuries, and a vast amount of international agreement and international law has been built around the definition of blockade and the rights of neutrals in respect to it.

President Wilson, in the second of his Fourteen Points of January 1918, gave probably the most complete formula covering the question that has yet been made. He proposed:

Absolute freedom of navigation upon the seas outside territorial waters alike in peace and in war, except as the seas may be closed in whole or in part by international action for the enforcement of international covenants.

This proposal was rejected by the British Government in November 1918, and received no consideration at the Versailles Peace Conference.

On September 11, 1941, President Roosevelt, speaking of the long-established American policy of freedom of the seas, said:

It means that no nation has the right to make the broad oceans of the world at great distances from the actual theater of war unsafe for the commerce of others.

In the Churchill-Roosevelt declaration of August 1941, it is said:

Such a peace should enable all men to traverse the high seas and oceans without hindrance.

However, this expression applies only to peace and, therefore, does not solve the real problem which is during war.

22. Just and humane rules of the sea during war should again be revived. The rights of neutrals should again be established. They could no doubt be made to hold in secondary wars. But if total war is to be a part of the calendar of humanity, they have little hope of use in such wars except so far as they hold by fear of reprisals. Nevertheless, such standards should again be erected in the world, and President Wilson's formula is the most effective starting point.

There is one segment of freedom of the seas, of vast importance to humanity, which should be worked out and might be so set that it would hold even in total war.

The food blockade has proved to be an endless chain of brutality, fear, hate, revenge, reprisals, and stimulation to armament. It should be stopped if there is to be any hope of lasting peace. A large part of naval building arises from the determination of nations to protect their overseas food supplies and to deprive the enemy of them.

Total war in 1914 brought the extension of food blockade to whole nations. In that war, blockade of civilian food by the Allies contributed a secondary factor only to the defeat of Germany and Austria. That defeat was brought about by armies. The countersubmarine blockade

of England even at that time came perilously near to defeating her, but
for American intervention. The food blockade does not deprive government officials, soldiers, and munition workers. They have a priority and
are always fed. The burden falls upon women, children, and the infirm.
Those mutual food blockades, with the stunting of children on one
side and ruthless killing of sailors on the other, left hate indelibly im-
printed on generations in both peoples.

Germany and her allies, having had the experience of the first World
War, prepared for the present war by intensifying agriculture and building up stocks. Today Britain is experiencing at least as much danger
and suffering from the submarine and air blockade as is Germany from
surface craft. The day is gone when the food blockade is a worth-while
weapon in war.

The physical and spiritual degeneration from it will last another generation. It is all a futility and a brutal folly.

In 1929, Mr. Hoover proposed a remedy. That was to vest the overseas food supply of all combatants in the hands of the combined neutrals,
to be delivered in full cargo lots, the ships to be free from attack on
both sides. The plan was welcomed at that time by the great majority
of nations, but rejected by a few, who prevented unanimity. It had been
tried in a practical way in the first World War and saved the Belgians.

It is true, agreements making for more humane war survive only
through fear of reprisals and fear of neutral opinion. This plan would
invoke both, and neutrals would be interested not only in the humane
aspects, but in keeping their markets open.

With the again proven experience of the almost equal futility of the
surface blockade against the Axis and the submarine blockade against
the British to produce anything but damage to the health of women,
children, and aged of both nations, it would seem that now the fear of
reprisals would uphold such an agreement. Certainly, the first to violate
such agreement would incur the denunciation of every decent person
in the world.

*23. We believe such action should be taken in the peace, for it would
lessen brutality, minimize the incentives to build great navies, and open
to the world a new hope of lessened hate and revenge.*

XII THE FOUNDATIONS OF LASTING
PEACE (*Concluded*)

Nationalism

As we stated in Chapter I:

Nationalism has developed from the deepest of primitive instincts and emotional forces in mankind.

It gathers from a thousand springs of common race with its common language, religion, folklore, traditions, literature, art, music, beliefs, habits, modes of expression, hates, fears, ideals, and tribal loyalties. It expresses itself in patriotism, which is itself built from the fundamentals of love of family, love of country, pride in racial accomplishments. Men fight for their hearths and their homes. They fight for their flag.

From all these racial instincts and mores rises the eternal yearning for independence from foreign subjection or domination. Thus, the subjection of races is one of the most potent of all causes of war. Nations are eternally striving for independence—self-determination. The oppressions which they suffer harden their souls and invigorate their resistance. All the thousands of years of human history are punctuated by wars of independence. . . .

Nationalism will not be stilled by battle or defeat. It is fired to greater heat by every war and every peacemaking. A fiercer nationalism flares out of every defeat and every victory.

Victorious peoples who have marched to the defense of their homes and country to the stirring words of their national songs, who have followed their flags on the battlefield, who have sacrificed their sons and their wealth are little inclined to accept abrogation of their independence of action or of their sovereignty.

Nationalism can be both a cause of war or a bulwark of peace and progress. The values of nationalism cannot be ignored because of its secondary evils.

Where it is an impulse to strive for independence from oppression, for defense against aggression, it makes for war. But independence and spiritual unity, pride of country, constructive rivalry, the building of national cultures out of cohesive mores, the better conduct of government in areas of unity of thought and purpose being the flowering of progress and the expansion of cultural institutions, scientific research, art, music, and literature. Nationalism, in the best sense, is a satisfaction, a fulfillment.

Extreme nationalism does have liabilities to peace and progress. As among individuals, there are ambitions in races for glory and for power of the race. Dignity, honor, and aggrandizement of his country is a satisfaction to the individual. To gain a place in the sun is an inspiring call.

Nationalism can readily expand into dangerous forms—greed in exploitation of the resources and foreign trade of other peoples and in aggression which quickly runs into imperialism.

There are about sixty separate nations in the world. And in the deep currents of human emotion, the primary interest of every citizen of them is his own country, first and foremost.

Nationalism, with all its emotions, will continue as long as man inhabits this earth and will have to be embraced in any plan to preserve the peace (p. 160).

Nationalism, being fed with the earliest milk to every human animal, will not be stamped out by this war. It will continue as it has continued since the dawn of civilization. It will be even more heated after the sacrifices of this war.

Small Nations. We Americans, through "self-determination" and "self-government" of nations, were pledged to sustain the theory of nationalism in the last World War. This sprang from our desire to see men free from oppression. Fifteen new nations sprang into independence from that' victory. We have renewed those pledges in this war—and more new nations will spring to independence, or at least self-government, at the peace.

Success has expanded Japanese ideas to embrace the hegemony of one billion Asiatics, controlling, molding, and pitting them against the Western World. No other Asiatic race of consequence possesses a skilled military class. The others can be depended upon to pursue peace if freed from this domination and leadership. But upon that defeat, other problems of Asia will arise to meet our pledges of independence and self-government. The self-government of India is assured by the British undertaking to establish Commonwealth status. But Burma, Indo-China, the Malay States, and the peoples of the Dutch Indies will also be asserting their claims to independence. It would seem unlikely that the American people will wish to sacrifice their sons to restore them to subjection. That would be repugnant to our whole national ideal.

Moreover, we have pledged ourselves "to restore sovereign rights and self-government to those who have been forcibly deprived of them." That pledge will demand restoration of the independence of the Norwegians, the French, the Danes, the Finns, the Estonians, the Latvians, the Lithuanians, the Poles, the Czechs, the Slovaks, the Slovenes, the Croats, the Serbs, the Greeks, the Albanians, the Dutch, the Belgians, the Luxemburgers, the Koreans, the Ethiopians, the Persians, the Arabs, the Siamese, and the Filipinos. In any event, the moment the enemy's power crumbles and the bugle of victory sounds, they will instantly resume their own governments.

They will wait for no peacemakers to act upon the needs of their peoples. Their economic, boundary and defense policies will present great problems.

24. All these nations and peoples of Europe and Asia will insist upon their independence and their own cultures. To deny them will bring no lasting peace. But there must need be better organization of them if they are to keep the peace.

The problem lies in finding methods of averting so far as possible the elements of conflict that arose from the creation of many new countries at the end of the last war. These countries must come to the peace table for recognition of their independence, or at least for necessary political and financial assistance, which amounts to much the same thing. This affords a fleeting opportunity to exercise a restraining influence.

We have seen that unrest and suspicion were increased in Europe by the way in which the multitude of new states hedged themselves about with economic barriers; by their building up of military forces and the making of military alliances which gave concern to their neighbors; and by their difficulties with their racial minorities. These three problems must be examined separately.

Many of these smaller eastern European states are in reality part of larger natural economic areas. Such is the case of the states in the Danube Valley—Czechoslovakia, Austria, Yugoslavia, and Hungary. From every standpoint of raw materials, complimentary agriculture, manufactures, and transportation, they should be in one economic unit. After the last war, the barriers they set up against one another impoverished them all. There are other economic unifications which would make for prosperity and lessened friction, and thereby for more lasting peace.

At the end of the last war, all the newly independent countries set about building up strong armies and making military combinations and alliances. This meant not only that they were living beyond their means and making full recovery impossible; it also meant that they were causing suspicion and apprehension in neighboring countries and encouraging them in turn to increase their armed forces. These alliances proved worthless in any event.

25. History has shown us that the possession of highly developed armed forces by small nations is disastrous in all its consequences. These forces do not suffice for successful defense against a powerful enemy. They serve for the most part as a real or fancied provocation, and eventually lead to military disaster.

The problem of irredentas also plagued these small states, for minorities were included which they could neither absorb nor control. We mention this further later on, as it concerns larger states as well.

It may be that there is a lesson to be learned by the smaller nations of Europe from the history of Switzerland. Here three divergent races grouped in a cantonal government with a very great cantonal autonomy have dwelt in peace among themselves and in independence for centuries. Switzerland has always been a force for peace. There were, of course, certain factors which favored the success of the Swiss experiment. But the fact remains that the Swiss have set up a small country composed of several races with different languages and traditions, and that by the exercise of tolerance and local government they have succeeded. If they had acted according to the methods current elsewhere in Europe, they would have had an Italian, and perhaps a French, irredenta. For centuries they have avoided this mistake and probably thereby averted the destruction of their country. Perhaps the secret of their success is that they accorded equal rights to all racial elements regardless of their importance in percentages of population.

It was the original intention at the Paris Peace Conference that Czechoslovakia should be organized on the Swiss model. Indeed, this was proposed in writing by Dr. Beneš. It is perhaps too much to hope that some sort of cantonal, federated, or economic unions be set up in these areas.

26. Certainly, the experience of history, and notably of the last peace, would seem to show at least the desirability of making the independence of these small countries conditional upon their accepting certain definite undertakings to refrain from building up the sort of economic barriers and military action which contributed so powerfully to their own collapse and the collapse in Europe after the last war.

Irredentas. The nations of Europe will be faced with problems of mixed populations on their borders.

27. Bitter experience for a hundred years shows that these European irredentas are a constant source of war. Consideration should be given even to the heroic remedy of transfer of populations.

The hardship of moving is great, but it is less than the constant suffering of minorities and the constant recurrence of war. The action involved in most cases is less drastic than the transfer of the Greeks and the Turks after the last war—and the lessening of tension brought about by that transfer measurably improved both the prosperity and amity of the two nations. A careful study should, of course, be made as to the possibility of real and final remedy.

German Unity. A still larger question of nationalism will arise over Germany. Any survey of the history of Europe will show that, in its periodic defeats, this race has been dismembered into separate states.

There is a widespread feeling that a united Germany constitutes a menace to peace and that the obvious solution lies in dividing the country and keeping it divided—at least isolating the Prussians who have provided the motive power for repeated aggressions. Advocacy of this proposal is described as being realistic.

Before committing ourselves to such a course we should try to satisfy ourselves as to whether it is realistic. The Germans, like all virile races, are cohesive. The incubation of movements for unity has usually exploded a European war. That was the case in 1866, 1870, and 1939. The more realistic interpretation is that it is the division of Germany that feeds her militarism and breeds wars.

Another test of dismemberment proposals is whether the solution could be maintained. In other words, can we be confident that the United Nations, once they have imposed a partition of Germany, will maintain for all time an identity of interest and purpose among themselves and be at all times prepared to exert their united strength to prevent by force any movement toward German unity? We find nothing in history to justify any such hope. During a great war allied nations are held together by a common peril and a common purpose. Once the peril is past and the common purpose achieved, conflicts of interests come to the fore. And dismembered Germany uses and widens these conflicts of interest in her efforts toward unity. Within a few years after Versailles the identity of interest disappeared and the carefully prepared measures for holding Germany down not only lost all their efficacy but resulted in ferment over all Europe.

Change of relationships among governments is one of the few things that are certain in international affairs. We should therefore be on our guard against assuming that we can establish a new *status quo* to our own taste opposed to living forces and then maintain it indefinitely.

28. There can be no lasting peace in Europe with a dismembered Germany, any more than there could be a lasting peace in North America if other nations tried to separate the states or to put parts of them under Mexico. In the light of historical experience, the sound course is to give the Germans an incentive for abandoning their old ways and becoming a peaceful nation.

Imperialism

We said in Chapter I:

Another of the larger forces moving in all history is imperialism. It may, for our purposes, be defined as the movement of races over their racial borders.

It is part cause, part effect. It springs from excessive nationalism, militarism, thirst for power, and economic pressures. They all feed upon one another. Old as the Chaldeans and as modern as this morning, its purpose has not changed, although its form has altered. At one time, part of the motivation of imperialism was dynastic or racial glory; at another, zeal to spread religious faith—for instance, Mohammedanism or Christianity. But in modern civilization, its motivation has been chiefly economic.

Modern imperialism has developed into three varieties, of which one is justified by modern moral standards, the second may be justified, and the third has no justification in morals or hope of peace. The first variety is expansion of races into the settlement and development of areas mostly unpopulated; the second, into areas of uncivilized races incapable of self-government; the third, sheer conquest of civilized races. The last two have always embodied one purpose—that is, to secure superior living by exploiting other races and their resources.

Whether its impelling force be glory, prestige, spread of religion, ideology, development of backward races, or exploitation of labor and resources, imperialism is not essentially an appendage of the Divine Right of Kings or the attribute of dictators. Democracies have been no less imperialistic than kings, emperors, or dictators. Rome was imperialistic before the Emperor was invented. Britain and France and the United States have expanded steadily. But wherever imperialism has been successful over long periods, it has always rested upon class government.

There can be no doubt that domination and exploitation of other races is one of the eternal causes of war. We know of no case where it has made for durable peace. Even in the phase of expansion over backward races or into open spaces, the rivalries between imperialisms have made for war. In the spread of civilization, it has compensations. But as a method of advancing peace, it cannot be given a great deal of credit. Much can be said for a satiated empire like Britain, which has arrived at a point where it becomes a stabilizing force. More especially that Empire, being liberal in instinct, makes for representative government among its components.

But imperialism as a theory of maintaining peace in the modern world has the disturbing consequence of setting up a dozen rival forms of Pax Romana to fight one another (p. 163).

The war-perpetuating monster, imperialism, is present in this war in a large way—and it will be present at the peace table as well. It was greatly weakened in the last war by freeing thirteen nations from Germany, Austria, Russia, and Turkey. It gained some strength through territories acquired by Britain, Italy, France, and Japan. But with victory for the United Nations in this war, Germany, Italy, and Japan should be finally cured of imperialism through restoration of the occupied and oppressed states.

29. The political basis of imperialism is being steadily destroyed by self-determination and the consequent independence of nations. The incentives of glory and power will be greatly dimmed by the suffering that will come to imperialistic nations from this war. Moreover, the economic pressures to imperialism through foreign trade, exploitation

and emigration of excess population can be ameliorated for the future.
In any event, with victory in this war, imperialism will be at the lowest
point in history, at least for a while.

With United Nations victory the only important peoples who will
probably be left under other states will be the Polynesian Islands and
largely unsettled areas of Africa, who will at their present state of
political development lay little claim to self-government.

Africa may well be called the "Dark Continent" in view of the preva-
lent ignorance of its problems. There is urgent need for study of the
varied and intricate questions which will demand answers after this war.

Africa could long be considered a sort of Atlantis so far as the affairs
of other continents were concerned. But even during the present war,
with the spread of hostilities and the staggering development of aviation
all continents are brought into a new and closer relationship. There are
within Africa's borders vast spaces adaptable to white settlement and
vast resources of raw materials needed by the world. Without exagger-
ating the growth of our immediate interest in other parts of the world,
it has become obvious that it behooves us as a matter of common pru-
dence to study the problems we have hitherto neglected, with a view to
averting the growth of future threats to peace.

It is not our task to judge the record of the colonizing powers. There
is much that is both good and bad in that record. To some, the good
far outweighs the evil: the establishment and maintenance of public
order; abolition of the slave trade; the development of national resources; greater markets for native produce; better health conditions;
the cessation of tribal wars with all their cruelties; and greater opportunities. And last, but by no means least, the spiritual, educational, and
social benefits from the spread of the Christian religion.

There are grave liabilities as well—in the introduction of new intoxi-
cating liquors, the spread of diseases not known before, the breaking
down of old customs and taboos of ethical value, and the evils arising
from organization and industrialization.

The true picture is to be found, if anywhere, in a composite of the
good and bad.

The problems of Africa are further complicated by the dfferent
degrees of civilization of its peoples. These problems are too compli-

cated to be settled at the peace table. There will be neither the time nor the objectivity needed for the task.

30. Perhaps the course that offers the greatest hope of sound achievement would be for the United Nations to negotiate agreement, before the end of the war, as to principles, and leave details to be worked out by international commissions. But experience shows that if such commissions are to achieve anything substantial they must have a clear mandate. They cannot operate successfully on the basis of general declarations which each nation is free to interpret for itself.

31. It is worth considering whether some of these latter areas in particular should not be put under international government with equal access to all nations for immigration, trade, and development of natural resources. Particularly could their open spaces, with proper organization, be made a refuge settlement for the oppressed of every kind and as an outlet for immigration from overpopulated nations without harm to the interests of the native populations.

Militarism

We said in Chapter I:

Man is a combative animal. He loves contest. He hates easily. He is an egoistic animal, and in the mass becomes more egoistic. His beliefs in superiority are quickly transformed into arrogance. And that is one of the stimulants of aggression. The pomp and glory of war have an appeal to man. He loves adventure, and to great numbers of people war becomes a wholesale relief from the dull routines of life.

Common defense is an age-old instinct. It started with the defense of the family and spread to the tribe and finally to the nation. By reason of this need of defense, every nation must have some degree of military organization, even among the most peaceful peoples. The possession of armament however, no matter how necessary, breeds suspicion, fear, counterarmament, and hate.

And out of military organization there often comes a military caste. Its hopes of renown lies in war, not in peace. And its voice in government is more often for settlement of grievances by war than by the processes of peace.

The militarism we describe is an aggressive force. It always makes for war.

But military organization can have two quite different spirits. The one defense, the other aggression.

Like individuals, some peoples are naturally pacific and some naturally aggressive. China has been outstandingly the most pacific of all nations. So pacific has she been that in 3,000 years she has been conquered and ruled by foreign dynasties in all but two comparatively short periods.

Moreover, there is in some races a definite aggressive warrior strain. It grows in an aggressive race to a glorification of war for war's sake. The "reinvigoration" of the race through war has long been preached in Germany, Italy, and Japan. The "warrior concept" is deeply rooted in Germany, particularly in Prussia. This may be because of the constant threat of invasion. On the other hand, it has been argued that the trouble with the Germans is that, unlike the French and the Britons, they were never conquered by the Romans and given the advantages of that form of education. Tacitus was eloquent on the subject of Germany nearly 2,000 years ago. The Order of Teutonic Knights carried their thirteenth-century ideas with fire and sword. Their ideas of an aggressive military caste have come down through the centuries, with periodic modernizations, through Frederick the Great to Bismarck, with his "blood and iron," to Hitler, with his "master race," his "guns instead of butter."

The same could be said of the Japanese. Their two feudal military clans—the Choshu and the Satsuma—are represented today in the control of the Army and Navy respectively.

Probably 80 per cent of the German and Japanese people are no more militaristic than any other. But by their very docility they are constantly overridden by the warrior groups.

And we must not overlook the Pied Pipers, consumed with ambition, who call their countrymen to glory and conquest. These men, seeking power on earth and a place in the eternity of history, are the apotheoses of militarism and aggression. They are the Alexander the Greats, the Genghis Khans, the Julius Caesars, the Charlemagnes, the Gustavus Adolphuses, the Napoleons, the Kaiser Wilhelms, and the current exhibits (p. 161).

32. Our experience since 1919 points to some profound deductions confirmed by even earlier history. One of them is: Disarmament offers the only effective way to bring militarism under control.

The problem falls into two phases: the disarmament of the enemy countries, and the reduction of arms in the victorious countries.

It is not to be expected that the victorious countries, having defeated aggressive militarism at infinite cost, are going to melt their swords and allow the enemy to return to the practices of the last hundred years.

Therefore, the first part of the problem resolves itself into disarmament of the enemy; the second part is disarmament among the Allies.

Disarming the Enemy. The first lesson that we may well draw is from the experience in disarming the enemy states in 1919. By the Armistice and the Treaty of Versailles, their arms were destroyed and their navies were surrendered. Germany was permitted to retain a professional army of 100,000 men, supposedly for purposes of maintaining internal order. She was permitted to have a navy severely limited in tonnage and types of ships.

We have pointed out earlier that the huge mistake was that it perpetuated her professional armies and navies. It perpetuated the warrior caste and all its traditions. It afforded a skeleton army and navy of skilled men ready for quick expansion. It insured the continuity of the German General Staff and all their military skill, brains, and ambitions.

Repeated experience with this warrior caste in its bluffs, intimidations, aggressions, blitzes, and attacks without even declaration of war should be enough for the world in this particular. We must make a better job of it this time.

33. The complete idealistic view would perhaps be the total dissolution of the military establishments of all enemy nations and the substitution, for purposes of a civic order, of a constabulary of the police type, excluding the whole officer and military caste from such organization and thus assuring their disappearance from the world.

That is, no doubt, too much to be hoped for in this world, but it will serve as an ideal toward which men can strive.

General Disarmament. The Treaty of Versailles contained a pious pledge of all the Allies to disarm sometime but made no provision for when or how.

The opposition among the victorious nations was rooted partly in fears that security could be provided only with overwhelming armies and navies. It came in part from mutual distrust among the former Allies themselves. Military alliances sprang up at once. The essence of military alliance is large armed force, and alliances are at once a block to disarmament. The heightened nationalism which arose inevitably from the war also contributed to each country's desire for arms. Arms were made easily accessible to the liberated nations by extensive sales from the larger Allies on credit. And there was the grim fact that masses of professional soldiers had been created who wanted to hold their jobs. To some extent, war industries wished to continue their markets. This was particularly the case in France, where a vicious combination of arms manufacturers with press and banking connections deliberately cultivated war scares and pressures to promote sales at home and abroad. America was not free from this taint, as witness the transactions around the Naval Conference of 1927.

Human nature and national mores being what they are, all this will happen again unless positive measures are taken immediately while the world is sick of killing and wants action to end it. The opportunity for comprehensive action will be of short duration. Unless this opportunity is seized upon, all these same obstructions will grow again—nationalism, imperialism, military alliances—and the witches, fear, hate, and revenge will mix a new brew. They all demand armies and oppose disarmament. Experience at the last peace showed that once the flame of war horrors had died down, forces quickly sprang up which destroyed all hope of real disarmament. It required but a short time for these oppositions to grow and mobilize.

34. Therefore, experience shows if there is to be a reduction of arms among the victorious nations, it must be agreed upon in advance and action should take place within weeks, not months or years, after the firing ceases.

The victorious nations will automatically demobilize a great part of their huge war establishments. But even after that was done following the last war, enormous peacetime establishments remained. The burden of them to the taxpayers and to national economy by separation of men from productive labor was a contributory cause to the general economic collapse. When this war is over economic necessities will cry even more loudly for relief from such burdens.

35. If the rate of $20,000,000,000 spent annually in the world on arms before this war could be reduced to small dimensions immediately with the end of the war, that alone would ensure the recovery of economic life and civilization. The people of Germany, Japan, and Italy would surely have every reason to welcome that relief.

To be realistic, we must conclude that some military establishment will be retained, at least by the United Nations. The problem falls into two stages : first, the minimum necessary to assure defense, and second, the comparative armament of other nations.

Before discussing the character of disarmament, we must digress to mention the great shift in war methods. The developments since the last war have had a profound effect, not alone on the whole method of this war, but also an enormous effect upon the problems of disarmament.

These changes in the main lie in the advance of air power. It has tended to make the offense of armies more powerful than the defense. Land armies without large air contingents are at a great disadvantage. At the same time, it has enormously strengthened defense against naval attack.

The whole question of the effectiveness and value of surface ships is now in doubt. Without accepting the view that capital ships are now wholly useless, it can be said that naval attack upon land defenses is now extremely difficult if not practically impossible against adequate land-based air power. Nevertheless, the question of naval arms to be retained will also be modified by the whole shift in the relation of air-craft to surface warships. The sinking or disabling of a large number of first-class battleships and a host of cruisers and lesser craft, from the air in this war, all accumulate at least to raise a grave question as to the future utility of large surface navies. And, therefore, naval disarmament becomes an easier dose for the Powers to swallow.

The naval situation with victory should also be still more simple than that after the last war. Germany, Italy, and Japan will, or should, lose their entire navies with defeat. The French, who proved so great a stumbling block in naval disarmament after the last war, are not likely to oppose effectively any United Nations program. The only consequential remaining naval powers will be the United States, Great Britain and Russia. But Russia did not have much of a navy at the beginning of this war, has lost much of what she had, and does not appear to have been engaged in substantial naval building during the present war. With victory, the substantial navies remaining will presumably be those of the United States and Britain.

There will, however, be the old question of relative naval strength as between the victorious nations. The huge naval strength maintained after the last war, as we have said, was not out of fear of the disarmed enemy, but out of fear of one another felt by the Allies. The whole painful negotiations of naval limitation of certain ratios are proof of all that. At least this problem will be much simplified by our being no longer compelled to compromise with the wishes of France, Italy and Japan —and having already established the principle of parity between the United States and Britain.

The preservation of order on the seas from pirates, and assistance in the preservation of order in semi-barbaric countries fronting the seas could be done with only a small fraction of the naval strength provided in the naval-limitation treaties of 1922 and 1930.

With victory, the problem of land disarmament will be further simplified at the end of this war as compared to the last war. The land and air forces of Germany, Italy, Japan, Rumania, Bulgaria could be disarmed as far as necessary by the armistice itself. Hitler has destroyed every other army in Europe except those of Russia, Turkey, and Spain. The only consequential land armies after the armistice will be American, British, Chinese, and Russian.

The opportunity to disarm enemy countries to a reasonable degree, the lessening of the number of armed nations to be consulted, and this rise of air power open another avenue of thought on the whole question of reduction of armament.

36. The sole possessor or possessors of military air power could stop anyone from going to war. And international action to enforce peace would be enormously simplified. We refer to this later on.

There enters into this question an element arising from commercial air power. During this war, the design and effectiveness of war airplanes have shifted away from the design and effectiveness of commercial planes to a degree almost comparable with the divergence of types of warships and merchant ships. This divergence in design and equipment in the two categories of airships has gone so far that types of civilian planes probably no longer can be used for military purposes. The contrary is also true to a large extent. Therefore, it is possibly not necessary to limit commercial planes in order to secure air disarmament. Nevertheless, this question is not so definitive as not to require reservations. It calls for discussion and study.

There enters into this question of relative arms among nations an additional approach to the problem. As we have stated, in 1932, Mr.

Hoover, through Mr. Gibson, chairman of the American delegation to the Disarmament Conference, proposed the abolition of all offensive arms—that is, bombing airplanes, submarines, large mobile guns, tanks, and poison gas. All but a few large nations agreed to it at that time— some forty-five of them. This proposal was revived and earnestly advocated by President Roosevelt in 1933. And battleships might now be included.

The effect would be to make the defense ascendant over the attack. While nations may violate such agreements to some extent secretly before war or after war begins, yet it is impossible to make these instruments so quickly and in such large quantities as to be overpowering. Had that proposal for the abolition of aggressive arms been accepted and enforced as provided in the American proposals, the blitz would not have been possible.

37. In any event, victory will offer an unparalleled opportunity to disarm and thereby reduce the cost and dangers of arms to the world to the lowest ebb for a whole century—and that would contribute much to quick recovery and lasting peace. But if it is to be done, it must be done at once at the peace table, not postponed.

The Forces of Fear, Hate, and Revenge

In the first chapter we stated:

Fear, hate, and revenge play a large part in the causes of war. . . . Fear of invasion, fear of starvation by blockade in war, fear of economic disadvantage; age-old hates from wrong, from rivalries, from oppression; yearnings for revenge for past wrongs and defeats—all press toward violence.

These great forces of violence lie deep in the recesses of racial consciousness and racial experience. These emotions are the inheritance from all previous wars. Wrongs live for centuries in the minds of a people. There are traditional age-old hates between nations which are burned into their souls. From these emotions, wars have bred new wars. They have seldom settled anything. Fear of stronger races by their weaker neighbors born of invasions and defeat keeps them in constant sacrifice for the burdens of defense.

It keeps them in constant agitation, seeking diplomatic action, seeking support and military alliances. And the humiliations and privations of defeat and punishment create an undying demand for revenge.

The defeated are always humiliated. They are always impoverished. Either in reality or belief, the national pride, the national hopes, the national economy, or the national dignity of the vanquished have suffered. No nation ever recognizes or admits that it is wrong. No leader of that nation would dare suggest such a thing. Hate lives on, and it becomes entrenched in the mores of a people.

These emotions are eternal inheritances and causes of war. They, too, will sit at every peace table (p. 164).

These total wars of the last generation are far greater breeders of hate than ancient wars. No longer is there chivalry of armed men for women, children, the aged and infirm. Starvation of nations has brought not only agony to civilians, but stunting of their children and decimation of millions from inevitable pestilence. Women and children have been killed in tens of thousands by bullets, fire, and bombs from the air. The hideous cruelties of blitz surprise, the sinking of seamen without compassion by submarines, the attacks upon helpless Jews, murder of hostages, the refusal of liberal governments to allow food to their conquered allies—all not only make a ghastly picture of barbarism, but they raise the emotions of peoples to heights of lasting fear and hate.

The whole experience of Versailles shows that these forces will not only sit at the peace table, but will influence international relations for generations unless there are statesmen far more elevated in spirit than sat at the last peacemaking.

Shrill cries for punishment will echo through every part of the peace deliberations. Yet we must realize that the mass of Axis peoples are no more responsible for starting this war than the last one. We must remember they have been under dictatorship, their people have been misled, wrongly educated, and were allowed to have no will in this war. They have been terrorized and deprived of the truth. But there is a large question of the personal responsibility of heads of state and their associates for violation of treaties and agreements, entered into with free will, in pursuit of militaristic and imperialistic designs which result in the killing of millions of human beings.

38. There is just one discrimination that can and should be made. The leaders of the nations who brought this situation upon the world must be made to realize the enormity of their acts. There can be no moral distinction and there should be no legal distinction between such men and common criminals conspiring to murder. Too long has it been assumed that there is something sacred about the heads of state who project or provoke war and wholesale murder.

It may well be borne in mind that defeat and disarmament of a nation is in itself the greatest humiliation that comes to a people. To continue punishment or to try to hold peoples in bondage is not only statesmanship terrible in its consequences, but is an allusion.

39. Nations cannot be held in chains. In the end there can be no trustworthy security except by giving the decent elements in a people a chance to co-operate in the work of peace.

Reparations. The problem of indemnities and reparations will arise. Aside from the loss of life, the cost of the war to the victorious nations will be more than the whole national wealth of the Axis Powers. The debts alone of the United Nations will not be less than $500,000,000,000, and the continuing cost of pensions and interest will add other hundreds of billions. Therefore, there can be no real reparations. The first World War proved that no considerable sums could be collected in any event. The total payments of Germany on reparations were not much more than the money she borrowed from the Allies and subsequently repudiated. After this war, some minor sum might be had.

40. Defeated people simply will not produce to pay huge reparations. And they cannot be made to do so. If the peacemakers resolve to take a few billions over a few years to give as a bonus to their widows, orphans, and maimed, with a few articles of vertu as mementos of the war, they will save much worry at the peace table.

Further, debts from one Allied Power to another are valueless. With the doors of free speech and propaganda open, people will squirm out of them somehow. Moral justification will be found by every demagogue against payment. It will be an issue in every election.

41. The fact is that there cannot be any continuing intergovernmental debt of consequential amounts between governments in either reparations or loans.

We may go back to the peace made after the other two great crises in modern civilization for experience in this matter. Historians find that mankind had some surcease from world war after the Treaty of

Westphalia in 1648, and after the Treaty of Vienna in 1815, but they can find no peace from the Treaty of Versailles in 1919.

The two previous great treaties avoided one error of the Treaty of Versailles. They did not try to punish the vanquished nations or put them into economic bondage. That may possibly explain the fact that they prevailed so much longer than the Treaty of Versailles.

42. Certainly, experience shows that no nation can be punished as a whole and at the same time leave any hope of lasting peace. This endless treadmill of punishment must be stopped in the world if there is to be real peace. Victory with vengeance is ultimate defeat in the modern world.

We can have peace or we can have revenge, but we cannot have both.

XIII METHODS OF PRESERVING
PEACE

IN the last three chapter we deduced some conclusions, from world experience, upon the foundations which must be laid for peace by allaying the destructive action of the six dynamic forces of ideologies, economic pressures, nationalism, imperialism, militarism and the complexes of fear, hate, and revenge. After these foundations are laid, a superstructure must be built where the seventh force, the will to peace, shall preside. Not only at Versailles, but time and again, it has been proved in the history of the world that unless these foundations are rightly built, no international co-operation for preservation of peace can be successful. But there must be such a structure. It is one of the great obligations upon the peacemakers.

The purpose of this chapter is not to advocate any particular form of such international action, but to present the different proposals objectively. World experience is more positive in the requirements of the foundations than in the architecture of the temple itself.

In describing the will to peace the outset of this essay, we said:

Against all the forces which make for war stands the will to peace. Ever in the background of men's minds is the infinite suffering of war. It kills or maims the best of the race. It brings the deepest of all griefs to every home. It brings poverty and moral degeneration. It brings these poignant ills to victor and vanquished alike.

The Sermon on the Mount launched the transcendent concept of compassion, of peace and good will among men as a fundamental of the Christian faith. And despite all his violation of the spiritual concepts, man has received from them an undying inspiration to strive for peace.

The search over centuries by men of good will for methods of lasting peace testifies to the yearning of peoples for relief from the world's greatest blight. The multitude of peace treaties, the establishment of embassies and legations, the Holy Alliance, the Concert of Europe, the balance of power, the development of international law, the Hague Tribunal, the processes of settlement of controversy by negotiation, by meditation, by arbitration, the League of Nations, and the World Court are all exhibits of the impelling will to peace.

And indeed the spiritual concepts of peace have brought it to pass that every war must be justified by its leaders as a war of defense and for the purpose of securing peace. And the end of every war is received with joy and the ringing of the church bells (p. 165).

There are several methods for preserving peace which we believe should in a sense be added to the foundations of peace by incorporation into all the actual agreements directly between nations in addition to their operation by the instrumentality set up to preserve peace.

The peace treaty must necessarily make political, military, and economic settlements. It must provide some sort of international machinery or organization for preserving peace.

43. But the step we here suggest is that there should be direct agreements between signatories which would tend to settle many controversies before they need reach any such international body. That is, each nation should agree to refer all disputes to arbitration or to refer them to judicial settlement or to establish cooling-off periods with independent investigation.

Such direct treaties have been current between enlightened nations for many years and have served a great purpose. This suggestion is to make them universal, and thereby localize disputes and burden the international organization only in cases where these means of direct settlement of disputes should fail. Important in this category is the necessity to provide in the foundations of peace provision for adequate revision of onerous treaties.

Revision of Treaties

Certainly, experience shows that peace can best be preserved, not by preventing change and putting the future in a straitjacket, but by seeking to control change and direct it. Obviously, any attempt to maintain the *status quo* indefinitely is a direct invitation to war—for peaceful means being denied, the change can come only through force. War becomes the only available solvent. If provision is made that there will be revision of treaties by adequate orderly methods, it can be hoped such revision will be done peacefully.

44. It is, therefore, suggested that the objective should be to build the concept of revision into the body of international law to a place of equal importance with the other pacific methods, alongside of conciliation, mediation, arbitration, judicial decision, and cooling-off periods. It is further suggested that the application of any nation for revision of treaty provisions, not sooner than ten years after its conclusion, should be implemented by the appointment of a committee of outstanding statesmen not interested in the dispute to report and negotiate a reasonable settlement.

International Machinery to Preserve Peace

The preservation of peace, however, must finally rest upon some sort of co-operative international organization which will continuously allay and keep in check the vicious elements of the dynamic forces which make for war and will constantly strengthen those forces which make for peace.

History is probably less instructive on what to do in the future than it is on what not to do. Nevertheless, experience is the substance of reason and a better guide on what to do than is Utopian emotion. If we go back over all these centuries of mankind's contriving of machinery to preserve peace, we find they divide into two categories.

The first method, historically, is to maintain peace by force. The Pax Romana, the balance of power, military alliances and counteralliances have been used to make aggression at least more cautious. These methods may have served as a check upon war, but in the end they crashed by their inherent stimulation of militarism, nationalism, imperialism, fear, and hate. And as their processes involve many nations not direct parties to the conflict, they cause a wider spread of war. The League of Nations was by "collective action" to set up force differing from other forms in that it proposed the use of military or economic force by common action of all the other nations against aggressors.

The second category of peace preservations sprang from the growth of civilization itself, the very spiritual and moral basis of which lies in the control of the conduct of men by law and justice. After all, the preservation and advancement of civilization cannot be based on force.

These processes, which we have called the pacific methods, are based upon the prevention of war by establishing respect for international law, fidelity to agreements, and settlement of controversies by pacific methods of negotiation, conciliation, arbitration, and judicial decision, and by agreement to abandon all war in favor of such pacific methods.

But rather than discuss the philosophy and methods of these two different ideas of peace preservation, we believe the reader will obtain a more direct approach to the problem if we take up the more important actual proposals that have been made for international action.

The plans for preserving peace, and which have been suggested, fall into eight major categories:

1. Restoration of the League of Nations under the Covenant as it stands.
2. Restoration of the League with a revised Covenant giving it absolute military power to enforce peace.
3. Restoration of the League of Nations with a revised Covenant constituting it as an effective Council of Nations to preserve peace solely by pacific settlements and for building international co-operation
4. Proposals for a separate military organization by the leading allied nations to preserve order.
5. Proposals that each great region of the earth should separately organize its own preservation of order while co-operating in pacific settlement through some form of the League, Council of Nations, or other world organization for pacific settlements.
6. Extreme isolation.
7. Federation of nations.
8. Pax Americana.

We do not enumerate these possible courses in order of their importance—every student has a different view upon that. Some may prefer to mix the ideas into different forms.

These plans are in process of evolution. There are certain positive lessons from world experience with them which can be deduced. There are arguments for and against each of them. The best form cannot be determined until nearer the end of the war, when we have a clearer view of things to come and until there have been wide public consideration and debate. From such discussion will come better understanding of the problems. Without here expressing opinions of our own, we give the arguments, pro and con, and state such experience as the world has had with such methods.

1. *Restoration of the League of Nations under the Covenant as It Stands.* The League of Nations represents the greatest and most comprehensive experiment in all history in deliberate organization of nations to bring lasting peace. Indeed, we can grasp the value of this experiment only if we realize that the world has to learn its lessons in preservation of peace by trial and error.

The League failed to preserve peace. Yet it was by no means wholly a failure. We have sought to analyze fully its workings in Chapter VIII, to which we refer the reader for the background of these immediate observations.

There were many causes for this failure. Among them were the failure of the Treaty of Versailles to allay the six dynamic forces which make for war; the disastrous political climate arising out of the competition of power diplomacy, balance of power; military alliances which constantly ignored the League; the failure to support representative government in the enemy countries; and, finally, the economic miseries of Europe.

Despite these handicaps from outside, the League did succeed in developing a considerable measure of accomplishment in one field and an unparalleled measure of success in another. It did settle many controversies by pacific means; it did advance the technique of such settlements. Its outstanding success was in the development of co-operation between nations in the fields of public health, in advancement of welfare, in intellectual exchanges, and in economic improvement.

We have referred to the outside influences which militated against the success of the League. There were, however, weaknesses in the League itself. We have analyzed these weaknesses elsewhere, but we may condense them here.

1. The Covenant of the League was at the same time too elaborate, too precise, and not precise enough in its provisions. The text became a yoke under which nations chafed or became fearful concerning

their sovereignty. The attempt to commit nations to certain procedures and at the same time to give them each a veto power over action led to destructive effects. In consequence, there were incessant disputes over interpretation, jurisdiction, and authority.

2. The original theory of the League was that all controversies between nations should be submitted to pacific settlement and that if any nation refused and began military action, it was to be dealt with as an aggressor. Thereupon, collective economic or military force should be applied by the other members. This definition of an aggressor proved to have great difficulties. But more important, the compromises in the Covenant by which nations did not bind themselves to this procedure and with the provision of a full veto power to each member the original theory never had a chance.

3. The League was thus founded upon two different concepts, one organizing the preservation of peace by economic or military force; and the other, for the prevention of war by settlement of controversy through pacific methods. The two concepts clashed. In any event, the attempt to summon economic and military force against important aggressors proved beyond the practical capacity of an international body, and with these failures the strength and prestige of the League in the field of pacific settlements were fatally injured.

4. The League did not recognize, or was prevented from undertaking, one of the first functions of preserving peace: that is, the need for comprehensive consideration of the political forces in different areas which were developing strains and the formulation of long-view policies and action for their correction. Regional development of such policies in Europe and Asia comparable to the work of the Pan-American conferences in the Western Hemisphere was a constant and urgent necessity.

5. The League failed to provide for or secure any reality in the revision of onerous treaties or those made from the heat of war which could not endure. Thus, it became the defender of the *status quo* and left to war the dissolution of such strains.

It seems improbable that the membership of the League could be voluntarily restored without considerable amendment to the Covenant.

Even if nations were forced to join, they could obstruct and withdraw unless the whole Covenant were revised.

Two categories of amendments are proposed. The one would take the League fully into the field of military force, the other would take it wholly into the field of pacific settlements.

2. Restoration of the League with a Revision of the Covenant Giving It Absolute Military Power to Enforce Peace. One proposal for revision of the Covenant is to preserve most of its present structure but with revision so as to give the League complete power by making arbitration or judicial determination compulsory in all disputes; making refusal the sole criterion of aggression; making the economic and military sanctions follow automatically upon military action of such an aggressor; doing away with the veto power of each nation; making League decisions by majority or two-thirds vote; and giving the League an international army, navy, and air force to enforce its decisions.

It is asserted that this would "put 'iron teeth' in the League" and would make peace impregnable. This method would assume that "aggression" can be defined in these terms, but the experience which we have discussed indicates that it is not this simple.

And such an armed force would necessarily have to be larger than any combination of other armies, navies, or air forces, all of which implies that the disarmament of all nations must be very thorough, or, alternatively, that the League force be a very large one.

These ideas were discussed at length and rejected at Versailles. They, of course, mean a wholesale surrender of national sovereignty. The refusal of nations to join or abide by the much milder provisions of the present League would seem to indicate that it would not have many voluntary members. It would, in fact, be a blind acceptance of super sovereignty which nations in practice would probably refuse to accept, or, if they were compelled to accept, they would not abide for long.

A further criticism is that a majority of nations would not necessarily represent a majority of population. And that a combination of small nations, even if a two-thirds vote were required, might use the machinery for aggression on the larger ones. A further objection is that such an army, navy, or air force would have to be commanded by human beings of some nationality, and they would not be likely to attack their own people; and conversely, they might on nationalist or other grounds be influenced to attack others. When such proposals were raised at Paris in 1918, they were rejected, partly because no considerable adherence could be expected, and partly because it was recognized that a group of nations or the commander in chief of such an army could become dictators of the world.

3. Rastoration of the League of Nations with a Revised Covenant Constituting It as an Effective Council of Nations to Preserve Peace Solely by Pacific Settlements and for Building International Co-operation. Another proposal is made for amendment of the Covenant which takes account of the weaknesses of the present League idea and its structure and seeks to build up and strengthen it in the directions where it has proved to have been the most successful. The proposal amounts, in fact, to a transformation of the League into a continuously sitting Council of Nations—each nation to be permanently represented by the highest-caliber men of more than ambassadorial rank, with the purpose of the League confined to developing broad regional policies for peace; to bringing about settlement of controversies under existing treaties through negotiation, arbitration, and judicial settlement; and to promote revision of onerous treaties. The use of force would be divorced from its proceedings. The League is to be, it is suggested, a continuous round table of nations through direct representatives of chiefs of states and Ministers for Foreign Affairs.

This would also be a radical departure from the practice of the League, which was seldom to convene the nations until after a crisis had arisen.

Broadly, it is proposed to preserve the name and that the Covenant be revised:

1. To eliminate all clauses dealing with military and economic sanctions.
2. To eliminate all clauses presuming to commit nations to specific procedure in the settlement of disputes.
3. To substitute for these clauses the simple declaration that it shall be the duty of the League to promote pacific settlements.
4. To substitute for the Council and Assembly as at present constituted a body composed of ambassadors from all nations, resident at all

times at the seat of the League, with no binding votes except upon procedural questions.

5. To elect annually a President from its membership with an annually elected Executive Committee on procedure and organization.

6. The Executive Committee to appoint subcommittees from its membership upon a regional basis to formulate regional policies of peace. For Europe, for instance, it would be, in effect, a Concert of Europe constantly operating. Its President, upon such regional committee's failure to secure settlements, to have power to appoint a more general committee from members not parties to the dispute.

7. All committees simply to negotiate, conciliate, urge adoption of pacific methods, report on facts and recommend to the whole body, with no penalties or obligations.

In fact, the proposal seeks to get away from rigid organization to a constantly functioning clearinghouse and round table of international questions, where each nation is effectively and at all times present in the person of a leading personality acting in close collaboration with his own Foreign Office.

Fundamentally, this is a modernization of diplomacy. It would tend to hold the heads of states and their Foreign Ministers more directly in the picture of responsibility instead of in a stand-off attitude negotiating with a separate body, as the League was regarded. It is proposed that the League should preserve and encourage all the treaties of arbitration, all the machinery of the World Court and the Hague Tribunal —it being one of the purposes of the League to secure that controversies be referred to and solved by such agencies or special committees as the occasion might require.

The plan proposes that the admirable organization of the existing Secretariat be re-established with all of its excellent machinery of international co-operation under the direction of this reorganized League.

No machinery of enforcement is suggested. It would rest solely upon good faith, world opinion, and the value of immediate discussion directly between nations rather than through the intervention of an outside body.

Carrying no commitments or delegations of sovereignty, it is contended not a single voice in any country could object to full membership.

It is held that such a Council, out of experience and successful precedent, could be expected to build up the fabric of international law and steadily guide the movement of nations toward abolition of war.

One objection to this plan is that some organization of force methods to preserve peace will be necessary for some years to come, but the contentions of its advocates are that experience has demonstrated that the two functions of force and pacific settlement are incompatible and mutually destructive when exercised by the same organizations, and that ultimate hope must be in the growth of pacific methods. The proposers hold that force measures to preserve international order should be separately erected elsewhere, somewhat as described next.

4. Proposals for a Separate Military Organization by the Allied Nations to Preserve Order. The history of 140 years amply indicates that among the multitude of nations in Europe and Asia there must be some kind of military restraints if there is to be peace. The long catalogue of a hundred military alliances and interventions of the balance of power intended to prevent war is in itself ample proof of this.

After the Napoleonic wars the Quadruple Alliance performed this function during the readjustment period. After the first World War the military power of Britain, France, and Italy served after a fashion until their joint relationships began to disintegrate and the League failed with "collective security." The job was bigger in 1919 than in 1815 partly because of the multiplication of independent states.

The organization of economic, military, or other force action to preserve peace is, however, the most difficult problem that civilization has to confront. The world is today not only divided by its nationalisms, but it is also divided by militant ideological groups whose emotions and devotions to their ideas are not going to evaporate with peace.

One lesson the world should have learned by this time. That is that economic sanctions mean war when they are applied to a strong nation and therefore can be abandoned as a method of force more likely to make for war than peace.

The foundation of any police measures must first be laid in general disarmament. Technically, for reasons given elsewhere, this is simpler than hitherto. The possibility after general disarmament of stopping aggressive action by a comparatively small air force as distinguished from large armies and navies offers more arguable approach to the problem than hitherto.

Most students agree that it is a reasonable deduction from all history that after the present war, with its even larger number of states which "self-determination" will create, and the increasing hates from total war, there must again be some strong military supervision if Europe and Asia are to keep the peace, at least until the malignant forces in those areas have had time to abate and the constructive forces to dominate.

The proposal of those advocating the transformation of the League into a Council is that the Allied Powers must, after the peace, take on the burden of policing the world for some period after the war, but should act only after the League, reorganized as above, had exerted its full energies to keep the peace.

In any event, if the realistic experience of former world wars is any criterion, even without definite organization, the victorious powers will, with military means, jointly dominate the world for so long as their interests do not clash. They will need to do so at least during a period for political and economic recuperation.

5. *Proposals of Separate Continental Organizations to Enforce Peace.* These proposals are that each great area—the Western Hemisphere, Europe, and Asia—should be organized for its own preservation of order, but co-operating in world pacific settlements through the League formed into a council of nations or other organization of the world for pacific settlements.

The proposers of these plans have in mind the separate problems and interests of the three great areas—Europe, Asia, and the Western Hemisphere. And they contend that not only are they thus separated, but that universal world organization for more than pacific settlements, such as the Council form of the League, are bound to break down.

The Western Hemisphere for a century, down to 1937, pursued a broad policy of separation from the conflicts of the other continents, with the exception of the one period of 1917 to 1920. And this policy was successfully maintained even in times when the Old World was wholly dominated by aggressive military dictators. The Spanish-American War, far from being an intervention in Europe, was another step in this hemispheric separation, which would have been completed with the independence of the Philippines. The Monroe Doctrine and the United States Navy served to maintain the separation by protection of the other states from Old World aggression. And the foreign policies of the other American republics were largely determined by their ability to count on us for protection against Old World aggression.

During the whole of the last century, the United States and the other nations of the Western Hemisphere co-operated, and at times gave the lead in co-operation with nations in the other continents in building up the body of international law and the settlement of conflicts by conference and other pacific means. At least as contrasted with Europe, a large degree of peace without fear has been maintained in the New World. This is well indicated by the fact that over this last century and a half in wars among the twenty-one nations of the Western Hemisphere, not more than 500,000 men have been killed, whereas in twenty-one nations of Europe alone, probably more than 15,000,000 have been killed. The broad arguments that are advanced to the Western Hemisphere for the readoption of separate organization for the future are:

1. That behind the two oceans the Western Hemisphere can, with moderate modern defense measures, be kept free from Old World encroachment.

2. That power politics and wars on the other continents are unending, and thus the Western Hemisphere would be eternally involved in the inevitable destruction resultant from these wars.

3. That it is neither within the knowledge or capacity of the people of the Western Hemisphere, so far removed from the actual problems of the other continents and so divergent in their ideals, to engage in foreign power politics.

4. That their form of government, with recurrent changes of administration, cannot have the continuity of foreign policies necessary.

5. That the American weight thrown into Old World balances serves to disturb rather than steady them.

6. That civilization in this hemisphere can make progress only if it is

unhampered by the setbacks of recurrent wars with their tolls of death and impoverishment.

7. That, while a policy of hemispheric separation involves non-interference in European and Asiatic politics and wars, this in no way precludes our co-operation with all countries in pacific means for maintenance of peace.

8. That unless we refrain from taking part in the wars of Europe and Asia, far from saving civilization, we shall only contribute to its destruction everywhere.

9. That the Western Hemisphere has no self-imposed mission, responsibility, or strength to compel peace on the other continents.

10. That the Western Hemisphere already has its foundations of organization in the Pan American Union and conferences.

11. And that by keeping the lamp of liberty burning brightly in this hemisphere, there is a beacon and a sanctuary to the whole world.

The arguments against such a policy are:

1. That communication, transportation, and trade interdependence of the two hemispheres have narrowed our great ocean barriers so that former physical separation is greatly reduced.

2. That the military airplane has reduced the defensive value of the two oceans.

3. That advanced bases necessary for our protection bring us into European problems.

4. That the growth of aggressive centers within Europe and Asia threatens the Western Hemisphere's independence.

5. That the Western Hemisphere cannot suffer the engulfment of liberty-loving nations of Europe and Asia without lasting harm to itself.

6. That the spread of liberty throughout the world is a prime concern to this hemisphere, both in self-defense and spiritually.

7. That this is a responsibility which we cannot avoid.

8. And further, that having now departed from our traditional policies by entering foreign power politics and joining in this war, we have created lasting hates and economic issues which require us, for some time after victory at least, to continue our involvement in Old World politics in order to protect ourselves.

The proposers of these plans of continental separation, except for co-operation in pacific means, believe that each continent should set up its own police force or, alternatively, that the Allies in this war should do the policing, each in their own hemisphere.

It is interesting to observe that through the history of both the United States and Great Britain there are recurrent waves of determination to be dissociated from wars between other nations. The movement toward involvement is always a reluctant process. And with the end of each war, with its deep wounds and huge losses, comes an inevitable reaction toward separation and aloofness.

For 300 years, Britain has lived cheek by jowl with these problems through her nearness to European conflicts. After participating in long and costly wars, she always reverts to a period—usually a long period —of deliberate separation. It sometimes goes further as a consciously adopted national policy eulogized as "splendid isolation." This was amply evident in the Peace Ballot of 1934–35, and the vote of the Oxford Union, pledging that its members would not fight in foreign wars. But sooner or later the cycle begins again, until the pressures for war become too strong to be resisted.

In our own case, the first real departure from our traditional policy in 1917 to 1920 also led to the inevitable reaction in the growth of a strong determination to keep out of foreign wars forever after. This reaction is inherent in the whole consequences of war and can no doubt be expected again.

6. *Extreme Isolation.* Isolation of the continental United States from all other nations has never been a policy of our Government. In strict logic, it means getting ourselves behind a Chinese Wall, trading and communicating gingerly over the top. It means no less than complete abandonment of the Monroe Doctrine.

The arguments in favor of such a policy are found in our fortunate geographic position, in our large measure of self-sufficiency, the lack of military dangers from our immediate neighbors—Canada and Mexico —and the ability to protect ourselves from serious invasion by any combination of nations from overseas.

The argument against this policy is the danger of overseas domination of Latin-America by European or Asiatic nations, and would require each Western Hemisphere nation to become an armed camp with all those dangers to liberty. Such a policy has never been tried and is more a descriptive term than a reality.

7. *Federation of Nations.* Another group of proposals for the maintenance of peace are those which advocate some form of federation between nations. There is a broad range of such plans.

The simplest envisages a Federal Union of the United States and the British Empire. Some expand to include all democracies. The most comprehensive of all urge world-wide federation, including all civilized states.

Most of the plans for federation have certain fundamentals in common, with variations in detail. They all provide for a supergovernment over the member nations to be conducted by representatives of the member states.

The proposals vary as to how the supergovernment should be composed and chosen. They rest usually upon extending the Bill of Rights and the general authorities of the American Constitution to the supergovernment. Some advocate that representation of the different nations should be based upon population, some on equal representation from each nation, some on a compromise by an upper house constituted like our Senate, and a house of representatives based on population. They vary in ideas as to where the seat of the supergovernment should be, but generally favor some neutral spot outside Europe and outside the United States.

It is usually proposed that citizens or subjects of any member state are to enjoy the privileges of citizenship within the boundaries of all other member states; that there is to be a common nationality. These plans usually provide for the maintenance of national governments subordinate to the supergovernment. But all questions of peace and war are to be vested in the supergovernment, which has full control of the armed forces of the member state and of its foreign relations. These plans also generally envisage the removal of all tariff and economic barriers, of the restrictions on immigration among the member states, and provide for a common currency and for other matters of common concern.

The more important plans limit the member states to the democratic nations or to those which may become democratic.

There are eight major arguments advanced in favor of federation:

1. That such a great military power would assure freedom from attack and could prevent the rest of the world from disturbing the peace.

2. That experience of the American Union shows that members of the supergovernment would stand to gain in the same way as did the states of the American Union through surrender of powers to the Federal Government.

3. That it would curb excessive economic nationalism and promote economic prosperity.

4. That non-democratic nations, impressed by the advantages of membership in the federation, would adopt democratic forms and methods and seek admittance—and thus increase the area of law-abiding nations.

5. That it satisfies the deep yearning to provide more sure survival of democracy and some escape of the world from its heartbreaking vicissitudes.

6. That if peace is to become the natural state of the world, we must outgrow the system of a community of separate states, each exercising full sovereignty, the right to make war, to create trade barriers and restrict immigration; that these and other rights must be surrendered to a central authority in return for greater security.

7. That a nation can no longer be final judge in its international controversies and that, as in the case of the individual, it must submit to the jurisdiction of recognized tribunals; that the use of force for self-defense is justifiable, but that the nation cannot be sole judge as to what constitutes self-defense.

8. That nations must recognize that the world has become an economic unit and forego the right to carry on a separate economic policy within each watertight compartment.

A host of objections are raised from an American viewpoint, which comprise the following major ideas:

1. That, next to religious faith, the deepest of spiritual emotions are love of country and patriotism; that these emotions are embedded

in struggles and sacrifices to maintain independence; that they embrace constructive ideals, unity of purpose, and symbols, all of which would be greatly injured or reduced in vitality by being melted into a foreign alloy; that their submergence in a new formation cannot be taken lightly.

2. That our nation has in 300 years grown apart from even the democratic ideals of other peoples. In some of them, class government still lingers; in others, democracy is little better than oligarchy.

3. That what relief we enjoy by the separation of two oceans from the age-old frictions and hates of Europe and Asia would be lost and their problems would be brought within our frontiers.

4. That several of the other democratic nations are burdened by the vast imperialistic problems of hundreds of millions of people of backward races, such as those of Africa, also of hundreds of millions of alien races, such as those of India and Malaya; and many of the democracies suggested for membership are themselves of different language and ideals and political development altogether.

5. That, being a minority in a supergovernment, the political, economic, and social control of our country would ultimately pass from our own hands, and all the assurances of our fundamental institutions would be lost.

6. That this more distant authority in conducting our foreign relations, in making war and peace, and in military service takes such control further from the people.

7. That we have a host of unsolved economic, governmental, and social problems, the solution of which would be determined or influenced by majorities from these other nations, and as we have the major natural resources they would sooner or later be divided among others with great lowering of our own standards of living.

8. That we are a strong-enough country, if we do not go to sleep, to defend the Western Hemisphere from invasion by any aggressor, and that if we want military support, it can be had by military alliance.

9. That the economic shocks of the arrangement would be too great to bear in time of national impoverishment which must follow war.

10. That the setting up of such a federation on the basis of democratic

ideology would, sooner or later, result in military counteralliances or in federations among nations of other ideologies, and thus reduce the world to groups of gigantic armed camps.

It is also advanced that American opinion alone does not suffice to bring about such a federation. It must be desired by others. Under some of these plans, it is proposed that the component parts of the British Commonwealth would have independent membership in the supergovernment. This would seem to require more thought, as it would mean no less than dissolution of the Empire by transference of their loyalties to the supergovernment just as would be the case if the forty-eight American states were given direct membership.

From the British side, Viscount Cecil, one of the most confirmed of internationalists, in a careful analysis[1] strongly opposes the whole federation idea as entirely unsuitable for the British Empire.

8. Pax Americana. The various proposals for some sort of military mentor for the world in the words of some of our spokesmen range into the idea "America must police the world for a hundred years" or "American democracy must rule the world"—a sort of Pax Americana.

The inevitable end of this latter idea, realized or unrealized by its advocates, is a sort of imperial America, establishing garrisons over the world and undertaking to direct the conduct of foreign nations. Those who think in this direction contend:

1. That it is the American destiny to rule the world with a new and more humane form of domination.
2. That traditional peacemaking and building up of the will to peace have proven a failure, and are outmoded.
3. That the world requires a wholly new order of peacemaking.
4. That America would do it all idealistically and for the good of the people concerned and of lasting peace.
5. That the British Empire and her stabilizing influence is passing and that some nation must dominate if the world is to have peace.
6. That America could, by directing development of the world, so increase its wealth as to repay our great costs of the war.

[1] *A Great Experiment,* Oxford University Press, 1941.

There are a number of objections raised by those opposed to these ideas:

1. That it is the same "master race" ideology that pervades Germany, Japan, and Italy.
2. That it violates our pledges of "self-government" and "self-determination."
3. That it would mean that the New Rome would be at perpetual war.
4. That nations, though disarmed and helpless before tanks and planes, still value their independence to the roots of their racial souls; they would find a thousand ways of resistance to what in their minds would be subjection and oppression.
5. That such a system applied to civilized races would ultimately bring about a combination of all the world against America—and there are 2,000,000,000 people against 130,000,000 Americans.
6. That history repeats and repeats that the role of Imperator over civilized nations (no matter under what name) inevitably devitalizes the governing people and revitalizes the subjected nations.
7. That our people would be divided over the idea of such tremendous responsibilities and would be divided about the conduct of every enterprise.
8. That if America remains a representative democracy, and with changing government every four years, the electorate would probably shed these responsibilities somewhere along the line even if the task were otherwise possible.
9. That no government of personal liberty and representative structure can survive in the United States if we undertake the imperial role.

In these plans, the two hundred years of peace held by military domination under the Pax Romana are sometimes recalled. There is, however, a certain difference in the two situations. The Romans were, for the most part, engaged in imposing peace and civilization upon barbaric peoples. To apply it to civilized peoples is a different job. And certainly, representative government withered in Rome under this regime.

XIV THE METHOD OF NEGOTIATING

LASTING PEACE[1]

FROM world experience it is not difficult to predict the situation that will exist in the liberated and enemy areas immediately after the United Nations armies are victorious.

Our pledges of "self-determination" and "restored sovereignty" will countenance and encourage the creation of even more independent nations than at the end of the last war. These twenty-five or more liberated peoples in Europe and Asia will at once set up their own governments. They will no doubt call their representative assemblies into session to deal with their emergencies. They will immediately create some military force to maintain order and to hold the boundaries which they think are justly theirs. They will appoint diplomatic agents to support their claims in the peace settlements. Their industries will be damaged or ruined. Their ports, railways, and canals will be demoralized. They will seize all the rolling stock and canal boats they can secure to assure transportation to their people. They will all be short of food or actually starving. There will be devastating unemployment. They will be without credit or raw materials. Their long and terrible suffering will express itself in hate and violence toward enemy countries.

In the enemy countries, with defeat leaders and government will be overthrown. Revolution will march and new men will come into ascendancy among whom there will be great ideological and political differences. These governments will have no credit; their industries will be paralyzed; unemployment will be general. The machinery for distributing and rationing what food they may still possess will break down, and, like the liberated nations, they also will be starving.

Therefore we cannot assume that the building of orderly government

[1] Some misunderstanding of the exact proposals in this chapter having arisen, the authors have revised it for clarification.

348

and the resumption of peace, industry, and production will proceed easily and smoothly in any of the war-ravaged areas. This time, as in the last, they will be retarded or undone by disorders, uprisings, wars, and passions.

45. From our examination of world experience in peacemaking, we believe it has been demonstrated that after world wars peace cannot be made adequately by such assemblies of scores of statesmen and diplomats as were convened at Vienna and Versailles.

The dynamic forces in many ways reach their most destructive point immediately after the cessation of hostilities. There are clamorous economic pressures for haste, that industry and trade may be resumed. There are the pull and haul of interests, the intrigues of nationalism and imperialism, the dangers arising from the white heat of fear, hate, and revenge, and the infinite complication of negotiation among a multitude of representatives of nations with divergent interests. All this tends to destroy and debilitate constructive effort and to drive toward improvised solutions, destructive compromise, and disregard of the fundamental forces in motion. Thus, the peacemakers are at the most disadvantageous moment to do their work.

General conferences of this character must consume time, and while debate and negotiation are in progress the whole world wallows in uncertainty, economic paralysis, political stagnation, and moral degeneration.

These past experiences show clearly the desirability of making peace under more favorable conditions, of giving time for destructive forces to abate and gaining time for reflection and negotiation in solving long-range problems.

46. We suggest that there should be a new and different approach to the whole machinery of peacemaking. We suggest that the peacemaking be divided into three stages:

(1) That instead of the usual military "armistice" with its deferment of peace, there should be substituted a "conditional" peace which would include not only the usual armistice provisions for ending combat but also the settlement of certain urgent problems which would reconstitute the forces of peace.

(2) An intermediate period—a breathing spell—for the rebuilding of political life and economic recovery.

(3) A further period for settlement of the long-view problems which require a cooling off of emotions. Without such a period we cannot hope for deliberation and careful development.

Such a "quick" and "conditional" peace as we suggest would take no more time to impose than the usual military armistice. In fact, it could be imposed by the military authorities on the battlefield, if the United Nations were agreed and prepared in advance. It would result in much quicker restoration of political institutions, public order, and economic life, all of which, as we have said, are weakened by the usual unsettling armistice followed by long and difficult negotiations.

47. Therefore, regardless of the character of the settlements to be made, we are convinced that there is one essential preliminary to any peacemaking; that is, before the end of hostilities there should be clear and unequivocal agreement between the victorious powers not only as to peace aims but also as to the methods to govern the peacemaking.

Such a "conditional" peace should include:

1. The instant surrender of arms and demobilization of all enemy military forces.
2. Repatriation of military prisoners and civil populations who have been driven from their homes.
3. The removal of all blockade measures against neutrals and liberated nations—and the removal of blockade against enemy areas the instant they have surrendered their arms and demobilized their forces.
4. Temporary restoration of pre-war commercial treaties pending general economic solution.
5. The designation of provisional boundaries of all states, liberated and enemy.
6. The immediate call of freely chosen elective constitutional assemblies or parliamentary bodies.
7. Immediate reduction of the armaments of the United Nations themselves to the minimum forces needed to maintain international order and to enforce ultimate peace provisions.

8. Acceptance by all liberated and enemy states of such future determinations as may affect these conditional arrangements.
9. Agreement by the liberated and enemy states to accept the machinery for the preservation of peace when it is settled.

Instead of a general peace conference of all these scores of nations the United Nations should create a number of separate international commissions to deal with such revisions of conditional arrangements as may be found necessary and with long-view problems such as the following:

1. The building of international machinery to preserve peace.
2. The definitive boundaries of liberated and enemy states.
3. The formulation of measures for the protection of racial minorities and provision for the transfer and resettlement of the populations in the irredentas where such solution is imposed by conditions.
4. The settlement of private property questions, damages from war, the return of plunder, compensations in machinery, plant, animals, etc., that have been ravished, including materials with which to rebuild destroyed areas.
5. Study of the various intricate problems of Africa with a view to agreement upon an enlightened course for the protection and development of the native population; the use of sparsely settled regions to relieve the pressures of European populations and the development of natural resources for the benefit of the world as a whole.
6. The settlement of intergovernmental debts.
7. The settlement of long-view economic questions of international trade which affect lasting peace.

These conclusions can be far better arrived at after political and economic life has had a chance to recuperate and destructive emotions have been given time to cool off. Thus such assemblies as Versailles, with all its surroundings of false pomp, emotion, propaganda, high-pressure groups, and log-rolling governments can be avoided.

With victory and even a minimum of armed force in the hands of the victors alone, there need be no doubt of their ability to secure adherence to these conclusions.

48. We believe that during the interregnum period required for the growth of political order, economic recovery, the solution of these long-view problems, and the setting up of machinery to preserve peace, the victorious powers must:

(a) Assure order in the world by military force.

(b) Instantly provide credits for food and its transportation in order to stay famine and pestilence. Otherwise there will be stunted minds and bodies, decimating death and anarchy upon which no lasting peace can be builded.

(c) Provide at once credits and raw materials in aid to the restoration of industry and employment and to enable the prostrate peoples to pay for their food supplies.

The cost of these last two provisions will be much less with a quick conditional peace than with a demoralizing armistice, for they would allow the national credit to revive and production and exports to begin, and would lessen the demands upon the generosity of the few remaining strong nations.

49. The purpose of this war, the most terrible of three centuries, is to make a lasting peace. We must first win the war. But we will not win lasting peace unless we prepare for it. And we can prepare only by full and free public discussion and the cold surgery of analysis.

The historian can discuss the growth of the impelling forces, good and bad, which preceded the first two great convulsions in Western civilization when world-wide wars ended for a while in the peace treaties of 1648 and 1815. He can evaluate the relative weights of the forces which moved in those times, but we are still in the midst of this third explosion. It may be that the era of growing human freedom and economic materialism which began four hundred years ago with the Renaissance and has continued down to the present explosion is now in a crisis of change which will bring other concepts of civilization.

50. We have pointed out that if we scan these former convulsions of the modern Western world we can see that, following these long periods of general war and disorder, new shapes of civilization and new forms of nations have emerged. Civilization has taken new impulses and new directions. We must expect new forms and new directions from the gigantic explosion that began in 1914. No one can pretend to see these shapes clearly.

We know, however, that whatever forms evolve, the seven dynamic forces will have a part in their shaping. And even if we are emerging into another era of civilization, then also we shall need peace. And this time the foundations of peace must be so laid that destructive forces are allayed, or again the structures that we erect to preserve peace will fail.

In the making of that peace will come a fleeting chance for leaders of mankind to bind the wounds, to restore faith, and to bring new hope to the world.

In the words of Washington to the Federal Convention:

Let us raise a standard to which the wise and the honest can repair— the event is in the hand of God.

APPENDIX

FOR convenience in reference, the authors have sought to tabulate the major and minor successes and failures of the League of Nations. The events of twenty years of League activity do not always lend themselves to hard and fast classification.

In the field of prevention of war, for instance, some sixty disputes were brought before the League. Some were delegated to the League for settlement by the peace treaties, some were submitted by member states, and some were passed along by the Council of Ambassadors. They differed widely in character and importance and in many of them it is difficult to determine the exact extent and effect of League action.

In some cases, it is true, war was stopped after fighting had begun (Yugoslavia and Albania, 1921; Greece and Bulgaria, 1925; Turkey and Iraq, 1924–26; Colombia and Peru, 1932). In some cases we find both success and failure. This is clear in the case of Vilna, where the League succeeded in stopping hostilities, but over a long period failed to end the quarrel and re-establish relations between Lithuania and Poland. In still other cases, disputes languished and died with no public evidence of effective League action; but there was sometimes a feeling that abstention from action had served a useful purpose and permitted controversy to die down without loss of face for either side. This will suffice to show the difficulties of hard and fast classification.

In addition to the settlement of wars and the preservation of peace, the League had large areas of success and failure in the field of non-political activity—a wide range embracing such different subjects as disarmament, financial reconstruction, the movement and protection of refugees, and health and social questions. These are perhaps even more difficult to classify. The following lists are therefore limited to League efforts to prevent wars and preserve peace and are offered as no more than an approximate outline of League activities in that field. Each reader remains free to make his own classifications and evaluations.

1. Major Successes

Mosul dispute, 1924–26. An admirable example of League activity. Dispute between Turkey (not a member of the League) and Great Britain (representing Iraq). The Council succeeded in stopping the fighting and securing the withdrawal of Turkish troops, which had crossed the frontier. Provisional frontier was drawn. Commission of Inquiry sent. Permanent Court consulted. After informal negotiation with both parties, the League solution was embodied in Treaty of Ankara, 1926.

2. Major Failures

Italian-Greek dispute—Occupation of Corfu, 1923. Italians murdered while fixing frontier line between Greece and Albania on behalf of Council of Ambassadors. Italy sent ultimatum and bombarded and occupied Corfu. Greece appealed to League. Italy rejected Council's proposal of arbitration, but accepted mediation by Council of Ambassadors. For fear of disrupting the League, the Council dealt gingerly with Italy and limited its show of authority to Greece, which was made to take the blame and pay damages.

China-Japan, 1931–33. Friction between the Chinese authorities in Manchuria and a Japanese garrison guarding the railway ended in Japanese attack and the seizure of several towns (1931). China appealed to the League. While the League was endeavoring to find a solution, Japan occupied the whole of Manchuria and set up the puppet government of Manchukuo, invaded Shanghai, and occupied various other points. Japan refused all offers of pacific solution and, on being designated and condemned as the aggressor by a resolution of the Assembly, withdrew from the League.

Italy-Ethiopia, 1935–36. A frontier incident at Walwal in late 1934 led to Italian demands of reparation. Ethiopia appealed to the League. Italy acquiesced in negotiation while preparing for war, counting on differences among the great Powers. Italy opened hostilities and, despite the application of sanctions, persisted until victory.

3. Minor Successes

Åland Island settlement, 1920–21. Conflicting claims of Finland and Sweden, settled by acceptance of solution proposed by League commissions.

Polish-Lithuanian dispute, 1920. League succeeded in preventing spread of armed conflict when Vilna was seized by the Poles in 1920.

Albanian-Yugoslav War, 1921–24. Under Council threat of economic blockade, fighting was stopped. The League followed up this action with various reconstruction activities, health organization, and famine relief.

Jaworzno, 1923–24. Frontier dispute between Poland and Czechoslovakia. Council, with advice of Permanent Court of International Justice, produced solution accepted by both sides.

Salgótarjan frontier dispute between Hungary and Czechoslovakia, 1923.

Burgenland frontier dispute between Hungary and Austria, 1923.

4. Minor Failures

Polish-Lithuanian dispute, 1920. Although the League was successful in preventing the spread of war, it failed in its efforts to reconcile the two nations and bring the quarrel to an end.

Eastern Karelia, 1921–22. Dispute between Finland and Soviet Russia over terms of Dorpat Treaty. League failure inevitable as Soviet Government refused to co-operate in seeking advice of Permanent Court.

Mur territory boundary dispute between Yugoslavia and Hungary, 1923.

Chaco dispute, between Paraguay and Bolivia, 1928, 1936. League efforts at conciliation and embargo of arms proved unsuccessful, and Paraguay finally withdrew from the League. Later settled by Conference of American States at Buenos Aires (1936).

5. Peacemaking Actions Outside the League Involving Several European Powers

April 1920. The San Remo Conference of Allied Powers dealt with various questions, one of which was a request of Germany for revision of part of the treaty, which was refused. Decided to leave settlement of the Fiume question to Italy and Yugoslavia.

June 1920. Hythe and Boulogne Conference of Allied Powers on Near Eastern questions.

November 1920. Treaty between Italy and Yugoslavia altering the Versailles Treaty setup of Dalmatian Islands.

May 1922. Genoa Conference of Allied Powers over Russia failed of agreement by French opposition.

November 1922. Washington Arms and Far Eastern Conference of nine Powers.

July 1923. Second Lausanne Peace Conference. Principal Powers made peace between Turkey and Greece.

November 1923. Lausanne Peace Conference between Greece and Turkey which proved abortive.

October 1925. Locarno Conferences of Britain, France, Germany, and Italy settled various questions.

June 1927. Naval Conference of United States, Great Britain, and Japan at Geneva.

August 1928. The Kellogg-Briand Pact signed.

February 1929. Agreement signed at Moscow by Russia, Poland, Rumania, Estonia, and Latvia, renouncing war.

January 1930. London Naval Conference: United States, Great Britain, France, Italy, and Japan.

July 1931. European nations agree to President Hoover's moratorium proposal on all intergovernmental debts.

August 1931. Principal Powers agree to President Hoover's proposal of a standstill agreement on all German private international obligations.

October 1932. Four Power Pact between England, France, Germany, and Italy.

July 1933. World Economic Conference was assembled at London upon the original proposal of President Hoover to deal with currency stabilization and trade barriers, but blocked by President Roosevelt's repudiation of it in a message to the Conference.

January 1937. British-Italian agreement on interests in the Mediterranean and Spanish affairs.

April 1937. Britain's recognition of Italy's sovereignty over Ethiopia.

September 1938. An agreement signed between Germany, France, Britain, and Italy at Munich, assenting to German occupation of Sudetenland.

6. *Military Alliances or Non-Aggression Pacts or Mutual Guarantees of Frontiers Made outside the League*

June 1919. Defense treaties between Britain, France, and the United States. (The United States did not ratify.)

August 1920. Military alliance between Czechoslovakia and Yugoslavia, subsequently including Rumania—The "Little Entente." Promoted by France.

February 1921. Military alliance between Poland and France.

March 1921. Offensive and defensive treaty between Poland and Rumania.

March 1922. Military alliance between Poland and the Baltic states.

April 1922. An alliance between Germany and Russia, agreed at Rapallo.

January 1924. French-Czechoslovakia military alliance.

October 1925. Renewed military alliances between France and Czechoslovakia, and France and Poland.

December 1925. Turkish Alliance with Russia.

April 1926. Treaty of "mutual security" between Iran, Turkey, Afghanistan.

November 1927. Treaty of friendship between Yugoslavia and France.

July 1933. A non-aggression pact between Rumania and Russia.

January 1934. German-Polish agreement of non-aggression (which marked practical abandonment of previous alliance with France).

February 1934. The Balkan pact, mutually guaranteeing frontiers between Turkey, Greece, Rumania, and Yugoslavia. It was, in fact, a limited military alliance.

March 1934. The Rome Protocols, organizing a Fascist Bloc of Italy, Austria, and Hungary, as opposed to the "Little Entente."

June 1934. Agreement by Rumania, Poland, and Russia, guaranteeing mutual frontiers.

September 1934. Military alliance for defense among Baltic states.

January 1935. Franco-Italian agreement settling African interests and co-operation in case of action by Germany.

April 1935. Stresa Conference of Britain, France, and Italy, establishing common front in view of German action in denouncing the disarmament clauses in the Treaty of Versailles the previous month.

May 1935. A military alliance between France and Russia.

May 1935. A treaty of mutual military assistance between Russia and Czechoslovakia.

June 1935. Britain signed a separate naval agreement with Germany, relaxing the Versailles provisions. France protested vigorously.

October 1936. Belgium denounced military alliance with France made during the war, and the German government guaranteed inviolability of Belgium.

October 1936. German-Italian military alliance—"The Axis."

November 1936. German, Japanese, Italian Anti-Comintern Pact. Japan practically joined the Axis.

March 1937. Treaty of non-aggression and mutual guarantees by Yugoslavia and Italy.

July 1937. Non-aggression Pact between Turkey, Iraq, Iran, and Afghanistan.

September 1937. Nyon Conference of nine Powers, establishing patrol zones around Spain.

November 1937. Poland and Russia renewed their non-aggression pact.

December 1937. Germany and France entered into mutual guarantees of their frontiers.

March 1939. Britain, France, and Poland entered into military alliance and agreement for mutual assistance.

April 1939. Spain joined Axis and signed the Anti-Comintern Pact.

April 1939. The Franco-British pledge extended to Rumania and Greece.

May 1939. Denmark, Estonia, and Latvia signed non-aggression pact with Germany.

May 1939. British-French-Turkish mutual assistance pact.

August 1939. Germany and Russia signed a non-aggression pact.

7. *Violent Actions During the Life of the League*

On the following acts of violence the League took no action.

April 1920. War between Poland and Russia.

June 1920. The Greeks made war on Turkey.

October 1920. Vilna seized in *coup d'état* by General Zeligowski.

March 1921. The French army occupied German cities.

October 1921. The Turks made war on the Armenian Republic and annexed it.

March 1922. A *coup d'état* overthrew the independent government of Fiume and annexed it to Italy. Armed rising in Upper Silesia under Polish Commissioner Korfanty to seize territory in spite of plebiscite.

January 1923. French and Belgians invaded the Ruhr. The British refused to take part.

January 1933. Italy shipped arms to Hungary despite disarmament treaties.

March 1935. Germany denounced the disarmament clauses of the Versailles Treaty.

March 1936. Germany reoccupied the Rhineland in violation of the treaties of Versailles and Locarno.

July 1936. In Spain, Germany and Italy give military aid to Franco. France and Russia to the Republican Government. France arranged a treaty of non-intervention which was freely violated.

March 1938. Germany annexed Austria.

October 1938. Poland seized certain provinces from Czechoslovakia.

January-March 1939. Hungary invaded and annexed Carpatho-Ukraine.

March 1939. Poland attacked Lithuania.

March 1939. Germany annexed Czechoslovakia.

March 1939. Hitler annexed Memel.

April 1939. Italy invaded and annexed Albania.

September 1939. Germany attacked Poland.

September 1939. Britain and France declared war on Germany.

The Price of

Free World Victory

BY HENRY A. WALLACE

from the new book
"The Century of the Common Man"

I OUR SECOND CHANCE

Wᴇ of the United States can no more evade shouldering our responsibility than a boy of eighteen can avoid becoming a man by wearing short pants. The word "isolation" means short pants for a grown-up United States.

Today we are not greatly concerned with the past except insofar as it furnishes a lamp to guide our footsteps in the future. The United States now has her second opportunity to make the world safe for democracy. During the first World War and the fifteen years which followed, our intentions were of the highest, but our judgment was not good. From the depths of our hearts we responded to the idealism of Woodrow Wilson. Our boys enlisted to save the democracy of Western Europe and the New World from encroachment by the imperialism of a militaristic Prussia. They thought they knew what they were fighting for. That is why they fought so well.

In that war, our nation fought well, believed profoundly and produced tremendously. Aside from that, our record was not so good. When the peace came, we refused to accept responsibility for the world we had helped to create. We turned our back on Europe. We said we were isolationists. During the war prices, taxes and wages had doubled. When the war ended, consumers wanted lower prices, employers wanted lower wages, and everybody wanted lower taxes. There was talk about getting back to normalcy. The desire for normalcy and for isolation caused our people to refuse to accept the world responsibility which had been brought to them.

Those who preached isolation and normalcy were skilled in their political insight. They appealed successfully to the blind prejudices of the people who were disillusioned when the war excitement stopped, when taxes went higher and prices fell and unemployment increased.

The people were hungry for isolation, high tariffs and normalcy—the very things which would make our problem worse.

Looking backward, we can afford to be charitable toward the isolationists and high-tariff men of the 1920's, but we can not feel so kindly toward those mistaken men as to encourage others in the future to repeat their mistakes.

The democracies, if they are to survive, must work out some way which, while holding fast to human rights, will at the same time permeate the individual souls with a feeling of responsibility so that the citizens of a democracy will be as willing to give wholehearted, unselfish service as the citizens of a totalitarian power. This we can do if in addition to holding firmly to our Bill of Rights, we formulate a Bill of Duties. Under the Bill of Rights and Duties, we can have a flexible structure into which each citizen may make his productive contribution to the general welfare. Youth now has a more intense desire to serve. Our governmental and business leaders must make it their first business of the peace to give our youth the opportunities to work and serve under the Bill of Duties, so that they may enjoy the privileges of the Bill of Rights.

Properly equipped with a Bill of Duties, the United States can shoulder her responsibility to the world in the peace that is ahead. Without such a Bill of Duties, I fear peace will mean world chaos. With such a Bill we can help build a Pax Democratica which will bless us and the whole world for a century to come.   (*April 8, 1941.*)

11 WHAT WE HAVE LEARNED

W E are now aware, after our experience of the last twenty-five
years, that the most careful delineation of national boundaries
is not in itself enough to prevent the world from suffering a repetition
of the catastrophe of general war. Nor can this be prevented simply by
the establishment of an international league. We know now that the
modern world must be recognized for what it is—an economic unit—
and that wise arrangements must be made so that trade will be encouraged. The foundations of democracy can be rendered safe only when
people everywhere have an opportunity to work and buy and sell
with a reasonable assurance that they will be able to enjoy the fruits of
their work.

Actually, the seeds of the present world upheaval were sown in the
faulty economic decisions that followed the war of a generation ago.
The vast sums of reparations imposed on Germany, however justified
they may have been on moral grounds, were an indigestible lump in
Europe's financial stomach. The war debts owed to the United States
by the Allies were equally a handicap to trade. All over the world the
old international gold standard had broken down, and nothing effective
was done to replace or restore it. Europe was left cut up into many small
national units, and each of these units was left free to erect tariff and
trade barriers as it pleased. Many nations, including our own, tried to
buy as little as possible from the rest of the world and to sell as much
as possible. European countries that normally bought wheat and meat
from overseas shifted their production policies with a view to becoming
self-sufficient in food. This not only lowered their own standard of living, but upset the economies of the exporting countries. The United
States, newly become a creditor nation, adopted tariff policies which

only a debtor nation could hope to live with, and in so doing helped make it certain that the world would go through hell.

In very truth this nation sowed the wind by its policies of isolation, high tariffs, unwise foreign loans, and high-pressure sales abroad. It could not avoid reaping the whirlwind. Hindsight is always easier than foresight, and millions of Americans now look back upon those earlier policies as tragically mistaken. It would be a prolongation of the present world agony if, after this war is over, any of us again put blinders on our hindsight.

Spokesmen for the isolationist point of view did not support President Roosevelt in his stand for a peace built around freedom of speech, freedom of worship, freedom from want, and freedom from fear. They were quick to condemn the President for having joined with Winston Churchill in subscribing to the Atlantic Charter. They saw dangerous foreign entanglements in such simple words of the President as these: "The cooperation which we seek is the cooperation of free countries, working together in a friendly civilized society."

We may wonder whether the long and bitter fight put up by the isolationists in the decade of the twenties to keep the United States from behaving as if it were part of the world is to be renewed when the time comes for building a new peace. What they do will have an important bearing on political alignments in the United States. The injection of such an issue into politics would ordinarily be nothing of which to complain, for surely the people have a right to choose the policies they want the nation to pursue. But the really serious aspect of the matter is that the whole future not only of this country but of human civilization itself may depend on the ability and willingness of the American people to take the broad view.

For my part, I believe that the American people have profited from their experiences of the last twenty-five years. I believe that they will perceive, with increasingly clear vision, the place of leadership in the world which the United States can scarcely avoid occupying; and that they will support policies and arrangements for sensible cooperation with other countries.

Now, what must be considered in establishing such "sound relationships" in peacetime? There are certain basic facts which can not be ignored. One of these is the universal necessity of access to raw materials and the need for an economic arrangement to protect the raw material producers of the world from such violent fluctuation in income as took place after the first World War. Another is the indispensability of markets for goods produced. A third is the present existence in all countries of tariffs and other barriers to imports. A fourth is the use of gold as a base for national currencies and as a means of settling international trade balances. A fifth is the place of credit in stimulating international trade. A sixth is the close relationship between stable national currencies and the exchange of goods and services. A seventh, and most important of all, is the essential role of adequate purchasing power within the various countries that are trading with each other— for full employment within nations makes broad trade possible with other nations. All these facts and factors are of prime importance in determining the state of the world's health, and they will naturally form some of the main ingredients of postwar economic planning, if it is to be done on a comprehensive scale.

As part of the effort to win the peace, I am hoping that what might be called the "ever normal granary principle" can be established for a number of commodities on a worldwide scale.

Thus far, there have been no definite arrangements between the United States and the British Empire or between the United States and Latin America with regard to handling the raw material problems of the world in such a way as to make for a just peace. A beginning was made along this line with the international wheat agreement meeting held in London in 1933. The world ought to move in the direction of an ever normal granary in wheat and similar arrangements for other raw materials, with export quotas and with prices stabilized at a point to be fair to producers and consumers.

The democratic countries are in splendid position to organize themselves for rapid relief work as soon as peace comes. I am confident that we can do this job and do it well. But we must be looking ahead to the longer future and laying plans on more than just a temporary basis.

In that part of the world where democracy and capitalism prevail, the permanent answer lies in finding ways to make our system of production and exchange work more effectively and more consistently. That can be done by removing trade barriers and enlarging markets; by stimulating and guiding investments where they can be productive;

by reducing—through appropriate fiscal policy and social security program—the inequalities in incomes, so that a higher and more stable demand for consumers' goods will be attained; by applying advanced techniques and skills to the development of undeveloped areas; by re-equipping our own industrial and transportation system; and by providing to those people in greatest need better housing, schooling, and recreation.

Most people do not want charity. They want paying jobs. They will be able to have paying jobs, with few interruptions, if prices, production, and purchasing power can be held in balance with one another, and the economic machine can be kept running steadily and smoothly. This is the challenge to the leaders of industry, agriculture, labor and government. It is a challenge to the highest statesmanship of our own and other nations. Of course, there are difficulties and obstacles. Only by recognizing and studying obstacles can they be surmounted. A "new order" is truly waiting to be created—not the "new order" which the Nazis talk about and which would cloak the new form of slavery they would impose, but a new order of democracy where security, stability, efficiency, and widely distributed abundance would prevail.

Many persons in the United States are deeply disturbed over the heavy government borrowing and the drastic shifts in our economy made necessary by the defense program. They fear an end of the war almost as much as the war itself, because they believe the return of peace would bring another bad depression. But one of the hopeful signs for the future is the very fact that the possibility of depression is so widely recognized. This increases the chance that action will be taken in time to prevent it or at least cushion the shock. The basis for such action can best be laid now, while the war is still in progress. It must be laid, at least in part, in the plans for expanding and regularizing world trade, world production, world consumption. This is the new frontier, which Americans in the middle of the twentieth century find beckoning them on. (*From "Foundations of the Peace," copyright The Atlantic Monthly, January, 1942. By permission.*)

III THE CENTURY OF THE COMMON MAN

THIS is a fight between a slave world and a free world. Just as the United States in 1862 could not remain half slave and half free, so in 1942 the world must make its decision for a complete victory one way or the other.

As we begin the final stages of this fight to the death between the free world and the slave world, it is worth while to refresh our minds about the march of freedom for the common man. The idea of freedom—the freedom that we in the United States know and love so well—is derived from the Bible with its extraordinary emphasis on the dignity of the individual. Democracy is the only true political expression of Christianity.

The prophets of the Old Testament were the first to preach social justice. But that which was sensed by the prophets many centuries before Christ was not given complete and powerful political expression until our nation was formed as a Federal Union a century and a half ago. Even then, the march of the common people had just begun. Most of them did not yet know how to read and write. There were no public schools to which all children could go. Men and women can not be really free until they have plenty to eat, and time and ability to read and think and talk things over. Down the years, the people of the United States have moved steadily forward in the practice of democracy. Through universal education, they now can read and write and form opinions of their own. They have learned, and are still learning, the art of production—that is, how to make a living. They have learned, and are still learning, the art of self-government.

If we were to measure freedom by standards of nutrition, education and self-government, we might rank the United States and certain nations of Western Europe very high. But this would not be fair to other nations where education has become widespread only in the last twenty years. In many nations, a generation ago, nine out of ten of the people could not read or write. Russia, for example, was changed from an illiterate to a literate nation within one generation and, in the process, Russia's appreciation of freedom was enormously enhanced. In China, the increase during the past thirty years in the ability of the people to read and write has been matched by their increased interest in real liberty.

Everywhere, reading and writing are accompanied by industrial progress, and industrial progress sooner or later inevitably brings a strong labor movement. From a long-time and fundamental point of view, there are no backward peoples which are lacking in mechanical sense. Russians, Chinese, and the Indians both of India and the Americas all learn to read and write and operate machines just as well as your children and my children. Everywhere the common people are on the march. Thousands of them are learning to read and write, learning to think together, learning to use tools. These people are learning to think and work together in labor movements, some of which may be extreme or impractical at first, but which eventually will settle down to serve effectively the interests of the common man.

When the freedom-loving people march; when the farmers have an opportunity to buy land at reasonable prices and to sell the produce of their land through their own organizations, when workers have the opportunity to form unions and bargain through them collectively, and when the children of all the people have an opportunity to attend schools which teach them truths of the real world in which they live—when these opportunities are open to everyone, then the world moves straight ahead.

But in countries where the ability to read and write has been recently acquired or where the people have had no long experience in governing themselves on the basis of their own thinking, it is easy for demagogues to arise and prostitute the mind of the common man to their own base ends. Such a demagogue may get financial help from some person of wealth who is unaware of what the end result will be. With this backing, the demagogue may dominate the minds of the people, and, from whatever degree of freedom they have, lead them backward into slavery. Herr Thyssen, the wealthy German steel man, little realized what he was doing when he gave Hitler enough money to enable him to play on the minds of the German people. The demagogue is the curse of the modern world, and of all the demagogues, the worst are those financed by well-meaning wealthy men who sincerely believe that their wealth is likely to be safer if they can hire men with political "it" to change the sign posts and lure the people back into slavery of the most degraded kind. Unfortunately for the wealthy men who finance movements of this sort, as well as for the people themselves, the successful demagogue is a powerful genie who, when once let out of his bottle, refuses to obey anyone's command. As long as his spell holds, he defies God Himself, and Satan is turned loose upon the world.

Through the leaders of the Nazi revolution, Satan now is trying to lead the common man of the whole world back into slavery and darkness. For the stark truth is that the violence preached by the Nazis is the devil's own religion of darkness. So also is the doctrine that one race or one class is by heredity superior and that all other races or classes are supposed to be slaves. The belief in one Satan-inspired Fuehrer, with his Quislings, his Lavals, and his Mussolinis—his "gauleiters" in every nation in the world—is the last and ultimate darkness. Is there any hell hotter than that of being a Quisling, unless it is that of being a Laval or a Mussolini?

In a twisted sense, there is something almost great in the figure of the Supreme Devil operating through a human form, in a Hitler who has the daring to spit straight into the eye of God and man. But the Nazi system has a heroic position for only one leader. By definition only one person is allowed to retain full sovereignty over his own soul. All the rest are stooges—they are stooges who have been mentally and politically degraded, and who feel that they can get square with the world only by mentally and politically degrading other people. These stooges are really psychopathic cases. Satan has turned loose upon us the insane.

The march of freedom of the past one hundred and fifty years has been a long-drawn-out people's revolution. In this Great Revolution of the people, there were the American Revolution of 1775, the French Revolution of 1792, the Latin-American revolutions of the Bolivarian era, the German Revolution of 1848, and the Russian Revolution of 1917. Each spoke for the common man in terms of blood on the battlefield. Some went to excess. But the significant thing is that the people groped their way to the light. More of them learned to think and work together.

The people's revolution aims at peace and not at violence, but if the rights of the common man are attacked, it unleashes the ferocity of a she-bear who has lost a cub. When the Nazi psychologists tell their master Hitler that we in the United States may be able to produce hundreds of thousands of planes, but that we have no will to fight, they are only fooling themselves and him. The truth is that when the rights of the American people are transgressed, as those rights have been transgressed, the American people will fight with a relentless fury which will drive the ancient Teutonic gods back cowering into their caves. The Götterdämmerung has come for Odin and his crew.

The people are on the march toward even fuller freedom than the most fortunate peoples of the earth have hitherto enjoyed. No Nazi counter-revolution will stop it. The common man will smoke the Hitler stooges out into the open in the United States, in Latin America, and in India. He will destroy their influence. No Lavals, no Mussolinis will be tolerated in a Free World.

The people, in their millennial and revolutionary march toward manifesting here on earth the dignity that is in every human soul, hold as their credo the Four Freedoms enunciated by President Roosevelt in his message to Congress on January 6, 1941. These four freedoms are the very core of the revolution for which the United Nations have taken their stand. We who live in the United States may think there is nothing very revolutionary about freedom of religion, freedom of expression, and freedom from the fear of secret police. But when we begin to think about the significance of freedom from want for the average man, then we know that the revolution of the past one hundred and fifty years has not been completed, either here in the United States or in any other nation in the world. We know that this revolution can not stop until freedom from want has actually been attained.

And now, as we move forward toward realizing the Four Freedoms of this people's revolution, I would like to speak about four duties. It is my belief that every freedom, every right, every privilege has its price, its corresponding duty without which it can not be enjoyed. The four duties of the people's revolution, as I see them today, are these:

1. The duty to produce the limit.
2. The duty to transport as rapidly as possible to the field of battle.
3. The duty to fight with all that is in us.
4. The duty to build a peace—just, charitable and enduring.

The fourth duty is that which inspires the other three.

We failed in our job after World War Number One. We did not know how to go about it to build an enduring world-wide peace. We did not have the nerve to follow through and prevent Germany from rearming. We did not insist that she "learn war no more." We did not build a peace treaty on the fundamental doctrine of the people's revolution. We did not strive whole-heartedly to create a world where there could be freedom from want for all the peoples. But by our very errors we learned much, and after this war we shall be in position to utilize our knowledge in building a world which is economically, politically and, I hope, spiritually sound.

Modern science, which is a by-product and an essential part of the people's revolution, has made it technologically possible to see that all of the people of the world get enough to eat. Half in fun and half seriously, I said the other day to Madame Litvinov: "The object of this war is to make sure that everybody in the world has the privilege of drinking a quart of milk a day." She replied: "Yes, even half a pint." The peace must mean a better standard of living for the common man, not merely in the United States and England, but also in India, Russia, China and Latin America—not merely in the United Nations, but also in Germany and Italy and Japan.

Some have spoken of the "American Century." I say that the century on which we are entering—the century which will come out of this war—can be and must be the century of the common man. Perhaps it will be America's opportunity to suggest the Freedoms and duties by which the common man must live. Everywhere the common man must learn to build his own industries with his own hands in a practical fashion. Everywhere the common man must learn to increase his productivity so that he and his children can eventually pay to the world community all that they have received. No nation will have the God-given right to exploit other nations. Older nations will have the privilege to help younger nations get started on the path to industrialization, but there must be neither military nor economic imperialism. The methods of the nineteenth century will not work in the people's century which is now about to begin. India, China, and Latin America have a tremendous stake in the people's century. As their masses learn to read and write, and as they become productive mechanics, their standard of living will double and treble. Modern science, when devoted whole-heartedly to the general welfare, has in it potentialities of which we do not yet dream.

And modern science must be released from German slavery. International cartels that serve American greed and the German will to power must go. Cartels in the peace to come must be subjected to international control for the common man, as well as being under adequate control by the respective home governments. In this way, we can prevent the Germans from again building a war machine while we sleep. With international monopoly pools under control, it will be possible for inventions to serve all the people instead of only the few.

Yes, and when the time of peace comes, the citizen will again have a duty, the supreme duty of sacrificing the lesser interest for the greater interest of the general welfare. Those who write the peace must think of the whole world. There can be no privileged peoples. We ourselves in the United States are no more a master race than the Nazis. And we can not perpetuate economic warfare without planting the seeds of military warfare. We must use our power at the peace table to build an economic peace that is just, charitable and enduring.

If we really believe that we are fighting for a people's peace, all the rest becomes easy. Production, yes—it will be easy to get production without either strikes or sabotage, production with the whole-hearted cooperation between willing arms and keen brains; enthusiasm, zip, energy geared to the tempo of keeping at it everlastingly day after day. Hitler knows as well as those of us who sit in on the War Production Board meetings that we here in the United States are winning the battle of production. He knows that both labor and business in the United States are doing a most remarkable job and that his only hope is to crash through to a complete victory some time during the next six months.

And then there is the task of transportation to the line of battle by truck, by railroad car, by ship. We shall joyously deny ourselves so that our transportation system is improved by at least thirty percent.

I need say little about the duty to fight. Some people declare, and Hitler believes, that the American people have grown soft in the last generation. Hitler agents continually preach in South America that we are cowards, unable to use, like the "brave" German soldiers, the weapons of modern war. It is true that American youth hates war with a holy hatred. But because of that fact and because Hitler and the German people stand as the very symbol of war, we shall fight with a tireless enthusiasm until war and the possibility of war have been removed from this planet. We shall cleanse the plague spot of Europe, which is Hitler's Germany, and with it the hell-hole of Asia—Japan.

No compromise with Satan is possible. We shall not rest until all the victims under the Nazi yoke are freed. We shall fight for a complete peace as well as a complete victory.

The people's revolution is on the march, and the devil and all his angels can not prevail against it. They can not prevail, for on the side of the people is the Lord.

"He giveth power to the faint; to them that have no might He increaseth strength . . . They that wait upon the Lord shall mount up with wings as eagles; they shall run, and not be weary; they shall walk and not be faint."

Strong in the strength of the Lord, we who fight in the people's cause will never stop until that cause is won. (*May 8, 1942.*)

IV RUSSIA

FROM north, south, east and west, Americans pay tribute to our Russian ally. It is right that we should do so. The Russians have thus far lost in the common cause of the United Nations at least fifty percent more men killed, wounded and missing than all of the rest of the European allies put together. Moreover, they have killed, wounded and captured at least twenty times as many Germans as have the rest of the allies. In all of Russian history, there is no more striking example of courage and willingness to sacrifice than Russia presents today.

It is no accident that Americans and Russians like each other when they get acquainted. Both peoples were molded by the vast sweep of a rich continent. Both peoples know that their future is greater than their past. Both hate sham. When the Russian people burst the shackles of Czarist absolutism, they turned instinctively to the United States for engineering and agricultural guidance. Thanks to the hunger of the Russian people for progress, they were able to learn in twenty-five years that which had taken us in the United States one hundred years to develop.

The first person to sense the eventual significance of Russia and the United States was the French author, de Tocqueville. One hundred and seven years ago he wrote:

"There are at the present time two great nations in the world which seem to tend towards the same end, although they start from different points. I allude to the Russians and the Americans. . . . Their starting point is different and their courses are not the same, yet each of them seems to be marked by the will of heaven to sway the destinies of half the globe."

Russia and the United States today are far closer than de Tocqueville could possibly have imagined when he traveled across the United

States in 1835. The continental position of both countries and the need for developing rich resources unmolested from without have caused the peoples of both nations to have a profound hatred of war and a strong love of peace.

We in the United States honor Maxim Litvinov, when we recall how as Foreign Minister of Russia he worked for "collective security." Litvinov, in those days when Hitler was rising to power, wanted to preserve the peace by banding together the non-aggressor nations so they could take a decisive stand against any ruthless nation that might be out for loot. He saw Russia bounded by fourteen different nations, many of which were unfriendly for definite historical reasons. He knew that Germany would use one or more of these nations against Russia when she attacked. Litvinov failed for a time, but now he has come into his own again because he was right.

Russia has had her bitter experience with isolationism. So also has the United States. In 1919 Republicans and Democrats alike sought through a League of Nations to express their belief in the collective security of that day. Taft, Hughes, Hoover, Lowden, and Root all wanted a League. Then isolationism came out of its cave and not only killed any possibility of our entering the League, but made it certain that we would adopt international policies which would make World War Number Two almost inevitable.

Both Russia and the United States retreated into isolationism to preserve their peace. Both failed. Both have learned their lesson.

Russia and the United States have had a profound effect upon each other. Both are striving for the education, the productivity and the enduring happiness of the common man. The new democracy, the democracy of the common man, includes not only the Bill of Rights, but also economic democracy, ethnic democracy, educational democracy, and democracy in the treatment of the sexes.

The ferment in the world today is such that these various types of democracy must be woven together into a harmonious whole. Millions of Americans are now coming to see that if Pan America and the British Commonwealth are the warp of the new democracy, then the peoples of Russia and Asia may well become its woof.

Some in the United States believe that we have overemphasized what might be called political or bill-of-rights democracy. Carried to its extreme form, it leads to rugged individualism, exploitation, impractical emphasis on states' rights, and even to anarchy.

Russia, perceiving some of the abuses of excessive political democracy, has placed strong emphasis on economic democracy. This, carried to an extreme, demands that all power be centered in one man and his bureaucratic helpers.

Somewhere there is a practical balance between economic and political democracy. Russia and the United States both have been working toward this practical middle ground. In present-day Russia, for example, differences in wage income are almost but not quite as great as in the United States. The manager of a factory may be paid ten times as much as the average worker. Outstanding artists, scientists, and writers are usually paid even more than factory managers or political commissars. The chief difference between the economic organization of Russia and that of the United States is that in Russia it is almost impossible to live on income-producing property. The Russian form of state socialism is designed not to get equality of income but to place a maximum incentive on each individual to produce his utmost.

A third kind of democracy, which I call ethnic, is in my opinion vital to the new democracy, the democracy of the common man. Ethnic democracy means merely that the different races and minority groups must be given equality of economic opportunity. President Roosevelt was guided by principles of ethnic democracy when in June of 1941 he issued an Executive Order prohibiting racial discrimination in the employing of workers by national defense industries. Russia has probably gone further than any other nation in the world in practicing ethnic democracy. From the Russians we can learn much, for unfortunately the Anglo-Saxons have had an attitude toward other races which has made them exceedingly unpopular in many parts of the world. We have not sunk to the lunatic level of the Nazi myth of racial superiority, but we have sinned enough to cost us already the blood of tens of thousands of precious lives. Ethnic democracy built from the heart is perhaps the greatest need of the Anglo-Saxon tradition.

The fourth democracy, which has to do with education, is based fundamentally on belief in ethnic democracy. It is because Stalin pushed educational democracy with all the power that he could command that Russia today is able to resist Germany. The Russian people for generations have had a greater hunger to learn to read and write, and when Lenin and Stalin gave them the opportunity, they changed in twenty years from a nation which was ninety percent illiterate to a nation of which nearly ninety percent are able to read and write. Russia has had a great admiration for the American system of technical education and public libraries. If she can continue during the next twenty years the progress made in the past twenty, she will surpass the United States. If, in the future, Russia comes wholeheartedly into the family of nations, we may expect Russian scientists to make contributions to human welfare which equal those of any nation in the world. In any event, the Russian scientists will most assuredly be doing their best to place the results of science more definitely at the service of the average man and woman. Patents based on Russian scientific work will not be held out of use to benefit international cartels.

With regard to the fifth democracy, the treatment of the sexes, most of us in the United States have felt complacent. It has taken the war experience of Russia to demonstrate the completeness of our failure. The Russian Revolution gave equality of economic opportunity to women. Those who have visited Russia recently say that about forty percent of the work in the factories is being done by women. The average woman does about as much work as the average man and is paid as much. Thousands of Russian women are in uniform, either actively fighting or standing guard. We in the United States have not yet in the same way as the Russians called on the tremendous reserve power which is in our women, but before this war is over, we may be forced to give women their opportunity to demonstrate that with proper training they are equal to man in most kinds of work.

The old democracy did not serve as a guarantee of peace. The new democracy in which the people of the United States and Russia are so deeply interested must give us such a guarantee. This new democracy will be neither Communism of the old-fashioned internationalist type nor democracy of the old-fashioned isolationist sort. Willingness to support world organization to maintain world peace by justice implemented by force is fundamental to the democracy of the common man in these days of airplanes. Fortunately, the airplanes, which make it necessary to organize the world for peace, also furnish the means of maintaining peace. When this war comes to an end, the United Nations will have such an overwhelming superiority in air power that we shall be able speedily to enforce any mandate whenever the United Nations may have arrived at a judgment based on international law.

The first article in the international law of the future is undoubtedly the United Nations' Charter. The United Nations' Charter includes the Atlantic Charter and there is little reason why it should longer be called the "Atlantic Charter" in view of the fact that the broader instrument has been validated by thirty nations.

This United Nations' Charter has in it an international bill of rights and certain economic guarantees of international peace. These must and will be made more specific. There must be an international bank and an international TVA, based on projects which are self-liquidating at low rates of interest.

In this connection, I would like to refer to a conversation with Molotoff. Thinking of the unemployment and misery which might so easily follow this war, I spoke of the need for productive public works programs which would stir the imagination of all the peoples of the world and suggested as a starter a combined highway and airway from southern South America across the United States, Canada, and Alaska, into Siberia and on to Europe with feeder highways and airways from China, India, and the Middle East. Molotoff's first reaction was, "No one nation can do it by itself." Then he said, "You and I will live to see the day."

The new democracy by definition abhors imperialism. But by definition also, it is internationally minded and supremely interested in raising the productivity, and therefore the standard of living, of all the peoples of the world. First comes transportation and this is followed by improved agriculture, industrialization and rural electrification. The big planes and skilled pilots which will be ours when the war comes to an end will lead us into a most remarkable future as surely as day follows night. We can make it a future of new democracy based on peace. As Molotoff so clearly indicated, this brave, free world of the future cannot be created by the United States and Russia alone.

Undoubtedly China will have a strong influence on the world which will come out of this war and in exerting this influence it is quite possible that the principles of Sun Yat Sen will prove to be as significant as those of any other modern statesman. The British Commonwealth,

England herself, the democracies of northwest Europe, Latin America, and in fact all of the United Nations, have a very important role to play. But in order that the United Nations may effectively serve the world, it is vital that the United States and Russia be in accord as to the fundamentals of an enduring peace based on the aspirations of the common man. The American and Russian people can and will throw their influence on the side of building a new democracy which will be the hope of all the world. (*November 8, 1942.*)

V WORLD ORGANIZATION

WE are beginning to learn what war privations mean. Abroad, our boys in ever greater numbers are coming to grips with the enemy. Yet, even while warfare rages, and we of the United Nations are redoubling our great drive for victory, there is dawning the hope of that day of peace, however distant, when the lights will go on again, all over the world.

Adolf Hitler's desperate bid for a Nazi world order has reached and passed its highest point, and is on its way to its ultimate downfall. The equally sinister threat of world domination by the Japanese is doomed eventually to fail. When the Hitler regime finally collapses and the Japanese war lords are smashed, an entirely new phase of world history will be ushered in. The task of our generation—the generation which President Roosevelt once said has a "rendezvous with destiny"—is so to organize human affairs that no Adolf Hitler, no power-hungry war mongers whatever their nationality, can ever again plunge the whole world into war and bloodshed.

The situation in the world today is parallel in some ways to that in the United States just before the adoption of the Constitution, when it was realized that the Articles of Confederation had failed and that some stronger union was needed.

Today, measured by travel time, the whole world is actually smaller than was our little country then. When George Washington was inaugurated, it took *seven* days to go by horse-drawn vehicle from Mount Vernon to New York. Now Army bombers are flown from the United States to China and India in less than *three* days.

It is in this suddenly-shrunken world that the United Nations, like our thirteen American States in 1787, soon will be faced with a fundamental choice. We know now that the League of Nations, like our own union under the Articles of Confederation, was not strong enough. The League never had American support, and at critical moments it lacked the support of some of its own members. The League finally disintegrated under the successive blows of worldwide economic depression and a second World War. Soon the nations of the world will have to face this question: Shall the world's affairs be so organized as to prevent a repetition of these twin disasters—the bitter woe of depression and the holocaust of war?

Woodrow Wilson gave up his health and eventually his life in the first attempt, a generation ago, to preserve the world's peace through united world action. At that time, there were many who said that Wilson had failed. Now we know that it was the world that failed, and the suffering and war of the last few years is the penalty it is paying for its failure.

When we think of Woodrow Wilson, we know him not only for his effort to build a permanent peace but for the progressive leadership he gave our country in the years before that first World War. The "New Freedom" for which Wilson fought was the forerunner of the Roosevelt "New Deal" of 1933 and of the worldwide new democracy which is the goal of the United Nations in this present struggle.

Wilson, like Jefferson and Lincoln before him, was interested first and always in the welfare of the common man. And so the ideals of Wilson and the fight he made for them are an inspiration to us today as we take up the torch he laid down.

Resolved as we are to fight on to final victory in this worldwide people's war, we are justified in looking ahead to the peace that will inevitably come. Indeed, it would be the height of folly not to prepare for peace, just as in the years prior to December 7, 1941, it would have been the height of folly not to prepare for war.

As territory previously overrun by the Germans and the Japs is reoccupied by the forces of the United Nations, measures of relief and rehabilitation will have to be undertaken. Later, out of the experience of these temporary measures of relief, there will emerge the possibilities and the practicalities of more permanent reconstruction.

We cannot now blueprint all the details, but we *can* begin now to think about some of the guiding principles of this worldwide new democracy we of the United Nations hope to build.

Two of these principles must be Liberty and Unity, or in other words, home rule and centralized authority, which for more than one hundred and fifty years have been foundation stones of our American democracy and our American union.

When Woodrow Wilson proposed the League of Nations, it became apparent that these same principles of Liberty and Unity—of home rule and centralized authority—needed to be applied among the nations if a repetition of the first World War was to be prevented. Unfortunately the people of the United States were not ready. They believed in the doctrine of Liberty in international affairs, but they were not willing to give up certain of their international rights and to shoulder certain international duties, even though other nations were ready to take such steps. They were in the position of a strong, well-armed pioneer citizen who thought he could defend himself against robbers without going to the expense and bother of joining with his neighbors in setting up a police force to uphold civil law. They stood for decency in international affairs, but in the world of practical international politics the net effect of their action or lack of action was anarchy and the loss of millions of lives and hundreds of billions of dollars in a second world war.

The sturdy pioneer citizen, proud of his own strength and independence, needed to be robbed and beaten only once by bandits to be ready to cooperate with his law-abiding neighbors. I believe the United States also has learned her lesson and that she is willing to assume a responsibility proportionate to her strength. England, Russia, China and most of the other United Nations are perhaps even more eager than the United States to go beyond the Charter which they have signed as a declaration of principles. The United Nations, like the United States one hundred and fifty-five years ago, are groping for a formula which will give the greatest possible liberty without producing anarchy and at the same time will not give so many rights to each member nation as to jeopardize the security of all.

Obviously the United Nations must first have machinery which can disarm and keep disarmed those parts of the world which would break the peace. Also there must be machinery for preventing economic warfare and enhancing economic peace between nations. Probably there will have to be an international court to make decisions in cases of dispute. And an international court presupposes some kind of world council, so that whatever world system evolves will have enough flexibility to meet changing circumstances as they arise.

As a practical matter, we may find that the regional principle is of considerable value in international affairs. For example, European countries, while *concerned* with the problems of Pan America, should not have to be *preoccupied* with them, and likewise Pan America, while *concerned,* should not have to be *preoccupied* with the problems of Europe. Purely regional problems ought to be left in regional hands. This would leave to any federated world organization problems involving broad principles and those practical matters which affect countries of different regions or which affect the whole world.

The aim would be to preserve the liberty, equality, security and unity of the United Nations—liberty in a political sense, equality of opportunity in international trade, security against war and business depression due to international causes, and unity of purpose in promoting the general welfare of the world.

In other words, the aim would be the maximum of home rule that can be maintained along with the minimum of centralized authority that must come into existence to give the necessary protection. We in the United States must remember this: If we are to expect guarantees against military or economic aggression from other nations, we must be willing to give guarantees that we will not be guilty of such aggression ourselves. We must recognize, for example, that it is perfectly justifiable for a debtor, pioneer nation to build up its infant industries behind a protective tariff, but a creditor nation can be justified in such policies only from the standpoint of making itself secure in case of war.

A special problem that will face the United Nations immediately upon the attainment of victory over either Germany or Japan will be what to do with the defeated nation. Revenge for the sake of revenge would be a sign of barbarism. But this time we must make absolutely sure that the guilty leaders are punished, that the defeated nation realizes its defeat and is not permitted to re-arm. The United Nations must back up military disarmament with psychological disarmament—supervision, or at least inspection, of the school systems of Germany and Japan, to undo so far as possible the diabolical work of Hitler and the Japanese war lords in poisoning the minds of the young.

Without doubt, in the building of a new and enduring peace, economic reconstruction will play an all-important role. Unless there is careful planning in advance, the return of peace can in a few years bring a shock even worse than the shock of war.

The magnitude of the problem here in the United States, for example, is indicated by the probability that in the peak year of the war we shall be spending something like ninety billion dollars of public funds in the war effort whereas two years later we may be spending less than twenty billion dollars for military purposes. In the peak year of the war effort, it is probable that we shall have around ten million men in the armed services and twenty million additional men and women producing war goods for the armed services. It would seem that within the first two years after the peace at least fifteen million of these thirty million men and women will be seeking jobs different from those which they had when peace came.

Our expenditures have been going at a rate fully seven times as great as in World War Number One and the conversion of our industry to wartime uses has been far more complete. Thousands of thoughtful businessmen and economists, remembering what happened after the last war, being familiar with the fantastic figures of this war, and knowing the severity of the shock to come, have been greatly disturbed. Some have concerned themselves with plans to get over the first year. Others have given thought to the more distant future.

It should be obvious to practically everyone that, without well-planned and vigorous action, a series of economic storms will follow this war. These will take the form of inflation and temporary scarcities, followed by surpluses, crashing prices, unemployment, bankruptcy, and in some cases violent revolution. If there is lack of well-planned and vigorous action, it is quite conceivable that the human misery in certain countries after the war may be even greater than during the war.

It is true that in the long run any nation, like any individual, must follow the principle of self-help, must look to its own efforts to raise its own living standards. But it is also true that stronger nations, like our own, can provide guidance, technical advice, and in some cases capital investment to help those nations which are just starting on the path of industrialization. Our experience with the Philippines is a case in point.

The suggestions I have made with a view to promoting development and encouraging higher standards of living are necessarily fragmentary at this time. But in some quarters, either knowingly or unknowingly, they have been grossly distorted and misrepresented. During the recent political campaign one member of Congress seeking re-election made the flat statement that I was in favor of having American farmers give away a quart of milk a day to every inhabitant of the world. In other quarters these suggestions have been referred to by such terms as "utopian," "soggy sentimentality," and the "dispensing of milk and honey." But is it "utopian" to foresee that South America, Asia and Africa will in the future experience a development of industry and agriculture comparable to what has been experienced in the past in Europe and North America? Is it "soggy sentimentality" to hold out hope to those millions in Europe and Asia fighting for the cause of human freedom—our freedom? Is it the "dispensing of milk and honey" to picture to their minds the possible blessings of a higher standard of living when the war is over and their own productivity has increased?

Among the self-styled "realists" who are trying to scare the American people by spreading worry about "misguided idealists" giving away our products are some whose policies caused us to give away billions of dollars of stuff in the decade of the 20's. Their high tariff prevented exchange of our surplus for goods. And so we exchanged our surplus for bonds of very doubtful value. Our surplus will be far greater than ever within a few years after this war comes to an end. We can be decently human and really hard-headed if we exchange our postwar surplus for goods, for peace, and for improving the standard of living of so-called backward peoples. We can get more for our surplus production in this way than by any high-tariff, penny-pinching, isolationist policies which hide under the cloak of one hundred percent Americanism.

Self-interest alone should be sufficient to make the United States deeply concerned with the contentment and well-being of the other peoples of the world. Such contentment will be an important contribution to world peace and it is only when other peoples are prosperous and economically productive that we can find export markets among them for the products of our factories and our farms.

A world family of nations cannot be really healthy unless the various nations in that family are getting along well in their own internal affairs. The first concern of each nation must be the well-being of its own people. That is as true of the United States as of any other nation.

During the war, we have full employment here in the United States, and the problem is not to find jobs for the workers but to find workers for the jobs. After the war, it will be vital to make sure that another period of unemployment does not come on. With this end in view, the suggestion has been made that Congress should formally recognize the maintenance of full employment as a declared national policy, just as it now recognizes as national policies the right of farmers to parity of income with other groups and the right of workers to unemployment insurance and old-age annuities.

Full employment is vital not only to city prosperity but to farm prosperity as well. Nothing contributes more to stable farm prosperity than the maintenance of full employment in the cities, and the assurance that purchasing power for both farm and factory products will always be adequate.

Maintenance of full employment and the highest possible level of national income should be the joint responsibility of private business and of government. It is reassuring to know that business groups in contact with government agencies already are assembling facts, ideas, and plans that will speed up the shift from a government-financed war program to a privately-financed program of peacetime activity.

This shift must be made as secure against mischance as if it were a wartime campaign against the enemy. We can not afford either a speculative boom or its inevitable bust. In the war we use tanks, planes, guns and ships in great volume and of most effective design. Their equivalents in the defense against postwar economic chaos will be less spectacular, but equally essential. We must keep prices in control. We must have continuity in the flow of incomes to consumers and from consumers to the industries of city and farm. We must have a national system of job placement. We must have definite plans for the conversion of key industries to peacetime work.

When the war is over, the more quickly private enterprise gets back into peacetime production and sells its goods to peacetime markets here and abroad, the more quickly will the level of government wartime expenditures be reduced. No country needs deficit spending when private enterprise, either through its own efforts or in cooperation with government, is able to maintain full employment. Let us hope that the best thought of both business and government can be focussed on this problem which lies at the heart of our American democracy and our American way of life.

The war has brought forth a new type of industrialist who gives much promise for the future. The type of business leader I have in mind has caught a new vision of opportunities in national and international projects. He is willing to cooperate with the people's government in carrying out socially desirable programs. He conducts these programs on the basis of private enterprise, and for private profit, while putting into effect the people's standards as to wages and working conditions. We shall need the best efforts of such men as we tackle the economic problem of the peace.

This problem is well recognized by the average man on the street, who sums it up in a nutshell like this: If everybody can be given a job in war work now, why can't everybody have a job in peacetime production later on? He will demand an answer, and the returning soldier and sailor will demand an answer. This will be the test of statesmanship on the home front, just as ability to cooperate with other nations for peace and improved living standards will be the test of statesmanship on the international front.

How thrilling it will be when the world can move ahead into a new day of peaceful work, developing its resources and translating them as never before into goods that can be consumed and enjoyed! But this new day will not come to pass, unless the people of the United Nations give whole-hearted support to an effective program of action. The war will have been fought in vain if we in the United States, for example, are plunged into bitter arguments over our part in the peace, or over such fictitious questions as government versus business. Such bitterness would only confuse us and cloud our path. How much more sensible it would be if our people could be supplied with the facts and then, through orderly discussion, could arrive at a common understanding of what needs to be done.

I have heard the fear expressed that after the war the spirit of self-sacrifice which now animates so many of our people will disappear, that cold and blind selfishness will supplant the spirit which makes our young men willing to go thousands of miles from home to fight—and die if need be—for freedom. Those who have this fear think that a return of blind selfishness will keep the nations of the world from joining to prevent a repetition of this disaster.

We should approach the whole question, not emotionally from the standpoint of either sacrifice or selfishness, but objectively from the standpoint of finding the common meeting ground on which the people of the world can stand. This meeting ground, after all, should not be hard to find—it is the security of the plain folks against depression and against war. To unite against these two evils is not really a sacrifice at all, but only a common-sense facing of the facts of the world in which we live.

Now at last the nations of the world have a second chance to erect a lasting structure of peace—a structure such as that which Woodrow Wilson sought to build but which crumbled away because the world was not yet ready. Wilson himself foresaw that it was certain to be rebuilt some day. This is related by Josephus Daniels in his book, "The Life of Woodrow Wilson," as follows:

"Wilson never knew defeat, for defeat never comes to any man until he admits it. Not long before the close of his life Woodrow Wilson said to a friend: 'Do not trouble about the things we have fought for. They are sure to prevail. They are only delayed.' With the quaintness which gave charm to his sayings he added: 'And I will make this concession to Providence—it may come in a better way than we propose.'"

And now we of this generation, trusting in Providence to guide our steps, go forward to meet the challenge of *our* day. For the challenge we all face is the challenge of the new democracy. In the new democracy, there will be a place for everyone—the worker, the farmer, the business man, the housewife, the doctor, the salesman, the teacher, the student, the store clerk, the taxi driver, the preacher, the engineer—all the millions who make up our modern world. This new democracy will give us freedom such as we have never known, but only if as individuals we perform our duties with willing hearts. It will be an adventure in sharing—sharing of duties and responsibilities, and sharing of the joy that can come from the give-and-take of human contacts and fruitful daily living. Out of it, if we all do our part, there will be new opportunity and new security for the common man—that blend of Liberty and Unity which is the bright goal of millions. (*December 28, 1942.*)

VI TRADE AGREEMENTS

U<small>NLESS</small> continuous, strenuous, and united efforts are made to attain economic justice, it will be impossible to prevent military war by any type of force. Force is important—but it is not enough. Force without justice would sooner or later make us into the image of that which we have hated in the Nazis.

We are now in the preliminaries of our battle for a just peace. The first round in this battle has to do with the reciprocal trade program—the program of sanity in international trade which was begun under an act of Congress in 1934 and which Congress extended in 1937 and 1940.

Within a few years after the war ends it is almost certain that farm product prices will fall very greatly. At the same time it will be apparent that the farmer is able to produce larger quantities of farm produce than ever before. Millions of farmers will probably be facing bankruptcy in all parts of the world.

Several of the United Nations have set a pattern for meeting this problem in the international wheat agreement which has already been signed. This international wheat agreement protects both farmers and consumers. If the same principle were applied to certain other raw materials that move in world trade, much might be done to prevent depression. The soldiers and sailors that come home after this war will not permit the paradox of bursting abundance on the farms and empty stomachs in the cities. A United Nations commodity agency can do much to prevent bankruptcy on the farms, unemployment in the mines, and hunger in the cities.

The farmers now have the technical ability to prevent hunger. The only question is whether the United Nations have the technical ability to put this productive power efficiently to use in serving the needs of hungry people.

I do not think it is the duty of the American farmer to feed the world. But I do think the American farmer is mightily interested in getting a market for his surplus production. I think he will want to cooperate with other farmers in the world in some sensible scheme whereby the surplus of the farms can be exchanged for the surplus that can be turned out by the enormous factories which will have been built. We just don't begin to realize the extent of the productive power both on the farms and in the cities that will be ours soon after this war ends. The only things that can prevent this productive power from giving a higher standard of living are individual selfishness, class selfishness, national selfishness, and plain dumbness. (*December 31, 1942.*)

VII THE NATIONAL DEBT

T HE only way we can really pay for the war is to see that people have jobs and full stomachs. Technologically, this is possible. Psychologically, it may be difficult because not enough people have looked at the simple arithmetic of the problem.

A nation that maintains full employment at useful production in peacetime has no problem of people going hungry. People then have income not only for food, but also for the rest of their budget, and the nation as a whole has income to pay debt charges that are not burdensome.

At present costs of borrowing, our primary fear should not be of the size of our national debt, even with the steep increase in that debt which the war inevitably brings—we need rather to make sure that jobs and adequate incomes are maintained.

It is conceivable that, as we push on to victory, the cost of the war will double the Federal debt over what it is now, raising the total to around two hundred billion dollars. It is also conceivable that private long-term investment, after the war, will increase the private debt to one hundred billion dollars. The burden of the annual interest charges on these debts, at present interest rates, would be about as light in proportion to income as in 1923 or 1929, provided we have full employment and a continued total national income of about one hundred and thirty billion dollars.

These simple figures will show what I mean: In 1929 we had private long-term debts amounting to eighty-seven billion dollars and an annual interest charge of five billion. We had a net Federal debt of nearly sixteen billion and State and local government debts of nearly fourteen billion, with interest charges amounting to one and one-fourth billion. These interest charges, totaling six and one-fourth billion, were the equivalent of seven and one-half percent of a national income of eighty-three billion dollars.

At present interest rates the annual carrying charge on a two-hundred-billion-dollar Federal debt would be five billion dollars, the carrying charge on a one-hundred-billion-dollar long-term private debt would be four billion dollars, and the carrying charge on a twenty-billion-dollar state and local debt would be six hundred million dollars, making a total interest charge of nine billion six hundred million dollars. This would be equivalent to a little over seven percent of a one-hundred thirty-billion-dollar national income (our prospective income for 1943) and would be approximately the same percentage of our national income as we devoted to paying interest on debt in 1929.

The real problem is to maintain full employment in peacetime production as we are now doing in war production.

As peacetime production expands and war production is contracted, the annual deficit will go down, and we can then begin to have substantial relief from the wartime burdens of taxation. But if ten million people should be thrown out of work, the result would be a reduction of national income by perhaps thirty billion dollars, and a proportionate reduction in both private and corporation income tax payments. The one criterion by which we should judge all fiscal, monetary, and taxation policies is whether they bring about an increased balanced production of useful goods.

Two simple facts for all of us to bear in mind are these: First, the more successfully private enterprise maintains full employment, the less government spending is required. Second, certain types of government economy, if they bring on widespread unemployment, can actually drive us deeper into debt instead of pulling us out.

We need not go hungry or unemployed if we follow sound policies, if experts in money and taxation match the technical competence of those who work on the farms and in the factories. As a matter of fact, the way to pay for the war is to utilize fully our greatly expanded farm and factory facilities, and to continue to expand the productivity of our agriculture and industry to the limit. If we do this, it is quite possible, within a few years after the war ends, in spite of the war-created debts, for the people both in the United States and in most other parts of the world to have a higher standard of living than they have ever had before.
(*January 18, 1943.*)

VIII BUSINESS MEASURES[1]

BUSINESS men realize that the shock of this war's end will probably be at least seven times as great as that which was felt beginning in 1920. Those of us who remember 1920 and the years which followed know now that there is just as much need of planning for peace as there was need of planning for war prior to Pearl Harbor. Peace unplanned could be a disaster worse than war, wrecking business, labor, and agriculture throughout the entire world and producing revolution and misery among the millions.

No business man can plan for the future with any certainty so long as there is the fear of war on the horizon. It is vital, therefore, that the United Nations' covenant must provide the machinery to assure "freedom from fear"—an international peace law, an international peace court, and an international peace force. If any aggressor nations take the first step toward rearmament, they must be served at once with a "cease and desist" order and be warned of the consequences. If economic quarantine does not suffice, the United Nations' peace force must at once bomb the aggressor nation mercilessly.

To guarantee the peace, the United Nations will need additional powers. We must prevent international cartels of the German type and perhaps substitute for them a United Nations agency to restore stable conditions in raw material markets, on price terms that assure producers fair incomes and promote expanded consumption.

To prevent worldwide unemployment, there will probably have to be a United Nations investment corporation, under whose direction public and private capital can be put to work for worldwide reconstruction. If unemployment could be prevented without the use of government funds, there would be no need for such a corporation. But the postwar impact resulting from the sudden cessation of tremendous governmental

[1] Most of the material in this chapter was included in a copyrighted article entitled "What We Will Get Out of the War," published in *The American Magazine* for March, 1943, and is reprinted by permission.

spending everywhere in the world will make it absolutely necessary for governmental investment capital to be used on a very large scale to prevent the sudden and complete destruction of the capitalistic system.

This will not necessarily mean the reduction of private initiative. On the contrary, private initiative probably will be increased.

In launching such an investment program, the establishment of a network of globe-girdling airways ought to be the very first order of business.

After the peace of the world has been made secure, it should be possible to internationalize the large airports. The war has already brought the construction of many new airports, most of them for military purposes. With the coming of peace, and the expansion of commercial air service, many more will be needed. Boldness should be the guiding principle in planning a worldwide airport construction program. When this war ends we shall be only at the threshold of the coming air age. Freedom of the air means to the world of the future what freedom of the sea meant to the world of the past.

The airways I visualize would have as their primary justification the safeguarding of world peace. They would be operated by the air arm of the United Nations peace force. To maintain a military air force with nothing to do but wait for some nation's act of aggression would be a big expense and would not give the young men composing such a force enough to do. Instead, after these young men have undergone the necessary military training, they can serve as the air and ground crews of the United Nations air network, which in peacetime would be commercial and would carry passengers and freight.

Doubtless there will have to be an "international air authority" to administer the large airports of the world and to safeguard the interests of the various nations in the expanded air commerce of the future.

Air travel will have an indirect but far-reaching effect on economic development. As people travel from country to country with greater ease, possibilities for utilizing the world's resources will be seen by men of daring and imagination, and they will lead the way in organizing new industrial projects of all kinds.

Boys and girls of the rising generation are already air-minded to a degree which is not possible for most of their elders who grew up earth-bound. Educational courses in the future might well include air-

plane trips to one or more foreign countries. It is infinitely more important to make the people of the United Nations space-minded for peace
than it was for Germany to make its people space-minded for war.

Rivaling aviation in its effect on future business development will be
highway transportation. We in the United States can realize from our
own experience what highways mean, for highways have been as essential as automobiles and motor trucks in the transportation revolution in
this country in the last three decades.

One great road project which has been under way for nearly twenty
years, and which is now within sight of completion, is the 9,330-mile
Pan American Highway, extending from Laredo, Texas, to Buenos
Aires, Argentina. This highway, known as the "lifeline of the Americas,"
is a monument to the cooperative spirit of the Western Hemisphere
republics.

There will doubtless be a close relationship between airways and
highways which follow the same intercontinental routes. To some extent
airports will be located along the highways, and both the airways and
the highways will be fed from the same streams of commerce.

Improved transportation will be the key that will unlock the resources
of the vast undeveloped regions of the world. We may expect the history
of those regions in the next hundred years to parallel our own history in
the last hundred years.

One of the great dramas of American history was the winning of the
West. Following the War between the States, the railroads crossed the
prairies at the rate of a mile a day. Farmers, ranchers, miners, cities,
churches, and schools followed.

A similar drama, unsung as yet, has been taking place in the Old
World, as Russia has been winning her East. Most of Siberia, at the
time of the fall of the Czars, was little more than waste land occupied
by Eskimos, herdsmen, and political exiles. Less than sixteen million
people occupied a land area twice as great as the United States. Today
over forty million people live in the same area, with its new Siberian
Pittsburghs, Bostons, Detroits. Great power dams, great mines, and
great factories are operated in a giant new industrial system. On the
farms are tractors by the tens of thousands.

What the United States has done and what Russia is doing give a clue to what is possible in such regions as China, Alaska, and Latin America.

China has coal, iron and other resources essential for industrial progress, but first must come improvement of agricultural production and transportation. More capital is one of China's primary needs, but even more she is in want of technical skill and guidance to utilize her resources effectively. It is in providing such guidance that the United States and the other United Nations can perhaps be of the most help.

Another region rich with new possibilities of industrial and agricultural development is the great Northwest—including Alaska, western Canada, and the northwestern portion of the United States. To such previously existing industries as fishing, lumbering, and mining, the war has added shipbuilding, aluminum production, and airplane manufacture. When peace returns, the Alcan Highway and other new transportation routes will lay the basis for further progress, and, with plenty of water power available, there will be the opportunity for great expansion in all the industries utilizing the mineral and forest resources which abound in the region.

Perhaps most challenging to the imagination of the modern businessman is the vast land of Latin America to the south.

An important point is the degree to which the projects can be made completely self-liquidating. Of course, in a broad sense, a loan to a government may be considered to be self-liquidating if it is used to build up the productive power of the country and results in an increased capacity for repayment. But many of the projects I have in mind would be self-liquidating even in the narrower sense.

The experience of our own Tennessee Valley Authority throws some light on what may be achieved through careful planning and skillful engineering. This experiment in regional planning, begun nearly ten years ago, has been a striking success.

There are practical people in the United States who believe that we have the "know how" to help many of the poverty-stricken peoples to set their feet on the path of education, manual dexterity, and economic literary. If American missionaries of a new type, equipped with this "know how," can work in cooperation with a United Nations investment corporation to develop flood-control works, irrigation projects, soil reclamation, rural electrification, and the like, it will make possible an expansion in half the area of the world reminiscent of that which was stirring in our own land during its rapid growth from 1870 to 1910.

The new missionaries, if they are to make their dreams come true in a really big way, must be able to grasp the enormous possibilities of combining governmental credit and organization with the drive of private initiative. The possibilities are all there—all just as practical and feasible as the growth of the United States.

In our foreign investments and activities, we have an opportunity to avoid the mistakes of the twenties. At that time the United States loaned billions of dollars abroad, but, through insisting on a high tariff, made it impossible for those dollars to be repaid. In effect, we gave away to foreign countries (perhaps even to Hottentots!) billions of dollars of our food and manufactured goods. The kind of investment policy I am suggesting for the future can be more practical and more to our interest than that which prevailed in the decade of the twenties, provided we manage our tariffs as a powerful creditor nation has to manage them if it is to prevent worldwide misery among the debtor nations, and eventually war.

But I do not mean to imply that the whole answer to our own problem, here in the United States, is to be found in economic development abroad.

To shift successfully from ninety billion a year war production to ordinary peacetime activity will require the greatest resourcefulness and determination, the greatest outpouring of industrial energy, and the finest cooperative spirit among businessmen, farmers, workers, professional people, and government officials that this country has ever seen.

Labor must go beyond hours, rates of pay, and working conditions, and through the appropriate agency of government, cooperate vigorously with business in programs for full employment.

Agriculture must, through the appropriate agency of government, see that the parity principle now written into law operates justly under changing conditions of production and is effectively applied to feed the largest number of consumers at a reasonable price.

Businessmen must, in their governmental relationships, go much deeper than the customary consideration of taxes, economy, and disdain for bureaucrats. They must work actively with appropriate agencies of government in the administration of policies which will best increase productive power, balanced by an ever-increasing consumptive power flowing from a prosperous agriculture and from labor fully and productively employed.

The war, with all its hardship and its pain, has brought one blessing— it is providing a job for everybody who wants a job. We should resolve now that victory will not rob us of this blessing.

After this war is over, it is quite possible that we shall have the same experience as after the first World War, when for nearly two years there was an advance rather than a decline. This time, after we have met the problems of the immediate transition from war to peace, we may enjoy a period of good business which may last anywhere from one to five years. There will be at least ten billion dollars in the hands of business men, which they can use to replace worn-out equipment and depleted inventories. There will be another ten billion dollars of consumer credit which can be tapped, since the old installment debts will have been paid off and the field will be clear for people to buy on credit again. There will be at least ten billion dollars of purchasing power in individual war savings. Automobiles, tires, furnishings, clothing, homes all will be worn out or run-down and needing replacement or repair. The combination of this pentup demand for goods and the thirty billion dollars or more of unusual purchasing power may produce full activity, or even a runaway boom if preventive measures are not taken. But, while such a period of good business and full employment might possibly last for several years, it still might prove to be temporary, because it would be based on a combination of war-caused factors that are only short-lived.

If a period of business decline should set in, not only will farmers desperately need a farm program, but business men and laboring men will desperately need a program to restore industrial employment and production.

Thus, on the economic side, the postwar planning that all of us are hearing so much about will probably have to cover three successive phases here in the United States. First will be the shock of transition from war to peace. Second will be the period of postwar prosperity, when restraining measures will be needed to prevent uncontrolled inflation and a runaway boom in stocks and land. Third will be the period of threatened decline, when strong action in advance both by private business and by public agencies may be needed to prevent a repetition of 1932 in this country and the rise of another Hitler abroad.

Much of the task of shifting to peacetime activity will have to rest upon the shoulders of the businessmen. In their task they will have the inspiration of the great progress of technology, accelerated by the war and the nation-wide research programs organized by men in the armed services.

If the business men are engaged in home construction, they will have many new materials and devices to work with. If they are in automobile manufacturing, they will be able, through the use of aluminum and plastics, to produce cars that are lighter, more efficient, more comfortable, and cheaper to operate.

If they are merchants, they will find a host of new products on the market, as the wartime accomplishments in making plastics are translated into peacetime goods. If they are in the food business, they will have the thrill of offering the public many new types of dehydrated and compressed foods, developed by the Army for the convenience of soldiers but adaptable to peacetime use. If they are in aviation, they can look forward to the introduction of the helicopter and the great changes and opportunities this type of plane will bring.

In nearly every country of the world one of the most feasible projects will be construction of low-cost houses on a scale never before contemplated. Few people realize the multitude of construction devices and gadgets of all kinds which are available to make houses livable at lower cost. Here in the United States the possibilities are enormous. The field for new and better rural housing has scarcely been touched. In cities, the problem goes far beyond the matter of slum clearance and rehabilitation of blighted areas. It involves the construction of houses for individual ownership and of houses for rent by those people whose work forces them to shift their residence frequently.

If each of the United Nations will do its duty for its own people on the housing front, a considerable part of the postwar unemployment problem can be solved. But no matter how far the respective United Nations go with regard to housing projects and the expansion of normal consumption goods industries, there will be wide-scale unemployment unless some united agency is prepared to plan and finance on a self-liquidating basis international airports and similar projects of the great-est significance to the peace and prosperity of the entire world.

With all the initiative and daring of the business men, it is doubtful if, in the short time they will have, they can make the ninety-billion-dollar shift by their own efforts alone. They will need the help of gov-ernment in various ways—the cushioning effect of "dismissal wages" for workers leaving war jobs, of "discharge bonuses" for men leaving the Army and the Navy, of plans for an orderly cancellation of war contracts, of provisions that will encourage the smaller companies to buy the war production plants from the government.

They will need the help of financial and tax policies which favor the maximum of individual incentive, but which do not shut out the rapid flow of government funds when these may be necessary for full employ-ment. They will need the protection of government insurance of busi-ness transactions, as so successfully worked out in the guarantee of bank deposits and in the insurance of home mortgages under the Federal Housing Administration.

They will need the protection of the social security system, broadened and strengthened. Social security is a splendid method of easing the individual worker and the business community over the rough spots. But we should recognize that the United States does not yet have a mature economy, and we should not look to a social security program as a substitute for dynamic, creative business energy and initiative.

In the situation that will face the United States and the world after the war, one might like to follow this course or that, according to his own personal inclinations. But, as is so often the case in the life of the individual, the decision comes down to a choice between very definite alternatives. On the one hand, the people of our country and of the world will have an opportunity to act boldly and imaginatively to organ-ize the greatest utilization of the world's resources that history has ever seen. On the other hand, we confront the alternative prospect of suffer-ing from a disillusionment like that which began in 1930—a disillusion-ment which will end inevitably in World War Number Three, if not in a collapse sooner in the form of an epidemic of insurrections and revo-lutions, or the loss of democracy and the sinking into a state infinitely more static and regimented than the life of the Middle Ages.

The American business man will rise to the challenge of the air age, to the challenge of the new frontier, to the infinite possibilities for development not only in our own country, but in the tropics and in Asia. Just as he has cooperated with government in time of war to build planes for the saving of civilization, so likewise will he cooperate with government to make air power the preserver of civilization.

More and more, everyone will recognize that business, labor, agriculture, and government have just one job in their four-way partnership: to lead the common man to full employment, a higher standard of living, and a peace which will be permeated by the exciting spirit of new frontiers. The creative business man of the future will recognize that, while government will play a large part in opening up these new frontiers, the government activity will be such as not to reduce but to increase the field for private initiative. Better government organization and more individual drive will go hand in hand.

The peace to come will be just as worthy of a supreme effort as the war is now. The men in the armed services are too intelligent to permit a dull, dead, dragging peace which will let the world drift into the maelstrom.

Airplanes and air power have eliminated the old significance of national boundaries. International airports and extensive international air travel will cause the American businessman to think in international terms as never before. The narrow selfishness of the past will more and more seem foolish and harmful. The seas will no longer separate the continents in the way they once did. Information and goods will flow with ever-increasing freedom.

Modern technology, the wings of the air, and the waves of the air mean that the common man will demand and get a better education and a higher standard of living. In serving the common man, the business leader will have opportunities for initiative such as he never dreamed of before. (*From "What We Will Get Out of the War," copyright The American Magazine, March, 1943. By permission.*)

IX THE NEW ISOLATIONISM

We cannot have national security if we follow an isolationist or excessively nationalist policy. With our country fighting for her life against aggressor powers on the other side of both oceans, hardly anyone in this country is now willing to admit openly that he is an isolationist. Nevertheless the country is being flooded with propaganda for new, subtle and therefore dangerous forms of isolationism which, if adopted, would lead straight to World War Number Three.

Here are some of the ways in which the old doctrine is taking new forms:

First: People are being told that a world war every generation is inevitable and that we can have national security only by maintaining the biggest army, the biggest navy, and the biggest air force in the world. Even if we could indefinitely stand the expense and the privation of such a program, it would not necessarily protect us. For though we might have the best and biggest army, navy and air force, other countries might and probably would combine against us. If they formed a combination stronger than our own, they would defeat us.

My view, and I am convinced that it is the majority view of the American people, is that rather than remain an armed camp, waiting for the inevitable World War Number Three, it is more practical for us as a nation to throw the weight of our influence behind worldwide efforts to prevent such a war.

Second: People are being told that anything which is done after this war to improve the standard of living of other countries will lower the standard of living at home.

Of course, while the war is on, the people of this country are making sacrifices, and making them cheerfully, to help our allies Britain and Russia keep on fighting. Doubtless our people will gladly continue these sacrifices for a short period after Germany is defeated, in order to prevent widespread famine in Europe.

But, for the long pull, the most effective assistance we can give is the kind which helps other countries to develop their agriculture and industry, and which at the same time increases our own prosperity. Those who really want to improve the standard of living of the American people know that the United States is now so much a part of the whole world that we can best help Americans by helping the peoples of all the world to help themselves.

Third: Another step in what appears to be a campaign of fear is the assertion that our government is preparing to take control of education everywhere in the world. This is nonsense. But all sensible people know that the United Nations in some way must prevent Germany from teaching the Nazi philosophy in the future as a preliminary to launching another German war for world conquest.

Fourth: A movement is already under way to abandon the sane tariff policy represented by our reciprocal trade agreement program, and go back to the Smoot-Hawley days of building a high-tariff wall around the United States. Economic warfare of the Smoot-Hawley type is the initial step toward military warfare. It leads first to totalitarian control of trade, then to shooting. To win the peace, we must follow through to establish the right kind of international trade relations. We cannot hope to maintain peace by force unless the peace we are maintaining is a just peace.

Fifth: It is urged that, after the war, American aviators ought to be permitted to fly everywhere in the world, but that not a single foreign plane should ever fly over any part of the United States. This astonishing idea seems to be first cousin to the fallacy that we can sell our goods everywhere in the world at the same time that we keep foreigners from selling to us. Many problems are bound up in the question of our post-war relationships with other countries in the field of aviation. We shall never solve them in a constructive way—and in a way that will promote peace instead of war—if we base our approach on such absurd and fuzzy thinking.

Recently I expressed the view that neither political party would want to be opposed to freedom of the seas or freedom of the air after the war. But I find that on January 5, 1943, an opposition leader set the tempo for orthodox opposition thinking with regard to American postwar imperialism when he said: "America must rule the air, and to do this it is necessary for the Congress to plan intelligently for this air supremacy following the war."

This visions an imperialistic fight for air supremacy between at least three great nations in the world—a fight which can end finally only in World War Number Three, or American domination of a type which will eventually make the United States worse hated in the world than the Nazis ever have been. Americans want peace, not war. Americans want sensible world cooperation—not isolationism or imperialism. By common-sense world cooperation the people of the United States will have infinitely more prosperity than in a senseless race for air power.

It is possible now to get votes, build prestige and even make money by shouting American supremacy of the air and seas. But when we yield to American imperialism of this type, we are working for the death of our children and grandchildren in World War Number Three. What we want is not imperialistic American supremacy in the air and on the sea. By cooperating with other nations, we can get security and peace, but by striving for imperialistic American supremacy of the air and sea we shall get insecurity and war at a tremendous outlay of taxpayers' money and our children's blood. (*March 8, 1943.*)

X THREE PHILOSOPHIES

THERE are three great philosophies in the world today. The first, based on the supremacy of might over right, says that war between nations is inevitable until such time as a single master race dominates the entire world and everyone is assigned his daily task by an arrogant, self-appointed Fuehrer. The second—the Marxian philosophy—says that class warfare is inevitable until such time as the proletariat comes out on top, everywhere in the world, and can start building a society without classes. The third—which we in this country know as the democratic Christian philosophy—denies that man was made for war, whether it be war between nations or war between classes, and asserts boldly that ultimate peace is inevitable, that all men are brothers, and that God is their Father.

This democratic philosophy pervades not only the hearts and minds of those who live by the Christian religion, both Protestant and Catholic, but of those who draw their inspiration from Mohammedanism, Judaism, Hinduism, Confucianism and other faiths. When we look beneath the outer forms, we find that all these faiths, in one way or another, preach the doctrine of the dignity of each individual human soul, the doctrine that God intended man to be a good neighbor to his fellow man, and the doctrine of the essential unity of the entire world.

Those who think most about individualism preach freedom. Those who think most about unity, whether it be the unity of a nation or of the entire world, preach the sacred obligation of duty. There is a seeming conflict between freedom and duty, and it takes the spirit of democracy to resolve it. Only through religion and education can the freedom-loving individual realize that his greatest private pleasure comes from serving the highest unity, the general welfare of all. This truth, the essence of democracy, must capture the hearts of men over the entire world, if human civilization is not to be torn to pieces in a series of wars and revolutions far more terrible than anything that has yet been endured. Democracy is the hope of civilization.

To understand the significance of these three philosophies dominant in the world today, let us look at each one in turn. During the last eighty years, the outstanding exponent of the sacredness and inevitability of war has been Prussia. By nature the common people of Prussia are simple and hard-working, and make excellent citizens except where they have become infected by the Prussian doctrine that might makes right. The Prussian philosophy causes its adherents to practice many of the highest virtues, but these virtues are all ultimately placed at the disposal of supreme evil. Hitler, seizing the Prussian militaristic tradition as a powerful instrument in his hands and putting it to use with his own religious frenzy, has become the anti-Christ of this generation—perhaps the most complete anti-Christ who has ever lived. It is not enough to bring about the downfall of Hitler. We must understand the origin and growth of the Prussian spirit, and do something to counteract that spirit, if we wish to bring permanent peace.

The Prussian attitude toward war and supremacy has strong roots. Whether it reaches back to the days of Caesar or whether it first took form under the guidance of the Teutonic knights in the Middle Ages, we are certain of this: by the time of Frederick the Great, the Prussians consciously adopted the doctrine of total war and the total state as the chief end of man. Bismarck and Kaiser Wilhelm II modernized and made completely deceitful and ruthless that which Frederick the Great had founded.

Shortly after Kaiser Wilhelm II rose to power, a generation before the first World War, one of the more tender-hearted of the German generals said, in addressing his troops: "Our civilization must build its temple on mountains of corpses, an ocean of tears, and the groans of innumerable dying men."

We know now, to our sorrow, that those were not just idle words. But God grant they will not be true much longer.

Bernhardi and Treitschke, through the printed page and through the classroom, preached the glory of war and the necessity of Germany picking a quarrel with England or France. Frederick the Great, Moltke and Bismarck were proclaimed as being superior to Goethe, Schiller,

Bach and Beethoven. Hegel laid broad and deep the philosophy of the totalitarian state. Other philosophers, and especially Nietzsche, seized on the Darwinian doctrines of natural selection and survival of the fittest to erect a seemingly scientific but false materialism to justify their ruthless acts.

In saying all of this, I do not mean to indicate that Prussia was the only wicked State in the world. England, France, Russia, Spain, and the United States were not always perfect. But Prussia and Japan were the only countries which systematically devoted the highest virtues of their citizenry, generation after generation, to the glorification of the State and to the ruthlessness of war.

The ancestors of many of the people of German origin in the United States were members of the minority in Germany who dissented from the extremist tendencies toward militarism. Thousands of these dissenters migrated to this country in the twenty or thirty years after the failure of the revolution of 1848. Their children, grandchildren and great-grandchildren today are among our finest American citizens. They are patriotically doing their part in the present war for freedom, and we honor them for the spirit they have shown.

It is in the years since 1848 that the liberal culture of the old Germany has been so completely submerged by the worship of strength and power. In this period of less than a century, under Bismarck, Kaiser Wilhelm II, and Hitler, Germany has launched five aggressive wars.

The result has been that, over the last thirty years, the spirit of Prussianism has cost the lives of at least twenty million men, has crippled at least ten million others, and has caused the nations of the world to squander hundreds of billions of dollars on death, destruction and hate. How different things would have been if this money had been spent instead on peace, prosperity and understanding.

Germans by blood are neither better nor worse than Englishmen, Americans, Swedes, Poles or Russians. But the Prussian tradition of the last century, and especially the Nazi education of the last ten years, have created a psychic entity so monstrous and so dangerous to the entire world that it is absolutely vital to exercise some control over German education when the war comes to an end. Prussian schoolmasters have been of greater importance to the German army than Prussian captains, and Prussian textbooks have had greater value than ammunition. It is the disciplined will to power and the worship of war as the method of power that have made the German army such a terrible instrument of force.

Just as Hitler took the Prussian military tradition and organized it into gangsterism, so he took the Prussian education system and streamlined it to marshal the millions of German boys and girls behind his evil conspiracy of world conquest. Hitler's children have been trained to believe implicitly that the State is more important than the individual, and that the individual must be willing and ready to sacrifice himself for the German Nation and for the Fuehrer. Starting with the young mothers and fathers, married or unmarried, and taking the children through the day nurseries and a series of schools for different ages, Hitler has indoctrinated the German children with what he calls his "leadership principle"—that among men as in nature there is an eternal struggle between the weak and the strong, and that the "decadent" democracies are destined to crumble before the superior might of the Nazi *elite*. German boys have been systematically trained in brutality. German girls have been systematically trained to believe that their supreme duty is to be mothers, married or unmarried, of children dedicated to the service of the Fatherland and the Fuehrer. Through the use of mystic ceremonies—pagan dances, bonfires, sun festivals on mountain tops, and many other types of ritual—both boys and girls have been trained to look upon Hitler as divine and they pray to him as God.

The evil influence of this systematic degradation of millions of German boys and girls cannot be counteracted in a short time. Even Hitler's death will not end it, because many of Hitler's children, conditioned as they are, will believe that he is still their leader, in the spirit if not in the flesh. Hitler dead may be almost as dangerous as Hitler alive.

This, then, is the vastly difficult problem with which the United Nations will have to cope, if the victory which now is coming closer is to bring more than just a short breathing spell before another Prussian attack is launched upon the world.

It is not up to the United Nations to say just what the German schools of the future should teach; and we do not want to be guilty of a Hitler-like orgy of book burning. But it is vital to the peace of the world to make sure that neither Prussianism, Hitlerism nor any modification of them is taught. There are many cultured German scholars with an excellent attitude toward the world who should be put to work on the job of rewriting the German textbooks in their own way. I believe these men would glorify peace and international honesty, re-establishment of the German culture of Beethoven, Schubert, Schiller, and Goethe, and the gradual preparation of the German spirit for an appreciation of the fact that a Bill of Rights for the individual is as vital as a Bill of Duties toward the State.

Doubtless thousands of German boys will come home from the war bitterly disillusioned of Prussianism and Hitlerism. Thousands of both young and old at home will feel the same way. They will honestly want to help build up a new democratic Germany, and we, without yielding at all to the old warlike spirit of Prussia, should encourage them to try. We shall need the help of all Germans who give convincing evidence that they do not subscribe to the "master race" myth and are genuinely opposed to the doctrine that might makes right. The re-education we insist upon should not crush out any sincere desire to practice democracy and live at peace among the world family of nations.

It will not be necessary for Americans to teach in the German schools. The all-important thing is to see that the cult of war and international deceit is no longer preached as a virtue in the schools. We cannot countenance the soft, lazy forgetfulness which characterized England and France in their treatment of Germany in the thirties. The cost of such short-sighted appeasement is too great in men and money. We must not go down that mistaken, tragic road again.

All of my discussion thus far has been concerned with Prussianism. Now I want to talk about Marxianism. This philosophy in some ways is the child of Prussianism, because Marx, its high priest, was molded in his thinking by Hegel, the great philosopher of the Prussian state. Marxianism has used the Cheka, just as Prussianism has used the Gestapo, but it has never preached international war as an instrument of national policy. It does not believe one race is superior to another. Many of the Marxian activities of the last ten years which people of the West have most condemned have been inspired by fear of Germany. The Russian people, who are the chief believers in Marxianism, are fundamentally more religious than the Prussians. The great mass of the Russian people is still hungry for spiritual food. The Russians have a better opportunity to find that spiritual food than have the Prussians under their regime, which glorifies the violence of the old Teutonic gods.

This question of religious freedom in Russia has been getting attention from the Church of England and from the Roman Catholic Church in this country. In a recent issue of the magazine *Commonweal,* which surely can not be said to have Marxian leanings, the managing editor discussed two books by exiled Russians on the status of religion in Russia. Quoting from both books, one written under the auspices of the Church of England, and the other by a professor at Fordham University, the editor came to the conclusion that the position of the Christian Church in Russia has definitely improved.

The future well-being of the world depends upon the extent to which Marxianism, as it is being progressively modified in Russia, and democracy, as we are adapting it to twentieth century conditions, can live together in peace. Old-line Marxianism has held that democracy is mere words, that it serves the cause of the common man with platitudes rather than with jobs, and that belief in it results in a weak governmental organization. And we who believe in democracy must admit that modern science, invention and technology have provided us with new bottles into many of which we have not yet poured the wine of the democratic spirit.

In some respects both the Prussians and the Russians have perceived the signs of the times better than we—and I hope that reactionary politicians will not quote this sentence out of its context, in an effort to prove that I have come out for dictatorship. The fact is that the Prussians have done an effective job of making their bureaucrats efficient in coordinating the social forces in the service of the state. The Russians have put great emphasis on serving and gaining the enthusiastic adherence of the common man. It is my belief that democracy is the only true expression of Christianity, but if it is not to let Christianity down, democracy must be tremendously more efficient than it has been in the service of the common man, and in resistance to selfish pressure groups.

After this war is over, the democratic capitalistic nations will need to prove that they are supremely interested in full employment and full utilization of natural resources. They will need to demonstrate that the consuming power of their people can be made to equal their productive power. The right to work at a regular job and for a decent wage is essential to the true dignity of man.

If the western democracies furnish full employment and an expanding production, they need have no fear of a revival of old-line communistic propaganda from within. If they do not furnish full employment, communistic propaganda of this kind is inevitable and there is nothing which the Russian government or our government or any other government can do to stop it. In the event of long-continued unemployment, the only question will be as to whether the Prussian or Marxian doctrine will take us over first.

I believe in the democratic doctrine—the religion based on the social message of the prophets, the heart insight of Christ, and the wisdom of the men who drew up the Constitution of the United States and adopted the Bill of Rights. By tradition and by structure we believe that it is possible to reconcile the freedom and rights of the individual with the duties required of us by the general welfare. We believe in religious tolerance and the separation of church and state, but we need to light again the old spirit to meet the challenge of new facts.

We shall decide some time in 1943 or 1944 whether to plant the seeds for World War Number Three. That war will be certain if we allow Prussia to rearm either materially or psychologically. That war will be probable in case we double-cross Russia. That war will be probable if we fail to demonstrate that we can furnish full employment after this war comes to an end and fascist interests motivated largely by anti-Russian bias get control of our government. Unless the western democracies and Russia come to a satisfactory understanding before the war ends, I very much fear that World War Number Three will be inevitable. Without a close and trusting understanding between Russia and the United States, there is grave probability after this war is over of Russia and Germany sooner or later making common cause.

Of course, the ground for World War Number Three can be laid by actions of the other powers, even though we in the United States follow the most constructive course. For example, such a war would be inevitable if Russia should again embrace the Trotskyist idea of fomenting worldwide revolution, or if British interests should again be sympathetic to anti-Russian activity in Germany and other countries.

Another possible cause of World War Number Three might rise out of our own willingness to repeat the mistakes we made after World War Number One. When a creditor nation raises its tariffs and asks foreign nations to pay up, and at the same time refuses to let them pay in goods, the result is irritation of a sort that sooner or later leads first to trade war and then to bloodshed.

The gospel of Christ was to feed the hungry, clothe the naked, comfort the sick, and visit those who were in hard luck. He said that treating your neighbor decently was the way to show that you loved God. The neighborhood in Christ's day was a few miles in diameter. Today the airplane has made the whole world a neighborhood. The Good Neighbor policy, whether at home or abroad, is a Christian policy. Those who preach isolationism and hate of other nations are preaching a modified form of Prussian Nazism, and the only outcome of such preaching will be war.

If we want peace, we must treat other nations in the spirit of democratic Christianity. We must make our religion practical. In our relations with China, for example, we must act in such a way as to enhance the material as well as the spiritual well-being of her people. So doing will not only be of spiritual advantage to ourselves, will not only do much to prevent war, but will give us more material prosperity than we can otherwise enjoy. And in saying this, I do not speak in the missionary spirit as a forerunner of a new imperialism.

Nearly half the people of the world live in eastern Asia. Seven-eighths of them do not know how to read and write, but many of them listen to the radio and they know that the world is on the move and they are determined to move with it. We can at their request help them to move in knowledge toward a higher standard of living rather than in ignorance toward confusion and anarchy.

Throughout history, every big nation has been given an opportunity to help itself by helping the world. If such an opportunity is seized with a broad and generous spirit, an infinitude of practical possibilities opens up. Thousands of businessmen in the United States have seen this kind of thing happen on a smaller scale in their own businesses, as their broad and enlightened policies have increased their prosperity and given jobs to their neighbors. Christianity is not star gazing or foolish idealism. Applied on a worldwide scale, it is intensely practical. Bread cast upon the waters does return. National friendships are remembered. Help to starving people is not soon forgotten. We of the United States who now have the greatest opportunity that ever came to any people do not wish to impose on any other race or to thrust our money or technical experts or ways of thought on those who do not desire them. But we do believe that if we measure up to the responsibility which Providence has placed on our shoulders, we shall be called on for help by many peoples who admire us. When we respond to this cry for help, we shall be manifesting not only a Christian spirit, but also obeying a fundamental law of life.

We of the Western democracies must demonstrate the practicality of our religion. We must extend a helping hand to China and India; we must be firm and just with Prussia; we must deal honestly and fairly with Russia and be tolerant and even helpful as she works out her economic problems in her own way; we must prove that we ourselves can give an example, in our American democratic way, of full employment and full production for the benefit of the common man.

By collaborating with the rest of the world to put productive resources fully to work, we shall raise our own standard of living and help to raise the standard of living of others. It is not that we shall be taking the bread out of the mouths of our own children to feed the children of others, but that we shall cooperate with everyone to call forth the energies of everyone, to put God's earth more completely at the service of all mankind. (*March 8, 1943.*)

Blue-print
for Peace

BY SUMNER WELLES

from the new book
"The World of the Four Freedoms"

I *

I DO not doubt that millions are asking—millions in England and in China; millions of enslaved peoples in Norway and in the other countries now temporarily occupied; millions in the countries which have not experienced war; yes, and millions in Germany and in Italy—are asking, what does the future hold for us after this struggle is over?

Does the end of the present carnage mean only a return to ruined homes, to the graves of slaughtered wives and children, to poverty and want, to social upheaval and economic chaos, to the same gray and empty years of confusion and bitterness, so barren in vision and in human accomplishment, which marked the decades after the termination of the last war?

It seems to me that those of us who are fortunate enough to be able to live as citizens of the free American Republics have our great responsibility in the framing of the answer to that question. For we all of us now see clearly, if we did not before, that no matter how great our American capacity for defense may be, no matter how perfect our hemispheric system may become, our future welfare must inevitably be contingent upon the existence in the rest of the world of equally peace-minded and equally secure peoples who not only will not, but can not, become a source of potential danger to us in the New World.

I feel it is not premature for me to suggest that the free governments of peace-loving nations everywhere should even now be considering and discussing the way in which they can best prepare for the better day which must come, when the present contest is ended in the victory of the forces of liberty and of human freedom and in the crushing defeat

* For a more extensive statement see the complete texts of the speeches from which the following paragraphs are excerpted in "The World of the Four Freedoms." *Columbia University Press.*

of those who are sacrificing mankind to their own lust for power and for loot.

At the end of the last war, a great President of the United States gave his life in the struggle to further the realization of the splendid vision which he had held up to the eyes of suffering humanity—the vision of an ordered world governed by law.

The League of Nations, as he conceived it, failed in part because of the blind selfishness of men here in the United States, as well as in other parts of the world; it failed because of its utilization by certain powers primarily to advance their own political and commercial ambitions; but it failed chiefly because of the fact that it was forced to operate, by those who dominated its councils, as a means of maintaining the *status quo*. It was never enabled to operate as its chief spokesman had intended, as an elastic and impartial instrument in bringing about peaceful and equitable adjustments between nations as time and circumstance proved necessary.

Some adequate instrumentality must unquestionably be found to achieve such adjustments when the nations of the earth again undertake the task of restoring law and order to a disastrously shaken world. But whatever the mechanism which may be devised, of two things I am unalterably convinced:

First, that the abolition of offensive armaments and the limitation and reduction of defensive armaments and of the tools which make the construction of such armaments possible can only be undertaken through some rigid form of international supervision and control, and that without such practical and essential control, no real disarmament can ever be achieved; and

Second, that no peace which may be made in the future would be valid or lasting unless it established fully and adequately the natural rights of all peoples to equal economic enjoyment. So long as any one people or any one government possesses a monopoly over natural resources or raw materials which are needed by all peoples, there can be no basis for a world order based on justice and on peace.

I cannot believe that peoples of good will will not once more strive to realize the great ideal of an association of nations through which the freedom, the happiness, and the security of all peoples may be achieved.

That word, security, represents the end upon which the hearts of men and women everywhere today are set. Whether it be security from bombing from the air, or from mass destruction; whether it be security from want, disease, and starvation; whether it be security in enjoying that inalienable right which every human being should possess of living out his life in peace and happiness, people throughout the length and breadth of the world are demanding security, and freedom from fear.

That is the objective before us all today—to try and find the means of bringing that to pass.

"Not in vain the distance beacons."

II

How can we achieve that Free World, the attainment of which alone can compensate mankind for the stupendous sacrifices which human beings everywhere are now being called upon to suffer?

Our military victory will only be won, in Churchill's immortal words, by blood and tears, and toil and sweat.

It is just as clear that the Free World which we must achieve can only be attained, not through the expenditure of toil and sweat alone but also through the exercise of all of the wisdom which men of today have gained from the experience of the past, and by the utilization not only of idealism but also of the practical knowledge of the working of human nature and of the laws of economics and of finance.

What the United Nations' blueprint imperatively requires is to be drafted in the light of experience and of common sense and in a spirit of justice, of democracy, and of tolerance, by men who have their eyes on the stars, but their feet on the ground. In the fundamentals of international relationships there is nothing more fatally dangerous than the common American fallacy that the formulation of an aspiration is equivalent to the hard-won realization of an objective. Of this basic truth we have no more tragic proof than the Kellogg-Briand Pact.

It seems to me that the first essential is the continuous and rapid perfecting of a relationship between the United Nations so that this military relationship may be further strengthened by the removal of all semblance of disunity or of suspicious rivalry and by the clarification of the Free World goals for which we are fighting, and so that the form of international organization determined to be best suited to achieve international security will have developed to such an extent that it can fully operate as soon as the present military partnership has achieved its purpose of complete victory.

Another essential is the reaching of agreements between the United Nations before the armistice is signed upon those international adjustments, based upon the universal principles of the Atlantic Charter and pursuant to the pledges contained in our mutual-aid agreements with many of our allies, which we believe to be desirable and necessary for the maintenance of a peaceful and prosperous world of the future.

We all envisage the tragic chaos and anarchy which will have engulfed Europe and a great part of the rest of the world by the time Hitler's brief day is done, and when he and his accomplices confront their judges. The United Nations' machinery for relief and rehabilitation must be prepared to operate without a moment's delay to alleviate the suffering and misery of millions of homeless and starving human beings, if civilization is to be saved from years of social and moral collapse.

"No one will go hungry or without the other means of livelihood in any territory occupied by the United Nations, if it is humanly within our powers to make the necessary supplies available to them. Weapons will also be supplied to the peoples of these territories to hasten the defeat of the Axis." This is the direction of the President to the Lend-Lease Administrator, to General Eisenhower, and to the Department of State, and it is being carried out by them to the full extent of their power and resources. The other United Nations, each to the full extent of its ability, will, I am sure, cooperate wholeheartedly in this great task.

Through prearrangement certain measures such as the disarmament of aggressor nations laid down in the Atlantic Charter must likewise be undertaken rapidly and with the utmost precision.

Surely we should not again resort to the procedures adopted in 1919 for the settlement of the future of the world. We cannot afford to permit the basic issues by which the destiny of humanity will be determined to be resolved without prior agreement, in hurried confusion, by a group of harassed statesmen, working against time, pressed from one side by the popular demand for immediate demobilization and crowded on the other by the exigencies of domestic politics.

If we are to attain our Free World—the world of the Four Freedoms —to the extent practicable, the essential principles of international political and economic relations in that new world must be agreed upon in advance and with the full support of each one of the United Nations, so that agreements to be reached will implement those principles.

If the people of the United States now believe as a result of the experience of the past twenty-five years that the security of our Republic is vitally affected by the fate of the other peoples of the earth, they will recognize that the nature of the international political and economic relations which will obtain in the world after victory has been achieved is to us a matter of profound self-interest.

As the months pass, two extreme schools of thought will become more and more vocal—the first, stemming from the leaders of the group which preached extreme isolation, will once more proclaim that war in the rest of the world every twenty years or so is inevitable, that we can stay out if we so desire, and that any assumption by this country of any form of responsibility for what goes on in the world means our unnecessary involvement in war; the other, of which very often men of the highest idealism and sincerity are the spokesmen, will maintain that the United States must assume the burdens of the entire globe, must see to it that the standards in which we ourselves believe must immediately be adopted by all of the peoples of the earth, and must undertake to inculcate in all parts of the world our own policies of social and political reform whether the other peoples involved so desire or not. While under a different guise, this school of thought is in no way dissimilar in theory from the strange doctrine of incipient "bear the white man's burden" imperialism which flared in this country in the first years of this century.

The people of the United States today realize that the adoption of either one of these two philosophies would prove equally dangerous to the future well-being of our nation.

Our Free World must be founded on the Four Freedoms: freedom *of* speech and *of* religion and freedom *from* want and *from* fear.

I do not believe that the two first freedoms—of speech and of religion —can ever be assured to mankind so long as want and war are permitted to ravage the earth. Freedom of speech and of religion need only protection; they require only relief from obstruction.

Freedom from fear—the assurance of peace—and freedom from want —the assurance of individual personal security—require all of the implementation which the genius of man can devise through effective forms of international cooperation.

Peace—freedom from fear—cannot be assured until the nations of the world, particularly the great powers, and that includes the United States, recognize that the threat of war anywhere throughout the globe threatens their own security and until they are jointly willing to exercise the police powers necessary to prevent such threats from materializing into armed hostilities.

And since policemen might be tyrants if they had no political superiors, freedom from fear also demands some form of organized international political cooperation to make the rules of international living and to change them as the years go by, and some sort of international court to adjudicate disputes. With effective institutions of that character to insure equity and justice, and the continued will to make them work, the peoples of the world should at length be able to live out their lives in peace.

Freedom from want requires these things: People who want to work must be able to find useful jobs, not sometimes, not in good years only, but continuously. These jobs must be at things which they do well and which can be done well in the places where they work. They must be able to exchange the things which they produce, on fair terms, for other things which other people, often in other places, can make better than they.

Efficient and continuous production and fair exchange are both necessary to the abundance which we seek, and they depend upon each other. In the past we have succeeded better with production than exchange. Production is called into existence by the prospects for exchange, prospects which have constantly been thwarted by all kinds of inequalities, imperfections, and restrictions. The problem of removing obstacles to fair exchange—the problem of distribution of goods and purchasing power—is far more difficult than the problem of production.

It will take much wisdom, much cooperative effort, and much surrender of private, short-sighted, and sectional self-interest to make these things all come true. But the goal is freedom from want—individual security and national prosperity—and is everlastingly worth striving for.

As mankind progresses on the path towards the goal of freedom from want and from fear, freedom of religion and of speech will more and more become a living reality. Never before have peace and individual security been classed as freedom. Never before have they been placed alongside of religious liberty and free speech as human freedoms which should be inalienable. Upon these Four Freedoms must rest the structure of the future Free World.

This time there must be no compromise between justice and injustice, no yielding to expediency, no swerving from the great human rights and liberties established by the Atlantic Charter itself.

In the words of our President : "We shall win this war, and in Victory, we shall seek not vengeance, but the establishment of an international order in which the spirit of Christ shall rule the hearts of men and of nations."

We won't get a Free World any other way.

III

It is not idealism that is the danger to the community. Grave danger does lie in the all-too-frequent unwillingness of the idealist to grasp the hard facts of national and international experience; but it lies equally, in my judgment, in the defeatist philosophy of the cynic who, because of the failures of the past, cannot envision the successes of the future.

It will help us to keep our perspective if, from the vantage point of the present, we frequently look back over the list of errors of omission and of commission of the past. Let me make a few brief statements with regard to recent history which, I hope you will feel, as I do, should be regarded as axiomatic.

Trade—the exchange of goods—is inherently a matter of cooperation, but a glance at the past is enough to show that in the policies of nations this simple truism has been more often ignored than observed. Nations have more often than not undertaken economic discriminations and raised up trade barriers with complete disregard for the damaging effects on the trade and livelihood of other peoples and, ironically enough, with similar disregard for the harmful resultant effects upon their own export trade. They have considered foreign trade a cut-throat game in which each participant could only profit by taking undue advantage of his neighbor. Our own policy at times in the past has, as we all know, constituted no exception.

After the last war at a time when other countries were looking to us for help in their stupendous task of economic and social reconstruction, the United States, suddenly become the world's greatest creditor nation and incomparably strong economically, struck heavy blows at their war-weakened, debt-burdened, economic structures. The shock was heavy, morally as well as economically. The harmful effects of this policy on the trade, industry, and conditions of living of people of many other foreign countries were immediate. Our high-tariff policy reached out to virtually every corner of the earth and brought poverty and despair to innumerable communities.

But the effects on American importers, and on American industries dependent upon imports, were likewise immediate.

Unfortunately, the inevitable effects on our export trade were obscured and put off for a number of years by lavish foreign lending, both public and private. The most important normal source of foreign purchasing power for American exports—other countries' exports to us—was being dried up, but what was really happening, as we all know, was that countless American investors were in effect paying American exporters for billions of dollars' worth of goods sent abroad. If the deficiency in normal foreign purchasing power derived from sales in this country had not been covered up by such vast sums advanced by American investors, we might have realized much earlier that our tariff policy was striking at the very roots of our entire export trade. We might have avoided the colossal blunder of 1930 and the less serious, but equally misguided, action of further tariff increases under the guise of the so-called excise taxes of 1932. Many foreign countries, which had not recovered from the shock of our tariff increases in 1921 and 1922 and were tottering on the brink of economic and financial collapse, were literally pushed into the abyss by our tariff action of 1930. Throughout the world this withering blast of trade destruction brought disaster and despair to countless people.

The resultant misery, bewilderment, and resentment, together with other equally pernicious contributing causes, paved the way for the rise of those very dictatorships which have plunged almost the entire world into war.

When human beings see ahead of them nothing but a continuation of the distress of the present, they are not apt to analyze dispassionately the worth of the glittering assurance of better times held out to them by a self-styled leader whom they would under more normal circumstances recognize as the shoddy adventurer which in reality he proves to be.

We thus helped to set in motion a whirlpool of trade-restricting measures and devices, preferences, and discriminations, which quickly sucked world trade down to such low levels that standards of living everywhere were dangerously reduced. Faced with the disappearance of markets in the United States for so many of their exportable products, foreign countries were forced to cut their economic cloth accordingly. They erected high tariffs and established restrictive quotas designed to keep their imports of American products within the limits of their reduced dollar purchasing power. They sought desperately for other markets and other sources of supply. In the process they entered into all sorts of preferential arrangements, resorted to primitive barter, and adopted narrowly bilateralistic trade-and-payments arrangements.

Obviously the totalitarian governments then being set up seized avidly on the opportunity so afforded to undertake political pressures through the exercise of this form of commercial policy.

They substituted coercion for negotiation—"persuaded," with a blackjack. The countries thus victimized were forced to spend the proceeds of their exports in the countries where such proceeds were blocked, no matter how inferior the quality, how high the price, or even what the nature might be of the goods which they were thus forced to obtain. They were prevented by such arrangements from entering into beneficial trade agreements with countries unwilling to sanction discriminations against their exports. By no means the least of the victims were the exporters of third countries, including the United States, who were either shut out of foreign markets entirely or else only permitted to participate on unequal terms.

This time our own export trade, unsupported by foreign lending on the part of American investors and unprotected against countless new trade barriers and discriminations, was immediately disastrously affected. Belatedly we recognized our mistake. We realized that something had to be done to save our export trade from complete destruction.

The enactment in 1934 of the Trade Agreements Act represented a new deal for our foreign trade, a reorientation of government policy on the basis of simple, obvious facts, one of the most simple and obvious being that a nation cannot continue to sell if it does not buy. I do not need to dwell on this phase. You who are meeting here have recognized in repeated resolutions of endorsement the merits of that policy and the simple truths upon which it is founded.

To that policy history will always attach the honored name of Cordell Hull. But time is required for such a reversal of policy to have its full effects, and in the meantime another shattering world war has again laid the whole international economic structure in ruins and has enormously increased the task of reconstruction.

So much for the past.

For the people of this country the supreme objective of the present before which every other consideration must now give place is the final and complete defeat of Hitlerism. We have been forced in self-defense to assure ourselves that the ever-growing menace to our free institutions and to our national safety cannot and shall not prevail.

For that reason the trade problems of the immediate moment have largely become problems arising out of our national emergency. As such their solution is imperative. You who are living daily with these problems before you are the last people who need to be told in any detail what they are. The function of foreign trade under present conditions is largely one of supplying the defenders of human liberty with the means of their defense and of obtaining, despite the shortage of shipping, the materials needed in carrying out our own defense program and in supplying the needs of our consumers.

There is likewise the acute problem of the essential import needs of our sister Republics of this hemisphere which are largely cut off from European sources of supply. Far too little emphasis, I regret to say, has as yet been placed upon the vital obligation of this country to co-operate to a far greater practical extent than has as yet been the case in assisting to the fullest degree possible our neighbors of the Western Hemisphere in the maintenance of their own national economies in the ever-increasing dislocation to which they are subjected.

There is also need for additional trade agreements which will help during the emergency and which will assist in establishing a sound foundation for international trade after the war. Your Government intends to go forward with this program.

But the future no less than the present presses itself upon our attention. It seems to me that there is nothing more urgently demanded than that the people of the United States, the governments of the Western Hemisphere, and the governments of all of the nations which have been assailed or menaced by the Axis powers should daily be considering and determining upon the policies and practices whose future enforcement could render the greatest measure of assurance that the tragedy which we now see being unfolded should not once more be brought to pass.

I can conceive of no greater misfortune than that the people of the United States and their Government should refrain from devoting themselves to the study of reconstruction until the end of the war, than that they should permit themselves to adopt the passive policy of "wait and see."

The period following the present war will be fully as critical for us as is the present crisis. Forces of aggression now menace us from without. But dangers of another nature here and elsewhere will threaten us even after the war has ended in the victory of Great Britain and her allies over the powers that are seeking to place the whole of the world under their own ignominious form of tyranny.

There exists the danger, despite the clear lessons of the past, that the nations of the world will once more be tempted to resort to the same misguided policies which have had such disastrous consequences. And in the economic field especially there is danger that special interests and pressure groups in this country and elsewhere will once again selfishly and blindly seek preferences for themselves and discriminations against others.

The creation of an economic order in the post-war world which will give free play to individual enterprise, and at the same time render security to men and women and provide for the progressive improvement of living standards, is almost as essential to the preservation of free institutions as is the actual winning of this war. And the preservation of our liberties, all-important in itself, is essential to the realization of the other great objective of mankind—an enduring peace. There can be no peace in a Hitler-ridden world.

In brief, in my judgment the creation of that kind of sound economic order which I have described is essential to the attainment of those three great demands of men and women everywhere—freedom, security, and peace.

The stakes are therefore tremendous in the task to which we must earnestly set ourselves. All of the talent of such organizations as this great organization of yours, of research institutions, and of the agencies of government must be brought to bear upon the solution of the post-war economic problems.

These problems are of two kinds: those which will present themselves as the immediate aftermath of the war and those involved in the
creation of a more permanent economic order.

In the immediate post-war period the task will primarily be one of
reconstruction. Food and material of all kinds will be sorely needed.
Both humanitarian considerations and self-interest require that we co-
operate to these ends to the fullest extent of our ability. So long as any
important part of the world is economically sick, we cannot be well.

Plans for meeting these requirements are already being considered.
In planning commodity agreements for stabilizing prices of basic commodities, such as the wheat agreement now under consideration by
several of the producing countries directly concerned, these unusual
post-war needs must be kept in mind in order that adequate supplies
may be available to meet them.

Both from the standpoint of immediate post-war needs and in the
longer-range aspect, we must give serious attention to the problems of
nutrition. Here again humanitarian considerations and self-interest
combine to make this subject one of outstanding importance to our
people. If the dietary needs of the world's population could be satisfied
to the extent necessary to meet minimum standards for sustaining health,
the burdensome surpluses which normally trouble producers of many
staple products would disappear. I am glad to be able to assure you
that this subject is being given preferential attention by agencies of this
and other governments.

These are some of the problems with which we shall be faced immediately after the war. But the basic problem in establishing a new and
better world order is to obtain the application by the nations of the
world of sound principles of commercial and economic policy.

The basic principles which, in my judgment, should guide the policies
of nations in the post-war world have been enunciated in the eight-point
joint declaration of the President and Mr. Churchill * at the historic
meeting of the Atlantic.

This set of basic principles, appropriately called "The Atlantic
Charter," deals with commercial policy in its fourth point, which reads,
"They will endeavor, with due respect for their existing obligations, to

* *Department of State Bulletin,* August 16, 1941, p. 125.

further the enjoyment by all states, great or small, victor or vanquished, of access, on equal terms, to the trade and to the raw materials of the world which are needed for their economic prosperity."

The basic conception is that your Government is determined to move towards the creation of conditions under which restrictive and unconscionable tariffs, preferences, and discriminations are things of the past; under which no nation should seek to benefit itself at the expense of another; and under which destructive trade warfare shall be replaced by cooperation for the welfare of all nations.

The Atlantic declaration means that every nation has a right to expect that its legitimate trade will not be diverted and throttled by towering tariffs, preferences, discriminations, or narrow bilateral practices. Most fortunately we have already done much to put our own commercial policy in order. So long as we adhere and persistently implement the principles and policies which made possible the enactment of the Trade Agreements Act, the United States will not furnish, as it did after the last war, an excuse for trade-destroying and trade-diverting practices.

The purpose so simply set forth in the Atlantic declaration is to promote the economic prosperity of all nations "great or small, victor or vanquished." Given this purpose and the determination to act in accordance with it, the means of attaining this objective will always be found. It is a purpose which does not have its origin primarily in altruistic conceptions. It is inspired by the realization, so painfully forced on us by the experiences of past and of the present, that in the long run no nation can prosper by itself or at the expense of others and that no nation can live unto itself alone.

IV

For example, let us reconsider the statement in Point Four of The Atlantic Charter, "access, on equal terms, to . . . the raw materials of the world which are needed for . . . economic prosperity."

Access to raw materials does not mean and cannot mean that every nation, or any nation, can have the source of all of them within its borders. That is not the way the world was put together. Coal and iron in combination are found in few locations. Much of the nickel of the world is in one great Canadian deposit. Neither coffee nor cinchona will grow in the United States. No nation can be self-sufficient by changes in its boundaries, and those who try by force to do so, as the Axis leaders have tried, bring on themselves inevitably only their own destruction. The path to plentiful supplies does not lie through physical control of the sources of supply.

The problem of raw materials is not exclusively, or even primarily, a problem of colonial or undeveloped areas. The great mineral deposits exist chiefly in countries that are already self-governing, such as the United States, the Soviet Union, Canada, Germany, Sweden, South Africa, Mexico, Brazil. Access to raw materials does not mean possession of a colony. It means effective power to buy in the world's markets.

The legal right to export raw materials has seldom been restricted by producing countries. True, the United States and other countries sometimes have been guilty of forbidding the export of certain things needed for production elsewhere, for fear that others might obtain the means to trespass on their markets. But those cases were rare. Countries producing raw materials desired normally to sell their surplus, and the problem usually was to find a profitable market. The right to buy was real, and satisfied peace-loving peoples. Belgium, Denmark, Sweden,

Switzerland, Czechoslovakia, Norway, not to speak of the United States and England, bought in the years between the wars great quantities of foreign raw materials, and none of them claimed that they needed greater resources to live. The countries that complained, and shrieked that they must have colonies or die, have shown now by their conduct that what they wanted was not prosperity and peace, but the materials for making war.

For war, indeed, one cannot count on overseas supplies, and an aggressor must first corner all he can of coal and iron and oil and copper, in the ground or out of it.

But the Atlantic Charter does not propose to aid aggression. It proposes, on the contrary, to make sure that aggression does not happen, and to that end the United Nations will create the necessary instruments —and this time they will be effective instruments and must be firmly used—to make it certain that any power that again threatens to enslave its neighbors is denied the means to do so. The materials of war must be denied to any future Hitler.

The access to raw materials of which the Charter speaks is access for the purposes of peace. For that purpose it matters little in whose territory particular resources are found. Access means the right to buy in peaceful trade, and it exists whenever that right is effective and secure.

What forces, then, have interfered with that right in the past or may interfere with it in the future?

Most raw materials are not subject to monopolistic practices because producers are too numerous; but there have been charges in the past, and there are charges now, that in certain cases the producers of some commodities with the support of the governments to which they owed allegiance have managed, by what our Sherman Law calls combinations in restraint of trade, to reduce supplies and enhance prices beyond reasonable levels or to discriminate among their customers. A world devoted to increased production and fair and fruitful exchange of all kinds of useful goods cannot tolerate such practices.

But monopoly in the field of raw materials is not the major problem. Most materials are plentiful in peace, and their producers want to sell them to any customer who has the means to buy. The real problem of consumers has always been the means of payment. In the world that emerges from the war that problem will be very serious indeed.

When this war ends, much of the world will be impoverished beyond anything known in modern times.

Relief cannot go on forever, and the day must come as soon as possible when the devastated areas again are self-supporting. That will require enormous shipments from abroad, both of capital goods and of the raw materials of industry. For these early reconstruction shipments no immediate means of payment will be visible. That means large financing, much of it long-term. The United Nations must arrange that too. But finally comes payment, both of whatever interest burden the loans carry and for the current purchases of raw materials and other imports. I need not tell this audience that international payments, on that scale, can be made only in goods and services. There is no other way. Access to raw materials comes in the end to access to the great buying markets of the world. Those who expect to export must take the world's goods and services in payment. I hope that the United States is ready now to act upon that lesson.

The United Nations have agreed to act upon it, and in mutual-aid agreements with a growing number of them we and they have promised to direct our common efforts to increased production, employment, and the exchange and consumption of all kinds of useful goods. We and they have promised further to attack the problem by removing discriminations in the treatment of international trade and by reducing unwarranted and artificial tariff barriers. The future prosperity and peace of the world and of the United States depend vitally on the good faith and the thoroughness with which we and they together carry out those promises.

During the war as fully as we can, and more fully after we have destroyed the madmen who seek to rule the world by force and terror, we of the United Nations will go forward in a loyal partnership to carry out the pledges we have made to each other and the world.

There is no limit, then, to the material prosperity which is within the reach of the United States and of mankind. The great thing that has happened in our time is that mankind at long last has taught itself enough of the means and techniques of production, of transport, and of scientific agriculture so that it is technically possible to produce and to distribute on this planet the basic physical necessities of health and decent living for all of the world's people. What remains, and it is a great and formidable task, is so to remake our relations with each other, in loyal and cooperative effort, that the great productive forces which are within our sight may function freely for the benefit of all. It is within our power to make a mighty start upon that road; we have laid down the principles of action; it is for the people of the United States to determine whether their Government is to be authorized to carry on.

For twelve tragic years after the close of the last World War the United States withdrew from almost every form of constructive co-operation with the other nations of the earth. We are reaping the bitter cost of that isolation.

For I am persuaded that after the victory is won, so long as the power and influence of the United States are felt in the councils of the world, so long as our cooperation is effectively offered, so long can one hope that peace can and will be maintained.

The blessings we have inherited from our forefathers do not constitute an inheritance that we may only passively enjoy. They can only be preserved by sacrifice, by courage, by resolution, and by vision. If the American people prove themselves worthy of their ancestors, if they still possess their forefathers' dauntless courage and their ability to meet new conditions with wisdom and determination, the future of this nation will rest secure, and our children and our children's children will be able to live out their lives in safety and in peace.